To Myra:

Julius Rosenwald

Best wishes,

Peter M. Ascoli

Philanthropic and Nonprofit Studies
Dwight F. Burlingame and David C. Hammack, editors

Peter M. Ascoli

INDIANA UNIVERSITY PRESS
Bloomington and Indianapolis

Julius Rosenwald

The Man Who Built Sears, Roebuck and Advanced the Cause of Black Education in the American South

This book is a publication of

Indiana University Press
601 North Morton Street
Bloomington, IN 47404-3797 USA

http://iupress.indiana.edu

Telephone orders 800-842-6796
Fax orders 812-855-7931
Orders by e-mail iuporder@indiana.edu

The paper used in this publication meets the minimum requirements of American National Standard for Information Sciences—Permanence of Paper for Printed Library Materials, ANSI Z39.48-1984.

Manufactured in the United States of America

Library of Congress Cataloging-in-Publication Data

Ascoli, Peter Max, date
Julius Rosenwald : the man who built Sears, Roebuck and advanced the cause of Black education in the American South / Peter M. Ascoli.
p. cm.
Includes bibliographical references and index.
ISBN 0-253-34741-6 (cloth : alk. paper)
1. Rosenwald, Julius, 1862–1932. 2. Businesspeople—United States—Biography. 3. Jewish businesspeople—United States—Biography. 4. Sears, Roebuck and Company—History. 5. Philanthropists—United States—Biography. 6. African Americans—Education—Southern states. I. Title.
HC102.5.R58A83 2006
361.7′4092—dc22

2005030411

2 3 4 5 11 10 09 08 07 06

To my late cousin,
Philip Stern,
who began the journey

Contents

Preface

Julius Rosenwald was my grandfather. Unfortunately, I never knew him. He died ten years before I was born. My mother, Marion Rosenwald Ascoli, told me some stories about her youth. I knew she had grown up in Chicago, that her father had been the president of Sears, Roebuck & Co., and that he had donated a great deal of money to numerous charitable causes. However, I had very little sense of my grandfather as a person. In fact, I knew almost nothing about him.

My ignorance about Julius Rosenwald was matched by that of my contemporaries. Most people today have never heard of this brilliant businessman and generous philanthropist. The man who largely was responsible for fashioning Sears, Roebuck into the greatest mail-order firm in the world, and who sought to assist African Americans at a time when relatively few white Americans thought of them in a positive light, is all but unknown today. His name graces one building on the campus of the University of Chicago and the library of the University of Chicago's Oriental Institute in Luxor, Egypt. He requested that his name be removed from the Museum of Science and Industry in Chicago, which he founded, and the charitable foundation that he created in 1917, the Julius Rosenwald Fund, went out of existence in 1948 at his expressed wish. There is a bust of Julius Rosenwald along with other notable Chicago businessmen in front of Chicago's Merchandise Mart. The former residents of the Michigan Boulevard Garden Apartments in Chicago, the African American housing project he created in 1929, still refer to the structure unofficially as "The Rosenwald." The "Rosenwald" schools for African Americans, 5,357 primary schools, shops, and teachers' homes he helped pay to construct in fifteen Southern states, are just being rediscovered. Otherwise his name is almost entirely unknown.

A few graduate students have written about some aspects of Rosenwald's life, primarily his philanthropy. Most have only written about the schools. Only one previous biography was ever written about Julius Rosenwald, and it was published in 1939.

In the last years of Rosenwald's life (1929–32), his family and associates made attempts to have a biography written. Stanley Rayfield was hired to conduct interviews with longtime Sears employees and top executives of the giant retail firm. Rayfield's credentials as a historian are unknown, but Rosenwald's biographer of the late 1930s, Maurice Werner, believed that most of the material he collected was worthless.

Ellery Sedgwick, editor of the *Atlantic Monthly,* which published two articles on philanthropy ostensibly by Rosenwald, suggested that the former Sears president write his autobiography. Rosenwald, who composed occasional articles and speeches, disliked writing, so the notion of penning an autobiography did not appeal to him. Around 1927, Rosenwald wrote a few pages about his youth, but then abandoned the project.

Rosenwald's children talked of engaging a well-known writer to undertake their father's official biography. The names of newspaperman David Lawrence and author John Gunther were mentioned, but nothing came of these efforts.

Following Rosenwald's death in January 1932, his children finally agreed on a biographer. Florence Kiper Frank was an acquaintance of Rosenwald's daughter Adele. She proceeded to conduct the necessary research and produced a manuscript, but for some reason, perhaps because the family members did not find it acceptable, the work was never published.

In the mid-1930s, Rosenwald's children engaged Maurice R. Werner, a professional biographer, to write the authorized biography. Werner, the author of works on William Jennings Bryan, Brigham Young, and P. T. Barnum, did a serviceable job. He researched his subject carefully and transcribed a large number of documents that no longer exist and that I refer to as "Werner Notes." The book is competently written. But some of the more interesting aspects of Rosenwald's life are not mentioned at all, and Rosenwald's first wife, Gussie, is not presented as the important figure she was in the life of her husband. Moreover, Werner's book is not a scholarly biography; it contains almost no footnotes and could hardly be considered the last word on its subject.

In the mid-1980s, my cousin Philip Stern, the son of Rosenwald's daughter Edith, decided that the time had come for a new biography of Rosenwald, and that he would write it. Stern, a journalist and political activist, had been one of the founders of the *Democratic Digest* and was at that time writing one of his best-known works, *The Rape of the Taxpayer.*

He began interviewing family members and hired a research assistant who commenced sifting through the large collection of Rosenwald's papers in the University of Chicago's Department of Special Collections and the papers of the Julius Rosenwald Fund at Fisk University. In 1988, Stern was diagnosed with an inoperable brain tumor. He valiantly continued work on the biography, but by 1990 he was dead.

Philip Stern stayed at our home near the University of Chicago when he visited the city to look up material at the university's Regenstein Library. After Stern's death, I asked his family if I could continue his work on the Rosenwald biography. They consented, and several boxes of material arrived shortly thereafter. When the fruits of Stern's research first arrived, I wasn't sure I really wished to embark on such a project. But once I started poring over the documents and reading Werner's biography, I realized that here was a story that needed to be told—the story of a talented and extremely successful business executive and a thoughtful and, in many respects, pioneering philanthropist who had played an important part in the history of America in the first decades of the twentieth century. Trained as a historian at the University of California, Berkeley, I utilized the skills I had learned to peer into archives Philip Stern had not approached. My research has taken me to numerous archival collections in many states from West Branch, Iowa, home of the Hoover Presidential Library (where the papers of Rosenwald's successor at Sears, General Robert Wood, are housed) to New Orleans. In the latter city I found the treasure trove every historian dreams of. In the home built by my aunt, Edith Rosenwald Stern, now a museum known as LongueVue House and Gardens, I found in the attic some thirty boxes of archival material. No one who knew anything about the family had seen this material before. It was a rich lode, and I trust I have made good use of it. The archive contained previously unknown letters of Richard Sears, Jane Addams, and others, as well as interesting correspondence between Rosenwald and his eldest daughters in 1910–11. The Chicago Historical Society, the Library of Congress, the American Jewish Archives at Hebrew Union College in Cincinnati, and various other archival collections around the country have also proved extremely helpful.

Once I completed the research and commenced writing, I decided that I would refer to my subject as "JR." This was a nickname he was called by many of his close friends and relations, except for his wife (who called him "Jule"). It seemed to me that referring to Rosenwald as JR made him more human, more approachable. I also decided to focus the book primarily on JR's philanthropy. That is because the vast majority of papers concerning JR's work at Sears have disappeared. They are not part of the collection at the University of Chicago, nor do the Sears archives possess much of great value, although Dennis Preisler, the former archivist at Sears, searched diligently on my behalf. I suspect, although I cannot prove it, that JR obtained all the records of his years at Sears and asked that they be destroyed because he wanted to be remembered primarily as a philanthropist.

Peter M. Ascoli
Chicago, Illinois
December 2005

Acknowledgments

This book has been twelve years in the making, and I owe many people a great debt of gratitude. Dan Meyer, the chief archivist in the University of Chicago's Department of Special Collections, and Beth Howse, archivist of the Rosenwald Fund Papers at Fisk University, have both been extremely helpful. Darwin Stapleton of the Rockefeller Archive Center at Tarrytown, New York, and Dwight Miller of the Hoover Presidential Library in West Branch, Iowa, both gave me valuable assistance. Laura Graedel, who was the archivist at the Museum of Science and Industry, became a close friend as well as a coworker, as eager to find out about JR and the history of the museum he founded as I was. The staff of LongueVue House and Gardens could not have been more gracious. The same adjective applies to the staff of the Joint Distribution Committee in New York, who assisted me in going through the archives of the Russian colonies project with which Rosenwald was so closely associated. Also helpful in numerous ways was the staff of the Chicago Historical Society Archives. Joy Kingsolver of the Chicago Jewish Archives has provided me with much valuable assistance and support. Beverly Calhoun of Chicago led me to her cousin Lee Ellen Cromer in California, and Ms. Cromer kindly supplied me with the memoirs of her uncle, Harry Kersey, Rosenwald's chauffeur. Kay Johnson introduced me to several former residents of the Michigan Boulevard Garden Apartments who described for me in vivid detail what it was like to grow up in that complex of buildings constructed for African Americans in 1929.

The resurgence of interest in Rosenwald schools in recent years has led me to meet a large number of historians and preservationists who are passionately enthusiastic about their subject. They have been eager to help me. Such individuals as Karen Riles of Texas and Angelo Franceschina of North Carolina each became fascinated by Rosenwald schools independently. Some, such as Karen, sought to document Rosenwald schools from a historical perspective; others, such as Angelo, have sought to refurbish and revivify the schools, transforming the vacant buildings into community centers, senior centers, and museums. My thanks also goes to the staff of the Southern Regional Office of the National Trust for Historic Preservation, notably John Hildreth, Nancy Tinker, and Tracy Hayes. By placing all Rosenwald schools on their "11 Most Endangered List" for 2002, the National Trust has sparked renewed interest in this subject throughout the South.

Other individuals have assisted me in a variety of ways. Patricia Powers provided me with important information on her relative Walker Lewis. Gayla Basham served as my research assistant so long ago that she has probably forgotten me and the entire project. Rabbi Emeritus Arnold Jacob Wolf of K.A.M. Isaiah Israel Congregation in Chicago aided my discussion of Reform Judaism and the philosophy of Emil Hirsch, the eminent Reform rabbi who so greatly influenced Rosenwald. Robert C. Blattberg of the Kellogg Graduate School of Management kindly read over the portions of the book that deal with Sears. Mary Hoffschwelle of Middle Tennessee State University read and commented on portions of the book that deal with Rosenwald schools. Emile Karafiol read the manuscript and gave me useful editorial advice. Any lingering errors that may exist are mine and should not in any way be attributed to them. Dr. Howard Platt of Loyola University of Chicago and Dr. Burton Bledstein of the University of Illinois at Chicago provided me with important bibliographical information. Elizabeth Varet, my wonderful cousin, not only let me see portions of the unpublished memoirs of her father, William Rosenwald, but also provided me with unflagging encouragement. My daughter, Elizabeth Tsapira, gave me inspiration, enthusiasm, and moral support. My beloved wife, Lucy, who has lived this project with me for the last twelve years and who has cheerfully urged me to persevere, read the first draft of the manuscript and made numerous suggestions that have proved invaluable.

Finally, this book is dedicated to Philip Stern, who started down this road and provided me with the inspiration to carry on and complete the task he so ably began.

Julius Rosenwald

1

Youth and First Business Ventures, 1862–1895

On May 12, 1854, Samuel Rosenwald, a twenty-six-year-old German Jewish youth, alighted from the ship *Wilhemine* in the port of Baltimore. He had come from the village of Bunde in Westphalia, where his mother, Vogel, owned a small general store. His father had died when he was a child. Like countless immigrants before and after him, Samuel Rosenwald was determined to make a good life for himself in the New World.[1]

The revolutions of 1848 in Europe brought hard economic times in their wake, and this was as true in Germany as in other countries. There were food shortages. Unemployment was rife. The second of four children, Samuel must have clearly realized that his options if he stayed in Bunde were relatively limited. By the mid-1800s, reports of the boundless opportunities available in America were filtering back to Europe. For a young man of brains and ambition, the lure of the New World was probably almost irresistible.

Life for the new immigrant was challenging. When he landed in Baltimore, Samuel had only $20 in his pocket. Like many Jews newly arrived in America, he became a peddler carrying an assortment of goods from watches to thread, his main route being the Winchester Trail in Virginia, West Virginia, and the Appalachian region.[2]

About two years later, Samuel began to work for the Hammersloughs, a German Jewish family who had begun arriving in America ten years earlier from a town near Bremerhaven. They set up a successful clothing business in Baltimore, and by 1856 they had branch stores in other towns. There were several Hammerslough brothers, each of whom journeyed to America when he was about thirteen. The eldest, Julius, chose to settle in Baltimore because he had distant relatives there. When the younger brothers arrived, they began working with him. In 1853, the brothers were joined by their twenty-year-old sister, Augusta. Samuel Rosenwald, whose story thus far had been that of the quintessential Jewish immigrant, departed from the norm by falling in love with his employers' sister. The couple were married in August 1857. A month after the wedding, they were headed west, for Samuel had been named manager of the Baltimore Clothing House in Peoria, Illinois, which the Hammerslough brothers had founded the previous spring. Managing a dry goods store was another prototypical job for a nineteenth-century Jewish immigrant, a post that many a peddler ardently desired.

The next few years were both difficult and peripatetic for the young couple. Their first son was born in Peoria but died in infancy. In 1860, the Hammersloughs sold the Peoria store and sent Samuel and Augusta to Talledega, Alabama, where another son, Benjamin, was born and survived. But the Rosenwalds disliked the alien culture, the heat, and the slavery of Alabama, and later that same year they left for Evansville, Indiana, where the Hammersloughs had purchased the Oak Hall Clothing Company, which was renamed S. Rosenwald & Co.[3] Although Samuel was successful in selling ready-made suits in Evansville, he stayed there only about six months. The Hammersloughs, who had opened a store in Springfield, Illinois, some years before, urgently needed Samuel to manage that store, which was doing a tremendous business selling uniforms to the Union forces mustering for the early Civil War battles. The Rosenwald family arrived in Springfield early in the summer of 1861. It was there on August 12 of the following year that Julius was born in a house one block from the home of Abraham Lincoln.

Contrary to the myth which developed that JR (as he was later called by his friends) was a Horatio Alger prototype who rose from rags to riches, he grew up in a solidly middle-class family. Probably because of the Civil War and the continued need for uniforms, Samuel's business flourished. In 1864, an ad in a Springfield newspaper boasted that his store had outfitted the Tenth Illinois cavalry regiment.[4] In 1868, the Hammerslough brothers sold the Springfield store to Samuel Rosenwald. The business continued to be very successful. In 1869, the family moved to a new home in Springfield, because it had outgrown the house in which Julius was born. There were five children in addition to Benjamin and Julius: Morris, Louis, Sammy, Selma, and Sophie. Then in 1872, tragedy struck. In an era when disease killed so many children, young Sammy, "the strongest and liveliest of them all," as his grieving mother described him, was carried off in an influenza epidemic.[5]

Even in the face of death, life and business had to proceed. In a letter originally in German to his family in Bunde, Samuel wrote in 1872:

> I have to do a very large business to meet my expenses; in the first place, it costs me $3,000 for my small family. . . . My expenses for the store are approximately $4,000. This has to be earned. And if one does not do a fairly good business one soon loses out. But really I must not complain. Last year my business was very satisfactory.[6]

By the 1880s, according to the R. G. Dun Company (predecessor of Dun and Bradstreet), which had agents in every town in America reporting on the creditworthiness of local businessmen, Samuel Rosenwald had an inventory of between $10,000 and $15,000 and a net worth of between $30,000 and $40,000. His house was worth $4,000 (a considerable sum at that time), and he also owned property in Kansas City from which he received rental income of $400 a month. He was considered an excellent businessman and a good credit risk. As the Dun agent reported in 1882, "[Samuel Rosenwald is a] very capable energetic man who, during a business career of about twenty years, has established an excellent trade and reputation."[7]

JR's childhood was unexceptional. His mother was evidently loving and very fond of him. There were not many amusements or distractions in small-town America. JR was too little to remember Lincoln's funeral, but he was old enough to recall the dedication of a memorial to the slain president. Amid the hoopla surrounding this event, which took place on October 15, 1874, a pamphlet was created entitled "History of the Monument." JR remembers selling this pamphlet and earning $2.50. He also sold lithographs of the Lincoln monument suitable for framing. "General Grant, who was President at that time, came to Springfield to dedicate the monument. I remember meeting him in an open barouche, and, in shaking hands with him, I was particularly impressed because he had on yellow kid gloves. He was the first man I ever saw who wore kid gloves," JR later wrote.[8]

The sale of the pamphlets and lithographs is one of the few authenticated instances of the young Rosenwald's business ability and entrepreneurship. Once he became president of a major corporation, numerous legends and stories arose purporting to demonstrate what a shrewd businessman he was even as a youth. Most of these stories, though charming, very likely are apocryphal. It is plausible, however, that JR assisted in his father's store on Saturdays selling paper collars.[9]

JR attended the Fourth Ward public schools and then the local high school for two years. In addition to a secular education, he also received a Jewish education. The Rosenwald family retained its religious traditions. Samuel was a leader of the Jewish community in Springfield and was president of Congregation B'rith Sholem from 1867 to 1873. Many years later, JR described his Jewish upbringing and education:

> Even though not a student of the subject of religion, I may lay claim to being deeply consecrated to the Jewish faith because not only was I Bar Mitzvah at thirteen, but it so happened that a year later, our congregation in Springfield, Illinois, dedicated a new Reform temple with confirmation exercises, and I was also confirmed. . . . I cannot claim that my parents were at all orthodox, as we understand that term. The parents and children attended Friday evening services regularly and kept the greater holidays. Most of the Jews of that city were members of the congregation. And I always believed that the respect in which the Jews of Springfield were held by their Christian fellows was largely the result of the congregational life and the fact that the Rabbi represented the Jews when an occasion arose.[10]

This passage would seem to indicate that JR did not personally experience any incidents of antisemitism growing up, but that was apparently not true of his brothers and sisters. In 1881, Samuel added in a postscript to his wife's letter to Elise Rosenwald in Germany, a note about antisemitism in Springfield: "In business one hardly ever hears anything like that, but the children often hear about it, and that is unpleasant enough."[11]

Despite occasional odd jobs, JR's first real employment occurred when he was fifteen. He described it as follows in his fragmentary autobiography written in 1927:

> My first regular job was during vacation in the summer of 1877 when I worked for two months in what was known as a 99 cent store, where everything was either 49 cents or 99 cents. There I waited on customers and also delivered packages. I remember taking out a 99 cent croquet set, or a glass globe with two gold fish in it for 49 cents and no end of other goods. It was during that summer that I managed to save about $20, and as my parents' china wedding anniversary occurred in August of that year, I invested my savings in an elaborately decorated tea set as a gift to my mother, who was especially delighted on account of my having earned the money with which to purchase it.[12]

This story which JR loved to tell about his youth reveals several interesting things. One is that instead of spending the money on himself, he spent it on a gift. And the nature of that gift is also significant. Although it was intended as an anniversary present, the only real recipient was JR's mother. Samuel Rosenwald is not even mentioned. The relationship between JR and his mother, which a Freudian would love, itself became the stuff of legend, part of the typical account of JR's life which appeared in numerous newspaper and magazine stories in the 1910s and 1920s. His intense devotion to her never varied throughout her long life. Finally, it is interesting to note that in JR's mind, it was his mother, not his father, who sought to instill in him the importance of saving the $2.50 a week that he earned.

In March 1879, after having attended high school for two years, JR departed for New York to serve as an apprentice for his uncles. The Hammerslough brothers had moved from Baltimore and had also changed professions. Instead of being the owners of clothing stores, they were now among the major manufacturers of men's clothing in New York City. JR never finished high school, something which was not unusual in America in the 1880s. He also never attended college, a fact which bothered him in later life. Despite the honors he was to receive and the prominence to which he rose, he always felt that he was not as well educated as most of the people among whom he moved.

New York

The seventeen-year-old from sleepy small-town Springfield suddenly found himself in the biggest, most dynamic city in the country.[13] Although his father often traveled to New York on business trips, JR had never ventured beyond the borders of his hometown. To the young midwesterner, the change must have been terribly exciting and slightly frightening. The Monday after his arrival in New York, he witnessed the St. Patrick's Day parade. Decades later, he vividly remembered the tremendous noise made by the hooves of horses pulling buses filled with revelers down the cobblestone streets of Broadway.[14]

New York, then as now, was a bustling metropolis, teeming with immigrants and filled with theaters and other amusements. It was a city of contrasts, of newly rich millionaires, such as Jay Gould, and the dreadful poverty of the tenements and the sweatshops.

One very noticeable change in the young man's life was that he moved from the pleasant bourgeois comfort of his parents' home into the house of one of his uncles, all of whom were extremely wealthy. As JR put it: "They all lived in much finer surroundings than I had been accustomed to." He now occupied a room in a town house with four stories and a basement in the newly fashionable area around East 58th Street.[15] The Hammerslough Brothers firm where JR worked was considered one of the premier clothing companies of New York. In 1879 the Dun correspondent said of it: "[They] claim a capital of $300,000. Julius Hammerslough is the senior partner in this firm. He is an active good merchant and is a man of considerable means and regarded as good for any engagements."[16]

Despite the lavish surroundings in which he lived, JR started as a stock clerk, earning $5 a week. To supplement this modest income, he made an additional $2 a week working Saturday evenings at either Rogers, Peet & Co. or Carhart, Whitford & Co., both retail clothing firms.[17] JR clearly was ambitious and hardworking, for he rose through the ranks rapidly, though family connections probably played a part in his success. Within two and a half years of his arrival in New York, he was traveling to cities such as Trenton, New Jersey, with a suitcase filled with Hammerslough Brothers wares.[18]

It was around this time, in 1881, that JR moved out of his uncle's comfortable home and into a rooming house where he paid $9 a week in rent.[19] The establishment was evidently one favored by upwardly mobile Jewish young men, for his housemates included Henry Morgenthau, later a lawyer, financier, and ambassador; Henry Goldman, later chairman of Goldman Sachs, who was to play an important role in his life at a crucial time; and Moses Newborg, son of a man who supplied goods to Samuel

Rosenwald and who became a clothing merchant in his own right. JR and Newborg became fast friends. Abandoning his Saturday night work, JR and his friends would go to Tony Pastor's variety theater where they would sit in cheap seats and take in the vaudeville shows. It is likely that they attended more serious theatrical fare as well, for it was possibly at this time that JR developed a love for the theater which he retained throughout his life.

JR maintained close relations with his family through frequent correspondence. Samuel sent his son letters he received in German from the relatives and reported back to them that his son in New York was enjoying himself. JR could not make it home for his parents' silver wedding anniversary in 1882, but he did send them a present, though not a very romantic one: a toilet seat.[20] Was this a belated statement of adolescent rebellion? There is no way of knowing, but it does seem a striking contrast to the tea set of five years earlier.

This young man on the make did not stop to examine the society around him and ask the probing questions that marked his later years. It is likely that the clothes made for the Hammerslough Brothers were stitched together by immigrant (mostly Jewish) tailors living in appalling conditions in tenements and paid abysmally low wages. Although reformers such as Lincoln Stephens and Jacob Riis were only beginning to write about the sweatshops, it is a fact that neither in his autobiographical notes nor anywhere else does JR make any mention whatsoever of these conditions. He probably did not see them or think about them. He was focused only on getting ahead.

After working five years for his uncles, JR decided to strike out on his own. In 1884, he was joined in New York by his brother, Morris, and the two had the interesting but unfortunate idea of opening a small shop a few doors down from Brokaw Brothers, the undisputed leader of men's clothing in the city. It was JR's notion that they could take advantage of the overflow business from the better known establishment. JR and Morris prevailed on their father to lend them the money to buy a small store, which they named "J. Rosenwald and Brother." It did not start out auspiciously. Samuel Rosenwald wrote his relatives in Bunde from New York: "My good sons, Julius and Morris, are here in business, but they are only doing fairly well."[21] Then the business worsened. As Mo Newborg remembered it many years later, "That idea was a *flop.*"[22] JR's memory of this enterprise thirty years later was "how anxious I was to sell a scarf and pin for ten cents and have handbills strewn all over the Bowery and Fourth Avenue."[23]

As Rosenwald and Brother was crumbling around him, JR had another idea that proved to be a good deal more sensible. It was based on a conversation he had with another clothing merchant. As JR describes it:

> I had occasion to buy summer clothing from the firm of Alfred Benjamin & Company who were large manufacturers in that line. One of the partners remarked to me that they had received over sixty telegrams for goods that day which they were unable to supply and that the demand was increasing constantly for such goods as they were supplying. I did not give it much thought at the moment, but during the night I awakened and thought of what he had told me and the opportunity entered my mind of embarking in the same sort of business. The idea took such hold of me that there was no more sleep that night for me and the next morning I presented my plan to my uncles, who thought it might be a capital idea to open a business for the manufacture of summer clothing in Chicago. My cousin, Julius E. Weil, was employed in the manufacturing department of my uncles' business, and together we planned to go to Chicago and begin the manufacture of summer clothing. After several months' planning, he and I left for Chicago, toward the end of September 1885 and rented a second floor loft.[24]

Several aspects of this account are characteristic of the later Julius Rosenwald. One is his ability to take advantage of an opportunity. JR was a modest man, but he never denied that this was one of his gifts. Second, once he had the vision, he was driven to make it a reality. But he did not do so on his own. In this case, he created a business plan and then presented it to his uncles for approval. And, just as he had not embarked on his first business venture on his own, he again sought out a family member, someone he knew well and felt comfortable dealing with, to be a partner with him. Having learned his lesson from the disaster of Rosenwald & Brother, JR acted conservatively and methodically and spent several months planning this new business venture. What he does not say in this autobiographical fragment is how he obtained the funding to start Rosenwald & Weil.

The previous quotation might lead one to assume that JR's Hammerslough uncles, having approved his plan, would put money into it. That did not occur. Instead, they did something just as important: they "gave the young men credit and guaranteed their purchases with other firms."[25] For immediate capital, JR turned again to his father, despite the failure of Rosenwald & Brother, and asked him for a portion of the money to launch the new firm. Fortunately, Samuel Rosenwald's store was continuing to prosper. In a letter to his family in Bunde dated December 1880, Samuel described his financial situation. In the previous three months he had taken in $11,000, which represented a profit of from 30 percent to 33.33 percent. He had two employees in the store, in addition to Bennie, the eldest son. One employee was given $1,000 a year, the other $900. Rent for the store was $1,100. Samuel estimated his total business expenses as somewhat over $4,000. Family and living expenses cost an additional $3,000 per year. In addition to his business, he had his investments in Kansas City. With his brother-in-law, Louis Hammerslough, he had bought two businesses and half of another. They provided him with an annual income after taxes and insurance of $4,000 a year. These figures belie the tone of the letter, which implies that by exercising great economy the family was just scraping by. This worry about expenses, however, seems to have been characteristic of JR's father. Having experienced poverty in his youth, he was determined not to face that situation again.[26] In short, Samuel Rosenwald had the money to invest in the creation of Rosenwald & Weil and was willing to do so. Nor did he keep this loan a secret. Even the Dun correspondent notes in 1886 that Samuel had lent money "to a son of his who is doing a lucrative wholesale clothing trade in Chicago."[27] The total amount of this loan was $2,000. Julius Weil's father put up an equal amount.

Rosenwald & Weil

There was good reason for JR's uncles to be enthusiastic about his plan to launch a store specializing in lightweight men's suits in Chicago. They knew the men's clothing market and could see that there was a niche to be filled there. Equally important, however, was the fact that Chicago was a boom town where an ambitious young man could indeed prosper, perhaps even to a greater extent than in New York.

The city had recovered miraculously from the disastrous fire of October 1871.[28] The stockyards were employing thousands of people and turning out meat for a nation, aided by the invention of the refrigerated rail car. The Pullman Company was building its famous sleeping cars in a planned company town just south of the city. Marshall Field had opened one of the largest, most lavish department stores in the world. And an interesting new method of retailing, selling items through the mail from a catalog, had been successfully developed by A. Montgomery Ward.

Ward had come to Chicago from Michigan in the mid-1860s and had worked briefly in a retail establishment. Then he became a traveling salesman for a St. Louis–based dry goods wholesaler journeying from one small midwestern farming town to another, going to the county stores that bought his wares. There, around the crackerbarrel, he listened to the frustrations of the farmers. They had much to complain about: the high prices charged by grain elevator operators and the low prices they received for their crops. They especially griped about the local stores, where the supplies were meager and overpriced. Ward listened to these complaints and realized that there had to be a better way of supplying these farmers. If he bought goods in bulk and sold them only for cash by mail, thus eliminating middlemen like his employer, he could provide farmers with a larger array of products and sell them at cheaper prices than the local stores. Eager to put his idea into practice, he returned to Chicago, purchased an initial supply of goods, and rented space from which to mail out the goods. Unfortunately, Ward chose exactly the wrong time to do this: October 1871. His entire stock of goods went up in flames. Without hesitation, he and his partner started over, using the network already established by the Grange movement, and in a relatively short time Ward could see that his experiment had proved successful. There was, indeed, a market in the hinterlands, hungry for goods by mail. To ensure that people would not be chary about ordering goods from a catalog, in a merchandising situation in which the customer could neither see nor feel the goods or deal with a salesman, Ward developed the policy that if the buyer was not satisfied with the purchase, he or she could send the item back free of charge. From a single sheet in 1872, the catalog grew to 150 pages by 1876.[29] The mail-order business had arrived.

While there was much for the civic booster to boast about in Chicago, the city also had its seamier side. Many of the immigrants lived and worked in conditions that were as appalling as anything the tenements of New York had to offer. Crime and prostitution were serious problems. Innocent farm girls from the prairie states to the West (like Dreiser's Sister Carrie) as well as immigrant girls who had not yet mastered the English language were both ensnared in the white slave trade. The politics of the

Figure 1. In 1886, Samuel Rosenwald sold his store in Springfield to Myers Brothers and moved to Chicago to assist his son. This scene depicts Samuel's store under the new management.

city was notoriously corrupt. Nevertheless, it was as good a city as any in America for a couple of ambitious, hardworking young men to open a clothing business.

The beginning of Rosenwald & Weil was difficult. JR remembered vividly how he made his first trip with suitcases crammed with samples of summer suits in January 1886. "I will never forget how bitter cold St. Louis was when I was on my first trip to sell clothes intended for the hottest summer weather, and the welcome I received seemed to me even colder than the weather, but as time went on, the prospects grew brighter and results comparatively satisfactory."[30] Still, it was hard work. Competition, even in such a niche market, was fierce. In the late summer of 1886, JR returned to St. Louis and once again was not very successful. In 1886, Samuel Rosenwald sold his Springfield store and came to Chicago to work with JR, Morris, and Julius Weil at the new firm. Eventually, Rosenwald & Weil became moderately successful.

Not far from Samuel Rosenwald's new home lived another Jewish family that had recently moved to Chicago from Plattsburg, New York. Emanuel Nusbaum, like Samuel, had emigrated from Germany, entered into the clothing business, and moved to Chicago in 1882 with his seven daughters and one son. He may have moved in order to remarry (which he did) or because it was easier to find suitable husbands for his daughters in Chicago than in tiny Plattsburg. Emanuel Nusbaum had lived in Plattsburg since the 1860s.[31] He and his brothers had gone into business with a New York City clothier named Stern. According to the Dun correspondent in Plattsburg, Nusbaum & Stern was fairly successful until Stern pulled out. From the Dun figures, it would seem that the Nusbaums were not nearly as well off as the Samuel Rosenwald family, but still were comfortably middle-class.[32] JR met Augusta "Gussie" Nusbaum, an attractive, intelligent girl, the third oldest daughter. They fell in love and became engaged on January 6, 1890, shortly after Gussie's twentieth birthday. Four months later, they were married and went off on a brief honeymoon to Niagara Falls.

As part of his work, JR was required to spend a considerable amount of time on the road. He made frequent trips to New York to examine and buy samples and to deal with his uncles. He also traveled to other cities to display his wares and take orders, for Rosenwald & Weil was not just a local Chicago firm, though it was small. A number of letters describing the business exist from the early years of JR's and Gussie's marriage. Although somewhat formulaic, they also contain vivid glimpses into the lives and characters of these two young people and of the German Jewish middle-class society they inhabited.

During his courtship and the first year of his marriage, JR provided Gussie with some glimpse into his world of work. Six months after the wedding, he wrote his wife from Pittsburgh: "The hour at which I write is a bad one for business, and for all the money I have made here, I might just as well have been on the cars today. . . . The most of the vast trade here is done by clothiers, and they will not interest themselves so easily."[33] This trip continued to be disappointing, as JR wrote from Philadelphia: "I visited the stores and found that none of the furnishers carried vests and that clothiers would not think of buying vests now."[34] A few days later, business had picked up a bit: "Just finished up with a customer with whom I succeeded in placing a few goods."[35] Several months later, business was again discouraging: "I fear . . . that my friends here meant what they said and will not place an order—for reasons which I cannot help but say

Figure 2. JR and Gussie shortly after their wedding in 1890.

are good."[36] After Christmas in 1890, JR was in his hometown. "Showing samples in a store is tedious work, as we were disturbed every moment. I sold Mr. Lange about $600 and will finish with him tomorrow, and then tackle my friends, the Myers [the people who had bought Samuel Rosenwald's store]."[37] The next day the business outlook was rosy: "I succeeded in selling by patience and perseverance about $1,200 today—$1,000 to Myers Bros. and about $200 to Lange and I want to increase the amount, so will remain tomorrow to do my duty."[38]

After the first year of marriage, however, descriptions of work become much more rare. Most of JR's letters are taken up with travel notes, but there were exceptions. For example, there is this note from a trip to Denver in September 1891: "I spent most of the morning with our best customer here. He took me out and showed me the principal buildings and they have really fine structures here. The afternoon I devoted to business, called on all the clothiers. In the evening, I invited our customer and his partner for dinner and theater."[39] Given his skill in dealing with people, one can imagine that this "schmoozing" with favored customers was something that JR was extremely good at and also enjoyed.

Evidently the volume of goods they dealt in was quite large, for Julius Weil cabled JR in New York: "Try induce Lange to have 5,000 vests made for us, seersuckers, alpacas."[40] As with many small businesses, there were apparently times when short-term loans were required, as Samuel Rosenwald wrote his son: "I think it would be well if you yourself were to go to the I & T Bank to talk to them and tell them that only twice during the year do we borrow money and that for such short periods we could not have such a big balance at the bank. In case they do not want to accede to this, you could go to the Fourth National Bank and find out what they do."[41] During a trip that JR and Julius Weil made to New York in the summer of 1892, Samuel Rosenwald wrote them daily. Clearly, JR was becoming more adept at getting goods at a reasonable price: "I am very glad that you, dear Julius, have got the alpaca somewhat cheaper. I hope that you can buy all the other goods cheap too. . . . We are getting along very well in the store. It is very quiet."[42] The next day, however, Samuel received bad news: "We have been very sorry that your trip was not as desired."[43]

In short, the business had its ups and downs. The original concept was a smart one, but Rosenwald & Weil suffered the vicissitudes of many small businesses, and there was nothing to suggest the brilliant future career of one of its founders.

One theme that runs through these letters is the question of money. JR and Gussie could certainly not have been considered wealthy at this stage. For the first few months after their wedding, they lived with JR's parents. Then they leased a house which, though it was very much within the city limits of Chicago, must have had a slightly rural feel to it, for there was a cow in a neighbor's yard.[44] Before they moved into the new house, Gussie wrote: "I will not be a slave to housekeeping cares. I will try and arrange matters so that if my home does not need my attention, I can devote it to improving myself in other important subjects, and with your help, love, I am in hopes of accomplishing this aim."[45] So they had a maid. And when Lessing, their first son, was born on February 10, 1891, they had a nurse as well. Nevertheless, money remained a concern. Faced with the reports about her husband's lack of success, Gussie developed a trope that appears in many of her letters: riches cannot buy everything; family love is more important. For example: "You know my views on having riches without true family love and union, which cannot be bought if it does not exist."[46] A few weeks later, she returns to the theme of being parsimonious, urging JR not to bring her a present. "You know that little house we are going to have. Well, a great deal will have to be expended, where, as yet, we do not know of. So it is best to be a little precautious. Not that we are going to save and hoard up money for money's sake. Not that we will wish to enjoy it later on, when we can appreciate it more."[47]

In January 1892, Gussie was shocked when Samuel Rosenwald announced that he had gone over the household accounts and found there were serious problems.

> Papa Rosenwald stopped in this A.M.—he says our expenses for the past year have been enormous. He says he only tells me in case there is a leakage we shall find it out and make it better. You and I, sweetheart, will have to have a good sensible talk on this question and see just where the biggest drain lies and try to correct it. Of course, last year [my] sickness [after the birth of Lessing] ate up a great amount, but this year, with but one exception, I do hope we cannot give this as an excuse for large expenditures.[48]

Her remedy, as in the past, was no presents: "Bring back no gifts to *anyone.* Then no one can feel slighted, and besides, there is nothing I really need, and to buy something I don't need is an extravagance we can't afford at present, for the money I have used for birthdays this month has been sufficient expense. This is not merely talk. *I mean every word.*"[49]

Actually, Gussie was not always parsimonious. Several months before the incident with Samuel Rosenwald, while JR was on a trip to the West, Gussie decided that she wanted a mink cape that cost $65. She said she knew it was an extravagance but it could be worn with anything.[50] JR replied:

I almost fainted, Gussie darling, when I saw the figures after that $ mark—in regard to Nettie's cloak or cape. But your reasons, I must say, are not well founded when you figure on being able to use it for full dress affairs. The few times that this occurs ought not, to my notion, be taken into consideration—as you shall wear a garment 50 times more for other purposes. I don't object to your having it, I'm sure, but be certain before you buy it that it's just what you want and not have cause to regret it afterwards, as was the case with your light jacket. It might be policy to get a more reasonable one now and next year get a seal skin—but do as you think best—these are only suggestions on my part.[51]

Gussie managed to both back down and stand her ground at the same time: "Now regarding that coat, I am going to get what I first intended getting, a real nice coat and not that cape—so that scene was all for nix."[52] It is interesting and slightly amusing to read these discussions about money in hindsight knowing that within a decade they would both be wealthy beyond their wildest dreams.

JR's letters are generally filled with news about family gatherings, the food he ate, the plays he attended. Occasionally, there are passages of real insight and humor, as in this description of a visit to an aunt in New York who seems to have felt slighted concerning JR's marriage.

I fortified myself, armed to the teeth with determination there "to beard the lioness in her den." I was announced, asked up by Uncle Sam, shook hands with the lioness, who asked for everyone in the family, that is, everyone who was in the family previous to my marriage, and then Uncle Sam and I drifted on to business topics, his wife sitting with a long face, uttering only an occasional word addressed to her liege lord. After about an hour, the battle was opened by Uncle Sam who said: "Now Emalie, don't sit there and moap [*sic*]. Give Julius HELL and be done with it." Then she let loose, and such vituperation (good word) you never heard. I admitted my mistake, but it was no go. She had done nothing wrong, and we had committed a crime to which murder wasn't to be compared. She had no forgiveness to offer, no matter what apology was offered. After a battle of about a half an hour, we drifted on to other matters, and the discussion was laid on the table.[53]

Or there were descriptions of cities he was visiting, as in this discovery of the newly built Plaza Hotel in New York: "On the way, a new hotel that has been built just at the entrance to the Park attracted my attention and

I went to see it. Such magnificence I cannot describe. We have nothing to compare with it—a perfect palace!"[54]

On his trip out west in 1891, JR describes many sights: the gambling houses in Albuquerque ("which are as open here as the clothing businesses and a good deal more busy"), a trip up Pike's Peak, and his first and presumably last prize fight in San Francisco ("It was a very exciting affair, but fearfully brutal").[55] He waxes eloquent about the beauties of the Bay Area, but when it comes to an Indian town in New Mexico, or a brief visit to Juarez just over the Mexican border from El Paso, he is shockingly blunt. On a trip he made to an Indian school in New Mexico with Gussie's sister, Miriam, and her husband, JR wrote: "You can't picture the inhabitants of this place. The dirtiest set of Mexicans and Indians—a lazy set."[56] Almost the same racial slurs were used to describe the people he saw on his excursion to Juarez.[57] Reading this with twenty-first-century sensibilities may be uncomfortable, but it is amazing to realize that this was a man who, twenty years later, was to start assisting black Americans in a way that few other white men were willing to do. Thirty-five years later, JR was to talk about building schools for Mexican children.

Gussie's life was a great deal more circumscribed. She did not do much traveling. And after Lessing was born in February 1891 and Adele in July 1892, she was really confined to the Chicago area. Although a maid did the housework, Gussie was not idle. She loved to read—not dime novels, but books such as George Eliot's *Daniel Deronda.* She took a class in Shakespeare sonnets. She took music lessons. She enjoyed the theater as much as her husband, and she also loved music and opera, for which he had to develop a taste. Often in the evening she would visit JR's parents and play pinochle or whist. Like other women of her social class, she held "at homes" where one would send invitations to a number of female friends and acquaintances and then wait to see who would present their card at the door. Success was evidently measured by the number of women who came. This kind of routine and the return visits to other women's homes could become rather tedious. As Gussie exclaimed in one letter to JR: "Please deliver me from all coffee klatches!"[58]

Gussie spent a great deal of time with JR's family and her own, for the three houses were within a few blocks of each other. She does not seem to have been particularly fond of her family. Her mother had died years earlier, and she never spoke particularly warmly of her father and stepmother. Sometimes she could be furious with them, as on one occasion in September 1890 when she waited all evening for them and "no one put in an appearance." Gussie declared that she was terribly angry and "they shall know it, for I am going down there."[59] Relations were also sometimes strained with her brother, Aaron, who was soon to play a very important role in JR's life. In January 1892, Gussie bought him a birthday present:

> Last evening we went to Nusbaums' for dinner, it being Aaron's birthday. I had the girls put the silk stockings in his room with love from Lessing. He didn't say a word to me about them, just as if I had not given them. I hate to receive thanks, but such bitter indifference hurt me terribly. I didn't say a word, but I will never allow him to give Lessing or myself a single trifle. I know I did wrong in not recognizing his previous birthdays, as he has always been kind and good to us girls, and he felt hurt to think that we, Miriam or myself, had not given him anything. Still, it does not excuse him for not recognizing a token at any time.[60]

Perhaps such slights should not be blown out of proportion, but in the hothouse atmosphere in which Gussie lived, it was easy to do that.

Gussie's relations with her in-laws were also ambiguous. On the one hand, she was thrilled that JR's parents treated her "like their own flesh and blood"[61] and, indeed, she seems to have often preferred their company to that of her father and stepmother. On the other hand, relations between JR and his mother must have made life difficult for the young wife. JR insisted that the letters he wrote Gussie should be brought over to his mother and read to her. At one point a year and a half into the marriage, Gussie pretended to be indignant, but there is a hint in this letter that perhaps she is partially serious: "Jule, love, who ever heard of such a thing as a husband writing to his wife that his letters are meant as much for her mother-in-law as for herself? Mama thinks so too. She feels insulted if I don't let her read every letter. She isn't satisfied if I merely tell her what is in them. To tell you the truth, I like to read them to her."[62] But the passage that would have delighted Freud occurred earlier in the marriage. JR had finished reading a book entitled "The Second Wife" and wrote his new wife about it, but he buried the name of the work in the bottom of a paragraph. He wrote Gussie: "After I finish with my first wife, I'll begin on my second." Gussie, after reading this, replied: "I didn't know what you meant, nor was I jealous. I thought you meant your mother, and it was not till I reread it that the real meaning dawned on me."[63]

While relations between Gussie and JR's mother were generally excellent, the relationship with Samuel Rosenwald was more problematic. JR himself almost never mentions his father in his letters, although he always inquires after his mother and often his brothers and sisters. It seems fairly clear that JR's father could be difficult. Gussie reported the following in July 1892: "[Mrs. Neufeld] is terribly hurt at [Papa Rosenwald's] actions. I know that last summer when she and her husband were at Sel[ma]'s to say good-bye, Papa came and went out as soon as he saw they were there. Of course I tried to smooth matters, but she knew better."[64] A friend of JR's from this period, speaking to a potential biographer many decades later, recalled that "Samuel Rosenwald always impressed me as being domineering and autocratic, demanding implicit obedience to commands in the household, and a man of irascible temper, good looking and good humored, but he would fly off the handle at the least provocation."[65] Although admittedly circumstantial evidence, there is something about this description that rings true.

Gussie comes across in her letters as a complex character. She is always the obedient little wife, and then every once in a while one finds her making decisions that are surprising, as when she is taking bids from contractors to fix up the house—the kind of task one would expect would be carried out only by a man in that period.

> I was so tired from the dressmaker and getting bids for the work to be done on the house. I had three men come and give me an estimate and all gave the same price: $16 for [the] sitting room and the hall—which I wasn't going to have done at first, but it looks worse than the rooms, as the walls are broken. . . . I don't know what you will say, Jule darling, that I am expending this money, but I wouldn't want to live in such looking rooms another year and a half. And I don't suppose there is any danger of our building till the lease is up on this house. You say I am usually right, and I trust you will think so now.[66]

There was a sad or self-pitying streak in Gussie that certainly did not border on the clinical but did occasionally cause her to become depressed. Her first letters to JR following their wedding are almost excessive in terms of sorrow at his departure and longing for his return. JR evidently told her to calm down and be cheerful even in his absence. But it was not always easy to bear his absence with equanimity. For example, in September 1891, she wrote JR that she felt old and separated from her peers in age because she was a wife and mother. What set her off on this train of thought was a song:

> "Backward turn, backward turn, oh twice in your flight, make me a child again, just for one night" were the words that came to me last night, and following their impulse, I joined the young people in calling on Helen and Lessing Rosenthal [close friends of JR and Gussie]. There were so many young people there, that at first I felt like sinking, but I soon regained my courage. How strange it all seemed, just as if I had never been one of them. . . . I like my present life too well, since it is devoted to my true good husband and a darling baby.[67]

A few months later, she wrote:

> I have so much reason to be dissatisfied with myself and my ill temper that half of my happiness with you and baby [Lessing] is overbalanced. By your gentle guidance, my darling husband, I am in hopes of reforming. This is not just idle talk, for in my own heart I know it is true. Only last night, just after I returned from the depot [presumably to see JR off] the Mr. Hyde of my character showed itself.[68]

In 1893, Gussie suffered what Werner delicately refers to as "nerves"—"too much responsibility—too much family interference with child-training—too much family in every direction. There is a definite longing to get away from it all—move way out—away from the family. There is the feeling of deprivation of 'fun' for a young thing—she is but 25—the feeling that romance is a little dimmed and within less than three years. Mostly it is a case of frazzled nerves—'I am all tired out.'"[69] Given her circumscribed existence and the presence of two small children, it would have been extraordinary if she had not felt this way at times.

However, this feeling could not last for long. Tremendously exciting events were occurring in Chicago just a few miles from where Gussie lived. The Columbian Exposition opened, one of the most successful world's fairs in history. Crowds poured into Chicago to view the gleaming White City of Daniel Burnham, proof that Chicago had overcome the fire twenty-two years earlier and was now one of the greatest cities in the world. One could not help but be caught up in the excitement, and Gussie was no exception. She wrote JR:

> Papa Nusbaum went around with me for a while and the rest of the time I went alone. I only went in the Agriculture Building and also saw the three ships Columbus sailed in. They are anchored in the water between La Rabida and Casino Hall. By the way, the French restaurant in the Casino failed. . . . I really think one can see more by being alone, but it is so lonesome that I prefer not to see so much.[70]

Unfortunately, there is no record of what JR thought of the Columbian Exposition.

Even before the Exposition had ended, Chicago was hit by an economic downturn that proved to be part of a nationwide depression. Homeless and desperately poor people crowded Chicago's streets. The English journalist William T. Steed wrote a blistering pamphlet entitled *If Christ Came to Chicago* in which he excoriated the political, social, and business leaders of the city for not doing enough to ease the economic crisis. Rosenwald & Weil survived the depression, but by the end of 1893 sales had begun a serious decline, a situation faced by many other small businesses. JR, breadwinner for a family of four with another on the way, knew that he could not take chances and thought he saw an opening for a new opportunity.

His close friend from New York days, Mo Newborg, was now a partner in a firm specializing in making cheap clothing, a business made possible by the sweatshop conditions then existing in New York.[71] Given the economic downturn, JR reasoned there would be a big demand for inexpensive clothes. He would found a branch of Newborg, Rosenberg & Co. in Chicago.

Shortly before he was to put these plans into operation, his father suffered a stroke in January 1894. Though very worried about his father's condition, JR left for New York in early March without telling Gussie or anyone else a word about his plans. He stayed there a week, so wracked with concern about his father that he could not sleep. This concern over Samuel Rosenwald's health might not appear to square with JR's earlier lack of love or admiration for his father, but it may be that there was a certain amount of guilt involved. Moreover, JR feared the effect Samuel's illness would have on his beloved mother. As soon as JR could leave, he returned to Chicago for a couple of days, assured himself that his father was recovering slowly, and informed Gussie of what he had been doing.

Then he journeyed back to New York to clinch the deal with Mo Newborg and to inform his uncles, who approved of this latest venture. The new firm, Rosenwald & Company, was capitalized at $100,000 and Rosenwald & Weil had a half interest in it.[72] The remainder of the money was put up by Newborg, Rosenberg & Co.

Sears

One day in 1886, a package of watches arrived at the remote community of North Redwood Falls, Minnesota.[73] The stationmaster and express agent who received the watches was young Richard Sears. His father, a Civil War veteran, was a blacksmith who, when Richard was about thirteen, bought a farm that ultimately failed. Like JR, Richard Sears never finished high school. At age sixteen he left home to learn telegraphy, went to work for the Minneapolis & St. Louis railroad, and eventually requested and obtained the position of stationmaster in North Redwood Falls. Shortly after arriving there, he set up a brisk business trading wood, coal, berries, and other products with the local lumbermen and Native Americans who lived in and around the small community. The watches from Chicago were to be sold on consignment, but the jewelry company in Redwood Falls for which they were intended refused delivery. Sears wrote the Chicago watch company and worked out a deal whereby he would buy the watches for $12 apiece. Familiar with the catalogs that came to the station, he wrote a description of the watches and offered to sell them to other station agents for $14 apiece. It was made clear that the station agents could then resell the watches for a higher price and keep the profits. Since such watches normally retailed for $25, the station agents could undersell the local jewelers and make a good profit. The first shipment of watches sold rapidly. So Sears himself ordered watches from another watch company and sold these in the same manner. Within six months, he had netted a profit of close to $5,000, moved to Minneapolis, and established the R. W. Sears Watch Company.[74] By the end of 1886, Sears abandoned writing letters to station agents and started advertising in newspapers. The ads were spectacularly successful, and it soon became apparent that Minneapolis was too small and not centrally enough located for a small but burgeoning mail-order concern, so in March 1887 Sears moved his company to Chicago, where he could take advantage of the excellent railroad grid. Business continued to boom, and Sears, who had been employing his sister as an assistant, decided he needed additional help. He advertised in the paper for an assistant who knew about watches, and the first candidate who answered was a young man from Indiana named Alvah P. Roebuck. He had had experience working with watches, and Sears, who admitted he knew nothing of the inner workings of the watch, hired him on the spot. Because Sears continued to sell his watches at a price well below that offered by most retail jewelers, he did very well. He also began to advertise in more varied publications, especially those directed at a rural audience. Moreover, he began to broaden his product line to include watch chains, general jewelry, and even diamonds sold on the installment plan. Orders poured in, and Sears opened a branch in Toronto.

Richard Sears was learning a great deal about the mail-order business and discovered that he had a real talent for marketing. However, he was still new at this profession and made some serious mistakes. In the beginning of 1889, he ordered sixty thousand watches from one company. Although the watches were relatively inexpensive, he was left with a huge inventory and a fairly large debt to pay for these timepieces. Though well aware that someone in the mail-order business had to appear to be honest, he began cutting corners. In a famous example that dated from this period, he advertised a suite of bedroom furniture at a fabulously low rate. Only in the most minute print at the bottom of the ad did he put the word "miniature." Gullible farmers saw the catchy come-on and a picture of the product, ordered it, and received in the mail a set of dolls' furniture. Richard Sears is alleged to have remarked one day after this occurred: "Honesty is the best policy. I ought to know. I've tried both ways."

Either it was a deep-seated conviction that the mail-order industry was short-lived, or economic worries engendered by his purchase of the sixty thousand watches, but Richard Sears decided to leave business and become a farmer in Iowa. In March 1889, at the age of twenty-five, he sold the R. W. Sears Watch Company to a Chicago concern for a reported $72,000, sold his share of the Toronto branch to Roebuck, and bought a farm in Iowa in his mother's name.

Sears quickly realized that he was not cut out for farming. No doubt he missed the busy pace of city life. In any case, a few months later he was back in Chicago founding a new business under the name of Henry Hoverson and Company because when he sold the first business, the sales agreement stipulated that he could not run a business under his own name for three years. But his stay in Chicago was also brief. His family did not like the city and persuaded him to return to Minneapolis. He did so in the fall of 1889 and founded a new business, the Warren Company, which, like its predecessors, sold watches and jewelry.

Sears lasted in the Warren Company until March 1891. Business was hard, competition was stiff, and he continued to fear that the whole company would come crashing down. Roebuck was still involved in the enterprise, so Sears sold the Warren Company to him and, for the second time, retired. This retirement lasted one week. Then he was back, begging Roebuck for a half interest in the business, which was now called A. C. Roebuck. In August 1891, Sears's share was increased to two-thirds.

Richard Sears had begun issuing small catalogs when he owned the R. W. Sears Watch Company. He continued this practice with the Warren Company. The 1891 catalog of the A. C. Roebuck Company was thirty-two pages long. Sewing machines were added to the line of merchandise. Sears wrote all the catalog copy himself.

In September 1893, the name of the business was changed yet again. The A. C. Roebuck Company, Inc. became Sears, Roebuck & Company. The catalog was now 196 pages, and a large number of new items had been added including "furniture, dishes, wagons, buggies, shoes, baby carriages, and musical instruments."[75] The company was successful. But the same problem that had plagued Sears in 1887 recurred. He needed the business placed in a more centrally located city. In December 1893, he decided to reopen a branch in Chicago. The 1894 catalog was 322 pages, and men and boys' clothing, among other items, were now being sold.

The arrangement of having a central office in Minneapolis and a branch in Chicago proved both cumbersome and expensive. In January 1895, Richard Sears left Minneapolis for good. Sears, Roebuck & Company was entirely located in a five-story building plus a basement in Chicago. It was not a great year to be in business. The depression that had begun a year and a half earlier had not dissipated. And although Sears, Roebuck & Co. was doing quite well, Alvah Roebuck was worried. He was not a wealthy man, he once again owned half the company, and if it crashed, as so many businesses were doing, he would be deeply in debt. Nor was that possibility remote. The company's liability in 1895 stood at $78,163, three times more than the limit imposed by the charter of incorporation issued in Minnesota. The net worth of the company was $54,570.[76] It was clear that without an immediate infusion of capital, Sears, Roebuck might not survive. Richard Sears was a workaholic who labored ten-hour days, seven days a week, and urged his colleagues to do likewise. Roebuck was not a healthy man, and the strain was beginning to tell on him. Moreover, although he admired his brilliant partner, he also realized that one of Sears's constantly changing and evolving schemes might go awry. Or perhaps Sears had finally persuaded his partner that the mail-order industry was going to be short-lived. In any case, Roebuck wanted out, and Sears was forced to find someone who would replace him and invest much-needed capital into the business.

JR and Sears, Roebuck

The story of how Julius Rosenwald became involved with Sears, Roebuck goes back to the Columbian Exposition of 1893 and starts with JR's brother-in-law, Aaron Nusbaum.

Aaron was an enterprising fellow. One day in 1892, he learned that Marshall Field, the head of the famous Chicago department store that bore his name, had lost a trainload of merchandise and was offering a substantial reward for its recovery. Aaron was determined to find this train and its cargo, and after an exhaustive search, he located it on a siding in Indiana.[77] He went to the department store magnate to give him the information and claim his reward, which turned out to be substantial. Field offered his informant the soft drink concession at the Columbian Exposition. Aaron eagerly accepted the offer, and by the time the Exposition closed he had amassed $150,000. He decided to invest this substantial sum in a business selling pneumatic tubes, devices designed to speed orders between floors in large stores. Eager to make a sale, he visited Richard Sears in Chicago. Sears was not really interested in pneumatic tubes, but he liked the enterprising salesman and he was looking for an investor. After several discussions over the course of the summer, the two men sat down to lunch at the Chicago Stock Exchange Restaurant on August 7, and Sears offered Nusbaum a half interest in the company for $75,000. As Sears figured it, half of the net assets of the company at that time were $60,000 and $15,000 was considered to be for goodwill. The money was to be used for a capital reorganization.[78]

Aaron Nusbaum was impressed by Sears and intrigued by his offer, but he did not want to invest such a large sum of money on his own. So he asked a number of friends and family members if they would be interested in coming into the business with him. Among those he asked was JR, the only person who expressed any enthusiasm.

In fact, JR had met Richard Sears himself and was busily supplying Sears, Roebuck with inexpensive men's suits, for he was now engaged in his venture with Mo Newborg.

Although Sears was a brilliant marketer, he was not well organized. He liked to experiment with ad campaigns and fliers, often selling products he did not have on hand. He would mail out his catalogs and circulars and then wait for the orders to come in. If the ad campaign was successful, he would have to obtain inventory in a huge hurry. This is apparently what happened with the men's clothes. As Mo Newborg told the story to Werner, Sears rushed to a Newborg agent in Chicago, Sam Heyman, and said, "Help, I need 10,000 suits right away." Heyman was flabbergasted at the size of this order, and he cabled Mo Newborg to come right out to Chicago and meet with Sears. Newborg hopped on a train, came to Chicago, and met with the young entrepreneur. Sears told him that he had advertised the suits at $10 apiece, and Newborg agreed to sell them to Sears, Roebuck & Co. for $6 apiece. Then he told Richard Sears that it would make more sense for him to obtain the product from the newly created Chicago branch of Newborg, Rosenberg, which was called Rosenwald & Company.[79]

Thus when Aaron Nusbaum asked JR if he would like to join with him to buy half of Sears, Roebuck, JR was immediately interested. He agreed to put up half of the requisite $75,000. JR did not have $37,500 readily available, but he quickly worked out a deal. Part of his interest was financed by Rosenwald & Weil and the other part by Newborg, Rosenberg & Co. In fact, with regard to the latter company, no cash changed hands because Sears, Roebuck owed Rosenwald & Co. and its parent store a considerable amount of money. The arrangement worked out with Newborg was that JR would hold the capital stock of Sears, Roebuck in trust for the benefit of Rosenwald & Co.[80] Once again, just as he had in New York when he developed the idea for Rosenwald & Weil, JR demonstrated that, confronted with a business idea that made sense, he was willing and eager to take advantage of it. Yet in later years he always modestly insisted that nothing had created this opportunity but luck.

A formal agreement between Rosenwald, Nusbaum, and Sears was signed on August 13, 1895. The thirty-three-year-old clothing merchant from Springfield, who had enjoyed a modest success, was about to discover his true vocation. And his $37,500 investment in the fledgling mail-order house would eventually be seen as one of the most brilliant decisions in American business history.

2

Early Sears Years, 1895–1908

Julius Rosenwald became associated with Sears, Roebuck in 1895 just as the country was emerging from a serious recession. It proved to be an excellent time to help manage a burgeoning mail-order company. Much had occurred in the business world, which made the current and future growth of Sears, Roebuck possible.

Two inventions were crucial: the railroad, which enabled the mail-order house to ship its goods, and the telegraph, which allowed the company to order the products that its customers wanted.[1] It was important that the mail-order store was located in Chicago, one of the major rail hubs in the country. Moreover, it was fortunate for Sears, Roebuck that it had a predecessor, Montgomery Ward. Although this meant additional work for Sears, Roebuck to overcome its rival, it also meant that the management of Sears, Roebuck could take advantage of any weakness on the part of its competitor, which was precisely what occurred.

The main customers of the mail-order houses were farmers. City dwellers had department and specialty stores where they could shop. But the farmers, who comprised the majority of the U.S. population in this period, had no shopping outlet other than the general store, where the selection was meager and the prices were high. The mail-order companies could take advantage of economies of scale to bring the prices of goods down substantially. Both Sears, Roebuck and Montgomery Ward could offer their customers a dazzling and ever-increasing array of goods. As William Cronon states: "Sears and Ward seemed the ultimate expression of advanced civilization." As Cronon also notes, the mail-order consumers were remote from the products they bought. Not only were they physically distant from Chicago in many instances, but they also ceased to think of the objects they purchased as anything other than a commodity whose source was Sears, Roebuck and whose origin or manufacture was of no interest to them.[2]

Starting in at Sears, Roebuck

For a year after purchasing one-quarter of Sears, Roebuck & Co., JR continued at Rosenwald & Co., winding up his business there. Aaron Nusbaum began working at Sears, Roebuck almost immediately, assuming the titles of general manager, secretary, and treasurer.

JR became involved with Sears, Roebuck at a most opportune moment. The period 1895–1907 was a boom time for the American economy. The lingering effects of the recession of 1893 had vanished, businesses were doing very well, and farmers were flourishing along with the rest of the population. With the money they now had in hand, many were willing to consider spending it on goods, implements, clothing, and even frills. And at this time, if they ordered by mail, they did not even have to go into town to collect their goods, thereby antagonizing the local storekeeper. For in 1896, rural free delivery became part of the U.S. Postal Service, meaning that goods ordered by mail could be delivered directly to even the most isolated house.

Moreover, as JR was to discover, Richard Sears was a marketing genius. His carefully crafted ad copy struck the kind of folksy note that appealed to farmers. He spelled out every detail of how to send in an order, and in the instructions printed in every issue of the catalog, Sears urged the timid not to be afraid: bad handwriting or poor English would be no barrier. One had but to fill out the order form, and the item(s) on it would be sent. However, in 1895 that was not necessarily the case.

As JR soon realized, the true problem at Sears, Roebuck was not persuading people to buy but filling orders satisfactorily. Two accounts of these early years show vividly the chaos that reigned in the offices of the company. R. Buchner joined Sears, Roebuck in the clothing division in

1895. At the time he started, Roebuck was still working for the firm. The inventory consisted of 300–400 pieces of clothing, all mismatched, and these were all there was on hand to fill orders. So if the sizes were not quite right or the colors of a suit did not quite match, it did not matter; the suit was sent out anyway. The price was certainly as low as possible, and because of that, it was believed that few customers would take advantage of Sears, Roebuck's generous return policy. Buchner noted: "The impression I gained at the time was that we were doing business on the plan that there is a sucker born every minute."[3]

Conditions had not improved by the time JR arrived in December 1896.

> Kitchen chairs were the seats; dry goods boxes the tables; chicken wire netting the partitions between compartments. . . . Only two telephones were available; no electric lights, no pneumatic tubes, no clever gadgets for opening mail. . . . Above all, there was no system. The growing business, that soon overflowed the two floors, at first sufficient for its needs and threatened to burst the very building with its exuberant demands, outgrew the systems faster than they could be invented. When Rosenwald came to work in the morning, he would find Sears absorbedly working at his desk in the large room that bulged with scattered heaps of merchandise. Boxes of watches, piles of clothing, samples of groceries in corners, files of correspondence, grimy with dust on the floor. . . . He found a harassed correspondence department doing its poor best with all manner of inquiries and complaints. . . . Still the orders poured in, faster than the factories could supply the goods, faster than they could be cleared through warehouses and shipping rooms. Departments fell behind—thirty days, sixty days, sometimes three and four months. . . . Reviewing this period from the eminence of calmer days, Rosenwald once said: "With a business on our hands that was growing so fast that we were fairly dizzy, without any previously developed system for handling such quantities, you can imagine the confusion. Our shipping rooms were in a state of chronic congestion; every warehouse in Chicago was choked with our goods; every shipping point in the country and almost every station was running over with Sears, Roebuck & Company's merchandise."[4]

The contrast between these vivid descriptions and the future clearly demonstrates that it was order and system that JR brought to the firm. As Cecil Hoge sums it up: "Rosenwald had a feel for internal efficiency as superlative as Sears had for sales."[5] It is doubtful that Sears, Roebuck could have survived without these attributes because impatient and dissatisfied customers would have taken their business elsewhere. The problem was that, if anything, Richard Sears was too successful, and in 1898 he hired a group of assistants, including the young Louis Asher, who learned from him and compounded his success. His carefully crafted ad copy and, above all, his incredibly low prices attracted thousands of customers and orders. The problem was Richard Sears's complete disinterest in administration or anything other than marketing.

The chaotic situation described above resulted in serious problems for the company. The sloppy dispatch of goods caused by chaos in shipping and storage facilities led to numerous returns, for though some customers were willing to abide by mistakes for the sake of cheap prices, many others were not. There were times when the piles of returned goods were almost as large as the piles of goods to be dispatched, and the large number of returns threatened to bankrupt the company.[6]

Almost from the beginning, there was a clash between two philosophies of business. Richard Sears, despite his successes, believed that mail-order shopping was a flash in the pan. Like other retailers and manufacturers of the time, he feared that an economic boom would lead to overproduction and crisis.[7] Sears, Roebuck & Co. had barely weathered the depression of the mid-1890s. Sears was afraid that those difficult times would recur. He was convinced that "the mail-order pot will never boil without a red hot fire all the time."[8] It was, Sears felt, his job to provide the fire, a constantly shifting series of ad campaigns and promotional gimmicks. He was astonishingly successful at these schemes, and the orders kept rolling in, so that by 1900, Sears, Roebuck had taken in $10 million in sales and surpassed Montgomery Ward.

That the relatively upstart company should have displaced its established competitor in such a short time is extraordinary. David Blanke attributes this to several factors. In the mid-1890s, the founders of Ward, including George R. Thorne, began to retire, leaving the company in the hands of Thorne's sons, who lacked the "common touch" that their father and A. Montgomery Ward had possessed. They began to emphasize quality over price, which provided a perfect opening for Richard Sears and his brilliant ad copy, emphasizing price over everything. Moreover, according to Blanke, who compared the catalogs of both companies around the turn of the century, Ward felt the need to explain everything in great detail and educate the farmer. Sears had the uncanny ability to ensnare the reader so that he was actively involved in the sales pitch. He persuaded his customers rather than educated them.[9]

In opposition to Sears's belief that innovative gimmicks were essential to keep the mail-order business healthy, JR and Nusbaum were convinced that sound business practices were important, that if supply could not keep up with demand it was time to cool down demand and ensure that goods went out correctly and in a timely fashion. Accordingly, when Sears came up with his "Send No Money" sewing machine ad campaign in 1898, JR and Nusbaum urged him to stop when it became clear that the sewing machines were not being manufactured fast enough to meet the demand. Sears and his assistants refused and derided JR and his brother-in-law as conservative and overly cautious. As Elmer Scott, one of Sears's chief assistants, noted, "The ideologies, business tactics, and personalities of the two [JR and Sears] were poles apart."[10]

The real problem in this early period, according to all accounts, was Aaron Nusbaum. Dapper and dashing, always well dressed, he was an able administrator who was also a martinet. He would monitor cash flow assiduously, and if it appeared that the company might be in trouble, he would tell Sears or JR, "Lay off this man and rehire him in about two weeks."[11] This cavalier attitude contrasted with Nusbaum's actions when he first came on board. According to Werner, he believed there was such a desperate need for employees that he stood on a soap box outside the company's offices and hired men as they came down the street.[12]

What really grated on Sears's nerves, according to Asher, the main source for all inside gossip, was that "Nusbaum, in discussions with his partners, did not like to commit himself on any important matter and thus was left in a position to say, 'I told you so,' no matter what the outcome."[13] As Asher relates, resentments against Nusbaum built up in Sears until, in 1901, he exploded, marched into JR's office, and delivered an ultimatum which, supposedly, left JR with a difficult choice: should he side with his brother-in-law or with Richard Sears? According to Asher's account, after agonizing over this decision, JR decided to throw in his lot with Sears.

There may well be some truth to this version of events, but letters to Nusbaum call some of it into question. In 1901, Nusbaum, who was ill, resigned as secretary and treasurer on February 14 and went on an extended vacation. He received several letters from his brother-in-law, Louis Rosenfield, head of a beer company, who knew many of the key players.

SEROCO TOPICS.

Vol. I. *CHICAGO, ILL., JAN. 21, 1899.* *No. 1.*

THE TRINITY WE DELIGHT IN SERVING.

JULIUS ROSENWALD,
Vice-President.

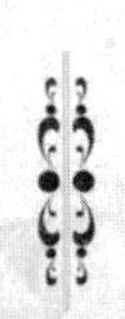

R. W. SEARS,
President.

A. E. NUSBAUM,
Treas. and Genl. Manager.

Editorial.

We gather here this evening principally for good cheer, but one of the ideas in bringing about this meeting of heads of departments, was primarily to afford a chance of becoming better acquainted with each other. Under the confining requirements of an exceedingly heavy business, it is impossible for men to know each other as they should.

There should exist between all heads of departments, and all employes as well, a firm bond of personal friendship, mutual interest and good fellowship. For this an organization of some kind is needed, and while it has been deemed wisest to start the ball a-rolling with a strictly social affair, it it is intended to organize, this very evening, an association of permanency which will bring us together regularly. While each meeting will tend to develop personal contact between us as men, the first and principal feature will be a frequent interchange of thoughts and ideas bearing upon our business activity.

We are free to say that the personnel of Department Managers of the house of SEARS, ROEBUCK & CO., INC., comprises the best aggregation of business talent that could possibly be found in so large and so young an establishment, of so wonderful a growth.

Each and every one of these men has thoughts and ideas of his own, which, if properly brought forth, will inure to the benefit of all. A better mutual understanding of our activity will afford to each interested member of such an organization, a wider horizon, and in the exchange of ideas, splendid results will speedily follow.

Such organizations exist in every progressive, large house of the country, and no case has ever been known where anything but the greatest good has resulted from such associations.

There are innumerable features that may be incorporated in the purposes of such an organization, which are, however, a matter of detailed attention. It being generally admitted that no harm can, and that only good will result from such an association, we should, this very night, apply ourselves to this idea, leaving the detailed parts and ramifications to be discussed at the first business meeting.

Connected with a house that may very truthfully be said to be the largest, most enterprising, most liberal and most progressive of its kind in the civilized world, inspiration for the greatest enthusiasm is furnished at the very start. In fact, it has been observed by a disinterested friend, that never in his large and varied business experiences, has he seen a collection of such enthusiastic men, from the members of the firm down to the managers of clerical departments, as in our house.

The reason is apparent. "There is nothing succeeds like success." There is nothing that stimulates a bright, active nature more than a wide, unlimited field for the display of individual ability where no limitations exist to the expansion of any man, no matter in what department he may be engaged.

Merchandise department managers view with surprise the rapid growth and progress of their respective departments, brought about by the most unique and constant advertising known in the business world.

To provide the proper merchandise, for a constantly growing demand calls for the very best activity on the part of all department manager, who thus are in touch with the markets of the world, more closely than the exclusive dealer.

It is an opportunity for gaining a thorough knowledge in each particular branch, such as is not even afforded to anyone conducting a similar line exclusively.

The same holds good in those departments which have to do with the handling of business only, in other words, the clerical departments. The ingenious system required to economically, speedily and satisfactorily handle such a vast amount of business, opens to the employee, whether he be engaged in the main office or the files and records, or anywhere, a vista such as cannot possibly be offered to him anywhere else. In short, a connection with this remarkable house is a rare education in all matters of business and business management.

Through the appliance of the very best and steadily improving methods, individual capacity is being constantly developed, and talents which might have remained dormant for all time to come are brought to the surface because of contact with so great and wonderful an establishment.

The quick recognition of worth, the speedy and unceasing promotion of employees to higher positions, are the best evidence of the spirit of progress at work in the house.

Many men have become bright, active factors in business life by being rubbed against the polishing and educational process in our wonderful establishment, who otherwise might have remained unconscious of their own capabilities.

Therein lies the most potent reason for congratulation on connection with the house of SEARS, ROEBUCK & CO.

It behooves us, not just to follow in the way of progress that has been pointed out, but to assume leadership as well, and for this purpose no better medium could be found than a strong, mutual and binding organization, affording a chance for the advancement of the best thoughts and ideas which each one may have to offer.

Proper advertising, proper merchandise and proper handling are the three principles that have made the phenomenal success of our house. Everlastingly keeping at it in each of these lines will still discount the success of the past, and toward the greater success of the future each and every member of the prospective organization will contribute his share.

Men of ideas are at a premium in this mediocre world, and men of ideas, that is of good ideas, will find their level just as surely and unalterably as water.

If you are a man of ideas you are the man we want. If you think you have no ideas to offer, join us and see how quickly the friction of mind upon mind will make you fruitful.

In signing our preamble not a man should be missing. Each signature should be attached, not merely on the enthusiasm of the evening, but with a firm determination to give every aid at command to foster and perpetuate this organization.

Figure 3. The first issue of *Seroco Topics,* the Sears, Roebuck in-house newsletter, with photos of JR, Richard Sears, and Aaron Nusbaum.

Rosenfield wrote Aaron that he had encountered Sears at a resort in Mississippi. Sears buttonholed Rosenthal and talked for hours about the business. "While he lauded your ability, he harped a good deal on things you did to him and J[R]" but he also indicated that 'you need not worry; take it easy until July 1 and by that time you will be asked to go back in harness, and J[R] will take a six month lay off.' S[ears] said this to me, but he said he can not broach it to J[R] just now but would later."[14]

The impression that JR wished to oust his own brother-in-law is reinforced in a letter that Rosenthal wrote Nusbaum two days later: "I don't know what J[R] would do if he had the power, but I will stake anything I have that S[ears] will not sanction anything wrong towards you."[15] A third letter from Rosenthal quotes JR's brother-in-law, Ernest Grunsfeld, as saying, "I *know* that Julius Rosenwald is trying to get Aaron out of the business. He got him 75% already and he'll get him out altogether. He's got Sears on his side."[16]

Such thirdhand information might not be trustworthy, but in the meantime, Nusbaum had heard from Richard Sears himself, a long letter, very friendly in tone. He informed Nusbaum about business conditions as if Aaron had still been working for the company. And he added this statement, which could be taken as mere politeness but does not sound like a man enraged at his correspondent: "I am sure it is not necessary for me to say that any time I can be of any service to you in the way of keeping you advised, or satisfying your curiosity (for I know one is always more or less curious about a thousand and one things when away from the show) I will consider it a pleasure to be commanded by you."[17] What all of this suggests is that it was not Sears but JR who staged what amounted to a coup to be rid of his brother-in-law.

There was a motive for JR's action if he, indeed, was chiefly responsible for Aaron's departure. When JR started work at Sears, Aaron had already been there a year and had assumed the titles of general manager, secretary, and treasurer. Sears was president and busied himself with marketing and advertising. JR was relegated to head of the men's clothing department, an area in which he did have expertise but which he might have viewed as second-class status. It is possible that JR resented this unequal treatment. He was supposed to be on an equal footing with Nusbaum, at least in terms of percentage of ownership of the company. He began to assert himself quickly, so that by 1900 it was evident that there were three partners. Still, he may have resented the treatment accorded him on his arrival when he was not even given the title of vice president, and Aaron's overbearing, slightly smug attitude must have grated on him as well as on Sears.

Regardless of who engineered it, Aaron's departure did take place, and it was stormy. JR and Sears offered their partner $1 million for his share of Sears, Roebuck, which had cost him a mere $37,500 six years earlier. Just when JR and Sears believed that the deal was concluded, Aaron demanded $250,000 more. The remaining two partners were furious, but eventually they complied. By mid-May, Aaron had taken his money and departed, but he never forgave JR.

Three years after his departure, Aaron was still brooding about Sears, Roebuck and hoping to return. Gussie wrote JR about a conversation she had had with JR's sister, Selma who was known as Sal: "She says Aaron is the most grieved man over his fallen pride. He hopes that by our becoming reconciled that it will ultimately lead to a reconciliation between him and you and then in that way he might get back into the business. Sal says he thinks and speaks of nothing else than his severance from the business and your treatment of him."[18] A few days later, Gussie returned to this theme after speaking to her sister, Sarah, but then had doubts: "I feared that a reconciliation would only lead to greater trouble if things did not play out as [Sal] expects. I do not believe that Aaron has such thoughts, that is, of returning to the store." Realizing the importance of this matter, Gussie wisely told JR, "I shall wait to hear from you before going to see him."[19]

Whether or not Aaron really wanted a reconciliation, it seems clear that JR did not. He appears to have asked his wife to keep away from her brother. Gussie, the dutiful wife, heeded this injunction, but nine years later, still stewing about the rift, she wrote a letter to Aaron asking for a reconciliation. The letter was never answered. Aaron spent much of the decade after his ouster traveling in Europe. In 1912 he returned to the United States, moved to New York, and spent the remainder of his life managing his money and investing in such companies as Inland Steel.[20]

The man chosen to replace Nusbaum was Albert Loeb, a lawyer who had drawn up the initial agreements with JR, Nusbaum, and Sears in 1895. He then served as the company lawyer. JR knew the Loeb family, part of the tightly knit German Jewish community in which he and Gussie moved. Loeb was, by all accounts, a perfect choice for vice president—a total contrast to the often acerbic Nusbaum. He was calm and easygoing, and he could mediate a dispute fairly. Everyone in the top management at Sears, Roebuck trusted him and listened carefully to his advice, including JR. With the departure of Nusbaum, Loeb became secretary and took charge of administrative affairs; JR became treasurer and vice president, concerning himself with financial affairs, the expansion of the merchandise line, the expansion of the company physically, and quality control. Sears remained in charge of marketing and advertising.

One area in which real improvement was made in this early period was record keeping and data gathering. For the first time, information was developed about sales in each department on a weekly, monthly, and even a daily basis. Reports were also available that showed sales for one week compared with sales for the same week one year previously. Part of the move toward systematic management that was sweeping American business, these reports, created and disseminated by new technologies such as the typewriter and the mimeograph machine, brought about both greater efficiency and control over workers by the top echelons of the corporation.[21] Such information enabled the top Sears, Roebuck management to eliminate unprofitable items or increase the advertising of proven moneymakers.

However, to balance this success, there were other chronic problems afflicting Sears, Roebuck. These difficulties were more intractable. One was cash flow, which had been one of the main reasons that JR and Nusbaum had been invited to join the company. Despite the best efforts of Nusbaum, this problem persisted until after 1900. In that year, JR wrote Mo Newborg and explained why he could not repay part of the debt owed him:

> I telegraphed you today you would not be able to count on us for much money for the present, and I hardly think we will be able to for much of anything before the latter part of September. . . . [F]or several reasons we will require all the money we can get up to that time. The great bulk of the expense of our catalog comes during that period; besides, we have bought the property adjoining our building and this will take considerable money. We have also made a very extensive bicycle deal, all of which is cash and will be required at once.[22]

Although this statement could be thought of as a mere excuse to avoid repayment, Mo Newborg was one of JR's closest friends, and it is unlikely that he would have put off repaying his debt unless he truly was unable to do so.

Another very serious problem was space. In 1895, the company's offices were located in a five-story brick building west of Chicago's Loop. On March 17, 1896, the company moved six blocks north to a six-story structure. The move gave them more space, but it was not enough. The phenomenal success of Richard Sears's marketing efforts meant that the other senior managers were constantly playing catch-up. In 1898, they added to their office building, more than doubling the space. In 1901, an eight-story structure with a basement was built adjacent to their office building and a courtyard was filled in. Nusbaum was supposedly in charge of the construction of this latest addition, which was even outfitted with electric lights. Thanks to the 1901 addition, the amount of space had been quadrupled since 1896. Still it was not enough. Albert Loeb, one of whose main jobs as legal counsel had been negotiating leases, had time for little else as Sears, Roebuck leased every conceivable foot of warehouse space available in a six-block radius. Still it was not enough, as the volume of business continued to increase astronomically.

Besides the issue of storage space, there were additional problems. Carts loaded with Sears, Roebuck merchandise were creating serious traffic jams around the nearby railroad stations. The shipping department was improved but still disorganized. The correspondence department was also better but needed further improvement. Above all, JR and Loeb agreed, there had to be some kind of system imposed so that from the moment an order was received to the moment it was shipped, everything was handled smoothly and efficiently. For all of these reasons, more space was needed—a huge plant covering a wide area near a railroad terminus. In 1904, following a year of deliberations, a forty-acre site was chosen and purchased at Homan Avenue on Chicago's West Side about five miles from the Loop. There were railroad lines in the vicinity, but much of the surrounding area was prairie.

Everything about the building of Sears, Roebuck's new plant was impressive. It was, wrote the contractor who built it in 1905–1906, "the largest mercantile plant in the world."[23] An army of seven thousand men worked night and day for a year to construct all the buildings and lay out the grounds. So much yellow pine was used that a sawmill was constructed on the site. "During the rush, a day's consumption sometimes ran as high as 30 [railroad] cars of bricks, 20 cars of lumber, and 10 cars of sand."[24] The architects were Nimmons and Fellows. They designed four buildings that added some three million square feet of work space to Sears, Roebuck's operations.

The heart of the plant was the administration building with its marble floors and wainscoting. Its rich brown brick exterior was decorated with a terra cotta frieze. Here were the main offices, including JR's. In this building arrived in 1906 more mail than was generated by the city of Milwaukee and its 300,000 inhabitants.[25] Envelopes at the rate of 27,000 per hour were opened by automatic letter openers that had been developed by the company. A phalanx of dozens of women wrote orders on color-coded tickets, answered letters, and kept meticulous records.

Orders were sent by pneumatic tube to the merchandise building, which was three blocks long, one block wide, and nine stories high. Here goods of every imaginable description except large pieces of machinery were stored, the larger, heavier items on lower floors. Extremely heavy machinery or such items as stoves were shipped directly to the purchaser from the factory. Merchandise was stored in bins according to the ninety-six departments into which Sears, Roebuck was divided. Each department was connected by a series of chutes, conveyor belts, and escalators. At the heart of the building was a rail terminus to which trains would bring merchandise and leave with orders to be shipped. However, a carefully designed system ensured that "the incoming merchandise never crosses or interrupts the progress of that going out."[26] There were two other buildings: a printing and advertising building in which nineteen cylinder presses turned out two million catalogs, and a structure housing the firm's own power plant. All of the buildings had heating and ventilating systems and excellent lighting.

A system was designed to have each order dispatched within twenty-four hours of receipt. When an order came in, it was stamped with the date and time and color coded according to the departments it was going to and the outcome—whether goods were to be shipped by express, by normal mail, or from the factory.

Another important undertaking that Sears, Roebuck was engaged in during these years was buying up factories that could produce goods for the company more cheaply and in greater volume, utilizing economies of scale. Often Sears and JR were able to negotiate deals with manufacturers whereby Sears, Roebuck would provide them with funds to purchase new, more modern equipment, and the factory would improve its productivity

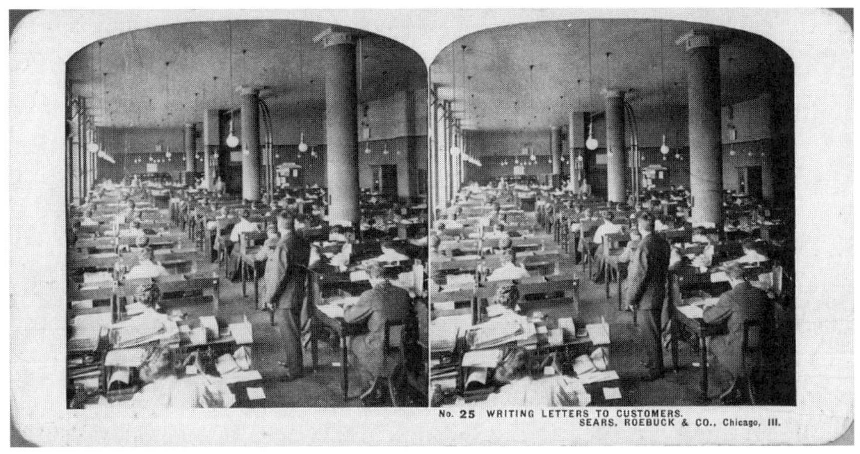

Figure 4. Stereopticon slides of the Sears, Roebuck plant. (*Top*) Hundreds of girls, some as young as sixteen, opened letters and recorded orders, part of the incredibly efficient system designed by Otto Doering. (*Bottom*) Part of the "campus," which afforded many amenities to Sears workers.

and efficiency. Thus stoves were manufactured exclusively for Sears Roebuck at a plant in Newark, Ohio; buggies were made in Evansville, Indiana; pianos and organs were built in Louisville, Kentucky. These companies shipped their goods directly to the customer after receiving the order from Chicago. Smaller items, such as guns, were also manufactured by Sears-owned plants, but these goods were sent first to Chicago.

The daunting problem of dealing with multiple orders in many different departments was solved efficiently in the new plant where one basket, representing a customer order, was sent via chutes and conveyor belts from one department to another. The architect of the entire ingenious system was Otto Doering, operations superintendent, who introduced it, at least in preliminary form, in 1906. The processing and shipping systems were so efficient that, according to legend, Henry Ford visited the plant and obtained ideas for his assembly line. And Ford was not the only visitor. The new Sears, Roebuck plant became a showplace. In his catalog copy, Richard Sears invited any reader who so desired to visit the facility, and many took advantage of this offer.[27]

To carry out the demanding shipping schedule, a large number of people were employed. In 1895, the company consisted of approximately eighty people who toiled extremely long hours at relatively low wages. By 1908, about eight thousand people were employed in the new plant. Although they did not have a union, they did enjoy definite advantages, such as the Seroco Mutual Benefit Association. It provided benefits for members who lost days to sickness or accidents. An employee savings plan was also established. The new plant even had a small hospital on the premises. A large canteen served excellent meals; one could eat three meals a day there for 35 cents. In the administration building there was a branch of the Chicago Public Library, "a recreation room for ladies, and a lounging room for men."[28] And the surroundings at the new plant were pleasing—there were flower beds, a pergola, and an athletic field where games were held in the summer. The new plant was like the modern corporate suburban campus decades ahead of its time.

All of these perquisites were part of a trend that progressive managers of American business were adopting. Called "welfare capitalism" by Stuart D. Brandes, this program of benefits (and others like it) was designed to discourage the formation of unions.[29] Although JR was not in favor of unions, it is not clear that this was the primary motivation behind his adoption of such worker benefits. He may have reasoned that it simply made good business sense to provide Sears, Roebuck employees with such perks.

JR was in charge of overseeing construction of the new facility, and although he had never undertaken anything like this before, the success of the project should be credited in large part to him. It was an expensive operation, especially given the cost of such modern equipment as conveyor belts and escalators. A total of $5.6 million was expended on the new plant, the equivalent of over $114 million in 2005 dollars. Yet the new facility was obviously needed, and it was money well spent.

Nevertheless, there was an urgent need for working capital. Some months after the company had moved into the new facilities, JR contacted his friend from New York days, Henry Goldman, the head of the banking firm of Goldman Sachs. JR and Sears visited Goldman and requested a $5 million loan. Goldman stunned them by suggesting that Sears, Roebuck go public and issue preferred stock based on the company's assets and common stock based on goodwill. The stock would be underwritten by Goldman Sachs and Lehman Brothers; $10 million of preferred and $30 million worth of common stock would be issued.

One reason that Henry Goldman was so willing to suggest the issuance of stock was that, by looking at some truly impressive numbers, it was clear that Sears, Roebuck was a real powerhouse in the merchandising business. In 1904 the net sales of the company were $27,601,738. One year later, net sales were $37,897,904. Net profits in those years were $2.2 and $2.8 million, respectively. What was unusual about the Goldman Sachs offer was that not many mercantile establishments up to that time had been transformed into public companies. Railroads, oil companies, and steel companies had done so, but not stores. Yet the public bought up the stock eagerly. As Emmett and Jeuck indicate, Sears and JR were once again fortunate in their timing. In 1906, the country was still enjoying an economic boom. A year later, a severe recession was beginning, so if Sears and JR had waited, the outcome might not have been so successful.

As a result of the stock issue, Julius Rosenwald and Richard Sears became instant millionaires. They had held private shares of stock when JR and Nusbaum had bought into the company. When Nusbaum departed, he sold his shares to JR. Now JR and Sears each received $4.5 million for these shares of the private stock.

Even in the midst of this windfall, JR thought about others. Shortly after the deal with Goldman Sachs was completed, he formed a stock syndicate to enable his relatives and a few friends to buy some of the stock at the initial offering. And he advanced money to help them do this. In January 1907, he also advanced $90,000 to allow a small group of older employees to buy stock in the company. Although the Sears, Roebuck profit sharing plan was still a decade away, it may be that the genesis of the idea started here.

Richard Sears and JR

Richard Sears was an imposing figure. Louis Asher, who worked closely with him for ten years and who greatly admired him, described him as "a man of large build, nearly six feet in height, well proportioned. His features were handsome, large lustrous eyes, a long straight nose. A pleasant agreeable voice with a tendency to rapid enunciation as he explained anything in which he was deeply interested."[30] Although the increase in efficiency brought to the company by JR and his associates helped to fuel the tremendous boom in sales, there is no doubt that a good deal of this growth came from the fertile imagination of Richard Sears.

In the years since he had started in the watch business, Sears had learned a number of lessons. One was that it was imperative to get good readable, somewhat bombastic ad copy into the hands of potential customers. To that end, he not only issued the big catalog, which soon grew to over a thousand pages, and smaller specialty catalogs, but he also bought numerous pages in cheap specialty magazines, consisting mostly of ads, that went directly to farmers. Thus the name "Sears, Roebuck" was constantly placed before the farmer.

Richard Sears also realized that low price and high volume were both essential to boost sales. An example is provided by the story of the cream separators. This handheld device, which efficiently separated milk from cream, was advertised in the 1903 catalog and sold in small quantities. The following year, Sears and Loeb were on a hunting trip to North Dakota.[31] They encountered a farmer who was using a cream separator he had bought for $100—not from Sears, Roebuck but from an agent of the manufacturing company. The farmer was extremely enthusiastic about this gadget. It saved him an enormous amount of time, money, and trouble, and he felt that the price was very reasonable for such a useful machine. Sears listened, enraptured, dollar signs dancing before his eyes, for he realized that the separator could be manufactured for about a third of what the farmer had paid for it. Sears and Loeb rushed back to Chicago. Sears started seeking manufacturers, and eventually he found a small company that was willing to meet his price given the enormous volume of the order. Sears started promoting the cream separators heavily, creating a special catalog for them, and they sold in amazing quantities. He had found the equivalent of the sewing machine (another best-selling Sears, Roebuck item) for the male farmer.

Another factor that helped boost sales was a large increase in the product lines. Groceries were added in 1895, and there was even a failed attempt at retail grocery stores. Although the groceries did not last long, many other newly added items remained in the catalog for decades. Indeed, the "big book" or "wish book," as it was called by customers, contained items for almost every conceivable aspect of life from baby clothes to tombstones.

Unquestionably there were contrasts in character and temperament between JR and Richard Sears, although Louis Asher probably paints them in overly glaring terms in his book *Send No Money.* Sears is pictured as brimming over with creative ideas. JR is portrayed as conservative and negative. All of this is meant to explain and prefigure the blowup that led to Sears's resignation from the company in November 1908.

There were undoubtedly disagreements between the two men over a variety of issues. One was quality control. Sears's gift for advertising led him to market items of truly questionable validity and utility. There was, for example, the electric belt that emitted a small charge that was purported to aid in weight loss. It was introduced in the 1898 catalog and Sears plugged it relentlessly. Sales of the electric belt reached their zenith in 1901, then started to slacken. Patent medicines were a fixture of the catalog from 1895 to 1908. Of course, they did no good, but people believed in them. JR was troubled by the sale of these quack remedies and sought to curtail their inclusion in the catalog. While Sears was away during most of 1907 and 1908, the number of pages in the catalog devoted to patent medicines declined dramatically. A trusted top executive at Sears, Roebuck, James F. Skinner, also was concerned about quality control, and he began systematically testing items to make sure that what was advertised in the catalog was honest and genuine. Sears knew about Skinner's work and praised it highly. Skinner's activity probably led to the creation of the Sears, Roebuck laboratory after Sears's departure.

Other areas of disagreement between Sears and Rosenwald were much more significant. One was the opening of the first Sears, Roebuck satellite plant outside of Chicago. Sears was determined that this step should be taken and that the plant should be located in Dallas. JR was vehemently opposed, and the reason was probably timing. The Dallas branch was to open in 1906, and JR, who certainly was more cautious than the flamboyant Sears, undoubtedly felt that the year of the move to a huge new facility was not the time to be opening a satellite. Moreover, except for satisfying Texas pride, there seemed no good reason for the choice of location. Elmer Scott was sent to Dallas to run the new facility. He rented office space, issued a Texas catalog, and commenced operations. JR opposed every step of this process and tried to throw roadblocks in Scott's way whenever possible, but he ultimately gave in. In the end, Sears proved to be right. The Dallas plant was a success, as JR recognized by later opening up other facilities in cities throughout the country. At the time, however, JR appeared to be an obstreperous naysayer regarding branch plants.

Of great concern to JR was a fundamental disagreement between him and Sears about the future of mail-order marketing. Sears believed that unless one constantly came up with new schemes, the business would collapse under the weight of customer indifference. JR believed that mail order was here to stay and that schemes such as the ones Sears kept concocting were unnecessary and counterproductive.

The two Sears schemes that brought about his downfall were "Iowizing" and the customer profit sharing plan, both brilliant innovations that were decades ahead of their time but unsuited to the realities of 1900s marketing. Both combined elements of "frequent flier miles" and "green stamps." Some of Sears, Roebuck's best customers were located in Iowa, and so Sears began his 1904 campaign with this state. The concept was simple. Each of the best customers in Iowa was given the opportunity to be a Sears, Roebuck "representative." If he agreed, he was sent twenty-four catalogs and asked to distribute them to his neighbors. He was then to send a list of the names and addresses to Sears, Roebuck. If the neighbors made purchases totaling a certain amount, the "representative" would receive a gift—for example, a free bicycle, depending on the dollar figure ordered by the neighbors. The genius behind this idea was that it was the farmer who would be doing the marketing because he could see that free item tantalizingly before his eyes and thus had an incentive to urge his neighbors to buy.

The "Iowizing" campaign was spectacularly successful. Thousands of additional catalogs were distributed. But it was one thing to "Iowize" a small state such as Iowa and another to Iowize every state in the country, as Sears desired. That would have cost the company a large amount of money not only in terms of catalogs but also in terms of prizes, not to mention the bookkeeping difficulties in this age, almost fifty years before computers. Catalogs in 1904 were free. Since each catalog ran to well over a thousand pages, it cost the company a fair amount to produce them in huge volume, even when they were printed on the Sears, Roebuck campus. Thus, when an economic downturn began in 1907 and worsened in 1908, and Richard Sears's only answer was to step up the "Iowizing" campaign, JR and Loeb began to question his judgment.

The customer profit sharing scheme should not be confused with the employee profit sharing plan that JR would introduce in 1916. The customer plan was similar in some respects to the "Iowizing" idea. The 1904 catalog informed readers in great detail about the exciting money-saving program. For each purchase made, a certificate would be sent to the buyer. Once enough certificates had been accumulated, one could cash them in and obtain a premium. Readers were urged to order items for friends, neighbors, and far-flung family members under their own names so they could obtain more certificates and thus more lavish gifts. The problem with this program was that it was too successful. Richard Sears continued to lower the minimum dollar figure at which certificates could be redeemed. By 1907, the cost of the premiums being handed out was $2.25 million, which was 40 percent of the total advertising cost.[32]

As with "Iowizing," the profit sharing scheme greatly overstretched the capabilities of the correspondence department. Even Richard Sears recognized that this plan had gone too far. When JR was in Europe in the summer of 1907, a decision was made to end the profit sharing scheme. Sears readily concurred, and in letter after letter to JR he lamented the fact that the company had ever become involved in such an unfortunate undertaking.[33]

A major factor that accounted for the break between Sears and JR was the amount of money spent on marketing. In 1898, it was $400,000; by 1902, it was $1.5 million. By 1908, the figure had jumped to $3.5 million. While it is true that advertising as a percentage of net sales had decreased from 13 percent in 1898 to 6 percent in 1906, Sears, Roebuck spent more on advertising than on payroll, doubtless at the insistence of its president. This large amount of money spent on advertising became a problem when, in 1907 and 1908, the worst economic downturn since the mid-1890s occurred. The company's customers stopped buying at the volume they had before. For the first time since it began operations, the net sales of Sears, Roebuck did not increase between 1906 and 1907. In the former year, net sales were $49,229,613. For the latter year, sales were down to $46,923,410. Profits declined almost half a million dollars between 1906 and 1907.

Sears was convinced that the end was at hand, and with increasing urgency he recommended that massive amounts be spent on advertising and catalog distribution. JR, who looked at the huge advertising budget, felt that such increases were unwarranted. He believed that the company should sit tight and weather the storm.

Louis Asher had been hired in 1898 as a correspondent, but Sears soon saw the young man's intelligence, and Asher rose quickly through the ranks, becoming general manager in 1906. Asher idolized his mentor. In the looming battle that seemed to be approaching between JR and Sears, there was no question on whose side Asher stood. In the book he wrote many years later about the early years at Sears, Asher was quick to denigrate JR at every turn. And yet, by August 1908, even Louis Asher had to admit that JR was right and Sears was wrong. In a letter to Sears, who was in Europe, Asher wrote on August 16, 1908:

> I believe in the spreading of schemes we are Cheapening our Merchandise Proposition and Dissipating our Goodwill faster than we have realized and perhaps to a dangerous extent. . . . Reviewing our advertising or order getting experience of the last ten years, watching the different methods rise up and fade away, I believe we are (or should be) done with all these schemes. They are expensive. Besides, the people have now seen all the Side Shows. They Won't Buy Any More Tickets. I believe we must depend upon simple straightforward merchandising. . . . I honestly believe we not only have a Good Show, we have a good business and that under a Good Merchandising, Good Service, Simple Advertising Policy, it will grow and prosper and pay Satisfactory Profits. I know that many things herein expressed are not your views, hence I am taking a bold position (taken, I hope, with proper modesty and respect) but it is the only Honest position I can take, for it is my humble belief. Times change, the people progress—enlightening influences work fast. . . . I have changed my ideas considerably in the last two weeks—swayed by results of a close analysis of our schemes.[34]

This was the straight JR line. By conceding these points, Asher had gone over to the other side. Sears admitted that some of these criticisms were well founded, but then he kept reverting to the notion of "Iowizing" the entire country.

The dispute that resulted in the departure of Richard Sears in November 1908 had an air of inevitability about it. In a sense, JR had been running Sears, Roebuck for some time. For much of 1907 and 1908, Sears was in Europe with his wife, Anna, who had suffered a serious accident. They went from doctor to doctor and spa to spa. Eventually Anna had to have her leg amputated. Even when he was in the United States, Sears seemed to spend less and less time in Chicago, either by design, to avoid JR, or by chance.

The notion that there was a lengthy period of disagreement between the two men which led to the blowup in November 1908—a view of history fostered by both Louis Asher and his son Frederick—may have to be revised. The letters that Sears wrote to JR when JR was in Europe in the summer of 1907 are not the epistles of a frustrated or angry man. They are typical Richard Sears letters, filled with news about the business. Both men shared the compulsion to know what was happening with the business while they were away. As Sears wrote JR: "I can, reflecting, sympathize with you and remember how different does the thing seem in Europe as compared with Homan and Harvard Street." And at the end of that letter, Sears told JR not to worry that his absence was causing the staff additional work. "Don't you censure yourself the least bit for burdening either Albert [Loeb] or me with work . . . for your humble servant is sort of floating with the tide, taking life very easy."[35] Subsequent letters belied the truth of that assertion, and, in fact, it would have been totally out of character, for Sears, while he was at "the plant," was the epitome of a workaholic.

These letters are also interesting because this was the time the downturn in sales was becoming truly apparent. Sears was scrupulously honest in reporting the news to JR, but also indicated that all hands on deck were busy trying to explain the downturn. Not yet realizing that there was a nationwide recession, they thought it was something that they were doing wrong, and Sears almost proudly wrote the solution that he and Asher had determined: they had not sent their old and trusted customers a notice telling them to send away for a new catalog. Thus people were using old and tattered catalogs or not ordering at all. There was a simple way to fix this. A circular that was going out informing people of the end of the profit sharing scheme would simply remind people that they needed to order a new catalog. In fact, the pessimism usually displayed by Sears is not evident in these letters. He seemed convinced that a bit of tweaking would fix everything. In almost every letter he mentioned approvingly the work of Skinner, who was going through the product line looking not only for deceptive items but also for those that were not selling well and eliminating them. Such descriptions were usually prefaced with the words "You will be pleased to learn." Sears knew exactly where JR stood on a host of issues, and he was happy to give him news he thought would please him. The impression conveyed by these letters is similar to the letter Sears had sent to Nusbaum in 1901: Business was going along basically fine; now let me tell you all the news about it—not the sort of missive one might expect from someone deeply angry at his partner.

Yet there was a showdown, and it is described by Louis Asher in his memoirs:

> The tension between Sears and Rosenwald increased; Loeb couldn't help the situation. Sears, by temperament a sensitive person, was the antithesis of Rosenwald. With the combination of the slower sales, JR's close presence in the adjoining office, his [JR's] open criticism, the very serious illness of Mrs. Sears, brought Sears to the limits of his endurance. Business had ceased to be fun. He could not stand to be at the offices of Sears, Roebuck & Co. JR got on his nerves terribly. The climax was inevitable. Sears sought JR for a "showdown" conference. They were closeted together in JR's private office about two hours. My office was just opposite, across the corridor. I noticed R. W. [Sears] stroll out nonchalantly; JR followed, apparently quite flustered, face and ears red, hurrying down the corridor. Sears later in the day came in, sat next to my desk, said he had told JR what was on his mind without mincing words: that he was resigning as president and would cease to take any active part in the business.[36]

At a meeting of the board of directors on November 21, 1908, Richard Sears formally resigned as president of the company he had created. JR was elected president of the company; Loeb became vice president; Louis Asher resigned. Sears agreed to remain as chairman of the board, and for the first couple of years after his retirement he did attend meetings. Then he ceased coming, withdrawing further from the company. In November 1913, Sears resigned from his titular position. He dabbled in a variety of businesses, including Florida real estate and a scheme for selling bonds by mail order, but abandoned them. Eventually he bought the Emerson

Typewriter Company, renamed it Woodstock, and even persuaded Alvah Roebuck to rejoin him. The two men were planning to expand the business when Richard Sears died on September 27, 1914, at the age of fifty. 

Sears had been in ill health for some time, and that was the official reason given for his departure from the company that bore his name. However, Louis Asher appears to be correct when he says that Sears left out of frustration. The economic downturn of 1907–1908 had not righted itself. Yet JR remained confident about the future of the business and knew that the schemes Sears kept devising were no longer appropriate for the mature company Sears, Roebuck had become. Averse to the constant criticism of his plans on the part of JR, Loeb, and finally even his own protégé, Asher, Richard Sears simply gave up.

The contrast between Richard Sears and JR is brilliantly encapsulated by Cecil Hoge:

> Sears was an opportunist and immediate benefit tactician. Rosenwald was a strategist, always with a long-term plan. Sears was a star and Rosenwald a team player. Sears overshadowed others. Rosenwald developed them. Sears was inclined to pour money into promotion and watch pennies in salaries. Rosenwald was more cautious in promotion and more generous in sharing profit with others in the organization. Sears lived for the mail-order moment and Rosenwald for the long-term pull. Sears had a flair for the publicizing of his entrepreneurial exploits. Rosenwald became a master of public relations for the organization. Gradually, those in the organization developed more respect for the soundness of Rosenwald's plans and gratitude for his being a fair divider. The effect of Sears's selling out was to allow one clear policy to operate in the firm.[37]

In the twelve years since he had started actively working at Sears, Roebuck, JR had accomplished a great deal. While he was not directly responsible for the huge increase in customers, he was largely responsible for creating order out of chaos and fashioning a smooth-running and efficient company. He did not do it alone. He had talented associates such as Doering, Skinner, and Loeb. His judgment was not flawless. He made mistakes, such as his opposition to the opening of the satellite plant in Dallas. Yet on the truly important issues, such as the need to retain the hundreds of thousands of customers Richard Sears had attracted to the company by efficiently and accurately delivering their purchases, JR was correct. JR was also right that the company was strong enough and well enough established to weather the economic downturn without resorting to frantic schemes to continually lure customers.

For the next sixteen years, JR presided over the largest retail establishment in the world. He did so with skill and grace; he was cautious but not afraid to take risks. Under his leadership, Sears, Roebuck continued to grow and prosper.

Little is known of JR's management style. In the early 1900s, he wrote a series of letters to his youngest brother, Louis, who, with a friend, had opened a small store in Salina, Kansas. JR was happy to give advice. But most of the advice is underwhelming. In one of the earliest letters, he sounds exactly like Richard Sears, telling the "boys": "You want to keep awake, thinking of something new all the time in order to attract the people." Then he provides an example that again sounds just like Sears: "It might possibly be a good scheme for you to give away a sewing machine. We can furnish you a genuine Davis sewing machine for $14, and you might give one away every month, if you cared to do so—by giving a man one chance for every dollar's worth of goods he buys."[38] Unfortunately, JR's advice was lost on the recipients of this letter. Louis Rosenwald, unlike his brothers JR and Morris, had no idea how to succeed in the business world.

More revealing of JR's management style is the story Werner tells about how JR selected a contractor to build the Homan Avenue plant. He interviewed a number of people, all eager to obtain one of the biggest construction jobs in the country. In walked young Louis J. Horowitz of the Thompson-Starett Company of New York. JR admitted that he was confused by all the different bids he was receiving. Horowitz said he understood JR's confusion and offered to have Thompson-Starett build the plant for a fee of $250,000. He further offered to have his firm make a contract for a fee of $1 and if JR and his associates were not satisfied with the results, they would be obligated to pay only the cost of materials plus $1. JR was stunned, but before accepting, he went to check with Albert Loeb, who told him that the fee had to be $30,000 instead of $1. When the plant was finished, JR sent Horowitz three checks. One was for $30,000, the contracted fee; the second was for $210,000, the verbal fee, and the third was a check for $50,000 because he and Sears were so pleased with the results of Thompson-Starett's work.[39]

This story is interesting for three reasons. One is that JR was honest and at ease enough to tell Horowitz of his confusion with the whole process; second, he carefully checked with Loeb before making the deal; and third, he generously rewarded a job well done. Although Emmet and Jeuck present a picture of JR in these years which is similar to that of Aaron Nusbaum—haughty, aloof, often critical, and overly conservative—such an image does not appear to be accurate. Rather, one can more easily picture JR eating in the cafeteria with the other employees, his office door open, always willing to consult and listen. In later years he did not favor a top-down style of management, and it is difficult to imagine him starting out in anything like that fashion.

Emil G. Hirsch and the Doctrine of Social Justice

Aloofness and conservatism were also not hallmarks of JR's early forays into philanthropy. And just as JR found a mentor for the business world in Richard Sears, so he found a teacher and ethicist to guide his initial steps in the world of philanthropy: Emil G. Hirsch, the Reform rabbi of Temple Sinai, which JR and Gussie joined during the late 1890s.[40]

JR had been brought up as a Reform Jew as a boy in Springfield. It is unclear whether he was concerned with religion when he lived in New York or only after he moved to Chicago. Gussie had been brought up in an Orthodox Jewish household, but at the age of fourteen she had started attending a Reform synagogue. Once married, JR and Gussie occasionally went to temple, though neither could really be called observant Jews. In JR's letters to Gussie there are references to not fasting on Yom Kippur and working on Saturdays.

Reform Judaism had begun in Germany at the end of the eighteenth century. It was initiated by laymen and was a consequence of the Enlightenment. That intellectual movement, which affected secular and religious life in both Europe and America, was based on reason and sought to sweep away what were regarded as those aspects of religious practice which had no relevance for contemporary life. In terms of Judaism, this meant that vernacular languages were substituted for Hebrew; men and women prayed together; music was supplied not merely by a cantor but by a choir or by the congregation singing what, in some cases were essentially Protestant hymns with the words slightly altered. The prayer services were shortened, and the rabbi preached a sermon during the service. Keeping a kosher home or wearing special garments such as the talith (prayer shawl) or yarmulke were no longer regarded as appropriate.

The criterion for whether or not ritual was to be maintained was whether it was truly a part of modern Jewish life, not something done by rote. As Hirsch stated, "Life and actual observance, not law or custom decide what rite shall be practiced."[41] What might be regarded as the ultimate change in ritual occurred in Hirsch's Sinai Congregation when he decided to hold the main service not on Friday night or Saturday morning but on Sunday morning. This change was made because many members of the congregation preferred to work on Saturday and pray on Sunday like their Christian colleagues. Reform Judaism, like other aspects of the Enlightenment, stressed progress and sought to discount commandments or miracles that could not be explained rationally. Judaism was recognized as one of many religions, and it was thought that mankind was progressing inexorably toward one religion, which would probably be strongly Jewish. Indeed, the idea of Jews as "the Chosen People" was now taken by Reform Jews to mean that Jews were to be the leaders of this new world religious movement.[42]

From its beginnings in Germany, Reform Judaism quickly spread to America, first to Charleston, South Carolina, and then to Baltimore, Philadelphia, and other major cities. By the 1860s and 1870s it had attracted the majority of the first wave of German Jewish immigrants and their children (including Samuel Rosenwald) and had become the largest branch of the Jewish religion in America.

Emil G. Hirsch came from a Reform background. He was born in Luxembourg, where his father, Samuel, was chief rabbi. Emil was a precocious genius. At a young age, he had mastered seventeen languages.[43] In 1866 the family moved to Philadelphia where Samuel became rabbi of one of the leading Reform synagogues in the country. Emil graduated from the University of Pennsylvania and then went to Germany to pursue rabbinical studies as there were no Reform seminaries in America. He studied in Berlin and Leipzig, and one of his teachers was the leading Reform rabbi in Germany. Returning to America in 1876, he became a rabbi in Baltimore, then moved to Louisville, Kentucky, and in 1880 became rabbi of Chicago Sinai Congregation.

Sinai was formed as the result of a split from Congregation Kehillath Anshe Maariv, the oldest synagogue in Chicago. In 1858, disaffected members began meeting with a young rabbinical student who had recently arrived from Germany. He was ordained and the Congregation was established in 1861. For a number of years up to 1879, its rabbi was a rising young star of Reform Judaism, Kaufmann Kohler. When Kohler moved to New York, Sinai chose Kohler's brother-in-law, Emil Hirsch, as its rabbi.

Hirsch remained at Sinai from 1880 until his death in 1923. In 1898 he accepted an offer from Temple Emanuel in New York, the leading Reform synagogue in America, but the outcry in Chicago was so great that he finally asked Temple Emanuel to release him from his commitment. During his tenure, Sinai became one of the most influential Reform congregations in the country. It also grew phenomenally, from a little over forty members in 1880 to almost nine hundred by 1923, a testament to Hirsch's charisma and changing population patterns.[44] Hirsch made Sinai one of the leading members of the recently formed Union of American Hebrew Congregations (UAHC), the influential body of Reform synagogues and rabbis.

The teachings of Emil Hirsch had a profound effect on JR, who noted: "When I went to live in Chicago, I naturally affiliated myself with Dr. Hirsch's congregation and I have sat at his feet every Sunday when he held services and I was in the City, during the past thirty-five years. . . . Never once in all that time have I left the Temple without feeling that I had carried away some helpful or inspiring lesson which would not have come to me except for having placed myself under such an influence."[45]

A man of towering intellect, Hirsch was one of the chief spokesmen for Reform Judaism in America. He influenced the development of this religious movement, playing a leading role at a conference in Pittsburgh in 1886 that defined the universal tenets of Reform Judaism. It was Hirsch who forcefully asserted that prophetic social justice should be a key element in these tenets.

In his carefully worded sermons, which were transcribed and printed in Sinai's newspaper, the *Reform Advocate,* Hirsch propounded his philosophy. He believed that Judaism could be reduced to an ethical and moral system. It was basically the religion of the prophets, who had excoriated Hebrew kings on ethical grounds. While he believed in the rights of man, he also believed that these rights imposed strict moral obligations. Above all, the rights of the individual should never take precedence over the rights of society. Unfettered, the rights of the individual could lead to despotism, to slavery, to the rampant capitalism of the Manchester school of Bentham and Mill, which most late nineteenth-century capitalists championed and which Hirsch deplored.

Hirsch was an unreconstructed Progressive, even radical for his day. He believed that "a legitimate program of state action would include a system of differential and progressive taxation, safety and sanitation regulation of factories, workmen's insurance, the cost of which would be borne primarily by capital, regulation of hours of work, prohibition of child labor, protection of women, strict control of monopolies and large corporations, and the guarantee to labor of the right to assemble and to organize."[46]

Hirsch's ideas were of particular importance to JR because they also touched on the special duties that capitalists and men of wealth owed to society. The notion of *tsadakah,* or charity and justice, is an essential tenet of Judaism, but Hirsch carried it a step further, declaring: "Property entails duties, which establishes its rights. Charity is not a voluntary concession on the part of the well-situated. It is a right to which the less fortunate are entitled in justice."[47]

Early Philanthropy

Although JR credited his mother for his penchant for philanthropy, it is more likely that it was Rabbi Hirsch who strongly influenced him in this direction. Gussie, in her correspondence of the early 1890s, occasionally mentioned a charitable event that she attended, but the young couple lived in straitened circumstances and did not have much money to spend on charitable causes. In this context, an often-repeated remark should probably be regarded as apocryphal. JR was reputed to have told Mo Newborg: "The aim of my life is to have an income of $15,000 a year—$5,000 to be used for my personal expenses, $5,000 to be laid aside, and $5,000 to go to charity."[48] In the mid-1890s, when this remark was supposedly uttered, JR was thinking primarily of how he could support his growing family.

Like John D. Rockefeller and other great millionaires and philanthropists at the end of the nineteenth century, Julius Rosenwald started by contributing only small sums to local and primarily religious organizations. An admittedly incomplete listing of all JR's charitable contributions shows that in 1899 and 1900 he donated $5 (the equivalent of $110 in 2005 dollars) each year to a local organization called the Hyde Park Protective Association, a sum that increased to $10 by 1902.[49] In this same period, he gave comparatively small sums to the Associated Jewish Charities, the organization formed in 1900 to systematize and organize the disparate German Jewish charities in the Chicago area. It was not until

1905 that JR's gifts to the Associated increased dramatically, when he donated $4,000 to that agency, the largest contribution it received that year, the equivalent of approximately $78,000 today.

In 1902, JR first made a contribution to an organization that was already of tremendous importance in Chicago, one of the earliest and best run settlement houses in the country, Jane Addams's Hull House. It is obvious how this gift came to be made, for the donation can be traced almost directly to Rabbi Hirsch's influence. Emil Hirsch was an early champion of Hull House, and he had invited Jane Addams to lecture at Chicago Sinai Congregation about her activities, the first non-Jewish woman ever accorded such an honor in an American synagogue. Another significant person who was in the circle of Rabbi Hirsch and a friend of Jane Addams was Judge Julian W. Mack, one of the founders of the Associated Jewish Charities with Rabbi Hirsch. Mack was also a founder with Jane Addams and Lucy Flowers of the Juvenile Court, which Rabbi Hirsch strongly supported. It is not clear how much JR's initial gift to Hull House was, but in a letter of 1906, Addams thanked JR for having contributed $100 for several years.[50] By 1908, his contribution had increased to $1,000. Gussie, too, made her own contribution, at least in 1906.[51] JR was to become a director of Hull House and serve on its board for over twenty years.

In addition to contributing to Hull House, JR also gave $100 a year to another settlement house, Chicago Commons, run by a University of Chicago sociology professor, Graham Taylor. Moreover, he made small donations to a Jewish organization, the Bureau of Personal Services run by Minnie Low, who was a noted social worker. The Bureau gave small sums to individual hard luck cases, and although JR rarely contributed to individuals, he did so through Minnie Low's organization. In the coming years, JR was to become more involved with both the Bureau of Personal Services and the Chicago Commons.

A donation pledged in 1904 was among the largest JR made up to that time and probably also involved Emil Hirsch. He gave the University of Chicago $6,782 to purchase for the German Department a privately owned library that had come up for sale. By 1904, JR lived within a mile of the twelve-year-old university, and his oldest children attended the newly opened University of Chicago Laboratory School under the direction of John Dewey. It is likely, however, that the inspiration for this gift came from Hirsch. Although the University of Chicago was officially a Baptist institution, its president, William Rainey Harper, a biblical scholar, sought to hire the best and most prestigious faculty he could find and thus had no compunction about offering a professorship in Hebrew studies to the gifted rabbi. Since Hirsch had studied in Germany, it is likely that he was interested in the affairs of the German Department, knew when this valuable collection came on the market, and persuaded his newly wealthy congregant to purchase the library for the university.

Word travels fast. A few months after the contribution to the University of Chicago, JR was involved in the purchase of another library, this time of Jewish sources, for Hebrew Union College, the only seminary for Reform Judaism in the country at that time. In one of his earliest extant letters to Hebrew Union College, JR stated: "A few years ago, I became a subscriber to the endowment fund of the Hebrew Union College through Dr. Hirsch."[52] It is not known how much JR donated before 1905. The amount of his gift to purchase Keyserling's rare collection of books, pamphlets, and manuscripts for the Hebrew Union College Library was $2,500.[53]

The largest philanthropic endeavor in which JR was engaged during the early 1900s was the expansion of Michael Reese Hospital, the preeminent German Jewish medical facility, which constructed a new building in its location south of Chicago's Loop between 1905 and 1908. JR joined the building committee starting in 1904, the first evidence of his service on a nonprofit board or committee. In addition to raising funds through his service on the building committee, JR contributed heavily to the Michael Reese campaign. In 1904, he gave $10,000; in 1905, he contributed $25,000, the largest sum he had donated to anything up to that time, and in a third wave of fund-raising in 1907 to finish the building, he gave $2,500.[54]

Another grant JR made in 1905 united two of his interests, Jews and agriculture. In February 1905, JR wrote a friend: "I am just now very interested in our Agricultural Aid Society work of placing Jewish farmers, and this work is progressing very nicely."[55] So involved was he in this project that he pledged $4,000 to aid a Jewish agricultural community in western Michigan if it could raise an additional $20,000. This is one of the first uses of a challenge grant by JR; it became one of the central mechanisms of his philanthropy. In the same letter to Lytton, JR indicated that most of the challenge money had already been raised. In future years, his interest in Jews and agriculture was to lead JR to Aaron Aaronsohn and to the Jewish agricultural colonies in Russia in the 1920s.

Generally in these early years of his philanthropy, JR does not say why he is donating to a particular cause. But in a letter accompanying a $100 gift to Chicago Charity Hospital in 1906, JR does give a reason: "When busy men, such as I know a number of your officers and directors to be, take an interest in work of this character, I believe the least the community can do, or at least such of us as can afford to, is give the work financial assistance."[56] But JR himself, who was clearly extremely busy during these years, was not above becoming thoroughly involved in an agency's work himself, as was the case with the Juvenile Court Committee, a group whose mission was dealing with youth who today would be termed "at risk." In 1905, JR was involved in a number of cases, including a young unnamed employee of Sears. As Sadie T. Wald of that organization noted when she thanked JR, "If more men gave of their personality, many conditions could be easily overcome."[57] This statement was not mere persiflage. JR's deep commitment to the causes he believed in was one of the hallmarks of his philanthropy.

In this period after he had initially acquired considerable wealth, JR had not yet reached a comfortable equilibrium between the amount he could contribute and the amount he wanted to donate. By the end of 1905, he had to acknowledge that even with regard to an organization he admired, such as the Juvenile Court Committee, he had reached the limit of his contributions for that year, which included Michael Reese, the University of Chicago and Hebrew Union College libraries, $4,000 for Jewish farmers, and $2,500 to aid Russians, presumably Jews caught up in the Russian Revolution of that year. Altogether, in 1905 JR donated approximately $45,450 to various causes, far more than he had ever given away before. As he wrote Sadie Wald in December: "You will no doubt be surprised that the check I enclose is only half of the amount that I have sent heretofore, and I hope you will not be seriously inconvenienced by the change. Owing to certain conditions which have arisen, I found it advisable to curtail in this direction for the time being."[58]

It is important to remember that 1905, a year of intense philanthropic activity, was also the time when the Sears plant on Homan Avenue was being erected. It is not at all clear, however, why JR should have made so many large contributions at that time, the year before the issuance of Sears, Roebuck stock, when he and Richard Sears suddenly found themselves multimillionaires. With the company's ever-increasing profits, JR must have felt more comfortable with Sears, Roebuck's future and his own place in the company. It is also possible that the preachings of Rabbi

Hirsch on the obligations and duties of the very wealthy members of the Jewish community were truly hitting home.

A contribution of 1906 suggests that JR did not simply respond to written appeals. He began asking advice, seeking information about some of the organizations he was thinking of supporting, as this letter to the head of the John Spry School illustrates: "I find upon inquiry that the work you are doing meets with the approval of people who have been contributors to your good work for some time, and I take great pleasure in enclosing my check for $255 to make up the deficit stated in your communication." In fact, this contribution may have been more in the nature of a thank-you for services rendered, as Henry Tibbets, principal of the Spry School, indicated that he had passed judgment "on the qualifications of many of the young people who find employment among you."[59]

One other aspect of JR's giving was becoming apparent even in this early period: he detested what he considered to be waste of any kind. While in Europe in 1904, he received a request from the YMCA asking him to contribute $5,000 for a new Hyde Park building. "The cable cost $25!" he wrote to Gussie. "I shall not even answer it."[60]

By the end of 1908, when Richard Sears resigned, Julius Rosenwald was beginning to assume a leadership role in the Jewish philanthropic community in Chicago. In 1908, after two years as a director, JR was elected president of the Associated Jewish Charities, a position he was to hold for the next four years.

Also in 1908, JR became involved in an organization that was to occupy a considerable amount of his time, talent, enthusiasm, and money, the Chicago Hebrew Institute. As Eastern European Jews arrived in Chicago in ever greater numbers in the early years of the twentieth century, they needed an institution where they could learn the language and customs of their new country, a center where they could have recreation, take classes, and gather to make their voices heard. A group of far-sighted Jewish immigrants recognized this need and formally established the Chicago Hebrew Institute in 1903. Many of the assimilated German Jews who had arrived in America decades earlier disdained these new arrivals, many of whom spoke little or no English, lived in poor conditions, were Orthodox rather than Reform, and expected their richer German cousins to assist them. Once again, it was Rabbi Hirsch who came to the Hebrew Institute's rescue in January 1907.[61]

As always when Rabbi Hirsch spoke, the audience was large and enthusiastic. Hirsch raised both money and awareness about the existence of the Hebrew Institute. He also very likely interested JR in this fledgling organization. Nathan Kaplan, president of the Hebrew Institute, and JR evidently met several times, and the conversation revolved around the Institute's proposed purchase of a building to serve as its home. In June 1907, JR proposed to Kaplan that he would be willing to assist in the purchase of this property under certain conditions, but this arrangement did not work out at that time. Despite the fact that the plan fell through, JR was sufficiently impressed with the Hebrew Institute to give them a small donation of $30.

The following year JR received a letter asking him to join the Institute's board of directors.[62] He agreed to serve and gave his reasons for accepting:

> It is unnecessary for me to say that I am in sympathy with any movement that will tend toward breaking down the social barrier which seems to exist between the Russian and German Jews, and with the thought in mind that my connection with the Hebrew Institute will be a step in that direction, I have concluded to allow my name to be used as a Director. I would not consent to do this were it not for the confidence I have in your earnestness in the cause and the belief that it will be lasting. Furthermore, I am attracted by the statement you made that the movement was to be a popular one and not one that was to be assisted financially from without.[63]

In other words, quite apart from the idea of unifying the Russian and German Jews, a goal toward which JR worked for many years, he was attracted by the fact that the Eastern European Jews were eager to contribute to their own organization and would not be totally dependent on their wealthier German brethren. The idea of self-help was to be an extraordinarily important element in JR's philanthropy, and this letter to the Hebrew Institute is one of the earliest manifestations of it.

JR was immediately elected to the board of the Institute. Since the building they wanted was still available, at a cost of $110,000, JR offered to take out a mortgage on the property for $75,000. No interest was to be charged on the loan for the first two years, and after that a rate of interest of 4.5 percent was charged. The Institute duly began making interest payments in 1910, but eventually JR announced that he would forgo repayment of both principal and interest, thereby giving the Institute an impressive gift. In addition to arranging for the purchase of the building, JR offered the Institute a personal gift of $5,000 if it could raise an additional $45,000, "so as to assure a fund for equipment as well as purchase [of the building]."[64] By September 1908, the Institute had moved into its new home, and the various adult education classes that had started the previous year continued and grew in size and popularity.

JR described his service on the Institute board, and its relationship to his other big charitable work, president of the Associated Jewish Charities, to a New York correspondent:

> Personally, I have not taken an active part in the work of the institution. I was elected a Director last spring, and was willing to assist the Society in the purchase of the property which they have recently acquired, but I took no part in the raising of money, or active work of any kind. Being president of the Associated Jewish Charities, which are our Federated Charities, my spare time is largely devoted to that work and the nature of the work is such that it necessarily prevents me from soliciting money for other purposes. However, my sympathies are with the Hebrew Institute, and whenever I can, I attend their meetings.[65]

This statement was not totally accurate. JR was, in fact, engaged in fundraising for the Hebrew Institute, for in May he received a check for the Institute for $200 from Samuel B. Goldberg, whom he had doubtless solicited. Goldberg's accompanying letter makes clear that JR's example was already beginning to have an impact on the Chicago Jewish community. "Permit me to say that it is through your broad idea of charity and philanthropy that our people can be thankful. If we only had a few more men with the same feelings and ideas that you have, I can easily imagine that our Jewish people of Chicago would have all the institutions they need."[66]

Rosenwald was to become increasingly involved in the work of the Institute. He also did a tremendous favor to the organization by bringing on the board Jacob Loeb, brother of his friend and associate Albert. Jacob Loeb eventually succeeded JR as president of the Hebrew Institute and remained in that capacity for decades.

In 1907, JR was one of the founders of a Jewish agency that was directly inspired by Emil Hirsch, the Jewish Home Finding Society. In the early years of the twentieth century, when most women were not employed, children from low-income families were taken from their widowed mothers and placed in orphanages, on the grounds that the mothers could not work and thus would be totally destitute. Hirsch preached sermons against this terrible practice, which the Jewish Home Finding Society sought to end, in order to keep such families together. Although Hirsch was not mentioned among the group of people who met to found the organization, he soon joined the board, and there can be little doubt that he gave the inspiration for the group's beginning. As a sign of his faith and interest in the fledgling organization, JR contributed $3,500 to it in 1908.[67]

Julius Rosenwald emerged as a philanthropist between 1900 and 1908. Clearly, Emil Hirsch was the guiding force behind most of the donations JR was making. There are, obviously, exceptions to this—gifts which cannot be traced to Hirsch's influence, such as the $8,000 given in 1908 to the Illinois Industrial School for Girls. Still, the fact remains that most of the large gifts in this period are either to Jewish causes or to organizations where there was a Hirsch connection. Once JR became more accomplished at philanthropy, he would look to other advisors to help him with his donations. But it was largely Emil Hirsch who set Julius Rosenwald on the road to becoming one of the preeminent philanthropists of the early twentieth century.

Hirsch, however, was not the only important influence on the philanthropy of JR in this period. Almost as significant was Julian W. Mack, who, along with JR, was a founder of the Home Finding Society. Judge Mack and JR became very close friends, and as the influence of Hirsch began to wane, he was replaced by Mack who remained one of his most trusted advisors even after he had left Chicago in 1912. Another influential figure was Minnie Low.

All of these people moved in the same social circles. For example, in 1905 JR founded the Book and Play Club, which met periodically at his house. Emil Hirsch was named honorary president, and Julian Mack was named the real president.[68] For Gussie, this enlargement of her social circle must have been a real blessing, a breaking of the tightly knit bonds of family which had so constrained her in the early years of her marriage. As for JR, he, too, seemed to thrive in this world of brilliant and dedicated men and women.

Family Affairs

The years between 1895 and 1908 were important not only for JR's business career but also in terms of his family. It grew and changed in important ways. As the children grew older, their father became an important factor in their lives. And both JR and his family had to adjust to a wholly new situation: sudden wealth and a definite change of lifestyle.

On October 19, 1899, Samuel Rosenwald died after a lengthy illness. Rabbi Emil Hirsch presided at his funeral. There is no record of what JR thought or felt, but one suspects that it was relief for the mother to whom he was so devoted. Even with the strong family support system that then existed, Samuel Rosenwald, not the easiest person to get along with in the best of times, must have been a great burden to his wife in his declining years.

JR's nuclear family grew in this period. In the 1890s, three children had been born to JR and Gussie: Lessing in 1891, Adele in 1892, and Edith in 1895. JR and Gussie evidently thought they had the ideal family size. In October 1897, JR wrote Gussie and reported on a pregnant relative: "Meta looks as if she weighed a ton." Then he added: "You see, my angel, you're through with that."[69] Thus Marion, who was born on March 19, 1902, was what one might today call "unplanned," and because Gussie and JR had Marion, they decided to provide her with a playmate, and so William was born August 19, 1903.

The seven years that separated Edith and Marion resulted in an interesting family dynamic. The three older children were brought up in modest circumstances. Their parents were present a good deal and devoted considerable time to them. For example, around 1900, it was Gussie who took the three children to the Art Institute to teach them art appreciation. "Edith is too young, but I expect to accomplish a great deal for the other two in order to make them lovers of fine art."[70] The two younger children grew up in luxurious surroundings, were raised mainly by governesses, and saw their parents much less frequently because both JR and Gussie were caught up in a whirl of social and philanthropic obligations.

One obvious way in which JR's increasing wealth affected the whole family was the building of a large house in the Kenwood section of Chicago not far from the University of Chicago. The house at 4901 Ellis Avenue was designed by George C. Nimmons and William K. Fellows, the same architects who shortly afterward built the Sears, Roebuck plant. The Rosenwald home was designed and built in 1903, although the family did not move in until February 1904. This mansion was located on one of the largest lots in Chicago. It has some elements of Frank Lloyd Wright

Figure 5. JR, Gussie, and their five children in 1909. From left to right are Lessing, William, Marion, JR, Edith, Gussie, and Adele.

and the Prairie School, but there are also flashes of an English architect, C. F. A. Vosey, who liked bare walls and banks of windows without sills or lintels.[71] The brownish-grey stone lent an almost industrial feel to the building, which led the younger children to refer to it as "the old pickle factory." But it had an enormous backyard with a sunken garden and large flower beds. In addition to rooms for the children and for JR and Gussie, the house had a ballroom on the top floor and numerous rooms for the servants, who were now a part of Rosenwald family life.

For Gussie, becoming wealthy meant that she had to manage a large household, which was an important responsibility. Wealth also conferred social respectability. In November 1900, Gussie proudly told JR she had been accepted as a member of the South Side Women's Club.[72] She also began to do volunteer work, joining the Women's Board of Michael Reese Hospital, among other organizations. Either because of her volunteer work or because of her husband's example, she also began donating small sums to charities on her own. Toward the end of this period, JR was writing frequently to family members that Gussie was at least as busy as he was.

Not everything in Gussie's life was social activity or managing the household. It was important for her to have time for reflection, time for reading and study, and time for letter writing. All three were important to her, but perhaps reading and study at times predominated, whether it was reading *Treasure Island* to the children or studying the book of Joel for a Bible class she was taking in 1906.[73] Gussie was not an intellectual, but she was thoughtful, and she liked to attend conferences on subjects that interested her. In 1906, she presented a paper at the March 12 meeting of the Council of Jewish Women. It was reprinted in the *Reform Advocate,* and it gives some insight into her thoughts.

The paper was about the religious education of children, and much of it demonstrates that, like JR, she had absorbed the lessons of Rabbi Hirsch, whom she quotes extensively. She starts with a distinction between morality and religion. Morality is something you teach your children so that it becomes automatic, and from the numerous letters she wrote her children, one can see that Gussie lived this dictum. Religion, on the other hand, involved conscious activity, and it, too, needed to be taught, preferably in Sunday school. The lessons of the Bible, Gussie asserted, were an important part of the curriculum, but they had to be structured. Also important for older children was a study of comparative religion. Indeed, religious education should go on for a longer time in a child's life than was usually the case, and it should also last longer than the hour and a half usually allotted to it, according to Gussie. Also important was the training of teachers, and even of parents, and Gussie advocated the kind of Bible study she herself was engaged in. She advised parents that the daily whirl of social activity, even going to clubs, could be deleterious. They should spend more time with their children, a maxim she did not always keep.[74]

Unfortunately, religious education was one thing in theory and another in practice. Marion often told the story of her one day in Bible class. Probably at the urging of her mother, she and William were sent off to Rabbi Hirsch's Bible class one Sunday when she was quite young. The biblical passage they were reading contained the word *stock,* as in cattle. Rabbi

Hirsch pointed a finger at Marion and boomed, "And what kind of 'stock' is that? Is that shares of Sears, Roebuck stock?" Marion turned crimson, and as soon as the class was over, she and William rushed home. She announced to her father that she was never going back, and JR must have agreed, for she never did.

Increased intellectual activity, increased household duties, and a wider social circle should have made it much easier for Gussie to deal with the numerous times when JR was away. Although the plethora of letters that marked the early years of their marriage is lacking, the brooding introspection that seemed to characterize many of Gussie's missives is not much in evidence. But occasionally it did surface—for example, on JR's trip to Europe in 1904. In a letter written on May 20, Gussie was clearly "down in the dumps":

> Responsibility increases with increase of pleasures, and so often I find myself robbed of many of the real joys we had in a more simple life. Mine is not the disposition to make light of life, and so I do not get full benefit of all my privileges, much to my own sorrow and discontent. . . . How I long for that power which would enable me to make the most of the great opportunities which our great good fortune presents to me. I am so discontented with myself and seem to make no strides toward a betterment of myself. . . . I don't want you to scold me and tell me I am all right. It seems I never accomplish anything. I fear that I haven't enough ideals, and allow too many trivial material things to fill my life and thus crowd out the important things. . . . You thought that when you were away I would have so much time for myself, and yet I am just as busy as ever and am seldom alone. When I plan to do this or that, something or somebody interferes. I try to make the best of conditions which confront me and am very patient but not contented. So now what will you say? You have nothing to do with this discontent. It is only I who am to blame.[75]

For the most part, however, Gussie's letters do not reflect such despondent moods, so that JR felt able to joke about these feelings. "Don't forget to worry if only a little every day and let me know what about when I get home," he wrote her in April 1897.[76] Moreover, as the first set of children grew older, Gussie was able to leave them in the care of JR and the nanny, as she did in May 1897 when she accepted an invitation from Mo Newborg to go fishing with him near Grand Rapids.

For JR, sudden wealth seems to have made little difference. He was still abstemious. In 1903, he wrote Gussie from Richmond, Virginia: "I was a little extravagant—I bought a trunk for myself—not quite so nice as yours but something I've wanted for some time."[77] This attitude is reflected most acutely when JR was trying to impart a lesson to young men, including his own son. In 1908, Lessing went off to college as a freshman at Cornell. He was urged to write every day, and his father also insisted that he keep a strict account of his expenses and send it home for paternal inspection. Consequently, Lessing was bombarded with letters such as the following:

> I am in receipt of your expense account, and am not at all pleased with it. In the first place, there is no reason at all why your account should not balance every evening. It is purely and simply a lack of willingness on your part, and if you cannot do any other way, mark down every cent as you spend it; but this should not be necessary. . . . There should be no occasion for you to buy 50 cents worth of mandolin strings at once. I am sure mandolin strings can be bought much cheaper here, and if you needed one or two strings, you could write here for the balance. Haircut and shampoo 75 cents looks entirely out of reason, and 40 cents for souvenir postals. All these things besides other extravagances are unsatisfactory to me. You are fully aware what my views are. . . . [Y]our account shows that you are not in the least trying to economize, but, to the contrary, are unnecessarily extravagant. If you had to earn one-half the money you spend, you would find it a hard job. . . . You are fully aware that I have no desire to deprive you of anything that is necessary and fairly within reason. . . . The above is all to be read as it is written—in the kindliest of spirit and with no intention to put a severe emphasis anywhere. Denying yourself unnecessary things will give you much more happiness than you will get from indulging yourself by satisfying every whim.[78]

The absurdity of this injunction to parsimony becomes apparent when one realizes that by 1908 JR was a multimillionaire. Poor Lessing received dozens of these letters, and it seems fairly obvious that after a short time, he simply ignored them. Interestingly enough, John D. Rockefeller Jr. had a similar experience when he went off to Brown University, but he appears to have taken the parental injunctions more seriously.[79]

Lessing was not the only family member to receive such homilies. Adele was not immune, although her treatment was far more gentle. After mockingly upbraiding her for using too much slang, JR added this admonition in the summer of 1906: "Have all the fun you can without being boisterous or infringing on the rights of others."[80] Nor were JR's children the only recipients of such advice. In a revealing letter to a distant relative, JR wrote: "I want to tell you that there are mighty few people who can stand prosperity, and I hope you have good sense enough not to allow your prosperity to warp your judgment to the extent of feeling that you are in too great a measure responsible for any success which you may imagine comes from your work." He goes on to admonish: "[A] young man who cannot manage his own affairs properly will never be able to manage another person's." What JR meant by "managing one's own affairs" was saving a percentage of one's income.[81]

This letter to young Harry Lipsis actually turned out to be part of a larger problem associated with JR's rise to wealth and prominence: relatives wanting favors. A couple of years after writing to Harry, JR received a letter from Harry's mother. The young man wanted to leave Kansas City and come to Chicago. Nettie Lipsis naturally expected that her relative, JR, would give Harry a job at Sears, Roebuck and look after him. JR replied that he could probably find a place for Harry at Sears, but at the bottom. If the young man was willing to live on $12–15 a week, he would be all right, especially if he had learned JR's lessons of thrift. As for looking after Harry, JR said that he would be happy to give the young man advice, but Harry was free to take it or leave it.[82]

Gussie was also not immune from such begging. Her sister Tessie wrote her in June 1908, saying that her husband, a clothing merchant in New York, was suffering from the ravages of the recession. He was going to ask JR for a loan of $15,000 to tide him over. But Tessie importuned her sister to put in a word so that the ante could be upped to $25,000.[83] In fact, JR was enormously generous with his large extended family. Many of his American relatives received Sears, Roebuck stock, and in 1904 JR went to Germany and met a number of his father's relatives. Many of them received monetary gifts and stock for years, interrupted only by World War I.

Pesky relatives begging for money or favors was a downside of great wealth, but there were a great many pluses. For one thing, it enabled JR and Gussie to do something they had rarely done before: travel. The Sears, Roebuck vice president made numerous trips to New York and had traveled to the West and Southwest on business. Gussie had chosen to honeymoon in New York, where she had been born, but immediately following her marriage, her travels had been confined to the Midwest. Thus she was thrilled by the trip to Mexico she and JR took in January 1900, their first journey outside the United States.

Their trip was a tour on which members of the group lived, ate, and slept on a train except in Mexico City. Gussie liked the amenities of train travel, but she exhibited the same kinds of prejudices as JR in his southwest trip of 1892. She wrote her children: "It means work to go on a tour of this kind, and yet this is the only way to go and be comfortable. In a more civilized country it is better to go independently and take as much time as one wishes for just sight-seeing and doing as you wish, but deliver me from going independently through this country. I would starve, and just think of poor me not getting enough to eat."[84]

JR had a fine time on this expedition, as this portrait, rather unappealing to twenty-first-century sensibilities, makes clear: "Our Papa dear is as jolly as can be and enjoys everything thoroughly. He is like a schoolboy, and is always having fun with the dirty little boys and girls, and is always throwing pennies for the children to scramble after. Everybody on the train likes him. They can't help it."[85] It is not certain how much Gussie learned from the trip. Her impressions seem to be those of the superficial tourist. She describes their visit to Pueblo as follows: "In the morning, we visited a most beautiful cathedral. It is a shame to see these gorgeously decorated structures, all bought with the money of the poor people, who are so very poor because they give so much money to the Church, which represents the wealth and only wealth of the country, and to see these dirty filthy people worshiping in these beautiful churches seems all wrong to me, but on the other hand, the Mexicans and these Indians are the happiest people under the sun."[86] For JR, it seems, the highlight of the trip was a meeting with President Diaz.

In the spring of 1904, JR made his first trip to Europe. A year earlier he had been extremely ill, and Gussie evidently regarded this as something of a rest cure. She remained at home with the children—the youngest, William, had been born only six months earlier. JR was thoroughly fascinated by the trip. His restless curiosity was put to use immediately on the ocean voyage over. He wrote Gussie from the ship: "I walk and talk a good deal with Mr. Schaffner—a very fine man. Yesterday he told us they—the other steerage passengers—were mistreating the Russian Jews in the steerage. We went at once, and gave a few of them—the offenders—the mischief, and since then there seems to be no trouble. Mr. S. and I went into the steerage this morning and had a pleasant half hour with some of the Russians. They are mostly men who have made some money and are going back for their wives and children."[87]

Three things really seem to have stood out for JR about this trip through France, Switzerland, and Germany. One was the importance of studying history and languages. Many of the letters he wrote home hammered on this theme, as if he regretted not knowing more of the history of the places he visited. He knew a little German, although he admitted it was exceedingly rusty. He knew no French and relied on his travel companions, relatives of Gussie's, who spoke quite passably. JR promised himself that he would learn French when he returned to the United States.

JR traveled through Europe by automobile, a relatively new mode of transportation. Although he had recently purchased a car in Chicago, touring around Europe by car was somewhat more exotic. Even before leaving, he bought what must have been one of the first guidebooks meant for auto travel, and he was so taken by it that he sent a copy to Gussie and the children and kept referring to it in his letters. Although captivated by the scenery, he was also completely enthralled by the cars. "I have the auto fever," he wrote his family. Toward the end of the trip, he went miles out of his way to go to Hamburg for an auto race. "I was within ten feet of every starter and got a good look at each before leaving. . . . I saw the Kaiser and Kaiserin. The former was there until about 11 [A.M.] and then left and returned about 4 [P.M.] to see the finish. . . . I enjoyed the experience immensely."[88]

The main purpose of the trip for JR was to accompany his mother to Bunde. Unfortunately, shortly before the long anticipated visit, JR's mother fell and sprained her wrist. Always something of a hypochondriac, she announced that she could not go. So JR and his sister Selma went alone. Although his letters to Gussie say little about the visit, the autobiographical sketch that JR wrote reveals that this was, for him, the most memorable part of the trip: "I slept in the house in which my father was born in the year 1905 [1904] and while it was still in the possession of the Rosenwald family. Since that time it has been sold. . . . I remember seeing a brass plate attached to a pump in the rear of the house where my father was born and lived until he left Germany."[89] A more tangible link to the past were the Rosenwald relatives whom JR met for the first time on this trip. From then on, he corresponded with them, sent them money, welcomed them and their children on visits to the United States, and visited them almost every time he was in Germany.

The trip was not all pleasure. On May 14, JR wrote from Paris: "I was busy in the morning, having several parties to see on business."[90] And although he was evidently having a splendid time, he could not get Sears, Roebuck entirely out of his mind. Five days later he wrote Gussie: "Tell Albert [Loeb] I think of the store often but don't find time to write to anyone except you."[91] Gussie, who probably had been eager to go to Europe, felt that JR was entirely too businesslike in his letters home, not affectionate enough to her, and so she responded with a touch of humor by writing what she called her "Business Letter." She spoke of the family as if it were a corporation and concluded formally: "With kindest regards to you and your traveling companions, I remain, sincerely, Augusta N. Rosenwald. All other members of the firm, especially the junior branch, wish to add their warmest regards."[92] JR was most amused.

In 1907, the entire family journeyed to Europe. Gussie, who wrote frequent letters home to her relatives, was fascinated by all she saw. She loved the hustle and bustle of Paris, especially the shopping, and she was both fascinated and repelled by the "immorality" she saw there. "One sees much that is beautiful on the one hand and so much that is indecent and immoral on the other hand. The demimonde are thick as mosquitoes at some of our own country's summer resorts, most of them elegantly gowned and are really the fashion plates. This is a most fascinating place for shopping."[93]

After Paris, the party went to spas in Baden-Baden and Marienbad. In Munich, the children refused to go to museums or galleries, but the whole family did go to the famous Hofbrau House, and even the "babies" got a taste of beer.

From Germany, the Rosenwald party traveled to Switzerland, and Gussie had this interesting observation about her fellow travelers: "Americans everywhere and three-quarters of the traveling population are Jews and they all seem to say the same thing: that they can travel here feeling that they are wanted and are treated as well as any other class of people."[94]

The three older children seem to have made friends easily and enjoyed themselves. Adele, captivated by Paris, wanted to stay there to perfect her

French, but her mother felt she was too young. The trip appears to have had little if any itinerary. If they liked a place, they stayed in it. On this trip, they did not see JR's German relatives. Gussie's excuse is that they were in southern Germany and it would have taken too long and been too much trouble to go to Westphalia. Interestingly enough, Gussie, also of German origin, seems to have had absolutely no interest in trying to locate her German relatives.

JR did not write much to relatives, except for a line in one of Gussie's letters in which he states that he is enjoying everything immensely. But from Gussie's letters, it sounds as if this trip was not nearly as enjoyable for him as the 1904 expedition. He was in charge of everything, placing the "babies" and governess on trains, arranging for cars that sometimes broke down, dealing with chauffeurs. Moreover, work and other duties were never far from his mind. On the boat trip over, he spent his time "schmoozing" (as he put it) for the Associated Jewish Charities among the other German Jewish passengers from Chicago, who must have been a captive audience.[95] Moreover, this was the summer of 1907, when the economy in the United States was heading into a recession. JR was bombarded by letters from Sears and Loeb, and he must have had "the store" constantly on his mind. In mid-August, he wrote them: "My greatest regret is that I am not with you to talk over the situation. . . . I have felt like cabling you to ask me to return. . . . I now make the request that you cable for me if I can relieve either of you."[96] One can imagine that JR heaved a great sigh of relief when he was back at work at the Sears, Roebuck plant and his family was safely back home.

Although JR worked hard in these years, occasionally laboring at his desk until late into the evening, it is likely that increased wealth also gave him a bit more leisure time. He and Gussie took up tennis and golf. And on a normal summer vacation, JR played as hard as he worked. Gussie describes a typical day at a resort in Michigan, where the family spent part of the summer of 1906: "Father has to get up very early in order to get in all there is to get in. He had a horse sent up here from the City, and goes horseback riding. . . . After horseback comes golf, then lunch, a nap, tennis, bathing, dinner, and then bridge."[97]

The years 1895–1908 can be seen as a period of apprenticeship for JR, in running a large business and in taking his first steps forward in philanthropy. He learned an enormous amount from Richard Sears, just as he learned a great deal from Emil Hirsch in the realm of philanthropy. In the coming years, he was to make some innovations in the business world, but the philanthropy would come to play a more and more dominant part in his life. That era was about to begin.

3

Blacks, Politics, and Philanthropy, 1908–1912

Sears, Roebuck

In November 1908, JR became president and CEO of Sears, Roebuck. Before Richard Sears resigned, JR and James F. Skinner had sought to curb the bombastic catalog descriptions of Sears and Asher. One of JR's first acts as president was to call a meeting of department heads. He told them that, henceforth, truth in advertising was to be the rule. Catalog copy had to be absolutely clear and aboveboard. The new catalog editor drew up a set of guidelines for ad copy that reflected the ethics of the new regime. For example, in the fur department, it had long been common to advertise fur coats as "Baltic seal," although the pelt of some other animal was used. Now, in the fine print, the discerning customer could learn that the sealskin coat was actually rabbit fur.

Truth in advertising led, in 1911, to the creation of the first retail laboratory, where products were tested to be sure that their catalog descriptions were accurate. The testing lab began with food and soon expanded to other products. Although Emmet and Jeuck claim that JR was never enthusiastic about the lab, the fact is that the letter to readers in the 1912 catalog featured an extended essay on the new facilities, indicating JR's enthusiasm for them.[1]

The letter to readers at the beginning of the catalog was another sign of changing times. JR wisely realized that to tamper with the name of the company, even though neither Sears nor Roebuck was now involved with it, would be a serious marketing mistake. The name had truly become embedded in the consciousness of American farmers. But JR went beyond refusing to tamper with the company's name. He effaced himself completely from the catalog. Ever since the company began, it had been customary for Richard Sears to write an introductory letter to readers. The practice of the letter was continued, but it was no longer signed. One can look through an entire run of Sears catalogs from 1909 to 1924, when JR resigned as president, and never see the name Rosenwald.

A possible explanation for this may be that JR, knowing that antisemitism certainly existed in the United States, believed that if his name were associated with the company, some of the farmers in the heartland, guessing that he was Jewish, might not be so eager to order from the catalog. This does not mean that JR, who had a keen sense of the importance of public relations, did not want his name associated with Sears, Roebuck in the press. Frequent stories and articles about JR and Sears, Roebuck identified him by name and noted that he was Jewish. However, JR may have thought it unlikely that his rural customers would be reading those publications. Although JR was generally self-effacing, the absence of his name in the catalog of the world's largest and most successful mail-order house appears to transcend mere modesty. Since the dawn of mail order, local country stores had waged ceaseless war against Sears, Roebuck and Montgomery Ward, going so far as to have public catalog burnings. Antisemitism could easily have been used to fan those flames, and JR doubtless knew that.

There were other innovations in the catalog as the product line continued to expand. In 1909, a Sears automobile appeared in its pages. Although attractive and well made, it did not last long. An analysis of costs versus sale price revealed that it was a money loser, and it could not compete with the new and cheaper product being manufactured by Henry Ford. A more successful innovation was the Sears House. The company had long sold home improvement tools. Now they sold prefabricated houses with all the fixtures and trimmings one could want. Each piece of the house was clearly marked, and kits and diagrams accompanying the lumber and fixtures made assembling the house comparatively easy. The Sears houses, which were popular and came in several shapes and sizes, remained in the catalog until the late 1930s, and many can still be found in the suburbs and countryside of America.

While items such as houses and cars were added to the catalog, other items were eliminated. Patent medicines were discontinued altogether, partly because of JR's antipathy to them, but also because the newly established lab could prove that they were utterly useless. JR also decided to eliminate the sale of handguns, gunpowder, and ammunition from the catalog.

Continuing the trend toward "welfare capitalism," two innovations occurred in 1912. One was the anniversary check system, which worked as follows: Employees who had been with the company for five years and earned a maximum of $1,500 per year would receive a check on their fifth anniversary for 5 percent of their salary. The bonus would rise to 6 percent for six years and so on up to ten years and 10 percent. The anniversary system was perhaps a precursor of the profit sharing plan, but it was designed to reward longevity among employees and to keep them contented. The illness allowance was also liberalized during this period.[2]

The year 1912 also marked JR's marriage of philanthropy, agriculture, and Sears in one of the largest gifts of corporate philanthropy ever given up to that time. Rosenwald had donated an occasional small check to some charity through Sears, Roebuck. In 1912, he pledged, in the name of his company, $1 million to provide for agricultural extension agents in counties throughout the country. The Rockefeller-funded General Education Board had begun funding such farm experts shortly after its founding in 1902, but its grants were confined to the South. JR was approached by the Crop Improvement Committee of the Council of Grain Exchanges, and he agreed to fund this program, which was to be run by the committee. The total outlay was to be $1 million, but the first round was for $100,000. Any agricultural county in the United States could compete. One hundred grants of $1,000 each were to be awarded.

In order to qualify, the county had to be able to match the Sears money. The match, to be pledged by the farmers, was to consist of a minimum of $100 per township, or a sum equal to 1 percent of the tillable land in the county. An equal amount had to be pledged by the local commercial club, bankers, and other businessmen. The combined funds would go to pay for the salary of the extension agent. He would be a farmer by birth who was educated at an agricultural college and was familiar with the latest information on farming methods. His job would be to travel around the county and advise local farmers on how to improve their crops, their yields, their use of fertilizer, etc. The General Education Board had proved that southern farmers could greatly improve their crop yields and hence their income using this system. Now such agricultural knowledge was to be made available to farmers across the country.

JR was blunt about his reason for making this donation. "Simply a business proposition," he was quoted as saying. "Our firm is readily willing to give the million dollars to help improve the farms because their improvement would add to their prosperity, and their prosperity would redound to the prosperity of the city, and to ourselves."[3] This grant, given in the name of Sears, Roebuck, was made before any U.S. corporation had set up a foundation, and it predated the Sears, Roebuck Foundation by six years. Yet the principle behind this corporate contribution—a grant that would benefit both the donor company and the recipient—remains true today.[4]

The full million dollars was never paid out. In fact, the company spent just $110,000 on the program, $19,000 in 1912 and $91,000 in 1913. The participating counties were located exclusively in midwestern states: Illinois, Wisconsin, Iowa, Indiana, Ohio, and Michigan. In 1914, the entire program was taken over by the U.S. Department of Agriculture, and Sears, Roebuck's involvement in it ceased. Although this pathbreaking corporate grant was not followed up until the creation of the Sears, Roebuck Foundation, it clearly could be deemed a bonanza for Sears, Roebuck from the public relations standpoint.

Julius Rosenwald was fortunate in the timing of Richard Sears's departure. By November 1908, the recession of the previous year and a half was ending. From November 1908 until 1921, a period of tremendous economic boom was to occur. The years 1909 through 1912 were especially spectacular in terms of sales and profits. With business booming and the success of the Dallas branch secure, JR opened a second satellite in Seattle in 1910. The capstone of this period was the introduction of parcel post, a mail service which greatly reduced the cost of sending packages of up to eleven pounds. Despite the intense lobbying of small country store owners, Congress passed the act in 1912, thanks to the active support of customers of the mail-order houses. When parcel post was inaugurated on January 1, 1913, JR was opposed to it because the vast bulk of Sears,

Roebuck merchandise was sent by freight. But the effect of parcel post on Sears, Roebuck was immediate. In the weeks surrounding the introduction of the new service, JR kept a detailed account of the business of Sears, Roebuck, and found that mail deliveries increased 15 percent.[5] From its inception, the savings caused by parcel post helped fuel the enormous growth of the mail-order company.

The dimension of that growth under JR's leadership was impressive. In 1909, the first full year of his presidency, net sales were $51,011,536, and net profits were $6,192,361. By 1913, net sales had climbed to $91,357,276, and net profits were $9,027,670. With a smoothly running administrative team in place consisting of people such as Loeb, Skinner, and Doering, JR could devote more of his time to other pursuits, and he took full advantage of that opportunity. Politics, and especially philanthropy, began to assume a role of growing importance in his life.

Black YMCAs

The first truly major landmark act of JR's philanthropy outside the Jewish community took place in December 1910 and united two of his interests: YMCAs and blacks.

Since 1904, when he moved to the Chicago community of Kenwood, JR had contributed approximately $50 a year to the YMCA of nearby Hyde Park.[6] He may not have used the facility, but he probably believed that this was a good neighborhood resource which needed to be supported. Eventually, he became acquainted with L. Wilbur Messer, general secretary of the Chicago branch of the YMCA. In 1908, he contributed $1,000 to the YMCA's Memorial Fund in honor of the organization's fiftieth anniversary.[7] Two years later, there was another YMCA fund drive to raise $350,000. As a member of the "metropolitan committee" along with other civic leaders,[8] JR issued a ringing endorsement of the YMCA:

> I have frequently asserted that in my judgment no philanthropy in Chicago is a greater power for good, or accomplishes better results than the YMCA. It is conducted in the true American spirit, in extending a welcome to all, regardless of creed, without any attempt to interfere to the slightest degree with the religious tendency of its members. If the citizens of Chicago knew how many thousands of young men have been morally strengthened and

guided by their contact with the Association, the $350,000 fund would be raised in twelve hours. It surely will be raised in twelve days.[9]

Perhaps as a result of this campaign, JR began negotiations with the Y leadership to build a new YMCA in the vicinity of the Sears plant. In a letter to his son, Lessing, JR noted: "We are figuring with the YMCA to put up a building on our property which will contain dormitories for about 300 men, and a regular YMCA outfit in addition."[10] The new facility, which could be viewed as yet another example of JR's penchant for "welfare capitalism," was to be for the benefit of Sears employees, who could use it for recreational purposes. Sears Roebuck & Co. agreed to deed two parcels of land to the YMCA for the building, to contribute $100,000 of the estimated $210,000, and to guarantee a net profit of at least 4 percent on the total cost.[11] Like the later agricultural extension program, this was both a very large corporate donation and a "win-win" proposition. Sears and its employees obviously benefited, but so did the Y because access was not restricted to Sears employees—the building was open to anyone in the neighborhood who wished to become a member.

African Americans constituted 1.9 percent of Chicago's population in 1900 and only slightly more by 1910.[12] Largely confined to the ghetto south and west of the downtown Loop known as the "black belt," they did not really figure in the world of JR and Gussie. The Rosenwalds were typical of the vast majority of white Chicagoans of that era for whom consciousness of racial issues was nonexistent. Interestingly enough, when a serious race riot erupted in JR's hometown of Springfield in 1908, it elicited no written comment from the Sears president.

Yet JR was not totally oblivious to the existence of African Americans, and he shared the prejudices of his day. In a 1908 letter to his family, he makes a jocular reference to "schwartze," the German term for "black" which has acquired pejorative meaning in our day, although JR's use of the word, having to do with gambling numbers, seems relatively benign.[13] Gussie displayed more overt racial prejudice. When her daughter, Adele, was on a trip to the South in February 1910, Gussie wrote her: "Speaking of the South, Adele dear, reminds me to tell you that you must keep any thing of value under lock and key, as the Negroes are known to be long-fingered."[14]

JR's attitude toward blacks was transformed when his friend Paul J. Sachs, a junior partner in the firm of Goldman Sachs, sent him two books during the summer of 1910 that changed his life. One was Booker T. Washington's autobiography, *Up from Slavery,* in which the black educator recounts his life and struggles. The other was *An American Citizen: The Life of William H. Baldwin Jr.* by John Graham Brooks. Baldwin, general manager of the Southern Railway, also headed the General Education Board, the philanthropy which dealt primarily with education for southern blacks and whites. A close friend and associate of Booker T. Washington, Baldwin had served on the board of Tuskegee Institute, the college in Alabama that Washington had founded. Baldwin died in 1905. His widow was a friend of Paul Sachs.[15] While JR was inspired and moved by Washington's autobiography, there was something about the Baldwin book that struck a chord in him, perhaps the fact that Baldwin had devoted time as well as money to his philanthropic efforts on behalf of blacks. An active fundraiser for Tuskegee, Baldwin had persuaded Andrew Carnegie to donate $600,000 to the black college.

JR's excitement on reading this book is reflected in a letter he wrote his two daughters, Adele and Edith:

> I just finished *An American Citizen* and it is glorious, a story of a man who really *led* a life which is to my liking and whom I shall endeavor to imitate or follow as nearly as I can. We have a great many views in common—but he, being college-bred and much of a student, had powers of analysis which I lack. But, Adele dear, you'll say, "What's Daddy raving about?" I was just thinking out loud, and you, my girlies, will bear with me, I know. He was a good friend to Booker T. Washington and made great study of the Negro problem along common sense, helpful lines. . . . I never read of a more interesting character.[16]

JR also sent a copy of *An American Citizen* to Lessing at Cornell and kept badgering the young man to read it, although Lessing, absorbed in his studies and other college activities, resisted starting the book and probably ignored his father's requests for comments on the work as he ignored his father's nagging letters to save money.

In 1900, twenty-one cities in the United States had YMCAs for blacks, but only five black YMCAs owned their own buildings.[17] A sixth was added to this list when George Foster Peabody, a white southern philanthropist, paid for the construction of a black Y in his hometown of Columbus, Georgia. Another black YMCA was planned for Washington, D.C., and John D. Rockefeller Jr. contributed $25,000, but the building ended up costing more than was anticipated, and when the YMCA leadership asked Rockefeller for an additional gift, he refused. The Washington Y remained unfinished.

These buildings filled a genuine need. In the Jim Crow America of the 1900s, blacks were not welcome at YMCAs in white communities. In many segregated cities, not only in the South but also in the North, African Americans suffered from a notable lack of recreational facilities. Moreover, there were no black hotels. Thus young black men who were beginning to come to cities such as Chicago in increasing numbers in search of jobs had no place to stay unless they had family or friends already living in the city of their choice. The black Ys not only afforded a place for recreation but also provided dormitories that would enable these young men to stay in decent surroundings while they put down roots in their new homes.

To assist the effort to stimulate the construction of black Ys, the YMCA leadership had hired two black ministers, William A. Hunton and Jesse E. Moorland. They had worked together since the 1890s to assist black YMCAs. Moorland's job was to aid black groups all over the country to build, staff, and maintain black YMCAs, although the running of such institutions was overseen by white Ys. Clearly Hunton and Moorland had sparked the creation of the black YMCAs that existed by 1900, and it was Moorland who had persuaded Peabody and Rockefeller to make their donations.

Sometime during the summer of 1910, Wilbur Messer began talking to JR about the possibility of building a YMCA for blacks in Chicago. It is likely that JR expressed interest. Messer invited Moorland to come to Chicago to launch a campaign for a black Y in January 1911. Yet Messer knew that he needed a spark to ignite the campaign, and he thought he had just the solution. He arranged an invitation for himself, Moorland, and William J. Parker, business manager of the Chicago Y, to go to Sears to meet JR and Loeb on December 16, 1910.

JR asked Messer about operating a black Y in Chicago. He then turned to Moorland and asked him about black Ys in general. Moorland probably told him about the Y in Washington and how Rockefeller had made his gift as a challenge grant with a one-to-one match. Then Messer made "the ask": Would JR consider giving a grant of $25,000 for the establishment of a black YMCA in Chicago? Without a moment's hesitation, JR offered to donate $25,000 to any YMCA in any major city in the country that could raise an additional $75,000. JR's guests were speechless. Their host turned to them and added with a smile, "Well, I guess you can't build more than one a month, but I hope you can."[18]

The entire program was to be conducted by Messer and Moorland. In every instance some of the matching money was to come from the black community. Messer, Parker, and Moorland had to determine if the communities applying for this grant could raise the matching money and maintain the building. Once JR had been notified that the $75,000 had been raised or pledged, he would contribute his share. These details were spelled out in the official letter of notification from JR to the YMCA of Chicago, dated December 30, 1910, which began:

> I have been considering for some time the question of the best method of assisting the colored people, particularly in our large cities, on securing such facilities for education and recreation as are afforded to others through your organization in Chicago and similar organizations in other cities. It has seemed to me that both in the interest of the colored race and in the interest of the country, it is essential that there should be in every community in which there are large numbers of colored people, a building, primarily for men and boys, devoted to such purposes for their use. They have not as yet, in their own ranks, a sufficient number of people whose means would enable them to establish and adequately equip such institutions, and it is therefore, in my judgment, the duty of the white people of this country, irrespective of their religious beliefs, to evidence their interest in these, their neighbors, by assisting to supply this need.[19]

In speeches, as in this letter, JR sought to convey the impression that he had been thinking of helping black Americans for some long, indeterminate period of time. The Chicago philanthropist could hardly say publicly that he had just discovered black Americans and their needs.

The formal announcement of JR's gift to the YMCA took place on New Year's Day 1911 at a meeting of five hundred carefully selected African American men. JR made a speech which strikes one today as glaringly insensitive but which explicitly made the connection between Jews and blacks. JR told his audience that blacks were much better off than Russian Jews, who were persecuted, killed, and essentially enslaved to a far greater degree than anything American blacks were currently experiencing. Citing antisemitism, he said that there were certain clubs that he could not join or be welcomed in because of his religion. All this was intended to be a message of comfort to American blacks: You see, there are others such as Jews who are as badly off as you are, if not worse off. One can only imagine the true feelings of the audience that heard these remarks. Nevertheless, JR received a welcome that was more than merely polite. After JR spoke, there was an appeal for funds, because this meeting was designed to kick off a campaign to raise the matching funds for Chicago's black YMCA. An elderly man arose, made his way to the podium, and handed the astonished Messer $1,000 in cash, his entire life's savings. His name was James Tilghman. Born into slavery, he had come to Chicago in the 1880s and worked at a variety of odd jobs, ending up as a janitor for the telephone company. JR was so moved by this act of selfless generosity that he went home and immediately dashed off a letter to the president of Illinois Bell praising the virtue of his employee.[20]

Tilghman's gift, supposedly the largest contribution ever made up to that time by a black man for a black YMCA, was precisely what JR hoped would happen as a result of his challenge grant. He was totally opposed to charity as a mere handout. Thus he would never have considered doing what Peabody did—contributing all the funds for a YMCA for blacks. He felt it was essential that blacks contribute to the endeavor, and that was what appealed to him about Moorland's approach. Moreover, JR expected that his gesture would stimulate white donations as well, as indeed occurred. Norman W. Harris, president of the Harris Trust & Savings Co. who had pledged $10,000 to the fiftieth anniversary campaign, announced that he would increase his pledge to $25,000 to match JR's, and that he wanted the entire amount to go to the black Y. Toward the end of January, Messer informed JR that Cyrus McCormick had also agreed to match the $25,000 gifts.

Reaction to JR's challenge grant was swift, and almost all of it was favorable. One of the first letters he received came from a young black San Franciscan and must have touched JR and reinforced the rightness of his offer: "After work and on holidays, we have nowhere to go, as we are not admitted into most places of amusement. Although I am not where I could enjoy such a good place, I am glad that there are so many that will be made so happy. If we only had a place like that here."[21]

Some Jews wrote to JR with gratitude, indicating that they understood his point about the affinity between blacks and Jews. Other Jews displayed their parochialism, as did an article in a Jewish newspaper that stated:

"[I]t would seem that all Jewish philanthropists ought to turn their attention to the Jew before they attempt to attend to the betterment of the larger world."[22]

The goal of the black campaign was to raise $50,000 in ten days. On January 17, Messer proudly sent JR clippings from the Chicago papers. The campaign had ended in triumph with $66,932 having been collected.

Within a few days of JR's offer, YMCAs in seven cities had sent Messer letters of inquiry.[23] One of the issues that quickly arose was whether smaller cities or cities with a relatively low black population could also qualify for the matching grant. The answer that Messer gave was a firm no. He told a correspondent from New York that this matter had been discussed with JR at the initial meeting in December. JR had insisted that there be a sufficiently large black population in each city to maintain and support a black Y.[24]

One of the letters Messer received in the days just after the announcement was from President William Howard Taft. The president praised the program, concluding: "Nothing could be more useful to the race and to the country."[25] A few weeks later, the president wrote to JR, requesting that the Washington Y be "grandfathered" into JR's program. The president assured JR that if he concurred, the black community in Washington would raise an additional $15,000, which would be enough to meet the $75,000 match. Taft's letter concluded: "Allow me to congratulate you on taking up a branch of that work which has not heretofore been efficient, but which has a very wide field of future usefulness."[26] Like his mentor, Theodore Roosevelt, who had been the first president to formally invite a black man (Booker T. Washington) to the White House, Taft felt a certain sympathy for Washington's black population and wanted to assist them.

JR, who was in Europe when Taft's letter was sent, never received it and thus never replied. Taft, realizing what had happened, decided to invite the Chicago philanthropist to the White House. JR was concerned that this was just a courtesy call, so he told Judge Julian W. Mack that he would not come to Washington unless the president "*really* desired me to come and not complementary."[27] Judge Mack investigated and reassured JR that this was real business and would not waste the president's time or his. JR and Mack took the train to Washington.

En route, JR was informed that part of the meeting would deal with the Washington Y, so as soon as they arrived in the capital, they met with black leaders of the Y, including Moorland. By 11:15, they were in the White House. "The president asked us to step into the Cabinet Room, where he joined us," JR wrote Gussie, "and with only one interruption . . . was with us until 12:45, and asked us to stay for lunch" and to see his newly painted portrait, but the two men had to decline because they had to catch a train back to Chicago. "I told him I would be glad to do what he asked for the YMCA. I should probably have done it anyway, as the conditions almost come within my offer. Altogether, it was a red letter event."[28]

A formal letter to the president, written a few days after JR's return, sealed the deal. A month later, there was a ceremony to celebrate the opening of the Washington Y. JR could not be present, but he was represented by Judge Mack, who wrote his friend: "I told them I was there really on your behalf and I caught them tremendously by saying that you were doing this thing not because they were colored or despite the fact that they were colored but simply as a man for his fellow men. They dislike as much as do we Jews to be talked to as a separate class."[29] President Taft was also present, and he made a short speech praising JR:

> [W]hat I wish to bring home to you is that in his broad philanthropy, in the wide spirit of his love of mankind, Mr. Rosenwald has not been deterred from giving money to that which he believes most useful to mankind, even though there may be a restriction in the management which a smaller or a more narrow-minded man might resent. This makes one rejoice that a man of his heart and soul and generosity has had the genius—for he has wonderful business genius—and executive force to build up a fortune that enables him to do what he would with his money for the betterment of mankind.[30]

Said Judge Mack of the president: "His whole manner was just as fine and earnest as his words and he told me in his cordial greeting in response to my thanks afterwards that he felt and meant it all."[31]

If Washington's black community was eager to build a Y and had enlisted the president to assist them, New York was a different story. About a month after the announcement of JR's offer, Messer received a confidential letter from the general secretary of the New York YMCA. Henry Orme stated that there was considerable opposition to taking up JR's offer, first because how could New York, the number one city, accept assistance in such a situation from a Chicagoan! Furthermore, the fact that JR was

Jewish was a thorn in the side of the members of the New York Y's board. For these and other reasons, the New York YMCA was not interested.[32]

After a year had elapsed, however, New York had changed its tune, and JR was writing to William Fellowes Morgan, president of the New York YMCA board: "It may sound trite to say that nothing would give me greater pleasure than to have New York take advantage of my offer to give $25,000 toward such a building, but it is really a fact that I would rather see such a building in New York than in any other city in the country." In fact, he added, New York deserved two black Ys.[33]

By January 10, 1912, a little over a year after his initial offer, JR could write excitedly that six cities had already met the terms of his offer: Chicago, Atlanta, Philadelphia, Indianapolis, Los Angeles, and Washington, D.C. Three others, Baltimore, Kansas City, and Nashville, were nearing the completion of their campaigns. Cincinnati also was interested.[34] Unfortunately, as JR was to discover, the momentum and the excitement did not last. All the six cities named as definite eventually opened black YMCAs, but the Atlanta branch did not open until 1920 and that of Los Angeles not until 1926. The YMCA in Nashville was never built at all.[35]

Having once started giving to the YMCA, JR found he could not stop, for Messer had another idea that greatly intrigued the Chicago philanthropist. It was the construction of a YMCA hotel for young white men coming to Chicago from the farms. The male equivalents of Sister Carrie would arrive in Chicago, unused to city ways, and would find lodging in cheap rooming houses, where they would fall in with prostitutes, alcoholics, and petty criminals. In New York, a refuge for such young men existed. It was called the Mills Hotel, and, in addition to inexpensive rooms, social services were provided to help the youths find jobs and, eventually, other lodgings. This information was relayed to JR in a meeting in early May 1911. According to JR, Messer called him up and said he needed to speak to him right away about a matter that was close to his heart. Messer told him about the problem and added that he had conducted an investigation using college students posing as newly arrived farm boys. They lived among their peers and documented what they saw and heard. The results of this investigation were in, and they proved that there really was a problem in Chicago.

JR was gripped by Messer's words and listened intently as the YMCA head described how the project could be funded. Because of the anniversary campaign of the previous year, Messer felt that he could not launch another massive and widespread fund-raising drive. But if ten men could be found to donate $50,000 each, Messer was certain the hotel could be built. With the impulsiveness that sometimes overcame him in the face of a good idea, JR signed on immediately, and before leaving Messer's office, he began the fund-raising drive.

The rest of the story is a fine example of how fund-raising could be carried on among the rich at that time—not very different from the way it is done today. "Knowing that John G. Shedd [the CEO of Marshall Field & Co.] was especially interested in bettering the condition of young men," JR told an audience at the dedication of the new facility in 1916, "I telephoned before I left Mr. Messer, and asked Mr. Shedd if he would see me that day." The meeting was arranged. JR presented the case (not as well as Messer, he modestly stated), and Shedd agreed. Not only did he agree, but he told JR that he would go with him the next day to solicit Cyrus H. McCormick, the CEO of the agricultural implement company. After thinking the proposition over for a day, McCormick also signed on.

Four days after JR's original meeting with Messer, an anniversary dinner was given in honor of the YMCA at which Booker T. Washington spoke. At that dinner, Messer announced this newest project, which was well reported in the press. The following day, Norman Harris telephoned JR. He said that he was so pleased with his collaboration on the black Y that he wanted to participate in this project as well. This unsolicited gift marked the fourth person who had signed up for a $50,000 contribution in five days. A week later, JR was invited to lunch by wheat magnate James A. Patten. Although JR declined to support the cause that Patten was promoting, he put forth the idea of the Y Hotel, and Patten too agreed to sign on, provided the $500,000 was collected in one year, that the hotel was built in the Loop, and that it serve as only temporary living quarters for its occupants—all conditions that JR had also recommended. In short, in just two weeks JR had, directly or indirectly, managed to secure half the funds necessary to build the hotel. He then departed to join his family in Europe, leaving the task of securing the remaining $250,000 to others. Eventually such families as the Swifts and the Wrigleys also joined this project, and the hotel was thoroughly funded and eventually built.[36]

It is easy to see what appealed to JR about this project: It was helping the sons of his customers. Moreover, like the black YMCAs, it was the sort of self-help project that would give the recipient responsibility for his own actions. The Y Hotel would provide services to assist young men, but they had to do their share as well, by seeking a job and other lodgings. As JR said in an interview about the black Ys in a statement that could be applied to much of his philanthropy: "No to alms giving, which tends to pauperization and degradation, but by offering to the colored young men of the land those opportunities for self-improvement, for education and recreation, for the acquisition of spiritual, moral, mental, and physical strength, that makes for manhood and self-reliance, can we of the white race be of the greatest aid in furthering this progress."[37]

JR and Booker T. Washington

It was L. Wilbur Messer who took credit for bringing together JR and Booker T. Washington. In a letter to Jesse Moorland written some five years after the fact, Messer claimed that he had encountered Washington on a train. The black educator had asked Messer to suggest a prominent white Chicagoan for the Tuskegee board of trustees. Messer had named JR, and after having made some inquiries, Washington informed Messer that he was eager to meet the Sears president. Messer then invited him to deliver the keynote address at the Chicago YMCA's fifty-third anniversary dinner. When Washington accepted, Messer asked JR if he would be willing to host a luncheon of Chicago business leaders to meet Washington. JR agreed with alacrity, and the luncheon was held at the Blackstone Hotel on May 18, 1911.[38]

The guest list of JR's invitees was a veritable *Who's Who* of Chicago business. No formal speeches were presented, but JR did give a brief introduction to his guest of honor, whom he called "a wise, statesmanlike leader." He went on: "He is helping his own race to attain the high art of self-help and self-dependence, and he is helping the white race to learn that opportunity and obligation go hand in hand, and that there is no enduring superiority save that which comes as the result of serving."[39] Washington, who gave a brief presentation about Tuskegee, was probably delighted with this elite audience.

In the evening, JR served as master of ceremonies at the YMCA dinner. In his remarks, he barely mentioned Washington, and referred to the black YMCAs only in passing, saying that he hoped they would serve to bring the two races closer together.[40] Much of the speech was devoted to the Y's work with immigrants and how this had inspired him in assisting the Chicago Hebrew Institute.

The following day, Washington and his friend Dr. George C. Hall, a prominent black physician, visited JR at Sears. In a letter to Gussie, JR described the visit in terms which showed that he had not yet shed many of the racial prejudices of the era: "Mr. Washington and Dr. Hall, another 'culled' gentleman came, and Max [Adler] and Mr. Skinner were my other guests, and it was unique if nothing else, to sit down in our restaurant with two darkies, but I'm sure it was an object lesson which will have its effect on prejudice in many forms. I afterwards acted as guide for them through the building and could see a number of curious faces wondering how I happened to be showing 'niggers' around. They only remained a short time after dinner."[41] This letter almost suggests that for JR in this early phase of his association with blacks, part of the thrill of being with them was the shock value it gave to others. It is significant that even in letters to Gussie, JR soon was to drop the racial epithets when speaking of African Americans.

Shortly after the Blackstone Hotel luncheon, Washington invited JR to join the Tuskegee board of trustees. JR declined, but he did express interest in visiting Tuskegee later in the year. Almost as soon as he returned home, the "Wizard of Tuskegee," a brilliant fund-raiser, decided to capitalize on his new friendship and see what his recent host might be willing to do for the school. He wrote JR, ostensibly to thank him, but actually to make two requests. One was money, so that he would not finish the Tuskegee fiscal year in the red. The second was a YMCA for Tuskegee.[42] JR replied immediately, gently turning down both requests. However, he added that he had recently had dinner with Dr. A. W. Harris, president of Northwestern University, who had promised to accompany him to Tuskegee sometime in the fall or winter.[43]

The trip began on October 24, 1911, and lasted four days. JR rented a Pullman car and traveled with Gussie, other family members, Messer, and Rabbi Emil Hirsch. The party first stopped in Nashville, where they spent a day visiting various educational and medical institutions. Then they journeyed on to Tuskegee.

Washington and his staff were accustomed to hosting important visitors, and the trip of JR and his group was planned in meticulous detail, probably by Emmett Scott, Washington's gifted and dedicated assistant.[44] The group toured the campus and met with faculty, administrators, and students.

JR was most impressed by what he had seen. As he told a reporter on returning: "I was astonished at the progressiveness in the schools. I don't believe there is a white industrial school in America or anywhere that compares to Mr. Washington's at Tuskegee."[45] When Washington again asked JR to become a trustee in early December, he accepted. Washington was triumphant. He wrote to former president Theodore Roosevelt, another trustee, that JR, whom he identified as "that Jew who gave so much money for colored YMCAs," had consented to become a trustee. He went on: "I think he is one of the strongest men we have ever gotten on our board."[46]

Even before he was formally voted onto the board, JR began to act like a trustee by aiding the institution. But if Washington expected a generous check from the new board member, he must have been nonplused by what arrived at Tuskegee at the end of December: a large crate from Sears, Roebuck containing 1,260 pairs of men's and women's shoes, remaindered or damaged, with instructions to give these goods to the neediest students. It is possible that, by sending this in-kind contribution, JR was testing Washington to see how he would respond. If all went well, he would be happy, later on, to give cash. If that was JR's intention, he certainly picked the right man. Washington knew all about what development professionals today call "stewardship," reporting to a donor and engaging that donor increasingly in the work of the organization.

Thus JR must have been delighted by a letter from Washington at the end of March, after another shipment of shoes had been received. Washington informed his benefactor that a committee had been set up to distribute the shoes. "I might add that whenever possible, we have made the students pay something for the shoes, even though a small amount, so as to make them not get into the habit of accepting something for nothing. I have been watching the matter pretty closely, and am glad to say that the gift of those shoes has enabled quite a number of worthy students to remain in school."[47] Although JR soon began contributing cash gifts, the in-kind contributions in the form of shoes and hats continued to flow to Tuskegee for several years.

After agreeing to join the Tuskegee board, JR consulted with Washington about which people to bring with him to his first board meeting at the end of February. This was an excellent way to introduce potential funders to Tuskegee, and Seth Low, former mayor of New York and chairman of the Tuskegee board, was bringing a trainload of East Coast prospects to the meeting. Shortly after returning home, these potential donors were sent group photos, a gentle reminder of the wonderful time they had spent. This soft-sell approach seems to have worked well.

JR's entourage on this February 1912 trip included Gussie, Lessing, Sophie and Max Adler (JR's sister and brother-in-law), Judge and Mrs. Mack, and H. H. Kohlsaat, editor of the *Chicago Record-Herald* and an unofficial public relations advisor to JR. The president of Northwestern University, A. W. Harris, who had been unable to make the trip in October, was now present. Also in the party were Charles R. Crane, heir to a plumbing fortune, and his wife, and Sherman Kingsley, director of United Charities and of a charitable foundation connected to the McCormicks.

While the trustees met, the visitors from both the East Coast and the Midwest were given extensive tours of the campus. On Saturday evening, everybody gathered in the chapel, where it was announced that JR had been duly elected to the Tuskegee board. In honor of his installation, JR was presented with a fifteen-pound sweet potato, "the largest such potato grown in the South that year."[48]

The trainloads of visitors from Chicago and New York departed the following day. Upon returning to Chicago, Gussie reported to her children that the trip was both "pleasant and profitable." She admitted that she had originally not wanted to go but "[n]ow I realize if I had not joined the party, we would not have met many notables and many interesting people. . . . In Tuskegee, everything was lovely. . . . Father . . . received great homage and great honors and seems to be a great favorite with the students, for they sang a long song about him and cheered him on every occasion."[49]

JR's guests also enjoyed the experience. A. Mitchell Innes of the British embassy in Washington, who traveled with the Rosenwald party, wrote: "Not only was what we saw intensely interesting in itself, but it does one good to see others devoting their lives to the service of mankind. Men . . . like Booker Washington . . . probably influence the course of the world more than most statesmen."[50]

Three weeks later, Booker T. Washington came to Chicago and stayed at the Rosenwald home. The emotion of the moment is captured in a letter from Gussie to Adele:

> This home has been all excitement this morning awaiting Booker T. Washington's arrival. Father was up at 6:30 and went to the station to meet him, and while he was gone there came a telegram from Mr. Washington stating that he had missed connections in Cincinnati and could not get here before 5 o'clock this evening. We are looking for him now. It was a great disappointment because he was to have spoken at our new Sinai Temple this morning and before the workers of the colored men's YMCA this afternoon, and is to speak tonight before the Sunday Night Club at Orchestra Hall. The Temple this morning could not take care of the crowd that poured in, and as many were turned away as were in the Temple and people had to sit on the platform. Many were so disappointed at not hearing Dr. Washington, but Dr. Hirsch gave a splendid sermon on "Shall Women Have the Vote." . . . This week we shall entertain rather simply and informally for Booker T., asking people interested in philanthropic work to be present. Booker T. will be here the greater part of the week, but we shall be rather quiet. Of course, his stopping here has caused a great many comments, but we don't mind. People will get over it.[51]

Despite the ever-present racism just alluded to, Washington's trip was a tremendous success. JR wrote to Scott: "I have just come from a luncheon at the Commercial Club where Dr. Washington was the guest of honor. At every meeting he has had here, there has been an overflow, no matter how large the place."[52] That included the first event Washington attended at Orchestra Hall; people had to be turned away.[53] The meeting at Temple Sinai was rescheduled, and a packed house heard Washington referred to as "a second Moses" by Rabbi Hirsch and listened admiringly to Washington's address, his basic speech summarizing *Up from Slavery.*[54] In between everything else, Washington saw potential donors. The fact that Washington was JR's guest for several days further strengthened the bond between the two men.

This bond had been demonstrated just a few weeks earlier, at JR's first Tuskegee trustee meeting. The Chicago philanthropist proposed that Washington have some of the fund-raising burden taken from him by the creation of a $50,000 fund over five years to which donors could make multi-year pledges. To kick off the campaign, JR pledged $5,000 a year for a total of $25,000, half of the goal.[55] Not content with that, he took an active part in advising Washington on how to solicit others, suggesting repeatedly that a list of those who had already made pledges to the five-year campaign be circulated to potential donors. Finally, he agreed to accompany Washington on solicitation trips to wealthy Chicagoans of his acquaintance.

Further evidence of the strong friendship between Washington and JR occurred in June when JR, who was becoming swamped with requests for money from black private schools, began using Washington as an unofficial advisor.[56] Washington took this role extremely seriously, knowing that his reputation as well as possible future funding from JR depended upon his performing credibly. On July 20, for example, he wrote JR that he had received three very strong letters from professors at the University of Missouri concerning the Bartlett Normal and Industrial School, which JR had asked about. Washington added, however, "I have learned by experience that very often southern white people endorse schools when they know little or nothing about the real work being done, and little about the character of the individual conducting the school. I am going to try to have somebody visit this school, and then I will be in a position to make you a report on it."[57]

Black Schools, Black Colleges, and the NAACP

At the same time that JR was becoming involved with Tuskegee and Booker T. Washington, he also was learning about small private black schools in the South. These schools, most of which were secondary, were often started by the graduates of the black colleges, Hampton, Fisk, Tuskegee, and Spelman. The schools hired teachers from these institutions, and their graduating students, if they went on to higher education, enrolled in the black colleges. Some of the schools were well run and had sympathetic white northerners on their boards, but most led a hand-to-mouth existence.

It is not clear why JR became interested in assisting these schools, but it is likely that Booker T. Washington was responsible. In February 1912, JR gave his first such grant to the Utica Normal and Industrial School in Utica, Mississippi—$2,000 to help rebuild a building which had been demolished by a tornado.

The same month, he visited the Berry School in Georgia, with the trainload of dignitaries who had just been to Tuskegee. He was impressed enough by what he saw to make an offer at the end of his visit. He would contribute $1,000 for five years if four other individuals could be found to match his gift. It took only three months for Miss Berry, the enterprising headmistress, to secure the necessary donors. In sending the check, JR noted: "I probably feel as happy over the result as you do, since the sowing of my $5,000 seed resulted in a $25,000 crop. Evidently the soil was very fertile, since the crop grew so rapidly after the seed was planted."[58]

Similar challenge grants were offered to other schools. At the urging of Booker T. Washington, JR cabled William Edwards, principal of the Snow Hill School in Alabama, that he would contribute $1,000 if an additional $6,000 could be raised. The match was met within a few days. A grateful William Edwards wrote JR a fulsome thank-you letter describing in detail some of the numerous problems faced by schools of this type. At the end of the academic year in 1911, Edwards was facing a deficit of between $21,000 and $22,000. He also had to raise between $18,000 and $20,000 for general operations. Somehow he managed to raise enough to eliminate the debt. Then three of his buildings burned down, and he knew it would take $15,000 to replace them. Nevertheless, he was optimistic, and he evidently had a dedicated board.[59] Snow Hill was not to be so fortunate forever. JR was still connected with this school in the 1920s when it was in much more serious trouble.

At the Tuskegee trustees meeting in 1912, JR proposed that feeder schools such as Snow Hill be tied more closely together and brought up to a uniform standard. He offered to pay the expenses of someone from Tuskegee who would visit these schools and make suggestions so that they could all be brought up to the same academic level. It took Washington a few months to agree to this idea, but eventually he wrote JR: "Acting on the suggestion made by you when here, we have taken measures to have all of the branch schools visited this Spring by some member of our staff and the results are very encouraging, bringing these schools up in a closer manner with our work here."[60] JR duly paid the expenses of the faculty engaged in this. Later, he would pay for an accountant who would not only put Tuskegee's books in perfect order but teach others who would then be sent to the branch schools to ensure that their accounting procedures were up to a satisfactory standard.

Black private secondary schools were not the only such institutions to benefit from JR's interest in African Americans and the South. Several institutions of higher learning other than Tuskegee were beneficiaries of JR's largess.

Fisk in Nashville was one of the premier black universities in the country. JR visited the school twice en route to Tuskegee. Following the first trip, which included a meeting with the school's white president, George Gates, JR proposed a complicated challenge grant. He would give $2,500 a year for five years if the rest of a fund totaling $10,000 a year for five years could be raised. But there were other conditions that made this challenge money hard to raise. The minimum matching amount had to be $1,000 and the money had to come from new donors.[61] Gates accepted the conditions, but the terms proved onerous and it was not until the end of 1912 that the match was secured.[62] This was the beginning of an association with Fisk that lasted many years and resulted in JR's donating a total of $74,600 to the school.

Meharry College, the leading black medical school in the country, also impressed JR when he visited Nashville. Following the 1911 trip, JR made an offer to the school's founder, G. W. Hubbard, that he would give $1,000 toward Hubbard Hospital, then under construction, if $10,000 could be raised. There apparently was some confusion about the $1,000. Hubbard informed JR that he no longer needed the money, but JR seems not to have read the letter very carefully and cheerfully sent him a check.[63] In March 1912 Hubbard visited JR. The Chicago philanthropist offered him $1,250 for five years if an additional $3,750 yearly for five years could be supplied by the Methodist Church.[64] These conditions were met and were part of a total of $13,000 that JR gave to the medical school.

Hampton Institute, one of the oldest black colleges in the country, which numbered Booker T. Washington among its graduates, also received a contribution from Rosenwald, who gave $2,000 a year for ten scholarships starting in 1911 and continuing for several years.[65]

JR's interest in the conditions of African Americans led to his involvement in a small organization that was soon to become very well known, the National Association for the Advancement of Colored People (NAACP). He first learned of the activities of this organization even before Messer and Moorland came to see him about the YMCA.

At the end of 1910, JR was sent two solicitations for the same purpose. One was from William E. Walling, a New York philanthropist. The other was from Oswald Garrison Villard, president of the NAACP and grandson of the abolitionist William Lloyd Garrison. Both men asked JR to assist in the case of Pink Franklin, a black man who had been convicted and sentenced to death for firing on a "constable" who had come to arrest him under the Peonage Statute of South Carolina. This law, which had been declared illegal by the Supreme Court, enabled local southern law enforcement officers to fine poor illiterate blacks and then force them to work for free to pay off the fine. Even a former U.S. attorney general felt that Franklin had been wrongfully accused. In what was one of its earliest cases, the NAACP needed $500 to hire a lawyer who would appeal Franklin's conviction to the governor and ask for clemency. JR agreed to contribute $100. The appeal was successful in that the governor agreed to spare Franklin's life.[66]

In 1911, JR gave the NAACP $250. In 1912, Villard made a personal appeal to the Chicago philanthropist over a luncheon, and JR responded by donating $2,000 for legal work. It was the second largest contribution the NAACP received that year. Only that of John D. Rockefeller Jr. was higher. In addition, JR again gave $250 for general operating expenses. Thereafter, for several years he gave $1,000 to the national organization. His reason for scaling back was that, in 1912, a branch of the NAACP opened in Chicago, and JR, who was involved with it from the very beginning, felt that the local rather than the national organization deserved his support. He was elected to the first board of the Chicago chapter along with his friend Jane Addams.[67]

In 1912, the NAACP held a conference in Chicago at Temple Sinai. JR not only helped arrange for the site but also gave $500 toward this event, half the money needed. He delivered an upbeat address in which he praised several Chicago newspapers for printing editorials urging that blacks "have their rights and be given better treatment."[68]

It may appear paradoxical that JR would support both Booker T. Washington and the more militant NAACP, which had W. E. B. DuBois on its staff. The philosophical and political differences between the two men were well known within the black community. Washington believed that blacks should receive an industrial education that would fit them for work in a Jim Crow world and that blacks should be accommodating to whites. DuBois believed that the black intelligentsia should receive the same education as whites and should oppose racial discrimination. JR was not the only white or Jewish philanthropist to support both Washington's Tuskegee and DuBois's NAACP; Jacob Schiff did the same thing. In JR's case his support was based on the belief that blacks deserved both legal rights and the right to a decent education.[69]

In less than two years, JR had started to make his name as a philanthropist who was concerned about the condition of black Americans. He was certainly not the first philanthropist to have this interest. Rockefeller,

Carnegie, and Jacob Schiff all gave money to black causes; George Foster Peabody was primarily known as a donor in this area. Rosenwald's reasons for interesting himself in the cause of black Americans was succinctly stated in a letter written in December 1911. It shows that he was not, at that time, in favor of racial equality, for he wrote to Caesar Cone: "What interests me particularly is that we have a problem to deal with: namely, bringing about a condition whereby the Whites do what they can to make of the Colored people a decent, respectable element, if not from a sense of justice, at least in self-defense. Equality is furtherest [*sic*] from my mind, but a nearer approach to justice toward these people must, in my opinion, be brought about through one method or another."[70] Yet JR, by his thoughtful use of challenge grants, was already making a name for himself in this area. Carefully nurtured by figures such as Booker T. Washington, this interest in blacks and race relations was to grow until it became one of the focal points of his philanthropy.

Jewish Causes

While the years 1910 and 1911 marked the beginning of Rosenwald's support of black causes, he did not abandon his primary philanthropic interest: funding various Jewish causes. He no longer confined himself to contributing to local or strictly midwestern Jewish agencies but became part of a national Jewish organization, met important leaders in the American Jewish community, and also began to support international Jewish groups and programs.

Between 1908 and 1912, JR was president of the Associated Jewish Charities. Chicago Jews of German origin were asked to contribute one sum to the Associated Jewish Charities, and the total funds collected were divided up among the constituent organizations according to need and other criteria, such as how efficiently the organization was operated. Much the same criteria are utilized by modern United Ways. The Associated Jewish Charities was among the first such federation of charitable organizations in the United States and predated by more than a decade the first community foundations and by three decades the founding of the first Community Chests and United Way organizations.

JR took his position as president of the Associated Jewish Charities very seriously. He was assiduous about attending meetings and tried to ensure that the federation, as well as the constituent organizations, operated in a businesslike way. JR valued the Associated Jewish Charities over all the other organizations with which he was connected at that time. As he wrote a friend in 1911: "[The Associated] is nearest my heart of anything in which I am engaged, simply because I believe it is a great step forward and places the raising of money for Jewish charity in a class by itself, and thereby reflects credit on the Jewish community wherever their system is in vogue, and it is gradually taking root in all the cities of the country."[71]

Then, as now, the most important part of any board president's job was fund-raising, and JR showed himself to be truly formidable in that activity. His letters to family members, particularly Lessing, refer frequently to taking an afternoon off to go on "schnorring" (i.e., begging) expeditions on behalf of the Associated. The goal, of course, was to induce people to increase their contributions (or, as they were then called, "subscriptions"). In 1910, JR announced that he would personally double large increases.

An article in the *Examiner* described, in a slightly fanciful fashion, how this system worked and how effective it was. JR ran into his friend Edward Morris, president of the giant meat-packing house of Morris & Co.

> "Ed, you ought to give more than $10,000 a year to the Associated Charities," said Mr. Rosenwald.
>
> "Let's see," said the packer, "I gave $3,000 last year, didn't I? How much do you think I ought to raise it?"
>
> "Well," said Mr. Rosenwald, "you can't raise it too high to suit me, but I won't suggest a figure—I leave it to you. There is a whole lot to be done with the money."
>
> The packer smiled. He remembered that his friend had promised to double any subscription made, and knew also that he would be as good as his word.
>
> "I think," said Mr. Morris, "that it will cost you just $20,000 to see my hand. I'll make my subscription $10,000 flat."
>
> On that instant, Julius Rosenwald grasped the hand of the big packer and the contract was sealed. Five minutes' conversation between men knowing the needs of the city's poor had contributed more heavily to the support of worthy charity than three months' preaching from a score of pulpits could have done.
>
> "On the strength of your generosity, I'll guarantee to get five more subscriptions of $5,000 each," said Mr. Rosenwald, and within a few hours he had secured four of the subscriptions. The fifth will be in hand today.[72]

JR did contribute $50,000 to the endowment fund of the Associated. It was the largest gift ever given to the organization up to that point.

There was a condition that had to be met before the $50,000 contribution could be made: the total collected for the year had to be $300,000 or more. JR's bold fund-raising tactics ensured that the goal was exceeded.

Although JR grew to detest endowments, his ideas about philanthropy were still evolving in this period. The first major public expression of his opposition to endowments was formulated and delivered in 1912.

Each year that JR was president, the amount of money donated increased substantially and the number of subscriptions rose. But in the speeches that he personally wrote for his president's report, JR constantly urged his audience to contribute still more, outlining all the wonderful programs that would be aided with the funds. Nor did he limit himself to speeches and personal solicitations. In October 1909 he reported to Lessing that he had invited twelve or fourteen gentlemen to his house to go over a list of names. Obviously, the men picked the names of friends to solicit. JR noted that they worked until 11:00 P.M. "with very good results."[73] It was probably because of his formidable fund-raising and organizational skills that JR was elected president of the Associated for five years in a row. In 1911, the bylaws had to be amended, for they had stipulated that no person could hold the same office successively for more than three years.[74]

JR also continued to donate to some of the constituent member organizations. One of his favorites was still the Home Finding Society. The idea behind it—that children whose fathers had died should remain with their mothers, and that true orphans should not be institutionalized but sent out to families that wanted them and could raise them properly—remained controversial. Even JR acknowledged that careful studies needed to be done to ensure that these theories were correct. In a 1910 letter he advocated the use of volunteer "friendly visitors" who, after proper training, could visit the various families where placements had been made and report back.[75] He gave liberally to the Home Finding Society and was almost certainly their most generous donor, contributing $14,000 in 1911 and $38,000 in 1912. And he used the "bully pulpit" of his position as president of the Associated to provide a strong plug for the agency in virtually every speech he delivered at the annual meetings, saying in 1911: "Commendable as is the work of all our organizations, that of the Home Finding Society is, to my mind, the most progressive and humane."[76]

Another Jewish organization to which JR remained devoted was the Chicago Hebrew Institute, although it went through some rocky times.

JR had been instrumental in recruiting the new executive director, David Blaustein, who began to put the Institute on a professional basis, established a synagogue as part of the offerings, and began publishing a newsletter. In February 1910, a fire swept through the main building of the Institute, gutting it. Fortunately for the institution, Jacob Loeb, whom JR had persuaded to join the board, was in the insurance business. The Institute thus had an excellent policy and received $57,000 after the fire, the equivalent of over $1.1 million today. A library was lost in the blaze, and classrooms were crammed into an annex that had served as the administration building.

In the wake of the fire, a dispute arose between Blaustein and the Institute's president. Blaustein resigned and was succeeded by the rabbi he had brought with him from New York to establish the religious program. Then, in May 1910, the president himself refused to run for another term. JR agreed to serve as president for two years, apparently on condition that most of the work be done by others, including Loeb.[77] As president of the Associated he felt that the bulk of his time and duties lay elsewhere. Upon assuming the presidency of the Institute, JR declared that he was interested in the Hebrew Institute because he intended to "remove the barrier which seems to exist between the different classes among the Jews of this city."[78]

Being president of the Institute, however, had its difficulties, for JR discovered that the financial condition of the organization was far worse than he had been led to believe. But he was ably aided by his associates, and eventually the financial situation stabilized. Although problems with executive directors continued until 1913, the Institute was a thriving concern. A typical Saturday night is described by Jacob Loeb:

> The dancing class on the top floor, numbering 120, the English Educational League listening to a lecture by Ella Flagg Young [a noted Chicago educator], a meeting which was addressed by Miss [Henrietta] Szold, the public dance in the dance hall, full to the limit, a barn dance in the basement by the senior gymnasium class, and in the library on the first floor, not a seat to be had.[79]

JR genuinely liked to go to the building of an evening to participate in this bustling activity. Letters to Lessing and other family members show that he and Gussie would go to see "a little play," spend part of a Sunday, or attend services.[80]

Finally, JR continued to support Minnie Low and her work with the Bureau of Personal Services, assisting hard luck cases. Through the Bureau, JR also set up a scholarship fund that loaned small amounts of money to deserving young Jewish men to help them pay for tuition and books. This fund, begun in 1911, lasted until 1922.

There was one other fledgling Chicago Jewish organization in which JR took a keen interest at this time. By 1909, the Eastern European immigrants had begun to develop their own institutions, one example of which was the Chicago Hebrew Institute. JR watched the development of these charitable organizations and tried to instill in the Eastern Europeans the notion of federation that was working so well in the German Jewish community with the Associated. At a meeting of the Associated board in March 1909, he appointed a committee including himself and Judge Mack to meet with the "Presidents and Secretaries of various Orthodox Jewish charitable institutions for the discussion of their ultimate amalgamation with the Associated Jewish Charities." The committee reported back that the Eastern European Jews wanted to start their own federation of charities.[81] It took a few years for this new organization to begin functioning, but by 1912 it was under way. JR wrote: "This is a greatly to be desired and much needed undertaking, and should be the means of placing the Orthodox Jewish Charities on the same plane as those acquired by modern and up-to-date organizations, thereby doing away with charity balls, fairs, etc., to say nothing of the other antiquated methods of raising funds for the purpose." To help the organization, he offered to meet with a group of wealthy businessmen to interest them in supporting this new cause.[82] JR was eventually named an honorary officer of the new Federated Jewish Charities, but his ultimate aim, as it had been since 1909, was to amalgamate the two groups, an event that did not occur until 1922.

In 1910, in his capacity as president of the Associated, JR began to travel to other cities in the country with Jewish federations to describe how successful fund-raising was done in Chicago. JR would make a rousing speech and then see how many new and increased pledges he could generate. These speeches also proved to be an excellent way for JR to meet Jewish leaders in other cities. After a trip to Cleveland, for example, JR received a letter from Charles Eisenman, who was to be his chief assistant at the Committee on Supplies during World War I: "It is with considerable pleasure that I report to you that we received from forty persons voluntary increased subscriptions to the Federated Charities in the last two days, all of whom, I believe, were influenced in doing this because of our meeting Sunday night, and I, also, want you to know, if you will permit me to say so, that your little talk and inspiring presence was to a large degree responsible for these results."[83]

The Cleveland trip was followed by visits to St. Louis, Baltimore, Cincinnati, and Kansas City.[84] Judge Mack accompanied him on the Kansas City trip, which JR described to Lessing: "It was a most enthusiastic meeting, and the people seemed very much elated over their success."[85]

Evidently, JR was not the only one who was enthusiastic about this event. Jacob Billikopf, a prominent local Jewish leader who was to become a lifelong friend, wrote to him a few days later: "The community is still under a hypnotic spell and at least a week or ten days will elapse before we get down on terra firma. Not since I was in Kansas City has there been such excitement in Jewish circles, and the effect of your and Judge Mack's presence in our city will be very, very far reaching."[86]

These trips demonstrate that JR was beginning to play an important role on the national stage of Jewish affairs. This had begun in 1906 with the creation of the American Jewish Committee. The group set out an ambitious program of lobbying, research, and diplomacy to improve Jewish conditions in Europe and to combat what they perceived as increasing antisemitism in the United States.[87] Two of the founding members from Chicago were Julian W. Mack and Julius Rosenwald.[88]

It took several years for the American Jewish Committee to begin to function effectively and to choose their first target—czarist Russia. Jews with American passports, it was alleged, were being denied entry to Russia, a clear violation of a treaty signed between Russia and the United States in 1832. The American Jewish Committee sought to have Congress abrogate this treaty. In November 1911, JR journeyed to Washington with Judge Mack and Louis Marshall, a highly respected lawyer also on the board of the American Jewish Committee. They and others met with President Taft and urged him to use his influence to pressure the House to pass the Sulzer Act abrogating the treaty. When Taft complied in December, JR was elated. "It is a question of whether American citizens, regardless of nationality, shall or shall not be discriminated against in Russia. American citizens are American, no matter to what nationality they belong, and they should be treated as justly as the Russian citizen is treated in this country. I heartily approve of President Taft's action," he said.[89] The somewhat subtle subtext to the lobbying for the abrogation of the 1832 treaty was a strong desire on the part of the AJC to keep open the lines of immigration for Eastern European Jews. There were many other Americans who were eager to see immigration halted.

JR served on the executive committee of the AJC and was named chairman of the finance committee. He paid dues of approximately $500 a year to the group, and while he attended occasional meetings in New York, the organization was not one of his highest priorities. Perhaps the chief importance of the American Jewish Committee to JR was that it provided him the opportunity to become acquainted with some of the pillars of the Jewish establishment in New York—men such as investment banker Jacob Schiff, jurist Louis Marshall, educator Cyrus Adler, and Judge Mayer Sulzberger, president of the AJC. JR became a close friend of Schiff's and they corresponded frequently. Schiff, the older, more experienced philanthropist, sometimes acted as a mentor to his younger AJC colleague.

It was through men such as Schiff and Marshall that JR became aware of projects involving Jews far beyond the borders of the United States. It was Marshall who wrote a letter of introduction to JR for Dr. Schmaryahu Levin, who was interested in establishing a technical college in Haifa, Palestine.[90] JR met with Levin and was captivated by his mercurial personality. As he wrote Lessing in February 1909: "[A] Dr. Levine [*sic*], a Russian who was in the first Duma, took lunch with me on Friday, and in order to entertain him I invited eight rabbis and also Judge Mack and Charles Schaffner to dine with me on Saturday evening. Mr. Levine is a wonderful scholar, and we had a most enjoyable evening listening to his experiences and theories. Dr. Hirsch told me that Dr. Levine is the type of man the profits [*sic*] were in biblical times. I will tell you some time of what his plans and dreams are."[91] Levin's plans and dreams were to build the technical college and serve in it in some capacity. Since he lacked a technical background (he had been a publicist), he thought of serving as head of the humanities division. JR was induced to join the American board of what was called the Technikum (it later became the Technion), and he served on it along with Judge Mack, Marshall, and Jacob Schiff's son, Mortimer. The elder Schiff, who was one of the project's biggest supporters, refused to join the board.

The Technikum was not one of JR's most successful charitable involvements. The Chicago philanthropist contributed $5,000 for part of Levin's salary over two years and $1,400 for his house.[92] He further pledged

$50,000 toward scholarships.[93] But this money was never paid because serious disputes arose between the American and European board members.

The root of this problem was Zionism, the concept that Jews should reestablish a homeland in Palestine. Zionism seemed to dog any international Jewish project with which JR was involved. In introducing Levin to JR, Louis Marshall, knowing that Rosenwald had no interest in or sympathy for Zionism, quoted Jacob Schiff by saying of the Technikum, "It is wedded to no 'ism' save Judaism." But this proved to be inaccurate. Levin was an ardent Zionist who, like many, tried to win over JR to this concept and failed, though he did make one important convert in Judge Mack.[94] The Zionist backers of the Technikum insisted the language of the school be Hebrew, and sought to wrest total control of the institution from those wanting courses taught in German. The American board, divided over this issue, resigned en masse in 1914 before the buildings had been completed and the school opened.

Cyrus Adler, president of Dropsie College in Philadelphia and a member of the executive committee of the American Jewish Committee, sent Aaron Aaronsohn to Chicago in 1909. Born in Palestine, the son of Rumanian immigrants, Aaronsohn had shown great promise. He had come to the attention of Baron de Rothschild, who had subsidized his university education in France and then employed him as the manager of an agricultural colony he had established near Haifa. The young agronomist was interested in wild wheat and had found some growing in the area of Mount Hermon. His idea was that the wheat could be cross-bred with cultivated varieties and planted in arid areas. He had written a paper on his discovery, which he sent to the U.S. Department of Agriculture. Those who read it were impressed and invited Aaronsohn to come to the United States. He did so, met with Adler, and then arrived in Chicago with Adler's letter of introduction addressed to Judge Mack. Mack instantly liked Aaronsohn and brought him to meet JR that same day.

JR was also highly impressed, but before the two men could become very well acquainted, Aaronsohn departed. On the agronomist's next visit to Chicago, JR invited him to lunch at his home, and then told Lessing: "I believe Mother wrote to you about Dr. Aaronsohn, who was at our house for dinner Sunday. He is a wonderful man. He took lunch with me yesterday; then . . . I went with him to the University [of Chicago], where he delivered a lecture in English. He has only been in this country since

June, and never spoke English until he came here. He speaks six or seven different languages and is only 35 years old. I expect to see him in New York when I go there."[95]

JR saw a good deal of Aaronsohn over the next several years. The young agronomist sought to set up an experiment station on land that was part of Baron de Rothschild's agricultural colony at Athlit near Haifa. He needed American backing, and JR was only too happy to provide it. An American board of directors of the station was formed in the spring of 1910 with JR as president and Cyrus Adler, Jacob Schiff, Julian Mack, Louis Marshall, Paul Warburg, Henrietta Szold (the future founder of Hadassah, the women's Zionist organization), and the noted Zionist Judah L. Magnes, among others. The board raised $50,000 on the spot, and, in addition, JR and Schiff paid for equipment for the station and JR purchased a valuable collection of 25,000 species of fungi.[96] JR and Schiff were the main benefactors of the Jewish Agricultural Experiment Station. JR contributed over $60,000 to the project over the next several years. Unfortunately, this venture, too, ended badly because of Aaronsohn's secret role during World War I when it was revealed that he worked as a double agent for the British.

Given JR's interest in Jews and agriculture, it is hardly surprising that he would have been attracted to the brilliant and charismatic Aaronsohn. Valuable work was done at Athlit in the areas of grain and wine production, and JR remained fascinated with Aaronsohn and his work until several years after the start of the war.

Social Service and Health Care

Between 1908 and 1912, JR continued and deepened his involvement with Hull House and the Chicago Commons and added other social service agencies to the list of his contributions. He also branched out into the field of health care, with a decided emphasis on assisting those too poor to obtain adequate care.

By 1908, JR was contributing $1,000 a year to Hull House. Two years later, he had joined its board of directors and was serving on the finance committee and sending out fund-raising letters. Jane Addams wrote him: "I shall never cease to be grateful for the help and vigor you have brought to our financial situation."[97] It is not certain what specific suggestions JR brought to his post on the finance committee, but he was gaining experience in charitable organizations from his work with the Associated Charities and the Hebrew Institute. As was the case with Minnie Low, JR used Hull House to aid individuals (usually anonymously) who desperately needed assistance.

Early in the summer of 1912, JR and Gussie became involved in a major Jane Addams project: a retreat in the countryside where working women and their children could go to escape the urban blight they lived in near Hull House. The site in Waukegan, Illinois, was donated by Jane Addams's close associate Louise de Koven Bowen. Gussie's contribution was $20,000 to build a cottage with ten rooms and a kitchen. Each room was large enough to accommodate a mother and four children. The thought was that each family would stay at the cottage for two weeks, enjoying the benefits of the country, then leave and be replaced by another. JR also contributed to this project, with funds for a playground and tennis courts.[98]

There was, however, one area where JR and Jane Addams disagreed. In May 1910, Addams informed JR that Hull House was embarking on a second $100,000 endowment campaign. The money was raised in two years. However, JR did not contribute to it. He was becoming increasingly opposed to endowments of any kind—he called them "perpetuities"—because he felt they unduly tied the hands of the organizations that possessed them. He favored funds where the principal as well as the interest could be expended. Jane Addams wrote Judge Mack in 1912 that she was perfectly willing to establish such a fund, but feared that she would cause trouble with her other friends and supporters, such as Mrs. Bowen, who strongly believed in the utility of endowments.[99]

JR had contributed $200 a year to Graham Taylor's settlement house, Chicago Commons, since the early 1900s, and in 1912 he increased his contribution to $500. He clearly admired Taylor, writing him in 1911: "You are among the few, comparatively, who feel for the underdog and fight and make sacrifices for him."[100]

JR encountered Taylor in another capacity—as the founder and director of the Chicago School of Civics and Philanthropy, one of the early social work schools in the country. The school had started in 1903 as a series of classes at the University of Chicago. Upon the death of president William Rainey Harper, the university had disassociated itself from the school, and the program had been absorbed into the Chicago Commons. In 1908, Taylor decided to make it an independent entity with its own board, which included Judge Mack, Jane Addams, Mrs. Bowen, and Julius Rosenwald.[101]

By 1910, JR was contributing $2,500 annually to this relatively new institution. As was so often the case, this donation was a challenge grant; the funds would be given provided an additional $7,500 was raised.[102] Moreover, starting in 1911, JR began contributing $1,000 to the school for two scholarships. He also was sending money to Julia Lathrop, the school's director, for a study on "mental hygiene."[103] All in all, JR felt he was doing enough for this organization, which was running on a relatively modest budget. So when he received a letter from Rabbi Hirsch asking him to do more, he refused. "I am sorry that I cannot suggest any way in which to help Mr. Taylor, and I would not feel warranted in underwriting the amount as I contribute $2,500 a year toward the School of Civics, and in addition, am paying for two students at $1,000 more. In view of the amount of their budget, I feel that this is rather a large proportion." He added that Taylor had "some very influential friends" who could be asked to help.[104] This letter indicates that by 1912, JR had enough confidence in what he was doing philanthropically to turn down his mentor. In general, he believed that he should not provide a disproportionate share of a charitable agency's budget. Nevertheless, JR was fascinated by the work of the School of Civics and Philanthropy. A few months after turning down Rabbi Hirsch, the Sears president met with Sophonisba Breckenridge, another teacher at the school, and agreed to help fund a study she was conducting.

In 1909, JR was invited by President Roosevelt to attend a conference on the Care of the Dependent Child, which he did. Chief sponsors of the conference were Judge Mack and Lillian Wald, the founder of New York's Henry Street Settlement. The conference urged the formation of a federal bureau to deal with the care of dependent wards of the state. It took a couple of years, but Congress did pass a law creating a Children's Bureau in 1912, and JR joined Jane Addams in lobbying for the appointment of Julia Lathrop as its first head, a task in which they were successful.[105]

In addition to aiding social service agencies, JR in this period also became involved in assisting agencies dealing with health care for poor individuals. One was the Lying-In Hospital, founded by a brilliant obstetrician, Dr. Joseph DeLee. What started as a clinic for impoverished women and infants in the Hull House area developed into plans for a hospital on the South Side of Chicago. JR made a financial transaction in 1909 with the obstetrician and his brother, S. T. DeLee, involving $30,000 worth of Sears, Roebuck stock.[106]

Construction was originally planned to start in 1910, but there were serious delays. By the time construction began in earnest in 1914, JR, as a result of his deal with the DeLee brothers and the rise in the price of Sears stock, was able to contribute $100,000 to the new hospital. In addition, he wrote fund-raising and lobbying appeals on behalf of the hospital to, among others, Mayor Carter Harrison. Citing some of the reasons that undoubtedly made the Lying-In Hospital appealing to him, JR told Harrison: "It is in the line of civic improvements, and saves the city annually a large sum of money in the care of women during childbirth and in preventing disease and despondency."[107] Because most poor women had, until this time, given birth at home and thus been prey to serious infections that afflicted them and their children, the Lying-In Hospital was a milestone in health care of the urban poor, both in Chicago and nationally. JR remained a supporter of the Lying-In Hospital into the 1920s, when it merged with the University of Chicago Hospital and relocated to the Hyde Park area.

In March 1911, JR received an unsolicited letter from a dentist of his acquaintance, Dr. Henry Schuhmann, requesting $500 for dental clinics in Chicago public schools. In a long, rambling document Dr. Schuhmann explained that studies had shown that some 95 percent of Chicago schoolchildren had teeth in appallingly bad condition and that other studies proved that children with such bad teeth not only were prone to attract diseases but also were often prevented from doing well in school.[108] JR was intrigued and replied expressing interest. At the end of March he wrote Schuhmann: "I will agree to contribute $2,500 if enough additional is raised within six months to create a fund of $25,000—no part of my subscription to be paid until the full amount has been contributed."[109] Clearly, the Chicago Dental Association could not raise the match because it was not until March 1912 that any movement on this front began.

Schuhmann once again solicited JR, since he had received a guardedly favorable response the previous year. This time, JR asked to be put in touch with someone who was not a dentist. He was worried that the dentists lacked the expertise to raise funds from other sources and that, though enthusiastic now, they would lose interest in the project. He also worried that the clinics were not organized on a sound basis. As he explained to Rufus G. Dawes, whom Schuhmann suggested he contact: "If this work is undertaken by practical men, some of whom are not professional men but who really have an interest in it, I should feel very much inclined to lend some encouragement. The trouble with many of these movements is that they are undertaken by enthusiasts who are temporarily interested."[110]

Dawes allayed JR's doubts. He said that five dental clinics had been started in schools, but these were nothing more than a pilot program. The dentists had every expectation that they would be successful.

JR was convinced. Spelling out the terms clearly to Dr. C. N. Johnson, head of the Dental Society, whom Dawes had praised as brilliant and visionary, JR made a grant offer that was unusual. Normally, JR gave challenge grants in terms of money raised from other sources. In this case, worried that no one would be in control of the clinics, and that dentists like Johnson, despite their zeal, would not have the time to devote to the project to ensure that it was done well, he set strict conditions that involved the actual mechanism of the plan. As he wrote to Johnson:

> I would want one or two men pledged to look after each clinic and keep in close touch with it so that the work would be properly done and no slipshod methods permitted to creep in. . . . If I can get satisfactory evidence that the organization for caring for these various clinics is well in hand and established along the right lines, I shall be very glad to equip six additional clinics at a cost not to exceed $500 each, and pay the salaries of ten men at $1,000 each, who are to devote their entire time every day the school is in session, for as many hours as your committee deems feasible.[111]

Details still had to be ironed out, but by October, Dr. Johnson reported that the rooms for the clinics had been set aside and outfitted, the operators of the clinics that JR had insisted upon had been chosen by competitive examination, and there were many dentists willing to serve.[112]

JR was attracted to this proposal for two reasons. One was that, for relatively little money, a significant difference could be made in the lives of children, especially disadvantaged children, throughout Chicago. Second, this was clearly a pilot program which, once it proved successful, would be taken over by the City of Chicago; thus JR's involvement need not be long term. This proved not to be entirely the case. JR supported six infirmaries for the 1912 school year and for the fall of 1913. A total of $14,750 was expended on the program from October 1912 through December 1913. During the 1912–13 school year, 22,671 children were examined, and 21,686 were found to need dental services. In 1914, the City of Chicago did take over the whole program, but by 1919 it was once again in serious danger. JR agreed to fund eight of thirteen clinics. By January 1922, all of JR's eight clinics had closed down, the City refused to fund them, and the dentists were feuding among themselves as to whether the clinics were even a good idea.

This program does raise questions about the limits of individual philanthropy and the role of government. In the short run, JR's backing of the clinics was an unqualified success. But elected city officials obviously must have asked: If a wealthy philanthropist is willing to take up this cause, why should the Chicago taxpayers have to pay for it? All attempts to induce the Dental Society to pay for the clinic program were equally fruitless. Thus JR's participation in this program may, in the long run, have been deleterious, for it created in the minds of the politicians the expectation that private philanthropy should pay for such a program, and if no individual stepped forward, then the program was not worth doing.

The Lying-In Hospital and the dental clinics marked the beginning of JR's involvement in the health care field, which would continue for many years.

The University of Chicago

JR had donated money to universities for specific projects, but higher education was not his primary field of interest. "I believe [universities] have friends enough among those who are interested, to care for their needs."[113] The one clear exception was the University of Chicago, to which JR had started donating in 1905.

By 1911, moves were afoot to appoint Julius Rosenwald to the University of Chicago's board of trustees. The active player was Judge Mack, who wrote JR in May, fearful that his friend was also being wooed by Northwestern University. Mack indicated that some months earlier he had mentioned JR as a possible candidate for the board to Judge Jesse A. Baldwin, who was then serving as a University of Chicago trustee. Baldwin stated that he and others had been talking about JR's candidacy for some time. There was, however, one problem. According to the University's bylaws, there could be only six trustees at any one time who were not Baptists. There was already one Jewish trustee, Eli B. Felsenthal.[114] Since trustees served three-year terms, Baldwin at first thought that he should wait until Felsenthal's term was up before he nominated JR. If some semblance of religious diversity on the board was a goal, it would not look good to have two Jews out of six non-Baptists. However, when Mack later told Baldwin of the Northwestern rumor, Baldwin was spurred to action.[115] On May 10, 1911, he and Rosenwald were at the same table at a dinner. As JR recounted the story to Gussie:

> He told me he was a trustee of the University of Chicago, and for some time they have been endeavoring to fix things so they could elect me a trustee, and wanted to be sure I'd accept. I told him I didn't like to pose as an educated individual—never having gone through high school. He said "That's a reflection on me, for I never went to high school at all." He spoke in such a charming manner, it was most gratifying. I told him I'd ask my wife.[116]

Gussie evidently said yes, because a year later JR was duly elected a member of the board of trustees, a position he held until his death. In June 1912, he attended his first commencement as a trustee. A friend wrote to him: "The cap and gown looked quite 'stunning.' I suppose before long they'll be 'Doctoring' you. The University is lucky to capture you."[117]

Politics

Prior to 1909, JR had not evinced any great interest in electoral politics. But between 1909 and 1912, JR became deeply involved in political campaigns—not always with very good results. He was very naive politically, but he knew that he was a reform-minded Republican, and the kinds of candidates he was willing to back. His new interest caused him to immerse himself first in local, then in national politics.

In November 1909, Mayor Fred Busse persuaded JR to serve on the Chicago Planning Commission along with over three hundred leading citizens. He was placed on the executive committee. This planning commission studied and adopted the famous Burnham Plan, which recommended, among other things, that certain key streets be widened and that the city keep a green belt along the lake front.

JR also was named to a commission to study Chicago's notorious houses of prostitution. In March 1910, he wrote to Lessing: "I was appointed to the Vice Commission. This is a thing, however, which I believe should be in the hands of people who have made a study of it more than I have, and I shall attempt to be released as soon as possible, provided I can get the Mayor's consent."[118] Either the mayor refused to release him, or he was persuaded to stay on, for he remained until it concluded its work a year later. Although Werner claims he "was not active in the work," going to meetings only rarely, JR testified at hearings in 1913 that he attended "a great many of the meetings"; he was named to the executive committee and agreed to serve in that post.[119] Yet JR had no hand in drafting its final report, which recommended, among other things, that a further study be made of the wages paid young girls by the city's leading employers. In addition, the report recommended that such an investigation should examine both the living conditions among such young women and the cost of living, and discuss the subject of a living wage. These recommendations would come back to haunt JR several years later.

JR was a member of numerous civic organizations, including the Civic Federation, the Municipal Voters League, and the Legislative Voters League. But the organization that really sparked his interest was the Bureau of Public Efficiency. In 1910, JR, as a member of the Civic Club, was on a committee that issued a plan to check on the expenditures and accounting system of the local governing bodies of Chicago. This direct attack on the patronage system resulted in the creation, in August 1910, of the Bureau of Public Efficiency, a body modeled after the New York City Bureau of Municipal Research. JR became chairman of this body and vigorously supported it for many years. Stating the case succinctly for the Bureau in 1913, JR said: "It is simply a case of applying business principles to the city and county government. . . . No city whose expenditures total millions should be without a committee, non-partisan and independent of the administration, to go over the budget, and then to go over the accounts after the money is spent to see if it has been used in an economical and practical manner. It is poor business for the merchants not to have such a committee."[120]

In 1910, the newspaper *Standard Opinion* began promoting JR as a perfect candidate for mayor of Chicago. The editor wrote to the prominent businessman: "Since our mention of you for mayoralty honors in the last two issues, many good men have spoken of their desire to vote and work for your election as mayor of Chicago should you decide to become the candidate of the business men of Chicago."[121]

JR was not interested in running for political office. He was very content running Sears, Roebuck. He did, however, have his own candidate in mind: Charles E. Merriam, a political science professor at the University of Chicago and a personal friend. Merriam agreed to run as reform candidate for mayor on the Republican ticket, and JR worked to support his candidacy with his accustomed gusto. He even ended a European trip early in order to work on the campaign.[122] On the return voyage, he composed a letter to Sears employees, urging them to vote for Merriam.

Arriving in Chicago, JR went almost immediately to the campaign headquarters. The mood, he reported to Gussie, was "sanguine. . . . The committee expressed themselves as very glad that I was back as there is lots for me to do. They said that I was badly wanted in the 'black belt' and in the Jewish wards, and could be very helpful in other places also."[123] This was only three months after JR's offer to the YMCA, and it is interesting that the Merriam campaign already believed that JR would be effective in the black community.

The next two and a half weeks were a whirlwind of activity. JR did speak in both black and Jewish wards and attended two huge rallies for Merriam. At the first one, Clarence Darrow spoke, as did Merriam. The latter was "enthusiastically received, and it looks to me as though he will be elected," JR reported to Gussie.[124] He remained absolutely convinced Merriam would triumph.[125]

In addition to making speeches and attending rallies, JR donated money and raised funds from others. He contributed almost $30,000 to the campaign. And he proved, as always, to be a superb fund-raiser. As he told Gussie: "I didn't go to the store as I had a date with Mr. Upham to go on a money raising tour for the campaign. We were successful as usual." After listing the various people he approached and the amounts they were contributing, he concluded: "So we are counting on $52,000 as our day's work. Charles Crane and I will fill in with what is short after we collect all we can."[126] Fred Upham, the fund-raising partner, was quoted as saying: "I was telling the fellows the other night that they couldn't want any better man on their Finance Committee than JR. Why, he can just walk down through the Loop wearing that happy smile of his and cash it most any place."[127] Finally, JR wrote an open letter to the people of Chicago, urging the election of his candidate, whom he compared to Lincoln. He stood, said JR, for good clean government and would be accountable to the people.

But all this work was in vain. As a reform politician for clean government, Merriam could not offer the patronage of the machine bosses. Carter Harrison, part of a dynasty that had ruled Chicago for decades, was elected by 17,000 votes. JR was crushed. He wrote Gussie: "I've just taken a few of the Merriam pictures off the windows of our house to lay them aside for four years—when maybe he'll try again. It's all over, and we must console ourselves with having fought in a righteous cause. It has at least quickened the public conscience, and will have a moral effect the value of which it is not possible to measure. I never felt worse about anything, except once and that was when I thought my reputation was endangered."[128]

Eventually, JR calmed down and wrote a letter of congratulations to Carter Harrison. "I told him I had no apology to make for my part in the campaign, but wanted him to know that if I could do anything as a citizen for the good of Chicago, he could have my cooperation."[129] Eight months after the election, JR was writing the mayor enthusiastically: "As a citizen who is greatly interested in the welfare of Chicago, I feel that I should express to you my gratitude for the magnificent work being done under your administration. In my judgment, your courageous stand in regard to the Police Department, and the splendid backing you have given your Civil Service board, is the greatest forward step toward good government that Chicago has ever known."[130] Still, JR felt badly burned by his foray into local politics.

Before 1910, JR had expressed little interest in national politics. Yet it was virtually inevitable that the head of the largest mail-order company in the United States would be drawn into the country's politics to some extent. Beginning in 1910, he attended a number of speeches given by Taft and met him on several occasions, including the trip to the White House with Judge Mack to discuss the Washington Y. By the end of 1911, Rosenwald was resolutely committed to supporting the reelection of the president.

On February 8, 1912, JR was named first vice president of the Taft Club. The press was spreading rumors that if Taft won the election, he would name Julius Rosenwald as secretary of commerce. JR responded strongly: "I feel highly complimented to be mentioned for such an honor, but there is not an office in the gift of the president or the people that I would accept—all I ask is to keep my good health and to be allowed to live in Chicago among my friends. I greatly enjoy the work in which I am engaged."[131] Taft immediately wrote to JR, expressing his incredulity that such a rumor had started and praising JR's response to the media.[132] Two weeks later, JR was again invited to the White House.

Whoever believes that Bill Clinton invented the use of overnights in the Lincoln bedroom for fund-raising purposes does not understand

American politics. The invitation for February 28 was to be for lunch only, but as soon as JR arrived at the White House he was asked if he could spend the night. He immediately assented, his bags were fetched from the hotel where he had planned to stay, and at 10:30 P.M. he excitedly wrote to Gussie on White House stationary: "Just think of it. Here I find your best fellow going to bed in the White House. I didn't dream of this." The long letter that follows is interesting in terms of what it does not relate. There is little mention of political discussions, though they did take place, and JR was uncharacteristically bitter over Theodore Roosevelt's statements that he was thinking of running as an independent. It was evidently Taft who tried to calm things down.[133]

Most of JR's letter to Gussie consisted of whom he escorted to dinner and what was served, "simple food and only one kind of wine—Rhine wine." This was his description of his hosts: "Mrs. Taft has a sweet face, does not speak much, and sometimes it sounds as though her tongue were heavy. She was very plainly dressed. He is as genial and kind as can be." The next morning, he reported, Mrs. Taft spilled coffee all over herself, but sat through breakfast anyway, drenched to the skin. The president was not present.[134] What is so charming about this letter is the writer's enthusiasm at being in the White House, in a canopied bed one and a half times the size of his normal bed. He was so excited that he did not sleep very well.

JR set to work to try to reelect Taft. He initially pledged $5,000 toward a local Chicago campaign goal of $25,000, and ultimately gave $10,000 to the local Taft campaign, one of the largest such donations in the country. He attended the Republican National Convention, which took place in Chicago, as an observer. But by mid-August, his enthusiasm had begun to wane, and he wrote Jane Addams, who had strongly supported Roosevelt for president: "[I]n choosing the political course you did, against the advice of your friends, I have no hesitancy in admitting that I now believe you acted wisely, and that I was mistaken."[135] Unlike the Merriam campaign, he had a sense of foreboding about this election, and wrote a friend: "Confidentially, . . . I am very much inclined to the belief that no matter what is done or what is not done, Mr. Wilson will be the next president."[136]

The election of 1912 soured JR on national politics for over a decade. Although he was involved in the Republican campaign of 1916, he did not throw himself wholeheartedly into a national political campaign again until Hoover's run for the presidency in 1928.

Lifestyle

During the years 1909–12, the older children were frequently away. Lessing was in college at Cornell, Adele and Edith were at finishing schools in Germany in 1911–12, and Adele, who was sickly, was packed off for "rest cures" to French Lick, Indiana, and Lakewood, New Jersey, around 1908–1909. Both parents spent a considerable amount of time writing or composing letters to their children. (JR often dictated his, which the recipients were not happy about because they did not want a stenographer to know the details of their lives.) Also Gussie and JR were often separated, either because of JR's frequent trips for business or to raise money for local Jewish charities around the country, or because, from March to June in 1911, Gussie was in Germany with Adele while JR was back in Chicago. This large volume of mail serves almost as a diary to describe daily life in the Rosenwald house, and what clearly emerges from it is the frenetic pace of daily life.

Both JR and Gussie frequently complain that they are so busy that they hardly know what day it is. JR very rarely mentions anything connected with business in his letters to family, other than to remark, especially to Lessing, that business is good and that Sears stock was continuing to go up. Most of what is described is an endless round of meetings and a busy social life. JR was board president or chairman of the Associated Jewish Charities, the Chicago Hebrew Institute, the Home Finding Society, and the Agricultural Experiment Station. He served on the boards of directors of Hull House, Tuskegee Institute, United Charities of Chicago, the Technikum, the University of Chicago (at the end of this period), and Rush Hospital.

JR was also first vice president of Sinai Congregation, a post he had held since 1902. This was an institution he loved. Not only did he give money for the new building that opened in 1912 (with Booker T. Washington as one of the first speakers) but he also undertook an important project. JR wisely saw that, if the Temple were to maintain its preeminent place in the Jewish community, it would have to interest and involve a whole new generation. He hosted several meetings of a group of young men in his home. The effort seems to have been highly successful. No doubt the young men were flattered that someone of JR's prestige took an interest in them and did start attending services and participating in the life of the Temple community.

In addition to his other obligations, JR was on the various civic boards and committees to which he was appointed, such as the Chicago Planning Commission and Vice Commission. And he was elected to membership in several clubs, such as the Commercial Club. Sometimes the meetings of these organizations, such as the Associated or the Hebrew Institute, would last past 11:00 P.M.

JR and Gussie attended a continual round of social engagements, some very lavish, such as cotillions or debutante balls. In the fall or spring there was the opera, which Gussie loved. JR was a generous patron. In 1910, he contributed $5,000 to the Chicago Grand Opera, and the following year he gave $2,646, his pro rata share to eliminate the company's deficit. The Rosenwalds had a box, and Gussie attended frequently. JR went on occasion, but since the performances often lasted until midnight, he left early. JR and Gussie also were patrons of the symphony, although JR does not seem to have been much of a devotee.

Finally, there was the theater, which JR truly loved. Amateur performances were presented by the Book and Play Club, which met periodically at members' homes. JR was ambivalent about this organization. As he confided to Lessing: "Tonight the Book and Play Club meets at our house. I never look forward to these evenings with very much pleasure, as I do not enjoy them, but they are all such good friends in the party that I don't like to take the chance of hurting their feelings by refusing to remain with them."[137] Yet just a few months earlier he had written his son: "Saturday evening was the Book and Play Club entertainment in which your Mother took part—not alone her part, but the entire performance. . . . It was splendidly performed and the lines were excellent."

Occasionally a speaker would spark JR's interest. In October 1909, he wrote Lessing: "Thursday evening we were at the 'Book and Play Club' at A. G. Becker's. Dr. Coit spoke to us about his friend Bernhard [*sic*] Shaw; it was very interesting. I heard him again yesterday at the City Club on the English Political Question, and shall try to hear him again tomorrow morning at the Ethical Culture; I don't know what the subject is."[138] There were other lectures to attend. At one point, he took Gussie to hear Mrs. Pankhurst, the famous English suffragette. Gussie was enthusiastic, but JR was not won over. "I think women have too many rights as it is, and not only young women," he wrote Adele.[139]

In addition to all his other activities, JR believed in being physically active. In the summer, he played tennis and golf. At other times of the year, he would arise at 6:00 A.M. and go for a brisk walk with Albert Loeb, who had built a home nearby.

Sundays were special. In the morning, JR attended Temple Sinai. Following the service, guests often came to dinner. In the evening there was always a family gathering. Birthdays were elaborate affairs, with costumed skits planned by the children. Such skits often took weeks to prepare and rehearse. Occasionally there would be costume parties where everyone dressed up in outlandish outfits.

Dinner parties would range from the small and intimate to the elaborate. Often visiting dignitaries would be present, such as Aaron Aaronsohn, Booker T. Washington, or Henry Goldman, the CEO of Goldman Sachs and JR's friend from his New York days, who came to Chicago with his wife in order to decide whether to raise the dividend on Sears stock.

Gussie, too, complained of being overly busy. She was on several boards, such as Children's Memorial Hospital. She had the household to run, the children to be seen to (especially the "babies," as Marion and William were called until they were teenagers), governesses to be hired, and shopping to be engaged in, especially for Gussie's own wardrobe, necessitating numerous trips to dressmakers. Gussie used her house as a venue for aspiring young musicians, such as the child prodigy Mischa Elman, an accomplished violinist. There were all those letters, painstakingly written by hand. And, of course, attending the opera, theater, concerts, and lectures also affected Gussie. No wonder she occasionally succumbed to general exhaustion and spent the day in bed, a practice that was considered perfectly acceptable for women of that social rank.

For JR there was no such release, but there were vacations. There could be short trips to fishing resorts in Wisconsin, or spas in Iowa or Indiana, or lengthy trips to Europe, where JR went in 1909 and twice in 1911. He and his family visited numerous German and Eastern European cities in 1911. Then JR returned to Chicago, ostensibly to participate in the Merriam campaign, but also to get back to running Sears, Roebuck. He debated with himself and with Gussie whether to return in June to rent a house in London for the coronation of George V. "I didn't cable about London," he wrote her. "That's for you to decide. I can't under any circumstances come before June and then only for two or three weeks. I've got to get into business again. It won't do at all. You know, sweetheart, what my position is on these matters, and I will not sacrifice principals [*sic*] for pleasure—even though it requires so great a sacrifice."[140]

The nearly three-month separation was hard on both JR and Gussie. "I will come if you say you want me," JR wrote his wife, "and I'll never do this again unless it's a question of life or death, or nearly so."[141] In the end, they did rent the house in London, and the occasion was a memorable one. The youngest children never forgot the jubilant crowds dancing in the streets.

When the family returned from London, they expected to rent a home in one of the northern suburbs of Chicago for the summer, as they had done the year before. JR's mother enjoyed going there because it was cooler. But they were greeted by the sad news that the house they had rented had burned down, and so they were forced to spend the hottest months of 1911 in the city. This fueled their determination to buy a house not far from the Ravisloe Country Club in the winter of 1911–12. A large estate was found in the Ravinia section of Highland Park, an area with woods and ravines and a house on a high bluff overlooking Lake Michigan.[142] The house was refurbished, and Gussie busied herself with the landscaping, aided by the noted landscape architect Jens Jensen. The family moved in during the summer of 1912 and thereafter spent part of every summer and many weekends there. They named the property "Tel Aviv" following their visit to Palestine in 1914.[143]

During the years 1909–12, the three older children came of age. Lessing departed from Cornell in 1911 without fanfare. He did not graduate. Although he had taken courses in science and shown an interest in conservation, he decided to work for Sears, Roebuck. JR, who had kept his son informed in general terms about the progress of the business, was probably delighted. However, he made sure that Lessing started at a suitably low position in the company—as a clerk in the shipping department. By the summer of 1912 he had become the manager of the billing department.

Adele had fallen in love with one of Lessing's roommates at Cornell, the scion of a German Jewish family well known to JR, Armand Deutsch. It is very likely that one of the main reasons Adele and Edith were packed off to Germany in the autumn of 1910 was to remove them from the attentions of potential boyfriends. If this was the plan, it failed miserably.

Armand and Adele were married in a private ceremony on February 11, 1912. Armand, who seems to have had no career goals or professional ambitions, oddly enough did not incur the wrath of his father-in-law, who was concerned only that his daughter should be happy.

Edith was the sweet-tempered and friendly daughter. The year after her sister's wedding, she married the feckless Germon Sulzberger. Of the two younger children, Marion was smart but somewhat bratty. In the spring of 1912, JR wrote Adele and Armand that the "babies" had come to visit the Sears plant. "Marion [age 10] is the most incessant talker you can imagine. After dinner we went over to see Lessing and when we walked into his department he was sitting on a table. She turned around to her Mother and said, 'He doesn't look as though he was overworked, does he; you needn't worry about him.'"[144] William was a bit of a problem in that he had nervous tics, which greatly concerned his mother. She took him to doctors who prescribed rest cures and near isolation from the family, solutions which only exacerbated the problems faced by this sensitive, intelligent boy. Both the younger children suffered by being largely brought up by governesses. They rarely saw their parents. They were, however, bolstered by a large and loving extended family.

Fiftieth Birthday

As the summer of 1912 approached, JR decided to take stock. On August 12 he would be fifty years old. This was a milestone event, and he wanted to use the occasion to make a bold statement about his philanthropy, as well as to clean up some personal matters. He was reputed to be the fifth richest man in Chicago, with an estimated $23 million, the equivalent of $455 million in 2005 dollars. And while this wealth brought benefits and pleasures, it also produced burdens.

One of these was how to deal with his own children in terms of money. JR's feeling of ambivalence on this issue is tellingly reflected in a letter he wrote to Adele and Edith in 1910. He sent them a clipping about a split in Sears stock, then tried to explain it: "You probably won't understand it, but it means simply this: that for every three shares anyone has, they will receive one share for nothing, and instead of getting $21 dividend each year, they will receive $28 because they then have 4 shares instead of 3. Just think what you, my dears, will get. Adele, by degrees you are becoming an heiress, and you, my Edie, shall, by the time you are 18, not

Figure 6. Portrait of JR around 1912.

be far behind your big sweet sister, if I can be on hand to arrange it." Then, sounding like Gussie fifteen years earlier, he continued:

> But these are only secondary to our love for one another and our helpfulness and kindness to others, and without these, the financial success in the world is scarcely worth having—without love and sacrifice, which means doing for others actively, the charm of success is lost. I don't mean to preach, but I see so many examples of people who are unhappy because they don't seem to realize this.[145]

Lessing also showed an interest in philanthropy, which delighted JR; he impulsively offered to donate a piano to a boarding school for troubled children located near Cornell University.

Figure 7. Portrait of Gussie around 1912. Courtesy of the Department of Special Collections, Regenstein Library, University of Chicago.

In matters of money, JR also had to deal with his sisters and brothers and with Gussie's sisters. Even for a man as devoted to family as JR, these siblings and in-laws could become grasping, demanding problems, always with an eye out for a piece of that large fortune. The most intractable case was that of JR's brother Louis, who ran a constantly failing store in Salina, Kansas. Louis repeatedly asked JR to help him with loans, and JR complied, but with less pleasure each time. Finally he hired someone to take over the business. He insisted that Louis and his family live on only $2,000 a month, and he kept urging him to adopt sound business practices. Generally these exhortations fell on deaf ears.

Other relatives, while not so impoverished, could be equally importunate. One of the worst was Gussie's sister Tessie. As his birthday approached, JR decided to put a stop to this family begging once and for all. The letter to Tessie was typical.

> We have reason to believe that you have long felt that, in our position as compared to yours, you should be a sharer in our good fortune to a greater

> extent than you have been, and this is probably only natural. For reasons which we deemed wise, we have not given you a stipulated or dependable allowance, although you have from time to time received shares of stock which have become of considerable value; all of which we took pleasure in giving you. We now feel that *under certain conditions* we would be glad to have you share further with us by allowing you a certain sum each year to be used for you and your family's comfort and for the education of your children.

Then come the conditions. (1) She and her husband were not to mention this letter to anybody. (2) "[Both of you] must refrain from criticism of either of us as regards our gifts *to you* or to *any* relative of ours." (3) Any allowance Tessie now received from her husband must not be lessened because of JR and Gussie's gift to the family. If all these and other conditions were followed, JR and Gussie would give them $5,000 annually "in installments at such times as in our judgment seems best. . . . If the conditions are violated, the allowance will cease without argument. We make these conditions in the interest of harmony and hope they will tend to that end and thereby add to your happiness and our own."[146] All this was on top of a stock arrangement worked out with Tessie's husband in May 1912. If this letter was intended to put a stop to all future appeals for money, it clearly did not work. The diaries of Tessie's husband reveal that by 1917, he was visiting Chicago, begging for additional assistance.[147] Similar letters were sent to JR's sisters Sophie and Selma.

In addition to dealing with his family, JR decided to systematize and streamline his philanthropy. It had become far too time-consuming for him to handle alone. He was being inundated with requests, and although he used such people as Judge Mack, Jane Addams, and Booker T. Washington to help him investigate prospective recipients, he needed someone who could devote all his time to this task. During the summer of 1912, he hired William C. Graves to fill that position. Graves had served as the superintendent of the James C. King Home for Old Men and as the secretary of the Illinois Board of Charities. Graves's office was in the Sears plant right next to JR's. It was Graves who increasingly took over the projects that JR had launched. He worked closely and compatibly with the Sears CEO for the next fifteen years.

Now that JR was donating fairly large sums of money, he was starting to think deeply about philanthropy. In November 1912, he made a speech before the American Academy of Political and Social Sciences in Philadelphia. In this address, JR made three important points. The first, which was truly surprising and points out once again the feeling of ambivalence that JR had for his wealth, was that the accumulation of large fortunes in a few hands was wrong and could have serious social repercussions. "The issue is excessive wealth. And I venture to make this suggestion because the social unrest is not only spreading but deepening, and because things *big* in the *social sense* are not to be expected of *big Americans.*"[148] This sentiment does not appear again in JR's writings or speeches on philanthropy. Second, he urged people not to make anonymous gifts, arguing that the name of the donor often carried as much weight as the gift itself and might encourage others to give. Finally, JR presented the idea that he was to formulate into a philosophy of philanthropy: his crusade against endowments. In this speech, the argument is not very clearly formulated, but the basic ideas are there: Charitable organizations should not place money in endowments that produce interest of only about 4.5 percent, but should be willing to spend down a certain amount of the principal along with the interest each year. If this means that the principal is gradually whittled away, so be it. A new endowment campaign should probably be conducted every twenty years in any case.

One of JR's main arguments against endowments was that they were often created by well-meaning donors for purposes which ended up having little significance in the future. In this speech he cited the case of orphan asylums, once thought to be the best place to put children whose father, usually the only breadwinner in the family, had died. Now, JR argued, society realized that the fatherless family should be kept intact, so numerous orphan asylums were no longer needed. The endowments given to such institutions were lying fallow, wasting money.

The Philadelphia speech was given to a small, select audience of academics. But several months before that speech, JR had decided that its main points should be presented to the American people as a whole. He concluded that the best way to do this was to give away a large sum of money to a variety of organizations. Each gift was carefully considered in order to provide an impact over and above the actual dollar amount donated. All were to organizations to which JR had a close connection. The ostensible reason for the contributions was to honor his fiftieth birthday.

It was because of JR's position as board president of the Associated Jewish Charities that he made one of the two largest gifts to that organization. At a board meeting in 1910, JR named a committee of five "to consider the establishment of a Central Registration Bureau and the securing or erecting of a Central Administration Building to house that Bureau," as well as other constituent organizations of the Associated, such as the Home Finding Society. This committee reported back at the September 15 meeting that a Central Administration Building should be "provided as soon as possible."[149] Over a year elapsed, but nothing was done.

JR decided to establish a Central Administration Building with his birthday gift. In a letter dated August 12, 1912, addressed to his fellow board members, he announced that he was giving $250,000 for the purchase of suitable land and the "erection thereon of a building to be called the West Side Charities Building adequate and suitable for the following philanthropic work": (1) office space for the Associated Charities; (2) office space for another federation of Jewish charities. Here JR was clearly thinking in terms of the Eastern European Orthodox Jews, and this was meant to be a gesture to help bring together the two Jewish communities; (3) space for a Central Registration Bureau for the German Jewish charities; (4) space for the offices of the Relief Department, the Bureau of Personal Services, the Employment Bureau of the Jewish Aid Society, and the Jewish Home Finding Society; (5) other constituent agencies of the Associated that needed office space. Once all the other conditions had been met, (6) room was available "for other philanthropic or civic work, whether Jewish, Protestant, Catholic, or nonsectarian but especially for work tending toward the improvement of the condition of the people in the section of the City in which the building is located"—the Hull House, Maxwell Street area. JR estimated that it would cost about $150,000 to buy the land and erect and equip the building. He urged that no unnecessary expense be incurred in the construction. If there was $100,000 left over, he wanted that money to be held in a building fund so that additions to the building could be made if necessary. Income from the building fund was to be used for maintenance. After ten years, whatever had not been expended for building purposes was to revert to the endowment fund of the Associated, which JR had helped to create. However, he stipulated that the principal and the interest from the former building fund had to be consumed in twenty-five years. Finally, JR insisted that he must approve the plans and that the contracts had to be entered into before he would release the money, except for the purchase price of the land. The thoroughness with which this entire plan was conceived is notable. Although he probably had assistance on details, it is likely that JR came up with the bulk of this plan himself.[150]

The structure, "a model of its kind" located at 1800 Selden Street, was completed in 1915.[151] As JR had hoped, it proved to be an extraordinarily useful addition to the philanthropic scene in Chicago.

A second $250,000 gift was made to the University of Chicago. Although he had just joined the board, JR knew the president, Harry Pratt Judson, and must have been acquainted with a number of his fellow trustees. He asked them what buildings the university needed most. Confronted with a list of three, he decided not to opt for any one himself, but to make the university choose. "The most pressing building requirements of the University at this time seem to be:

(1) A women's gymnasium (including possibly a club house)
(2) A building for the Geologic and Geographic Departments
(3) A building for the Classical Departments."

When two-thirds of the sum required to build and equip any one or more of the buildings would be raised, either in cash or pledges, JR agreed to donate his $250,000.[152] As it turned out, only one building was erected utilizing JR's money. The structure housing the Departments of Geology and Geography was built in 1914 and was called Rosenwald Hall. JR was opposed to having the building named after him, as he explained in a letter fifteen years later: "The building at the University was named for me contrary to my wishes while I was in the Orient and I felt that it would have been extremely discourteous for me to ask to have it changed, inasmuch as it was the wish of the family and trustees."[153]

Julius Rosenwald Hall was designed by the architectural firm of Holabird and Roche and was dedicated on March 16, 1915. It still stands today on the University of Chicago campus.

At the point at which JR was deciding what projects to fund in celebration of his fiftieth birthday, Jane Addams visited her board member. As she told Judge Mack, she pressed the idea of a "country club" for social workers. Social work was a relatively new profession in 1912. Its practitioners were almost entirely women who were poorly paid and who worked constantly in the front lines battling poverty and the evils associated with it: alcoholism, spousal abuse, child neglect, etc. Some followers of Jane Addams, like Mrs. Joseph T. Bowen, were wealthy and could es-

Figure 8. JR and University of Chicago president Henry Pratt Judson at the dedication of Rosenwald Hall, 1915. Courtesy of the Department of Special Collections, Regenstein Library, University of Chicago.

cape from the sordid scenes in which they worked. But the vast majority could not, and they would welcome a place in the country where they could relax that was peaceful, clean, and quiet. JR listened to Jane Addams state her case and believed that this was a worthy project that should be included in the fiftieth birthday package.

He decided that the "country club" should not be an adjunct of Hull House but an independent entity with its own board of directors, which he named: Jane Addams, Minnie Low, Judge Mack, S. C. Kingsley, the executive director of United Charities, and William C. Graves. His letter announcing this $50,000 gift to found the "country club" stated: "The proposed club house should be conveniently located; it should have all reasonable facilities for comfortable weekend, summer and winter vacations. It seems to me that a club of this kind might have a membership of social workers paying the minimum of dues required to support the enterprise." His money would be paid, JR continued, once he had approved a budget that proved that the purchase of the land and the building, equipping, and furnishing of the clubhouse could all be accomplished with the sum provided. Furthermore, the board had to prove that the "country club" would be self-supporting.[154]

The Social Workers Country Club was dedicated on June 20, 1914. It was located along the banks of the Des Plaines River in Riverside, Illinois, and consisted of a clubhouse and fourteen acres of rolling wooded land. The clubhouse had dormitory rooms that could accommodate twenty-four guests who came for weekends or longer vacations. The facility could also accommodate two hundred day visitors. The place was easily accessible by train and was built so that it could be operated year-round. It survived until the 1930s.

In 1908, when Dr. David Blaustein, recruited by JR to head the Chicago Hebrew Institute, came from the Educational Alliance in New York, he brought with him the athletic coach of that institution, Harry Berkman. JR became well acquainted with Berkman, who had a talent for turning poor Jewish children from the tenements into athletes. At one point, Berkman indicated dissatisfaction with the Hebrew Institute and talked about leaving, but JR persuaded him to stay. It was almost surely Henry Berkman who either convinced JR or planted the seed in his mind to donate a gymnasium to the Chicago Hebrew Institute.

As part of his fiftieth birthday contributions, JR informed the board of the Hebrew Institute that he would contribute $50,000 toward this gymnasium, provided the Hebrew Institute raised an equal sum to build and equip the facility. As with other such grants, JR required that the other $50,000 in cash had to be raised, the contracts had to be drawn up, and the whole project had to be within the $100,000 budget before JR would release the funds.[155] Controversy developed over the vagueness of this grant, centering on whether or not a "gymnasium" meant two swimming pools, one for men and boys, the other for women. The cost of the project also went up. JR was unwilling to pay the difference or even to undertake the project. It took a considerable amount of pleading from Jacob Loeb, JR's successor as board chairman of the Hebrew Institute, to persuade JR to relent and renew his offer. He did not increase it, however, and the additional $25,000 expense had to be borne by the Hebrew Institute. The new gym was opened on JR's fifty-third birthday on August 12, 1915.

Two other Jewish charities benefited from JR's largess in this fiftieth birthday round of grants. One was to an organization that JR did not even believe in. Because of his work with the Home Finding Society, JR found the very idea of orphanages repugnant. However, in 1909, the Marks Nathan Orphan Home decided to move to another area of Chicago, and JR was asked to give money to the new building. He offered, in essence, to make a sizable contribution if the Marks Nathan Home changed its mission, abandoned the idea of a new building, and agreed to the idea of boarding out children rather than institutionalizing them. This offer was refused. Some money was collected for the construction of the new building, and the cornerstone was laid in June 1911, but construction was slowed because sufficient funds had not been contributed. After great fund-raising efforts, the building was almost completed when JR was appealed to once again. The time was propitious, close to August 12, 1912. JR offered to contribute $25,000 to complete the building, although he did not disguise his basic disagreement with the whole orphanage concept. Moreover, as was true of most of the other grants, the funds were subject to certain conditions: "This offer is subject to the adoption by you of a financing plan that will absolutely insure the completion of the building, and provide for the proper maintenance of the institution, said plan to be acceptable to a committee which has been appointed by the Associated Jewish Charities." The building was actually completed by the time the Marks Nathan board agreed to accept the recommendations of the Associated committee, and in 1913, JR honored his pledge in full. It is interesting and somewhat remarkable that JR would give a large amount of money to an organization whose mission he did not believe in, but perhaps he realized that, having fought hard for his point of view and lost, he might as well be generous.[156]

Tuberculosis was a serious problem in the tenements of Chicago, where the highly contagious disease was easily passed on. At first it was thought that only in the pure air of such places as Denver could one be successfully treated for this dread disease. But the Jewish Consumptives' Relief Society proved that tuberculosis patients could also be cured in Illinois. This led to the building of the Winfield Sanitarium. JR became familiar with that institution through his service as president of the Associated Jewish Charities. On September 30, 1909, JR appointed himself to a committee to investigate the affiliation of the Winfield Sanatorium with the Associated. To further understand the issue of TB, the Associated president called a special meeting at which doctors discussed the disease and its cure. Still, it took an additional three months before the Winfield Sanatorium was accepted as a constituent institution, which meant that it could receive grants from that agency.[157] JR's $25,000 contribution to Winfield was also for a new building. He stated that he would give the last $25,000 once all the other needed funds had been collected.

The final two gifts were to non-Jewish institutions. One was the Glenwood Manual Training School, an Illinois institution JR had started supporting in 1910 with his contribution of $100. The fiftieth birthday gift was $12,500 to purchase a farm to add to the school's property. Clearly JR, with his interest in agricultural education, believed that a working farm would be a useful addition. Unlike most of the other grants in this series, there was no matching component for this one.[158]

The subject of southern black private schools interested JR. He had visited the Berry School in Georgia and had contributed to it and others. When Booker T. Washington stayed at the Rosenwald home, JR had discussed these schools with him. They decided that these private schools needed to be aided according to a common standard. In the midst of a relatively routine letter on July 15, JR dropped a bombshell: "I wish, when you have time, you would write me fully on the following subject: If you had $25,000 to distribute among institutions which are offshoots from Tuskegee or doing similar work to Tuskegee, how would you divide it?"[159]

One can only imagine Washington's delight upon receipt of this letter. Only a few weeks earlier, JR had pledged $5,000 a year for five years to

Tuskegee. Now he was proposing another $25,000 for a fund to be established and managed by Washington. When Washington replied to JR's letter, he used caution to demonstrate that he was not acting hastily or alone but was seeking the advice of others:

> I shall be very glad to send you my recommendation and opinion regarding the use of $25,000 in helping institutions which are offshoots of Tuskegee or are doing similar work. Such a sum of money will prove a Godsend to those institutions, and can be made to accomplish more good just now than any one realizes. I think I am not stating it too strongly when I say that a wise expenditure of such a sum of money will enable these schools to do 50 or 100% better work than they are now doing. Just as soon as I return to Tuskegee . . . I shall take up your suggestion with some of the heads of departments, and shall write you fully regarding the whole subject. It is most generous and kind of you to think of these schools in this way.[160]

Washington's carefully considered answer, dated August 3, has been lost. But JR did reply to that letter.

> The plan that I believe that I would favor most, providing you concurred in it, would be the following: You select such schools as in your judgment would participate, naming the amount for each and the purpose for which the money is to be used, if you so desire, and, as soon as any school which you have named has raised an equal amount, I will pay to it such an amount as you have designated. I will agree to pay a total of $25,000 to such schools as soon as they furnish a list of bona fide subscriptions equal to the amount you have designated.

After explaining that he was doing this for his birthday and wanted Washington to formulate an announcement of this gift, he added: "It is wise to make the condition as to the raising of an equal amount, because the incentive will be great for others to give and the trustees of the various institutions will put forth work under such conditions that they would not be likely to do otherwise."[161]

Three people besides JR were involved in planning and announcing the fiftieth birthday gifts: Judge Mack, Jane Addams, and the journalist H. H. Kohlsaat. It seems clear that Mack was the person with whom JR discussed the details of his eight grants. Kohlsaat was the editor of the

Chicago *Record-Herald* and had been editor of the *Inter-Ocean.* He had accompanied JR and his party to Tuskegee in February. JR had loaned him $10,000 at 6 percent interest to start his new paper.[162] JR, who had a keen appreciation of the value of the nascent field of public relations, used Kohlsaat when he wanted to place stories about himself, and it was in this capacity that the journalist was utilized now. As Judge Mack explained to Jane Addams: "I have suggested to Mr. Rosenwald to send you copies of the various letters. My thought about Kohlsaat was that you should give the information to him, not for the *Record-Herald* alone, but that he, as a newspaper man, might see to it that it got to all the papers in the proper form. I did not mean that you, personally, should bother sending to the individual papers. There is no necessity for your putting yourself to this trouble. I mentioned Kohlsaat rather than somebody else because of his close personal relations with Mr. Rosenwald."[163] Thus the texts of the letters announcing the gifts were to be sent to various newspapers by Kohlsaat, but it was Jane Addams who made the announcement of all the fiftieth birthday grants.

The choice was brilliant. Rosenwald, generally a self-effacing man, did not want to make the announcement himself, although he readily made himself available for interviews after the fact. Addams, by 1912, had a national reputation. She had recently spoken at the Republican National Convention, and many people had read her books, whereas few people outside of Chicago had ever heard of Julius Rosenwald.

Kohlsaat did his work well. He invented a catchy slogan, "Give While You Live," which was prominently featured in a cartoon entitled "Other Millionaires Please Note—This Form of Birthday Party Is Not Copyrighted," which ran in the *Record-Herald* on August 12, 1912. It showed a kindly Rosenwald introducing to an audience figures representing his recent donations. Moreover, stories about this Chicago millionaire's gifts to charity ran in newspapers throughout the country. Many of the Chicago papers, in addition to reporting on the contributions and reprinting the letters, published interviews with the man of the hour himself. This afforded JR the opportunity to come out with such aphorisms as "Never lose interest in something. Center your soul and mind power on something, grip it tight, work over it, develop that interest and it will yield you contentment, happiness and prosperity."[164]

JR affirmed that donating money was a truly enjoyable endeavor (clearly

Figure 9. Fiftieth birthday cartoon: "Other Millionaires Please Note—This Form of Birthday Party Is Not Copyrighted." From H. H. Kohlsaat's *Inter-Ocean,* August 12, 1912. Courtesy of the Department of Special Collections, Regenstein Library, University of Chicago.

part of the message he was trying to convey) and that he most enjoyed being with his coworkers and his family. Another part of this public relations effort may have been to demonstrate that millionaires who donate large sums of money are basically just ordinary folks.

The public reaction to the announcement of the fiftieth birthday gifts was largely positive. Family and friends hastened to write laudatory tributes. Most editorial opinion also was filled with praise. In an editorial entitled "Julius Rosenwald, Citizen," the *Chicago Tribune* declared:

> The objects of these gifts are in every case worthy and their selection indicates how broad, inclusive, and well considered is the spirit which animates Mr. Rosenwald's philanthropy. The social value of beneficence—to say nothing of its value to the donor—is doubled when it is the result not only of impulsive kindness but of patient thought and unselfish direction. To give money is a privilege, but to give oneself with it in the sense of giving time and interest in order that the giving shall be wise is a higher service by far. It is not only philanthropy but citizenship.[165]

Amidst the near universal adulation, there were voices of dissent, such as this "Letter to the Editor," which appeared in a New York newspaper. The writer correctly if satirically nails the public relations aspect of this event.

> He wept tears of joy at the great good he had brought to the community and reeled off a number of platitudes and hints for happiness to the reporters for the benefit of the reading public. It was a beautifully press-agented birthday affair, and the nice things the press said about him probably made his eyes dance and his chest swell. I wonder, however, if his ears burned from the wave of universal criticism voiced to the effect that his charity might have begun, as all real charity is supposed to, at home. No mention is made that he added a mite to the weekly pittance of the hundreds of young girls and women whose long hours of labor made it possible for him to contribute to already heavily endowed institutions.[166]

This argument was to haunt JR in the next few years.

Several papers stated that JR normally gave his gifts without any fanfare whatsoever, and so it is interesting to note that the $687,500 was, in fact, not the full extent of JR's birthday present. Undisclosed sums also were sent to Graham Taylor and Minnie Low for their own personal use. In characteristic fashion, Graham Taylor announced in his thank-you letter that he was turning JR's largess into a cash reserve fund that he could draw on to balance the constantly shaky budget of the Chicago Commons.[167]

The fiftieth birthday gifts were an important signal to the philanthropic world that a new man had arrived on the scene, a man with his own philosophy, in some ways not so different from that of Andrew Carnegie, who declared that a man who dies with his fortune intact dies disgraced. What distinguishes JR from Carnegie and Rockefeller is his comparative youth, his lack of corporate ruthlessness or bullying, and the fact that he started donating large sums of money while he was still very active in business. Both Rockefeller and Carnegie gave away the vast bulk of their fortunes after they had retired. JR was far from retired, but already in 1912, philanthropy, rather than business, was becoming the true interest and passion of his life.

4

Black Schools, Political Attacks, and the Profit Sharing Plan, 1912–1916

The Origin of the Rosenwald Schools

Julius Rosenwald's donation of $25,000 to Tuskegee Institute was to prove far and away the most important of all his fiftieth birthday contributions. The brilliant and charismatic Booker T. Washington shaped JR's gift to suit his purpose, the construction of small rural schools. Then, through clever and timely reporting, he managed to so completely captivate the Chicago philanthropist with this concept that expansion of the rural schools program was almost inevitable. It is clearly an example of consummate fund-raising. But it also shows JR's desire to support a program that so obviously worked successfully to educate black schoolchildren in the rural South. What began modestly in 1913 became a large program that had a profound impact on black Southern education in the Jim Crow era.

The state of public education for blacks in the rural South around 1912 was deplorable, but some rays of hope were beginning to emerge. Many black rural communities did not have public schools. If they did exist, schools were located in extremely dilapidated buildings. School supplies were meager if they were available at all. If there were textbooks (which was doubtful), they were woefully outdated. Teachers had almost no training and were paid minuscule salaries. The school year was usually only three or four months long because the agricultural cycle was paramount and the children were needed for work in the fields. It was almost impossible for children to acquire a year's worth of education under these conditions.

In 1902, one of the very first foundations in U.S. history, the General Education Board, was founded by John D. Rockefeller Jr. and a group of his advisors. The money for the foundation came from Rockefeller's father. The aim of the new foundation was to assist with education throughout the South. In theory, this meant blacks as well as whites, but the founders were so worried about offending Southern white sensibilities that, in the GEB's first decade of operation, very little money went to blacks.

A more hopeful development occurred in 1906 with the gift of Miss Anna T. Jeanes. A forthright and very wealthy Quaker, Miss Jeanes was solicited by Booker T. Washington, an alumnus of Hampton Institute, and Hollis B. Frissell, principal of the all-black college, to provide a sizable contribution to Hampton. Miss Jeanes, however, was uninterested in black higher education. She wanted to support rural public schools for blacks. At first she donated $10,000 to this cause and later increased the amount to $200,000, stipulating that the funds should be under the GEB but should be administered by Washington and Frissell. Initially, the two principals used the money to help construct small schoolhouses in the areas near their institutes. In 1907, the GEB, with the blessing of Ms. Jeanes, hired James Harvey Dillard, a classics professor and dean at Tulane, to manage the fund. The GEB also decided to utilize the Jeanes money to assist black teachers. Dillard discovered Virginia Randolph, a smart, well-educated black woman who knew how to teach and knew how to motivate other instructors. When Anna Jeanes died in 1909, leaving $1 million to the fund established in her name, Dillard essentially cloned Virginia Randolph. The funds went to her and to men and women like her who traveled from school to school in a given area, offering technical assistance and useful advice to other black teachers.[1]

In 1912, the GEB finally accomplished something meaningful for African Americans. They began paying for officers at the state level in the South to take charge of black public schools; these individuals complemented officials who had been supervising white rural public schools since the early 1900s. The "Negro school agents" were white males chosen by the state superintendents of education, but they understood their job, they were dedicated, and they knew the ins and outs of Jim Crow politics.[2] If anyone could help black schools at the state level in terms of funding and programs, these men could. By 1914, this program was in operation throughout the South.

Building black public schools in the farmland around Tuskegee was something Booker T. Washington longed to do. In addition to using some of the Jeanes money for this, Washington also interested Henry H. Rogers, a Standard Oil executive, in the project. Forty-six small one-teacher structures were built in Macon County, Alabama, with Jeanes money and Rogers's assistance before Rogers died in 1909.[3] Clearly, Washington was looking for somebody to restart this worthwhile program. He found his man in JR.

The two men had discussed the question of rural schools when Washington was in Chicago in mid-August 1912 making fund-raising calls for Tuskegee. Referring to this conversation, Washington wrote JR on August 31, 1912, noting that he was working on a plan on this subject which he would submit to JR shortly and enclosing an article he had written about black rural schools.[4]

The "plan" was still under consideration as of September 12, but Washington wanted to arrange some preliminary details and wished to obtain JR's approval for the funding. Noting that $2,800 of the original fiftieth birthday grant had not been appropriated, he suggested that JR agree to fund the building of six rural schools as an experiment. Washington estimated that each school could be constructed for $600. JR would put up half of this amount. Local blacks would then match that. JR would put in an additional $50 per school to pay for the traveling expenses of someone to "get people stirred up and to keep them stirred up until the schoolhouses have been built." Washington's letter concluded:

> One thing I am convinced of, and that is that it is the best thing to have the people themselves build houses in their own community. I have found by investigation that many people who cannot give money would give half a day or a day's work and others would give material in the way of nails, brick, lime, etc. I feel that there is nothing just now more needed in the education of the colored people than the matter of small schoolhouses and I am very anxious that the matter be thoroughly planned for and well worked out and no mistakes be made.[5]

In this letter, Washington showed himself to be an exceedingly shrewd if not overly truthful fund-raiser. By positing the building of the six schools as an experiment, he did not mention the previous schools built with funds from Jeanes or Rogers. He knew that JR would want to contribute to something that was new but not too risky. This "experiment" could be carefully monitored and modified if errors were found. This was precisely the sort of formulation that would appeal to the cautious Chicago businessman, who was able to take advantage of a good opportunity and make something spectacular out of it.

JR replied to Washington's September 12 letter four days later, agreeing to spend $2,800 on rural schools. Then, ignoring the last paragraph of Washington's letter, he said that he had been thinking about this subject and proposed that Sears furnish the materials for construction as a cost-saving measure. This was precisely the period in which Sears was beginning to make prefabricated homes, so it would be relatively easy to assemble the materials for a school. If Washington agreed to this scheme, JR asked the Tuskegee principal to send him an architectural plan of the sort of school he had in mind.[6]

Washington was not enthusiastic about this idea, which went against his notion of self-help, but he did not wish to alienate JR. So he promised that plans would be sent, and merely added that schools should be built to accommodate forty or fifty students because the schools would be the only ones in a district, and students would often have to walk three, four, or five miles one way to get to them. Thus there might be more students than originally projected. These early schools were simple one- or two-room structures with one teacher serving several grades.

It was not until December 20, 1912, that Washington finally replied to the prefab idea. He had been in touch with people at Sears, he wrote JR, but "after considering the whole subject very carefully and fully, we recommend that all of the rough and heavy lumber, bricks, etc., be gotten in the vicinity of the schoolhouses. In most cases it will be found that there is a small sawmill near the schoolhouse and the freight, in this way, will not amount to a great deal." He added that several schools had already raised the requisite amount of money and were ready to start building.[7] JR replied: "[T]he only thing to do is to build these at the lowest possible cost without sacrificing quality. By this I do not mean a cheap building, of course, but a good building at a low price. The cost of the building will, of course, be a great consideration as to the number we can assist."[8]

In the first five months of 1913, various letters sent by Washington enclosed information about the rural schools: a privately printed paper written by a Tuskegee instructor, showing how local blacks were raising money; a report by Clinton Calloway, head of the Extension Department, who was handling the school construction program, which showed that about $250 had been raised by the local blacks; an internal memo of mid-May stating that $953.60 had been spent thus far on three schools. Then on May 21, Washington sent the following letter: "I thought you might like to see the enclosed description of how the people in one of the country districts are raising money to meet your conditional gift. In addition to securing schoolhouses, the training that many of these people are getting in business methods is very valuable. Three schoolhouses are practically complete, and I shall be sending you a detailed report as well as photographs in a few days."[9] The photos arrived, along with an exact accounting of expenses of the funds raised by local blacks and given by JR, as well as letters of appreciation from whites living in the three black communities where schools had been built. Washington added: "You do not know what joy and encouragement the building of these schoolhouses has brought to the people of both races in the communities where they are being erected."[10]

This was a brilliant statement from "the Wizard of Tuskegee" because, just as he had hoped would occur with the construction of the YMCAs, JR now expected that the work of building and raising funds for these schools would somehow serve to bring the two races closer together. Washington's letter and its enclosures seemed to indicate that this goal was being accomplished. But it was not the letters from Southern whites that galvanized JR; it was the photographs. He wrote Washington on June 10: "The photographs came to hand and they are tremendously interesting. I believe if they were given wide publicity, without mentioning any names, it would be helpful in stirring up other communities. It might get some other people interested in making an offer to help build schoolhouses."[11] Such a statement was typical of JR. Washington had proposed showing the photos to the members of the Tuskegee board. JR was eager to have the photos more widely displayed, but he did not want his name used. He hoped that a pamphlet could be made from these photos accompanied by a well-written text that would inspire other philanthropists to give to the schools as well. Despite words of enthusiasm from Washington, nothing was accomplished until November 1914, when Washington sent William C. Graves a prototype pamphlet.

In September 1913, an article appeared in the Chicago *Inter-Ocean* about the rural schools. Doubtless on instructions from JR, it mentioned a donor "from the West" but never gave his name. The article was about the construction of a number of schools in Macon County, Alabama; some were among the six to which JR was contributing. The article emphasized that the building of these schools was breaking down religious barriers in the black community that had arisen between rival Protestant sects; moreover, the existence of the schools was serving to inform whites about the importance of black education. The article quotes the mayor of Notasulga, one of the first communities to receive a Rosenwald school, writing to Clinton Calloway of Tuskegee: "It [the new rural school] is a credit to the town and I feel sure that it will be the means of benefiting not only your race but ours as well. I am truly glad to see your people taking so much interest in preparing their young for the duties of citizenship."[12]

In December, just before JR went off on an extended trip, Washington wrote that he was planning to send JR a report on the schoolhouses, but did not have all the data ready. In JR's absence, Washington met with Graves on April 24, 1914, and Graves, describing this encounter, stated that Washington desired a meeting with JR in early June, primarily to discuss an extension of the school program if the Sears CEO judged it to be successful.[13]

In advance of the meeting date on June 10, Washington sent JR some additional photographs and this arresting description of the impact the schools were already having:

> Yesterday I spent one of the most interesting days in all of my work in the South. Through our Extension Department under Mr. Calloway, a trip was planned that enabled us to visit four of these communities where the schoolhouses have been completed. We traveled, all told, about 135 miles. At each one of the points visited there was a very large audience, averaging I should say 1,000 people of both white and black people. It may interest you further to know that two of the state officers from the Education Department accompanied us on the entire trip. It was a most intensely interesting day, and the people showed in a very acceptable way their gratitude to you for what you are helping them to do. I wish you could have been present to have noted how encouraged and hopeful they feel; and I repeat, how grateful they are to you. I have never seen a set of people who have changed so much within recent years from a feeling of almost despair and hopelessness to one of encouragement and determination.[14]

The meeting on June 10 was extremely successful. It resulted in an agreement that was refined over the next several months and that set the basis for a program that would run almost twenty years.

Rosenwald agreed to provide the funds to help construct an additional one hundred schools in three Alabama counties, although the door was left open for schools to be built in other areas of the state and of the South. JR pledged to spend up to $350 per school and up to $30,000 on the entire program. Money for travel and for mobilizing the local black populace was to come out of the $350. From six to one hundred schools was a large commitment, which clearly emphasized JR's enthusiasm for the program. But circumstances had also changed.

While the first six schools had been built under a loose agreement, with costs shared by JR, local blacks, and to some extent local whites, the new agreement was more formal, and another party had been added: the state. Article two of the agreement stated that the funds supplied by JR were "[t]o be used in a way to encourage public school officers and the people in the community in erecting schoolhouses in rural and village districts by supplementing what the public school officers or the people themselves may do."[15] Thus the bulk of the funds were to come from public school officials and local blacks and whites. Indeed, they were to provide money equal to or larger than the amount given by JR, whose contribution was to be made available only after the other funds had been collected. Moreover, the rural school agents for the state and for black schools were to be consulted and involved, in addition to the Jeanes teachers. In short, the revised program was to be much more of a coordinated and community effort than the initial six schools had been. Although no percentages were spelled out in the agreement, JR's contribution, which had been 50 percent for the original six schools, was to shrink to between 25 and 33 percent of the cost of each school. Schools larger than the original one-teacher structures could be built. Also important was the requirement that these schools must operate approximately eight months a year.

The June 10 agreement also marked a change in JR's direct involvement in the program. The Chicago philanthropist, who had been very personally committed in the early phase, passed more and more responsibility for it to Graves. Washington still wrote JR frequently, and the two men remained on cordial terms. But the bulk of Washington's correspondence on the schools and other Tuskegee matters now went directly to

Graves. This was similar to what had happened to the YMCA program and was to recur throughout the remainder of JR's life: he would become interested in a project or initiate it; then, once it was under way, he would delegate most of the work needed on his end to a member of his staff (usually Graves), coming back into the picture at key moments or when important decisions had to be made.

Despite this change of focus, Washington continued to make moves designed to ensure that JR's interest remained high. He prodded some of the residents in communities JR had aided to write expressing their thanks. JR replied to each of these letters. The fact that the busy Sears president had taken the time to do so understandably delighted Washington, who wrote JR:

> I am so glad that you took the time and pains to write an individual letter to the colored people of Notasulga, Ramor, Loechopoka, Auburn and Montgomery who wrote you. This will prove a great encouragement, and I am equally glad that you have given us permission to use these letters in a way to create further interest. The feeling of gratitude which these people have is something beyond description. They do not always know how to express this feeling, but nevertheless they have it.[16]

Washington was dedicated about filing reports, especially when he desired payment, but these reports were not always in the form that the fastidious Graves wanted. On November 30, 1914, Graves wrote the Tuskegee principal in answer to a previously submitted bill that he wanted the cost of each school divided into the amount for promotion, the amount coming from sources other than JR, and the amount due from JR.[17] After some complaining, Washington did submit a report on three schools to Graves in the format requested. This report indicated that the schools were coming out slightly under budget as far as the cost to JR was concerned and that the average spent on promotion was a paltry $5.40 out of approximately $700 or $800 expended.[18]

The issues of reporting and money spent on promotion opened up another topic about which Washington appeared uncertain—the scope of the program. The June 10 agreement had limited the next one hundred schools to three counties—with an escape clause. If, said Washington, we opened the program up and built schools only in communities that asked for them, then we would not have to spend money on promotion at all.[19] This subject of "widening the territory" concerned Washington, because two days earlier, he had written JR: "Owing to the very depressed conditions of the South, it may be that we cannot pursue the policy of concentrating quite as much in a few counties as we had planned to do: that is, for this year it may be that we shall have to widen the territory to some extent, but we shall not make any change in the first policy, unless it is absolutely necessary."[20] Washington probably feared that if this project reached beyond the three counties surrounding Tuskegee, the entire state would be fair game, and from there it would be only a short step to going out of state. If that happened, Washington may well have feared losing control of the entire enterprise.

In February 1915, Julius Rosenwald had his first opportunity to see a Rosenwald school. It occurred during the course of the now annual train trip that JR made to a Tuskegee board meeting with a number of guests, including potential donors. JR's forty-one guests on this trip were a veritable *Who's Who* of people who either were or were about to become important in his life: Jane Addams; Jacob Billikopf, president of both the National Conference of Jewish Social Workers and the National Conference of Jewish Social Service, a friend of JR and a notable Jewish fundraiser; Charles Eisenman, a Cleveland clothing manufacturer who would become JR's chief assistant when he went to work in Washington during World War I; William Parker, business manager of the Chicago YMCA; Harold Swift, scion of the famous meatpacking family, newly named trustee of the University of Chicago, who was to serve as chairman of the board for decades; Minnie Low, the Jewish social worker with whom he worked closely for many years; Mrs. Kellogg Fairbank, president of the Chicago Lying-In Hospital; and Grace and Edith Abbott and Sophonisba Breckenridge, all three on the faculty of the School of Civics and Philanthropy. William Graves also accompanied JR, Gussie, and their daughter Edith.

The idea of visiting a school came from the Alabama rural state agent for Negro education, James L. Sibley: "I am writing to urge that on your coming visit to Tuskegee to attend the trustees' meeting you arrange your schedule so as to allow one day to be spent in Montgomery County in order that you may see the progress that is being made in rural schoolhouse building. We have found the assistance given from your fund to be a great stimulus to the work in each community, and both the white and colored people are cooperating to make the movement a success."[21] JR approved the idea, and Graves, Sibley, and Booker T. Washington arranged the itinerary. The plan was to visit four Rosenwald schools.

Figure 10. Train trip to Tuskegee. JR and Gussie are in the center of the photograph. Courtesy of the Department of Special Collections, Regenstein Library, University of Chicago.

At 8:45 A.M. on February 21, a train pulled into the Montgomery station. The passengers were met by Sibley and a fleet of cars that took them on a sixty-mile trip through Alabama plantation country. "At each place not only the children, but all the colored community in the vicinity, and many whites were there to greet the party. They were lined along the road several tiers deep, waving evergreen branches and singing the old plantation refrains of their fore-elders. . . . At each of these stations definite reports were made of receipts and expenditures, length of school term, attendance, and 'the number of whitewashed and painted houses in the vicinity.'"[22] This last point is important because it was claimed by Washington and others that building a new school had a galvanizing effect upon the whole community. People painted or whitewashed their homes and cleaned up their gardens so that the community would be thought worthy of having a splendid new school building.

Figure 11. JR and Booker T. Washington walking on the campus of Tuskegee, 1915. Courtesy of the Department of Special Collections, Regenstein Library, University of Chicago.

At each stop, the visitors were seated, usually in a church adjoining the school. At each school, JR addressed the crowd. He "expressed his appreciation of the wonderful things that the pupils and teachers had done for themselves with his assistance, stating that their progress was far above his expectations." At the Pleasant Hill school, Jane Addams said a few words. "'I was told,' she said as she looked over the faces of the Negro children, 'that you know nothing but how to pick cotton. On my way here I saw cattle, sheep, hogs, hens, bees and evidence of many kinds of farming. . . . I believe you are on the eve of diversification.'"[23]

JR was very pleased. As he wrote to Judge Julian W. Mack: "Our Tuskegee trip was, if possible, better than any previous one; we had some exceptionally novel experiences. Arriving at Montgomery about 9 A.M. Sunday morning, we had automobiles that took us to four rural schools in the same county, which had been built through the efforts of Tuskegee Institute in connection with the fund they are handling for me. (I think about 30 of these schools are already under way or completed.) At each place the community had gathered to welcome us, and each had a short program arranged. Both the visitors and the visited were enthusiastic and seemed to enjoy the celebration."[24] Others also were tremendously impressed by the rural schools. Writing to thank JR, Jenkin Lloyd Jones, director of Chicago's Abraham Lincoln Center, noted: "It proves to me how much more potent and vital, long-lasting and profitable is constructive new work as compared to 'repair shop work' which at the best only ameliorates suffering and saves the wreck. . . . I am always grateful when I find people of means who also have brains and faith enough to augment their own generosity with the virility and vitality of others and thus help the life of the future."[25]

Part of the trustees' meeting dealt with the Rosenwald schools. An evening meeting of the whole school was devoted to the subject. The clear favorite of the evening was a short, stocky black woman from Notasulga, Mrs. Mary Johnson, who described in simple language how, nine years earlier, she had looked at the rickety building that passed for a school in her community and said to herself: "Those children ought to have a better school." She had sought the advice of Washington and followed it, despite the skepticism of her husband and other men. She and other women of the community had baked pies and other goods and sold them to raise money. The first treasurer of the organization had proved dishonest and run off with the money, so Mary and her friends went back to baking and selling.

Finally they were able to obtain enough money to buy a load of wood, but as they did not have enough to actually erect the building, the men, still skeptical, left the wood to rot on the ground.

> Once more she set out to "build a school if it takes me the rest of my life." One of the means followed this last time was to advertise a minstrel show which she planned to give; and the dogged earnestness of this woman began to lay hold of the audience as she told how she went from house to house advertising the show, and as she showed how she tried to give, on the night of the show, an imitation of the dance which she thought the people expected. But all the ludicrous aspect of such an elderly woman trying to engage in vaudeville was lost in the dawning appreciation of the deep earnestness which would make a pious woman of her order, with soul revolting against all dances, crucify her own feelings that "those poor little children wouldn't have to freeze in that old schoolhouse."[26]

At the end of nine years, Mary Johnson had accumulated enough to buy the lumber and pay for the construction. Every day she visited the site, and with her own hands passed boards or shingles to the carpenters. The school was one of those which was finished with JR's money. The evening ended with a magic lantern show of slides, narrated by Booker T. Washington Jr., who worked for the Tuskegee Extension Department, showing "before and after" photos of schools in communities aided by JR.

That the Chicago philanthropist was pleased by what he had seen on his visit to Alabama was clear, and Washington knew it. Less than a month after Rosenwald's return to Chicago, Washington sent him a modest proposal. In consultation with James Sibley, he proposed that the scope of the program be extended to five additional Alabama counties, bringing the total number of counties to be covered to eight. He further suggested that someone be hired to travel around this enlarged area, keep in touch with local officials and teachers, and help with fund-raising. If all of this were done, he wrote JR, Sibley predicted that an additional twenty schools could be constructed. The salary of this itinerant aide was a suggested $1,500 a year. Washington concluded: "Mr. Sibley and all of us are convinced that this school-house-building in the rural districts is 'taproot' work, and is reaching the bottom of the problem."[27] JR replied immediately with a cable on March 20: "Proceed immediately to select additional man to supervise and assist in increasing rural schoolhouse building. Will

Figure 12. JR at the Big Zion School, one of the first five Rosenwald schools constructed. This photo was taken during the Tuskegee trustees' trip in February 1915. Courtesy of the Department of Special Collections, Regenstein Library, University of Chicago.

allow you $125 a month for salary and expenses of such man until further notice."[28]

The person hired to fill the new position was Booker T. Washington Jr., who was already involved with the Rosenwald schools. However, this seeming act of nepotism turned out to work well. Booker Jr. was conscientious and filed periodic reports on his work, as Graves requested. These reports vividly show the joys and challenges faced by someone trying to arouse interest in constructing rural schools for blacks in the South in 1915.

First, it was essential to have leadership. People from the black community, like Mary Johnson, had to have the vision and drive to mobilize their neighbors, and this was not something that Booker Jr. or anyone else could artificially implant in a community. Often there had to be both black and white leaders. And yet, in some cases, leadership alone was not enough. For example, in Cedarville, Alabama, a black leader who owned two acres of land was willing to deed them to the county for a school. But "the people are not interested."[29]

Booker Jr.'s job was multifaceted. He issued bids and drew up plans for the Chester School. He not only attended fund-raising meetings and picnics but also went door to door visiting farmers trying to persuade them to come to a meeting. His job reports reveal different truths about building schools for blacks in the rural South in this era. For example, even in this Jim Crow era of lynchings, middle-class whites who were not plantation owners with share croppers—such as a druggist, a banker, and a merchant in Barbour County—were willing to give time and money to promote primary schools for black children.

"Held a meeting at Clayton Industrial School. At this meeting over 600 people were present. The people are thoroughly interested, and have raised altogether $100: $40 in cash and $60 in lumber. They started a two-story building over two years ago and have never finished it. The State has given $300 and they are now ready for the Rosenwald money. In today's meeting we raised $11 and subscribed in labor, material and cash."[30] The system of sweat equity for the blacks worked, just as Washington had predicted.

Working with the county supervisor was absolutely essential, but local blacks could be overly ambitious. It is clear that a number of schools were begun before JR made his offer but needed an extra spurt of funding. JR and the state provided these sorely needed extra funds. Yet not all communities were in dire straits. There were some black towns with relatively prosperous inhabitants.

> Tuesday, August 10, Church County, Alabama
> I held a meeting at Needmore Community in the old schoolhouse with several farmers, their wives and children. The men subscribed to give $50 in 3 weeks and the women promised to assist. It is interesting to note the good spirit existing in this community and the desire to improve their school facilities on the part of the patrons. The colored people own several acres of land and are living well. The County Superintendent is interested in the school conditions and is assisting.[31]

Booker Jr. concluded his August 1915 report:

> On the whole I feel very much encouraged with the work because of the interest which is being shown on the part of the people in their efforts to raise their share of the funds with which to build better schoolhouses. I have endeavored to keep the Rosenwald agents who are in the field[32] encouraged through correspondence and also by my presence whenever I found it convenient, and have watched the contributions of the schoolhouses to make sure that they were being constructed according to plans and specifications.

These reports were sent to Graves on a regular basis, and they must have impressed JR. For all of Booker T. Washington's fine words, these terse accounts provided basic facts about what was happening in the various local communities. Along with the evidence of what he had seen, JR had tangible proof that this program was moving forward rapidly and successfully.

During the autumn of 1914, Washington had had questions about whether to extend the schoolhouse program. By March 1915, he clearly had decided in favor of expansion and had increased the area covered to eight counties and fifty schools. But an occasional doubt still lingered—not so much fear of losing power or control but fear of white reaction. At the end of May, Washington wrote to Sibley:

> I think we will have to be very careful in putting up this large number of schoolhouses, not to put so much money into a building that it will bring about a feeling of jealousy on the part of the white people who may have a schoolhouse that is much poorer. I think, of course, the feeling of jealousy

> will gradually disappear in proportion as the white people themselves get better school buildings, but I can easily see that the white people who might have a very poor school building would have a feeling that the colored people are getting ahead of them, therefore something might be done to bring about an awkward position regarding the Negro school. . . . I think the more modest our school buildings are at present, at least, the more we are likely to avoid such a difficulty.[33]

These qualms soon dissipated because no adverse white reaction occurred. Moreover, there was a push to do even more. A financial report submitted by Washington at the end of July indicated that the first Rosenwald school outside of Alabama had been constructed in North Carolina.[34] By the time of Booker T. Washington's death in November 1915, the number of schools completed or under construction in three Southern states was seventy-eight. No formal signed agreement marks this expansion of the schoolhouse building program beyond Alabama. It seems to have occurred spontaneously, without JR's official blessing. Yet the Chicago philanthropist certainly approved.

Construction of the schools would, JR and Washington hoped, stimulate state government to become involved, and that did occur. The first stage in this process was the creation of the position of rural agents for Negro schools. Next came JR's program with its matching component and the strong implication that the state and local government were expected to add funds to the match. The fact that Washington cannily extended the area covered by Rosenwald schools to include Montgomery County, seat of the capital, may have had something to do with this. So did the enthusiasm of local county superintendents of education to aid black schools. On June 19, Washington reported to Graves that the $4,600 that JR had thus far expended on the school construction program had led state and local governments to expend $10,500—money earmarked for black primary education in the state of Alabama. Later in the year, the state legislature passed a bill authorizing $124,000 for the erection, repair, and equipping of rural schoolhouses. The bulk of this money doubtless was expended on white schools, but some of it surely went to blacks. There was a matching provision for these grants, just as there was with JR's funds, and in fact Washington credits JR with starting the entire program of state funding for black education.[35] Although the sum of $10,500 appropriated by the Alabama legislature appears modest, in fact it was crucial. A bridge had been crossed in terms of black education in the South. Black education was no longer being entirely ignored at the state and county levels. Although it is true, as scholars such as James D. Anderson claim, that blacks who paid for Rosenwald schools were, in essence, being taxed twice, once through taxation for services that were never performed, and the second time by giving their own hard-earned funds for schools that state and local governments should have provided in the first place, the fact remains that at last local governments were doing *something* for black education.[36] It may have been too little, and it was certainly too late, but it was a beginning, and the trend that began in Alabama in 1915 spread throughout the South in the years ahead. One could argue that it was not the actions taken by the usually timorous General Education Board but JR's challenge grants that finally mobilized local governments to action.

In addition to the reports of his son's work, Washington continued sending JR and Graves materials connected with the schoolhouse construction program that he thought would interest them. For example, on October 1, 1915, he noted: "It is impossible for us to describe in words the good that this schoolhouse building is accomplishing—not only in providing people with comfortable school buildings who never knew what a decent school building was before, but even in changing and revolutionizing public sentiment in the South as far as Negro education is concerned."[37] A few days later, he wrote:

> I often wish that you could have time to hear and see for yourself some of the little incidents that occur in connection with this work. I wish you could hear the expressions of approval that now come from white people—white people who a few years ago would not think of anything bearing upon Negro education. I wish you could hear the expressions of gratitude uttered over and over again by the most humble class of colored people. Let me repeat that we count it a great privilege to have some little share in this glorious work.[38]

He also invited JR to visit some more schools.

Washington was planning to travel to Chicago in November to talk to JR about the school building program, but JR announced his decision to accept Washington's offer to visit Tuskegee. At that moment, Washington was dying of kidney failure in a New York hospital. But he continued to try to control events. Knowing that JR would be in Tuskegee, he cabled

Calloway to be sure that JR was taken to the Chehaw School. JR did visit several schools on his trip. As he wrote to Gussie: "We went direct to the school [Tuskegee] but passed four new schools on the way—all were waiting to welcome me and had signs 'Welcome Mr. Rosenwald'—to school. I just stopped long enough to go inside and to thank them for the reception. Such enthusiasm as they evidenced! I am greatly pleased with this work. Not alone it helps them to help themselves but it will serve the community in many ways for years."[39]

JR did not realize it at the time, but over 5,300 schools were to be constructed as part of this program started on a modest scale three years earlier. Washington had showed himself masterful in engaging and maintaining the interest of the Chicago philanthropist. The result was a program that had enormous significance for black education throughout the South. It is true that the schools were segregated, but in that era there was no other way to accomplish anything meaningful in terms of black education in the South. It is also true that these primary schools taught shop, gardening, and dress making. To some, this meant preparing African Americans for menial jobs. But they also taught the "three Rs" and often did a fine job of that. Moreover, the schools did serve to start the slow process of bringing the black and white races together, which was one of JR's primary motivations in engaging in this project. As the decade wore on and black people moving to Northern cities increased exponentially as part of the famous "Great Migration," Southern landowners realized that the only way they could retain black sharecroppers on their land was to help provide schools for their children.

Started by a simple suggestion from Booker T. Washington, the Rosenwald schools were to be one of JR's most important and enduring achievements.

JR and Tuskegee

As long as Booker T. Washington was alive, JR took his service on the Tuskegee board very seriously, perhaps more so than any other board he was on except for the Associated Jewish Charities. This was because of the very special relationship he had with Washington. The two men were in many ways alike. Both were "self-made" men, although Washington had faced far more formidable obstacles, a fact of which JR was keenly aware. They both had an entrepreneurial spirit. Each was an expert in his area, and they began to rely upon each other for advice. For example, JR frequently referred letters he received concerning blacks to Washington; when he wanted to build up his own library of books about blacks, he solicited Washington's advice. In this case, as always, Washington complied, suggesting, among others, books by his rival W. E. B. DuBois. Washington valued JR for his business acumen and frequently consulted him on business matters. Thus, after going carefully over the school's books, he determined that Tuskegee spent approximately 10 percent of its budget on fund-raising, and he asked JR if he thought such a figure was appropriate. JR rightly replied that it seemed entirely adequate.[40] On another occasion, Washington sent JR the draft of a fund-raising appeal. JR looked it over and said he thought it was "very well worked out." But he added: "I believe every form of appeal ought to carry the names of the Trustees with it."[41] This important symbiotic relationship lasted until Washington's death.

The relationship between Sears and Tuskegee was also a close one. Hats and shoes continued to flow into the Alabama college. Sears provided ovens for the school's training kitchens. Books for the school were purchased through Sears at a substantial discount. In 1915, Rosenwald managed to secure a printing press for Tuskegee valued at $2,000 wholesale. Washington used his connection with Sears in other ways as well. In an effort to ascertain whether Tuskegee was paying too much for goods, he sent a series of bills to Sears accountants and asked them to determine whether the amounts paid were reasonable. JR offered $10,000 toward the cost of a much-needed new heating system. This offer served as the impetus that was needed to raise the rest of the money, and Sears experts were sent to Alabama to advise Washington on the best equipment to buy.

JR paved the way for Washington to meet some of his wealthy Jewish friends in New York. He wrote letters of appreciation to major donors he did not even know, such as George Eastman, the noted inventor, who gave the school $10,000. But he was best at persuading others to contribute.

The affection that JR and Gussie felt for the school after repeated trips there was almost palpable. As JR said in a speech in the Tuskegee chapel on February 22, 1915: "Nothing that comes into our lives during the year makes us happier than our visit to Tuskegee."[42] On that same trip, JR met with all the faculty. This meeting probably led to one of the more gracious gestures that JR ever made—a gesture which went way beyond the bounds that an ordinary trustee feels for an institution.

On April 21, 1915, JR wrote to Washington, "If you had an opportunity to divide $5,000 among the staff of Tuskegee, how would you do it?"[43] Washington was overjoyed, and responded with a number of suggestions. What was finally decided on was that any faculty member who had been with the institution a minimum of fifteen years would receive a bonus. Several staff members were also included, such as the cook who had been with Tuskegee from its inception. All told, thirty-four people received checks of between $25 and $275, the equivalent of between $460 and $5,066 today. JR personally drafted the letter that accompanied these checks, and stated that this was a gift that he and Gussie were making in honor of their twenty-fifth wedding anniversary. In thanking JR for his munificence, board chairman Seth Low, president of Columbia University and former mayor of New York, noted: "It is one of the thoughtful things of which one delights to hear because there is in it such a personal quality."[44]

Washington described the atmosphere at Tuskegee on the day the checks were delivered: "I have seldom, if ever, experienced a day when there was such an atmosphere of joy and happiness pervading the whole school grounds as was true of Saturday because of the receipt of your gifts."[45] The response of individual faculty was dignified but euphoric. George Washington Carver, the noted scientist, was thrilled at this "generous and gracious gift." He continued: "I do not feel, however, that I should be paid extra for doing my duty. Again, it adds a responsibility upon me that lies nearest my heart; this will enable me to get certain bits of apparatus, and also to carry out the unique task of showing to the entire South and to some other sections of the world, the wonderful riches that lie beneath their feet."[46]

JR's affection for Tuskegee and for Washington was evident as a result of this special anniversary gift to the teachers, and those concerned about Washington and the institution began to confide in JR rather than one of the other trustees, because it was becoming clear that something was seriously wrong with the principal's health. In early August 1915, JR received a letter from A. R. Stewart, a self-styled friend of Washington's, who said that he was writing to JR because of the gifts to the faculty. Stewart claimed that Washington was deeply worried about his financial situation, that he was $20,000 in debt, and that this was having an effect on his health.[47] JR had Graves send a copy of this letter to fellow board member William Willcox, who said that the matter should be looked into. In late October, the correspondent was the noted black Chicago physician, George C. Hall, who knew Washington well and who had been JR's guest on the train trip of 1913. Hall wrote that Washington was suffering from severe kidney problems and high blood pressure; he needed complete mental and physical rest.[48] This letter, too, was forwarded to Willcox, who reported back to JR that he and other trustees had talked to Washington about his finances and there seemed to be nothing amiss there; on the health front, however, Willcox acknowledged, "I am afraid that his condition is more serious than any of us had suspected, and I think we must at least look forward to an almost complete cessation of his trips about the country and of public addresses." Willcox had asked an abdominal specialist he knew to examine Washington, who was becoming more gravely ill by the day. By early November, Washington was in a New York hospital. He had planned to be at the inauguration of the new president of Fisk University, but instead Emmett Scott, Washington's assistant, represented Tuskegee.

On November 12, Washington's wife Margaret wrote JR a brief note: "Washington is very weak—very ill. . . . It is terrible, Mr. Rosenwald, to see him so broken all at once it seems, and yet he has not been well for a long time."[49] Washington, who knew he was dying, insisted that the end should come at Tuskegee. He barely survived the one-day train trip and died on November 13.

Having just returned from Tuskegee, JR was unable to hurry back for the funeral. However, he did deliver a eulogy at a memorial service at Tuskegee on December 12. "I believe there is no individual among the hundred millions of people in our beloved country whom we could spare less than we can spare Booker T. Washington. . . . I have tried . . . to think of someone whose life means more to the welfare of this country than his life. I am unable to think of one." Summing up what he felt was Washington's influence and legacy, JR quoted a newspaper editorial which said that the Tuskegee founder had started a movement whose goal was "interpreting one race to another."[50]

Almost before Washington was laid in his tomb, the question of his successor arose. William Willcox wrote to JR about the funeral and stated: "We found a very strong sentiment for Major Moton as a successor."[51] Robert R. Moton was the second in command at Hampton Institute. JR, however, was not at all in favor of Moton. His chosen candidate was

Emmett Scott. JR had been at the inauguration of Fisk's new president along with Scott, and he and Scott had shared a Pullman car to Montgomery following the Fisk ceremony. The two men talked late into the night, and the subject of the succession inevitably came up. JR made no promises, but his support for Scott was strengthened by this encounter and by several days of conversations in Chicago later that month. Other people began writing JR on Scott's behalf, including Washington's nephew, G. W. A. Johnston, and James C. Napier, a banker-lawyer from Nashville, friend and confidant of Washington, and one of the highest ranking black officeholders in America (Register of the Treasury). JR needed little convincing. He had spoken to various influential faculty members when he was at Tuskegee just before Washington's death and had asked them, confidentially, who they preferred as successor should the principal die. All had named Scott. In letters and telegrams to his fellow trustees such as Seth Low and Theodore Roosevelt, JR pleaded Scott's case. Quoting others, he said that Moton, who had often visited Tuskegee, could not be taken seriously. He was good at telling jokes and singing but had never delivered a substantive address. He said that Moton had a certain "bumptious" quality and lacked the gravitas that the office of principal demanded. But almost from the beginning it was clear that JR was swimming against the tide. Finally, Theodore Roosevelt wrote JR and said that he had gone to Tuskegee convinced that Scott was the right man. But he had met Moton on the train and talked to him for hours and was impressed by what he had seen and heard. Realizing that the cause was lost, JR replied to the former president that he was relieved by this good account of Moton and trusted Roosevelt's good judgment. Thus it was no surprise when a committee of five trustees chose Moton as the second principal of Tuskegee.

Although JR remained on the board of trustees of Tuskegee, he never got on well with Moton. The close bond that had existed between JR and Washington could not be duplicated. Although he did not hold grudges, JR felt that the trustees had made a major mistake in not naming Scott to the principalship. He may have been correct in his judgment. Moton was not a reincarnation of Washington. He was not a great manager, and he was not the gifted spokesman for blacks that the trustees hoped he would be.

Scott stayed on at Tuskegee for two unhappy years, then accepted a post as assistant secretary in the War Department and went on to become secretary-treasurer at Howard University. JR continued to encounter him through the years.

Embarrassments: Mound Bayou and "Birth of a Race"

JR was usually extremely cautious about investing money, but in one instance his friendship for Washington brought him into singularly unproductive and unfortunate territory. This was his investment in the town of Mound Bayou, Mississippi.

Mound Bayou looked and felt like the setting for a Zora Neale Hurston novel. The town was founded by Isaiah Montgomery, a former slave who had been a servant of Jefferson Davis. It was intended to be a self-sufficient black community filled with farmers and prosperous black-owned businesses. This was to be the epitome of Washington's principle of self-help in action. Unfortunately, this vision did not conform to reality.

JR encountered Montgomery at the funeral of a friend who had been a passenger on the *Titanic.*[52] Montgomery told JR that black farmers near Mound Bayou were being gouged by banks—they were being charged twice the rate of interest on a first mortgage as was charged to white farmers. JR offered, under certain conditions, to loan the Bank of Mound Bayou an initial $50,000 that could be loaned out at 5 percent interest. If this money were recovered, JR offered to give 1 percent back to the community. He added that, if the project were successful, he would increase the loan to a total of $250,000, provided another $250,000 could be raised from other sources.[53] Having made this offer, JR then sent the entire correspondence with Montgomery to Washington and asked for his advice. Washington replied that he had looked over the correspondence and thought the plan excellent. JR, however, began to have second thoughts about this scheme and let it drop. Affairs at the bank then took a decided turn for the worse. In response to the pleas of Washington, JR loaned the bank $5,000. But it was too late. A couple of months later, state regulators forced the bank to close. Although it reopened briefly in October the following year, JR never recovered his money.

Meanwhile, another player had appeared on the Mound Bayou scene, an associate of Montgomery, Charles Banks. Banks planned to start a mill to manufacture cottonseed oil. He had a building and machinery, but he needed startup capital. At a meeting that Washington arranged between

Banks and JR during the Tuskegee trustees' meeting of 1913, JR agreed to purchase $25,000 worth of 6 percent bonds in the cottonseed oil mill if an additional $15,000 in such bonds could be sold. Banks tried without success to sell the remaining bonds to companies that manufactured machinery used in cottonseed oil mills. He finally sold the bonds to B. B. Harvey, a rival white mill owner in Memphis who turned out to be an unscrupulous rogue. "Harvey secured a lease on the Mound Bayou mill and became, in effect, its manager," but Banks never revealed this fact to either JR or Washington.[54] In 1914, an economic depression hit the South brought on by World War I. Harvey's Memphis mill went bankrupt, but he used JR's money to milk the Mound Bayou mill for a time until it, too, went bankrupt in January 1915. Various efforts to enlist JR's assistance to restart it never succeeded. JR's beneficent $25,000 loan went up in smoke.[55] This was one of the few instances in which JR let his heart overrule his head in relation to an investment or a donation.

Another embarrassing incident that indirectly involved Booker T. Washington centered around the early days of the film industry. JR was deeply distressed by reports he heard about film director D. W. Griffith's racist epic *The Birth of a Nation,* and he wrote to Graves in April 1915 suggesting that a protest be drawn up and signed by everyone who had been to Tuskegee as his guest. Graves responded that the subject of the film was the topic of a meeting of the Chicago chapter of the NAACP of which JR was an important member and where Graves was filling in for his employer. The secretary reported that everyone was "'up and coming' for a vigorous fight."[56] Rumors abounded, complicated by the viewpoint of a new mayor, "Big Bill" Thompson, who had just been installed. Ultimately, Thompson did come out in opposition to presenting the movie. JR was delighted and wrote the mayor one of the few letters of praise he ever sent him: "[L]et me commend without reserve the splendid stand you have taken in declining the permit to present the play 'The Birth of the Nation' in Chicago."[57] Unfortunately, Thompson soon reversed himself, and the movie opened in Chicago anyway.

The idea of a counterweight to *Birth of a Nation* came up later that year, just before Washington's death. As JR and Emmett Scott were traveling from Nashville to Montgomery in a Pullman car, Scott told JR that he felt the best antidote to the Griffith film would be a movie based on *Up from Slavery.* Accordingly, he had secured the rights to the book and had contacted Edwin Barker, who had made several industrial movies for International Harvester. Scott said that Barker was enthusiastic about the idea. So was JR, but nothing really occurred until the summer of 1916 when Barker wrote asking for a testimonial from JR. By this time, Scott was involved in writing a screenplay, and the film was tentatively titled "Birth of a Race." JR hastened to give this project his blessing: "In my opinion, the creation of a photoplay designed to help remove misunderstandings between the White and Colored races, to make for more sympathetic and helpful relationships, and to show the best of both races rather than the worst of either is a task worth while undertaking."[58] This endorsement was to prove a mistake.

Barker turned the production of the film over to Giles Cory, a rascal who, to drum up money, issued a prospectus quoting JR and implying that JR had a financial interest in the film. Furious, JR had his lawyer approach Cory to threaten him with legal action if he continued to lie about JR's involvement. Although Cory promised to desist, JR was haunted by rumors of his financial stake in the movie for the next two years. *The Birth of a Race* was eventually completed and was both an artistic and financial disaster.

Black Organizations and the YMCA Program

Attempting to stop the showing of *Birth of a Nation* was perhaps the most actively involved JR became in the NAACP and the Urban League, but he played a very important role as a backer of both organizations, which at that time were in their infancy. He provided crucial initial support, guaranteeing 20 percent of their budgets. He believed that both the NAACP and the Urban League were engaging in effective work that was not being done by other organizations.

JR's interest in the NAACP dates from 1910. By 1913, he was donating $1,000 a year to the national organization, and he was on the board of the Chicago chapter. In that same year, he was instrumental in staging a mass meeting to celebrate the fiftieth anniversary of the Emancipation Proclamation. JR gave $100 toward the expenses of the meeting and $50 in cash on the spot to stimulate a fund drive. In addition, he disclosed that Sears was working to hire blacks, a significant development at a time

when most mainstream Chicago businesses refused to hire African Americans except as strike breakers.[59] Graves, who was active in the organization in JR's absence, suggested that the Chicago philanthropist agree to pay

$500 a year (one-quarter of the chapter's budget) for five years. JR acceded to that request.

Unlike the NAACP, which concentrated on the legal rights of African Americans, the Urban League was concerned with providing them opportunities for meaningful and gainful employment. JR was introduced to the Urban League by his friend Paul Sachs, the man who had first awakened him to the plight of blacks. At Sachs's urging, JR contributed $2,000 to the fledgling organization in 1912 and 1913. In June 1913, JR informed Sachs that he would donate 20 percent of the League's budget for five years provided the remainder of the budget was guaranteed by other sources. He followed through on his pledge, but the Urban League failed to raise enough additional money to justify an increase in JR's donation until 1918.[60]

Although JR did little more than contribute to these black organizations, the amounts that he gave in terms of the percentage of their budgets were critical in starting these groups on a sound financial footing. And when the local chapters began, he helped them with more than money. When the Chicago branch of the Urban League began in 1917, JR was on its board, and eventually he found himself deeply involved in tumultuous events.

Between 1913 and 1916, five black YMCAs opened as a result of the challenge grant that JR had launched in 1911. Ys were built in Chicago, Indianapolis, Philadelphia, Kansas City, and Cincinnati. Others were started in Brooklyn, Baltimore, St. Louis, and Columbus. All of these YMCAs opened after 1916.

The campaigns to meet the Rosenwald match were organized by Jesse Moorland and were conducted with vigor. Typical was the campaign in St. Louis, whose Y opened in 1919. There, $68,947 was collected in just ten days by twenty-two teams coordinated by Moorland. Donations ranged from 25 cents to $3,500.[61] In most cases, both blacks and whites cooperated in the fund-raising effort, although the results were not always what was anticipated. For example, L. Wilbur Messer evinced disappointment at the relatively small number of blacks who contributed to the Chicago Y. He claimed that only a third of the black pledges had been collected.[62] In St. Louis, the situation was reversed. More money was collected from blacks than from whites. Although he was happy with the results once the Ys were built, JR was aggravated by the slow pace at which the program proceeded.

The Wabash Avenue YMCA in Chicago formally opened on June 15, 1913. At the ceremonies JR gave another speech on prejudice. It was one of his better efforts at oratory.

He began by stating how pleased he was with the nationwide building campaign, named those cities which were in the process of erecting black Ys, and then paraphrased Lincoln's Gettysburg Address:

> We should here dedicate more than this building. We should dedicate ourselves to the unfinished work, to the great task before us of removing race hatred, of which, unfortunately, so much exists; of bringing about a universal acceptance that it is the individual and not the race that counts.

He ended by quoting Ralph Waldo Emerson and an unnamed orator in Washington, who said:

> The man who hates the black man because he is black has the same spirit as he who hates the poor man because he is poor. It is the spirit of caste. I am the inferior of any man whose rights I trample under foot. Men are not superior by the accidents of race or color. They are superior who have the best heart, the best brain. Superiority is born of honesty, of virtue, of charity, and, above all, of the love of liberty. Of one thing you colored men can rest assured: The best white people are your friends.[63]

Unfortunately, JR also added a supermoralistic passage. Blacks were responsible for each others' behavior just as whites were. Blacks should realize that those who frequent saloons "or other unwholesome places" were hurting not only themselves but the whole race. The real message that JR wished to convey, however, was one of patience ("you must realize that, in the evolution of a race, time counted by generations is necessary") and of hope. In an article written for the YMCA's newsletter in January 1914, JR reprised many of the themes (and some of the same words) used in his dedicatory speech. In the newsletter he stated that he believed the very presence of these new YMCAs was a reflection of hope.

> These buildings made possible by the gifts and labor of so many are only instances of the fact that conditions [for blacks] are improving and evidence that the contact of the white and Negro races will surely lead to a better understanding of each other.[64]

This theme, that the building of the Ys, like the construction of the schools, would bring the races together, was one that JR deeply believed, and he referred to it frequently. As he wrote a few months after the Wabash Y dedication: "I earnestly hope that out of this campaign and from the use of the new YMCA building there will grow . . . a feeling not of mere tolerance but of helpfulness; and that gradually the monstrous injustice caused by race prejudice will disappear."[65]

Compared to the vast majority of his fellow white Chicagoans, JR's views on racial prejudice were enlightened. Even such a reformer as Graham Taylor called blacks "depraved," and Jane Addams spoke of blacks' "lack of inherited control."[66] Given the prejudice of his fellow citizens, JR knew that an integrated Y was an impossibility. The way the program had been presented to him from the beginning had whites and blacks at the highest leadership levels of the YMCA working to solve a common problem. The manner in which he established his challenge grant program, with the white leadership of a Y in each city mentoring its black counterpart (which had its own leadership), meant that blacks and whites would continue to work together in this cause.

The Wabash Y was a magnificent building of five stories, made of solid brick. It contained a swimming pool with the attendant lockers and showers on the first floor; a reading room, billiard room, gymnasium, dining room, and offices on the second floor; and 114 dormitory rooms on the upper three floors. The Wabash Y was one of the few safe places in Chicago where a black man visiting the city with no friends or relatives could reside. The Pullman Company contributed $10,000 to the building so that its porters would have a clean and comfortable place to stay during layovers. Moreover, the Wabash Y was to become a hub of the vibrant black community on the South Side of Chicago that became known as "Bronzeville." During the terrible race riots of 1919, it became a command center. Moreover, during that turbulent period, the Wabash Y was a place where white businesses that employed blacks, such as the meatpacking plants in the Stockyards, could distribute much-needed paychecks to their black employees.[67]

Yet not everyone was overjoyed by the dedication of the Wabash Y. An article headlined "'Jim Crow' Y.M.C.A. Dedicated . . . Wealthy Jew Gives Money to Aid Establishment of the Color Line," appeared in a black newspaper, the *Cleveland Gazette,* with a rather different slant: "The idea of removing race hatred by establishing an institution which draws the color line! How can it be done? The trouble today is that the races are getting further and further apart. Race hatred can only be removed by free racial intermingling in religion as well as business."[68]

Who was right in this debate? The YMCAs clearly were segregated. Yet blacks did benefit, and even the black author admitted it was a beautiful facility. Moreover, unlike the black donors to the schools, who for the most part were truly impoverished, some urban blacks had become wealthy and successful, and they were motivated to donate on a level far above anything that had ever been seen before. Gifts from African Americans in the thousand dollar range were not common, but they occurred in virtually every city where a Rosenwald Y was built. The donors of these gifts are described in an article written by Booker T. Washington for the *Outlook* magazine in 1914. Washington described JR's gift: "[It] has proved to be one of the wisest and best-paying philanthropic investments of which I have any knowledge. In fact, I doubt if there is any single gift to any public institution that has brought a greater return to the community than this one single benefaction, which is all the more interesting because it is the gift of a Jew to a Christian religious institution."[69] After quoting Jesse Moorland to the effect that JR's only dissatisfaction is that more Ys in more cities had not taken advantage of his offer, Washington goes on to describe some of the wealthy blacks who contributed to Rosenwald Ys in their communities. For example, Mrs. C. J. Walker of Indianapolis, who became wealthy in the hair care and beauty product business, gave $1,000 to that city's Y. These black entrepreneurs had been stimulated to donate what for most of them were generous sums to the YMCAs because of JR's challenge grant and the well-organized campaigns conducted by Jesse Moorland in cities where the local white YMCA indicated it was prepared to launch a successful fund drive. The fact that they had had a hand in building such a structure did give members of the black community a feeling of pride. Thus, despite the criticism of some African Americans, which appears valid when seen from the standpoint of today, many blacks believed that JR's contribution had sparked an important force in their community.

JR himself was proud of this initiative and the way it was progressing. In a statement that he issued to Graves, the Chicago philanthropist said: "The products of these campaigns have been often of equal or greater importance than the definite object for which the campaign was conducted.

I am informed that in many cases, a better financial system has been adopted in churches and organizations controlled by the colored people as a result of these campaigns. There has also been a realization of ability to do things in a united way, under a well directed system that has surprised the colored people and their friends."[70] JR went on to list other benefits of the Ys. Membership had doubled in one year, boys were learning job skills and the work ethic, and men were taking classes in such advanced subjects as auto mechanics.

Sears, the Vice Commission Hearings, and Profit Sharing

At the same time that Julius Rosenwald was engaged in a multiplicity of philanthropic activities, he was still the CEO of Sears, and the company was enjoying unprecedented prosperity. This was also a time when JR became entangled with political opponents, determined to besmirch what, up to that time, had been a sterling public image. From these troubles emerged something that was more important and had more far-reaching implications than the reputation of one man: the Sears profit sharing plan.

Chicago in the 1910s was not only a center of the meatpacking industry and the steel mills, the city "of the broad shoulders." Its red light district also was notorious. Some 5,000 women and girls plied their trade in its saloons, dance halls, and brothels. Many were immigrants, newly arrived in America, who were lured into a life of degradation by pimps whom they encountered as they arrived at train stations. Others were "girls straight off the farm." There were myriad reasons why such women turned to "the oldest profession." Some reformers were determined to get at the root causes and alleviate the problem.

The 1910 report of the Chicago Vice Commission, on which JR served, suggested that there was an important link between low wages and women turning to prostitution. While the bulk of the report languished on shelves, this particular issue was examined with vigor by a commission of the state senate chaired by Lieutenant Governor Barrett O'Hara, a Democrat who was eager to play political hardball and tarnish the reputation of such staunch Republicans as Julius Rosenwald, the head of a Chicago concern that employed large numbers of young women. On March 7, 1913, JR appeared before the commission as a witness to present testimony on the salary scale and employment practices regarding women in effect at Sears, Roebuck. He intended to cooperate fully, and he presented the commission with masses of employee records. What JR, always naive in dealing with politicians, failed to realize was that this information and his testimony would be turned against him and that the picture of him that would emerge from his day of testimony would be that of a penny-pinching capitalist.

JR testified that as of March 8, 1913, Sears employed 4,732 women and girls. The average wage paid to the women was $9.12 per week. The number of males employed at Sears was 4,171; the average weekly wage paid to men and boys was $15.41, which even one of the commissioners remarked was "a much higher average than obtained in many other establishments."[71] The focus of the hearings was the wages and working conditions of girls ages sixteen to eighteen and over eighteen. The lowest wages paid to Sears employees went to 119 sixteen-year-old girls who were paid $5 per week. JR testified that all these girls, when interviewed, stated that they were living at home and were being supported by their fathers, although Sears did not conduct any background check to ensure that they were telling the truth. After six months at the $5 rate, these youngest girls were given a 50 cent raise. The vast majority of women and girls employed at Sears received a minimum wage of $8 per week, although women could rise to relatively important positions and some were receiving salaries of as much as $50 per week. The big issue before the commission was whether, by paying some female employees only $5 weekly, JR was driving them into prostitution as the only possible means of making ends meet. From other testimony, the commission determined that even $8 a week was insufficient for a woman to live decently in the Chicago of that era.

The questioning turned embarrassing when O'Hara asked JR what the profits of Sears were in 1911. Coming after hours of testimony about wages of $8 a week, the answer, over $7 million, was stunning.

> Q. Could you take $2 million from the total profits of $7 million and apply it to the wages of employees and still pay interest on the money invested in your business?
>
> A. I would say we could take $2 million and still pay some dividend, some income to the shareholders of the company.
>
> Q. What dividend are you paying now, Mr. Rosenwald?
>
> A. We are paying now 7 percent on all the preferred and common stock of the company.

Q. How much surplus have you after paying the dividend?

A. I would not want to state that offhand; I am not just sure what that figure is. I think our surplus according to our books was something in the neighborhood of $12 million at the end of the year 1912. . . .

Q. If, after investigating the matter yourself, you reach the conclusion that you can pay the girls enough money to live on decently, you will take money from the surplus fund and give it to them in decent wages?

A. I wouldn't say we will take it from the surplus fund. We endeavor to pay all our employees what we feel is fair wages and will always continue to do so.[72]

One can almost see JR bridling at this question. As he said many times during his testimony, he absolutely rejected the entire premise of the commission. And, although he was a generous philanthropist, he was also a hardheaded businessman who thought that business and philanthropy should not be mixed. He paid his employees what he knew was the prevailing wage.[73]

According to the testimony of others before the commission, entry-level female workers at Montgomery Ward were paid between $5 and $6 a week. A representative of Marshall Field's indicated that no woman over eighteen received less than $6 a week, which was actually worse than the case at Sears. Although JR raised the issue of competition in the hearing, it fell on deaf ears. So did his statements that working conditions at Sears were considered excellent. Instead, the commission heard testimony from two former Sears employees who had worked in the department that wrote address labels by hand. They said that there was a woman in charge whose job was to reprimand and scold girls who did not perform adequately or fast enough. This official scold was not accused of physically beating the girls, merely of issuing verbal tongue lashings that often left them in tears. Such a heartrending picture does not seem to be borne out by the facts.

Sears was no sweatshop operation. As JR testified, "If a girl is sick, we send a nurse to take care of her,"[74] which is better care than one would receive today. Working hours were long, but that was also true throughout the industry. Allowances were made for age. Girls under sixteen worked eight hours a day; those over sixteen worked eight and three-quarter hours. The maximum that anyone could work was nine and a quarter hours. The work day started at 8:00 A.M. and went to 5:30. Sunday work was not uncommon, and no overtime was paid. Again, however, these were common standards throughout the retail industry.

For a man as conscious of his image as JR was, the hearings were a public relations disaster. The following exchange was widely published and did not cast the Sears president in a good light.

> Senator Juhl: If you do not mind telling us, what is your personal income from the corporation?
>
> A. I would not want to answer that question.
>
> Q. Could you, Mr. Rosenwald, live on $8 a week?
>
> A. That is pretty hard to tell without trying.
>
> Q. Have you ever tried?
>
> A. No, I don't think I ever tried.[75]

Yet the premise at the core of the commission hearings was indeed spurious. Graham Taylor, who had served on the Chicago Vice Commission with JR, testified later, in a very scholarly presentation, and indicated that there were numerous reasons why women and girls turned to prostitution. Low wages was cited as a reason by some, but only a relatively small percentage. Even Jane Addams attacked the O'Hara Commission, thus coming to JR's defense: "Throughout the investigation, the paramount object of the committee seemed to be to develop a connection between the wages paid to women and girls and immorality. The questions that should have been considered are: (1) How much can a given industry afford to pay its workers, and (2) How much is required by a worker to enable her to live decently?"[76] It is obvious that JR could not have continued on friendly terms with Jane Addams if she felt that he was exploiting his female employees.

Still, much damage had been done to Julius Rosenwald's reputation, and for the next two years, his political enemies could gleefully point to the O'Hara Commission testimony as evidence that this supposed philanthropist was nothing but a hypocrite.

JR was aware of the political ramifications of the hearings, and when the commission traveled to Washington to press for a minimum wage law for women and arranged a meeting with Woodrow Wilson, JR wrote the president, denouncing O'Hara and his cohorts. "I conscientiously believe he has done more to injure the good name of the women of this country than any man has ever done or probably will do. He has led the women wage earners of this country to believe that they are justified in leading an immoral life if they do not earn a certain wage. He has given the mothers of these young women justification for condoning immorality in them for the same reason."[77]

Much the same point was made three months later in a statement issued to the press before JR's second appearance before the O'Hara Commission. In this statement, which was officially barred from the hearings, JR roasted his adversaries. He had tried to comply fully, but the commission had ignored all the positive information at hand; they had concentrated solely on attacking him politically.[78] In his testimony, before the commission the same day, JR was noticeably less forthcoming, saying that he would stick only to the facts, that Sears had nothing to hide, but he would not offer any opinions because these were clearly twisted in ways he did not believe were justified.

Whether the Sears profit sharing plan was, in fact, a direct result of the O'Hara hearings is far from clear. That plan was developed in 1916, three years after the hearings had concluded. Moreover, there may have been precedents for the profit sharing plan within Sears. JR testified about these in his first appearance before the commission, but the import of his testimony was drowned out by the attention given to the $5 a week apprentices. As he told the commissioners: "I would also like [the commission] to have this information, that all of our employees who have been in our employ five years or more receive, on the anniversary of their engagement in the service, an additional compensation of from 5 to 10 percent of their yearly earnings. I would also like to state for the benefit of the Committee that over one thousand of our women employees have savings accounts and a goodly number are stockholders in the company."[79]

Although it is unlikely that JR was lying, this statement cannot be corroborated from available evidence. One of the reasons the profit sharing plan was started was to induce people to save, although a savings bank for Sears employees paying 5 percent interest had existed since around 1907.[80] Perhaps there was some sort of pilot program occurring in 1913.

The profit sharing plan was part of the movement of "welfare capitalism" which JR and Richard Sears had championed. A number of companies including Procter and Gamble, U.S. Steel, and Ford had developed profit sharing plans between the 1880s and the outbreak of World War I. Of the 250 that did so, 60 had a form of stock ownership plan somewhat similar to that of Sears.[81]

Historians are divided as to the exact origins of the profit sharing plan at Sears, Roebuck. Werner believes that the idea came from a letter to JR from Mrs. Joseph T. Bowen written on February 11, 1915. JR served on the board of Hull House with Mrs. Bowen and knew her well. Mrs. Bowen wrote:

> As a stockholder, I am, of course, glad that the Company has had such prosperous years that it can afford to pay me such a large return upon my investment, but I must also confess to a feeling of responsibility as a stockholder—and perhaps some sense of guilt—that in these hard times so large a sum is to be distributed among the stockholders and that the employees are to have no share whatever in it. . . . [S]ome distribution of profits would not only tend to better the feeling between employer and employed, but would redound to the interest of the Company in better service, as the employee would feel that he was not only a cog in a machine, but a participant in the process of a business created by his work.[82]

Emmet and Jeuck cite the Bowen letter but also point out that JR was highly enthusiastic about a profit sharing plan that the Harris Trust & Savings Bank instituted for their employees on January 1, 1916.[83] A third possibility also exists. Graham Taylor had taught a course for industrial welfare workers in an early incarnation of the School of Civics and Philanthropy in 1906 and was clearly familiar with various aspects of "welfare capitalism."[84]

Emmet and Jeuck state that it was Albert Loeb, not JR, who was the officer primarily interested in the plan and that he was the one who worked out all the details.[85] Regardless of who initiated and developed the profit sharing plan, JR had to sign off on it, and he was enthusiastic about it. The plan formally came into existence on July 1, 1916. Immediately it involved more people in profit sharing than any company in America.

The terms of the Sears, Roebuck Employees Savings and Profit Sharing Plan were as follows: Any employee who had been with the firm three years or more was entitled to participate. To enroll, an employee had to deposit in the program 5 percent of his or her salary. The company then deposited in the employee's account an amount equal to 5 percent of its net earnings (before accounting for deductions paid to stockholders). Employees were forbidden to deposit more than 5 percent of their salary or more than $150 per year. This last provision was done so that the higher paid employees would not have the bulk of the money in the fund and reap the lion's share of the rewards.

An employee who worked for Sears for ten years could withdraw the full amount, including the company's share. An employee who worked for the company less than ten years could withdraw the amount he/she had deposited, plus interest at 5 percent per annum compounded semiannually. An exception was made for a woman who wished to draw her money out of the fund to marry. As was customary in that era, no married woman could work at Sears. If she had worked for Sears for five years, she could withdraw the full amount. If an employee vested in the fund died, his/her estate was entitled to the full amount. The fund was administered by a board of five trustees, three of whom were company officers: initially JR, Albert Loeb, and Otto Doering; the other two were employees who were not officers. The money in the fund was invested in shares of Sears stock, which rose rapidly until 1921, which meant that Sears employees vested in the fund benefited substantially.

The first year of its existence, the fund operated for only six months. The number of employees who participated in it was 6,064. Employee deposits were $136,311. The company's contribution was $412,215, and the value of the stock held by the fund was $545,893. By 1924, over 10,000 employees were participating in the fund, and the value of the stock had climbed to over $8 million. Typical of an employee's experience in 1916 was that of Frank Vesely, who began working at Sears in May 1913. He invested $14.30 in the fund, the Company put in $44.19, and at the end of the year he had $58.49 worth of Sears stock. The Sears profit sharing plan was far more generous than other similar corporate plans, which is presumably why it lasted far longer.

There were many reasons why companies started such plans. Among those that applied to Sears was that such plans would induce habits of thrift in workers and might lead to increased productivity.

A second reason, which might link the Sears plan to the O'Hara Commission investigation was its value as public relations. The profit sharing plan was prominently mentioned in two out of three important articles about Sears and JR that appeared between December 1916 and December 1917. Two of these interviews were widely quoted and helped to spread the image of JR as a kind and astute businessman, loving family man, and thoughtful philanthropist. In each article, the story of the rise of Sears, Roebuck was recounted, often with the facts slightly glossed over. Richard Sears always emerged as a fine, upstanding individual who, in 1908, simply resigned—no explanation was ever given.

One of these interviews, entitled "The Making of a 'Mail Order Menace,'" appeared in the *Nation's Business* in December 1917 and was widely reprinted. Asked about his philosophy of business, JR replied: "[I try] to feel that I am always selling merchandise to myself. I would stand on both sides of the counter, if we had a counter." Later he was asked about the still-burning charge from "mom-and-pop" retail stores that mail-order houses like Sears were ruining their business. JR noted: "Mail-order houses cannot monopolize the retail trade of the United States, but they can, in a measure, regulate it and improve it as to service."[86]

Other ideas about business infuse the newsletter of Joe Mitchell Chapple, part of a series of personal interviews with business leaders. Here, according to Chapple, is JR discussing the profit sharing plan:

> We never use the word "welfare" or "pension." The latter has a sort of decrepit worn-out sound that any man in the vigor of his mature years dislikes. Our cooperative and profit sharing plan works out the purpose of protection in declining years as a matter of just equity. It is what the man deserves, and is only a deferred payment in recognition of meritorious service.[87]

JR also told Chapple that part of the reason for Sears's success was that he liked to promote from within. Highlighting his usual modesty, he offered this advice, which still rings true today: "The man who acknowledges what his assistants have accomplished, rather than take all the credit himself, emphasizes his ability as an executive by getting their good will and continued loyalty."[88] Perhaps it says something about the personalities of American businessmen of that era that such a statement should have been regarded as extraordinary. Chapple, who was thoroughly smitten with his interviewee, summed up JR: "Unflagging and unfailing thoughtfulness is a keynote in the make-up of Julius Rosenwald. It is felt by even the smallest and most isolated friend or casual acquaintance. He has infused into business a soul and impulse that serve the highest and best ethical purpose."[89]

By far the most influential article that appeared at this time was by a young business writer, B. C. Forbes, who later founded his own magazine. Forbes believed he had "discovered" JR and that he represented the best of American business. He wrote several articles praising the Sears president. The first, part of a series that became a book entitled *Men Who Are Making America,* appeared in *Leslie's Weekly* on December 7, 1916. Calling JR a "miracle worker," Forbes highlighted JR's modesty in a fashion similar to Chapple. He felt that this story about JR typified the man and explained a good deal about the success of the business he ran. "A friend was riding home with Mr. Rosenwald one day as the more than 13,000 Chicago employees were pouring out of the principal establishment. 'How does it feel, Mr. Rosenwald, to have so many people working for you?' the friend asked. 'Why, I never think of it in that way,' he replied. 'I always think of them as just working with me.'" Forbes also describes how, when the Sears "plant" was built in 1906, JR's associates decided that his office was too austere and that it needed a fine Oriental rug to spruce up the place. They went ahead and purchased the rug—which remained rolled up in a corner for weeks and then disappeared. "If linoleum covered floors were good enough for his workers, they were good enough for him!" concluded Forbes. The enthusiastic writer called the profit sharing plan "perhaps his crowning achievement" and added, "Students of the subject have pronounced the Plan the best ever conceived."

Forbes summed up JR as follows:

> The most notable thing about Julius Rosenwald is not any superhuman business ability, nor any phenomenal smartness in seeing and seizing mercantile opportunities, nor any transcendent qualities as a merchant. *The greatest thing about Julius Rosenwald is not his business but himself, not what he has but what he is,* his character, his personality, his sincerity, his honesty, his democracy, his thoughtfulness, his charity of heart, his catholicity of sympathy, his consuming desire to help the less fortunate of his fellow creatures, be they black or white, Jews or Gentiles, young or old.[90]

These laudatory articles undoubtedly would have helped JR withstand another public relations disaster that occurred in this era: JR's political enemies had him investigated for tax evasion in May 1913.

The Bureau of Public Efficiency, of which JR was president, was a watchdog group dedicated to good local government. It became involved in investigating a scandal dealing with voting machines. The machines cost almost $1,000 apiece and were complicated to operate and faulty. JR was bound to make enemies from the members of the "political machine." They struck in May 1913. JR was denounced on the floor of the Chicago City Council as a tax cheat who had failed to file for thousands of dollars in personal property taxes. He was investigated by a tax commission, and it was alleged that these charges were true. The tax laws at this time in Chicago were exceedingly complex and open to all kinds of abuse. Many wealthy citizens routinely ignored them, believing them to be totally unfair. JR was asked to file a schedule of his personal property which, it was alleged, included 147,701 shares of Sears stock worth some $25 million. He pointedly failed to do so. A year and a half passed. Then, around New Year's Day 1915, a grand jury returned an indictment against JR. The charge was tax evasion.

An impartial observer could see that a group of political enemies was attempting to besmirch the reputation of JR. In 1913 his personal property taxes had amounted to $166,667, the highest amount paid by any citizen of Cook County. In 1914, he was assessed on personal property worth $2.5 million and refused to pay the tax. The fine for failure to comply was all of $200. JR was willing to serve as both scapegoat and example in the hope that his case would demonstrate the fallacy of the system. The press was filled with stories about this case. Some newspapers rallied to his defense, and many friends backed him, such as Judge Harry Fisher, who wrote JR: "I hope that the only motive for this prosecution was to select a man about whose fair dealing there could be no question, and thereby demonstrate that our best citizens cannot adjust themselves to such a pernicious law. To demonstrate that the law is at fault and not the man."[91] JR never had to appear in court. His lawyer ably argued his client's case, and the judge dismissed it without any possibility of appeal. It was a victory for JR and the cause of reform, but the label "tax dodger" continued to be raised occasionally by JR's political enemies.

The Bureau of Public Efficiency did score a victory with the voting machine scandal when Judge Kennesaw Mountain Landis ruled against the City on that issue in 1915.[92]

Jewish Causes

JR had been president of the Associated Jewish Charities from 1908 through 1911. Following a year's hiatus, he served as president again from 1913 through 1917. During this time, donations to the organization rose considerably. Moreover, JR was proud of the fact that administrative costs were kept exceedingly low.

During his second term, JR was concerned with the Federated Orthodox Jewish Charities. The newer organization was constantly struggling financially. JR and the Associated helped provide technical assistance to the Eastern European Jewish organization. The Associated board also agreed to raise $35,000 for it for two years. JR requested even more help, which was forthcoming and which further served to cement the bond between the two communities of Judaism.[93]

JR continued to be active in various national and international Jewish organizations, but what primarily attracted his interest in the period from December 1913 through 1915 was the Leo Frank case, one of the more notorious miscarriages of justice in American history. 

On April 26, 1913, Mary Phagan, a teenage girl who worked at the National Pencil Factory in Atlanta, was murdered. A number of suspects were arrested provisionally, including Leo Frank, a twenty-nine-year-old supervisor at the factory who was president of B'nai B'rith in Atlanta's burgeoning Jewish community. Although the evidence against Frank was circumstantial at best, prosecutors decided that he was guilty. The trial ran from July to August, and Leo Frank was sentenced to death. The case was appealed to the Georgia Supreme Court, but Frank lost. Then the case was appealed to the U.S. Supreme Court, which declined to hear it. At the end of June 1915, the outgoing governor of Georgia, John M. Slaton, besieged with letters to spare Frank's life, commuted the sentence to life imprisonment.

Antisemitism was a serious problem in the South, and it quickly became apparent to Jews throughout the country that Frank was innocent and that he needed financial assistance to press his appeals. JR was approached on behalf of Frank by his friend Albert J. Lasker, and in December 1913 he agreed to match what Lasker gave dollar for dollar, starting with a $1,000 contribution. He ended up giving almost $10,000 to the case, although Lasker, who became so involved that he went to Atlanta and hired detectives to try to find the true murderer, presumably gave more.

JR did not merely give money. In May 1915, after Frank's appeal had been turned down by the U.S. Supreme Court, JR received a letter from his friend Louis Marshall, who had represented Frank before that august body pro bono because he was convinced of Frank's innocence. Marshall urged JR to write Governor Slaton to ask for a pardon. He also asked JR to contact other prominent people to write to the governor. But, reflecting the great delicacy of this case for American Jews, Marshall added that appeals for clemency should not come from Jews because the charge "has been made that the Jews, in seeking commutation, are attempting to save one of their faith irrespective of his guilt or innocence."[94] JR did write these letters to non-Jews. His appeal to William Howard Taft was turned down on the grounds that Taft was not familiar enough with the case, which seems dubious, since the case had been prominently featured in the press for months. Charles G. Dawes did write to the governor. The impassioned letter that JR wrote to Judge Walter Fisher is probably typical of what he wrote to all those on his list—although in writing Fisher, he was defying Marshall because Fisher was a very prominent Jewish jurist. JR's main point was that at each step of the judicial process some lawyer or judge involved had expressed doubts about Frank's guilt. He concluded: "In view of this really tragic situation and to help prevent what the future will undoubtedly prove to have been a great calamity in the judicial taking of innocent life, I ask you, in the interest of justice, to write at once in behalf of Mr. Frank to the governor and also to the board of Prison Commissioners at Atlanta, Georgia."[95]

Leo Frank wrote to JR to thank him for his assistance in July 1914. JR was disappointed with this letter, perhaps thinking that it was a standard thank-you note and that he deserved something a bit more personal.[96] A year later, Frank wrote again:

> Allow me to assure you how profoundly grateful I am for the interest you have taken in my case. I am cognizant of the fact that you have given unselfishly and so largely of yourself to the end that my preservation and vindication become realities.
>
> My life, thank God, has been denied the hue and cry of the unreasoning mob. I am in an environment which, through the kindness of the warden and his staff, has been made as bearable as the circumstances will permit. I am gaining rapidly in health and strength, storing up vitality for the next phase of my battle against ignorance, prejudice, and unreason to the goal of liberty and honor—justly mine, even now.
>
> Surely the day cannot be far distant when, Right and Justice holding complete sway, my vindication and the acknowledgment of my absolute innocence will of necessity result![97]

A week after this letter was written, Frank was stabbed by a fellow prisoner. On August 16, while he was still recovering from his wound, the prison he was in was attacked by an angry mob. Frank was dragged from his bed and lynched.

JR was appalled. The *New York Evening Post* quoted him as follows: "It is almost beyond belief that such a crime committed in Georgia should be possible within the borders of a great nation like ours. It indicates that, with all our boasted freedom, our civilization is not complete, that there are communities, and people in them, to whom due process of law . . . means nothing." He called for all guilty parties, even those who incited the deed in the press or by oratory, to be punished.[98]

The University of Chicago Medical School

Between 1912 and 1916, JR did relatively little for the University of Chicago besides perform his duties as a trustee. He remained on cordial terms with university president Harry Pratt Judson and invited him on the train trip to Tuskegee in 1913. In 1916, however, a project connected with the university was presented to him that genuinely sparked his interest.

JR's close friend Abraham Flexner, an advisor to the Rockefellers, takes the credit for linking JR to the University of Chicago Medical School. Flexner was an expert on medical schools. At the request of the Rockefellers, he had conducted an exhaustive study of American medical education and had discovered that, with the exception of Johns Hopkins, Washington University, and the newly established Rockefeller Institute, American medical schools were deplorable and lagged far behind their European counterparts. Because of his interest in both medical schools and the University of Chicago, to which the Rockefellers had contributed so much, Flexner was eager to establish an outstanding medical school with a national reputation on the South Side of Chicago. The university had a loose affiliation with the Rush College of Medicine, to which JR had been appointed a trustee in 1908. But the affiliation did not work well. Rush was several miles from the University of Chicago campus, and Flexner was convinced that the university needed its own clinics. He approached Judson, who was dubious about this proposal. Judson told the Rockefeller advisor that an attempt had been made by Dr. Frank Billings, a noted physician, to raise money for a medical school, but he had not progressed very far. Flexner asked Judson, "Have you ever asked Rosenwald?" Judson said he had not, but remained doubtful about the outcome. Flexner replied that he would solicit JR.

JR invited his friend to have lunch with him in the dining room of the Sears "plant," where executives and department heads sat around a large communal table. JR placed his guest between himself and J. F. Skinner, one of his chief aides. Skinner, who was feeling ill, asked Flexner what he thought he should do. "Go to Johns Hopkins," replied the Rockefeller aide. After the lunch, JR took Flexner up to his office and asked, "What do you want to see me about?"

Flexner replied, "Mr. Skinner."

"What! You never saw him before in your life."

"Right, but why do you suppose I advised him to go to Johns Hopkins?"

"Because we have nothing like it in Chicago."

"Exactly. How would you like to establish a Johns Hopkins here at the University of Chicago? You have the laboratories. All you lack is the clinics."

"Oh," JR said, "that would make a powerful appeal to me. Come to Ravinia tonight and explain it to Gussie and me."

Flexner traveled to JR's country house and explained why the Rockefellers had put money into Johns Hopkins and Washington University medical schools. He said that to build a showplace medical school at the University of Chicago would cost about $5 million. The Rockefeller Foundation and the General Education Board were prepared to put up $2 million. He asked JR to spearhead a Chicago campaign by pledging $500,000. JR turned to Gussie and asked: "What do you think?" She replied, "I shall be glad to have you do anything that you think is right."[99] It is notable that JR wanted Gussie to participate in the decision. In fact, the gift to the medical school was given in both their names, which was not JR's usual practice.

According to Flexner's autobiography, JR agreed on the spot, but the reality was more drawn out. First, JR was given a tour of the Rockefeller Institute by its head, Abraham Flexner's brother, Simon, and he was much impressed.

Several months went by. Then Flexner informed Judson that JR had summoned him once again to Chicago, presumably to discuss the medical school, and he would be on the next train. Shortly after the meeting between Flexner and JR, Judson offered to accompany JR to view the medical school at Washington University. He also extolled the idea of the new medical facility. JR replied somewhat noncommittally: "The plan is undoubtedly a most worthy and glorious conception."[100]

He was, however, drawing closer to a commitment. On November 13, JR agreed to contribute $500,000 to the new facility.[101] A delighted Judson cabled back: "[This splendid gift] gives an impetus to the movement at just the right time."[102]

JR was not only committed; he was exceedingly enthusiastic. On November 21, he wrote to Judson: "We feel that we are enjoying a rare privilege to be associated in so noble a service for not only the people of our home City but for the 'life of the whole nation,' as one of our friends put it."[103] He also offered to write solicitation letters on behalf of the medical school.

Abraham Flexner had been proved correct. JR's gift did spark numerous other donations from prominent Chicago families. However, because of World War I and the fact that Flexner and the university planners had underestimated the cost of the medical school and then had trouble collecting the funds, the new facility first discussed in 1916 did not actually open until 1927.

Personal Life

JR was engaged in other pursuits besides business and philanthropy before World War I. He continued to be an inveterate traveler and an avid tourist but also more than a mere tourist, for he had a genuine interest in learning about the places he visited and meeting the people who lived there.

A curious honeymoon occurred in early 1914 when JR, Gussie, and various members of the Rosenwald family traveled to Europe, Egypt, Palestine, and Syria. The family was awash in weddings. On November 6, 1913, JR's eldest son, Lessing, married Edith Goodkind. Six days later, daughter Edith married Germon Sulzberger. At the end of December, the two newlywed couples, plus JR and Gussie traveled to Venice, whence they sailed to Alexandria and an extended stay in Egypt.

JR kept a diary of this journey, and there are flashes of personality that shine through it. For example, on their arrival in Cairo: "Drove through the Musky and Bazaar districts of Cairo; our necks gave out—straining to see new things every moment."[104] The party journeyed down the Nile, marveling at the scenery and the wonders they beheld on the way. Edith wrote to her sister Adele: "Our trip is lovely. Of course, I can't rave like Mother over thirteen ruined temples, all alike, but the boat trip is ideal and I love being with the folks. But I never thought of honeymoons as getting up before seven to go sight-seeing."[105] Lessing's new wife also wrote Adele: "Really that Nile trip, as much as I loved it, I realize now that it was work."[106] The honeymooners were only part of the party for the boat trip down the Nile, and even then the various family members were given considerable latitude, so the reality of a honeymoon with one's parents was not as bizarre as such an idea sounds.

After a few days of rest in Luxor, JR and Gussie journeyed back to Cairo alone and then embarked on a nine-day trip in the desert by camel and donkey. On the second day out, JR wrote in his diary: "Like camels so well we think of exchanging our autos for them when we get back." But even the beauties and exoticism of the desert had its disadvantages. When they returned to the comforts of modern civilization on February 13, JR noted "the bathtub looked like the promised land."[107] JR was joined on the expedition by his friend Aaron Aaronsohn, who turned out to be an amateur archeologist among his other talents. JR clearly enjoyed his company. Various members of the Aaronsohn family accompanied JR and Gussie throughout the rest of their visit to the Middle East.

Because of Aaronsohn, they visited Palestine and had an extended visit at the Agricultural Experiment Station at Athlit. JR was clearly impressed by what he saw.

Unlike the typical tourist, JR made an effort to meet the people in the areas in which he was traveling. In Cairo, he spent some time with the leaders of the Jewish community, which was extensive. In Haifa, he invited thirty-three of the leading citizens, including some of the professors at the nascent Technion, to join him for dinner.

When JR, Gussie, and some of the Aaronsohns visited Damascus, the only negative note in the whole diary occurs: "Went to theater in the evening, the worst building I have ever seen for the purpose, and the performance consisted of women and men playing and singing Arabic music—monotonous in the extreme. Later, stupid dancing—nothing vulgar but all senseless; only men in the audience, very few, all smoking nargilahs (water pipes)."[108] Two days later, the group visited some schools in the Jewish quarter of Damascus: "a kindergarten of 250 children in four or five rooms—no apparatus at all—then to an older school, 700 crowded and poorest excuse of teachers' salary $5 a month. Kindergarten teachers $4 a month. Principal $16—excellent teacher." The next day, JR got a lecture on "statistics about conditions existing in Damascus," drove on the Baghdad Road, "a road older than history," and before leaving Damascus gave one of the local Jewish leaders £100, "a very good sum," to use for the schools.[109] JR was generous even as a tourist, donating money where he felt it would do the most good.

What is interesting in JR's account of this journey, aside from his enthusiasm at encountering new sights and experiences, is the total lack of any sense that Europe and the Middle East were hurtling toward a cataclysmic crisis. True, JR was a tourist, but he did try to understand what was happening in the countries he visited. This demonstrates what a shock the outbreak of World War I was to Europeans and residents of the Middle East. Ordinary people did not seem to have any inkling that the old order was about to collapse.

In August 1915, JR was off on another excursion with Gussie, Marion, and William. Their goal was the San Francisco Exposition. But en route they stopped in Glacier National Park, and JR showed a side of himself that was not often visible—the lover of natural beauty. Gussie was the one who wrote at great length about the flowers and grounds of Ravinia and who hired the famous landscape architect Jens Jensen to plan out the gardens. It was Gussie who insisted on having the younger children taught about nature, hiring a woman who was to instruct them about bird calls by waving around stuffed birds on sticks while emitting strange shrieks, much to the hidden hilarity of the children. And it was Gussie who one night uttered the family's memorable line: "Children! Children! Come and see Venus on the front porch!" But JR, it turned out, was a lover of nature, too. On the Egyptian trip he wrote in an aside: "The wild flowers through entire Palestine are fabulously beautiful, and especially coming up on the train."[110] But the trip to Glacier made a profound impression on JR. He still remembered it vividly four years later:

> The fine location and limpid waters of McDermott Lake, which we beheld with joy from our rooms in the Many Glacier Hotel, Iceberg Lake, with its blue floes, to which we made our first horseback trip, the interesting journey (lured on by the whistling marmots) over Swiftcurrent Pass to wonderful Granite Peak, more than 7,000 feet above sea level, from the heights of which we looked out over an expanse of country stretching from Canada to Idaho, our restful excursion upon Upper St. Mary's Lake to Going-to-the-Sun chalets, around which typical Swiss scenery abounds—these and many other things all fascinated us. We loved the ruggedness of the views, the variety of the landscape, the simple grandeur of the mountains, the Alpine lakes, the glaciers, the woods, and with it all there was the comfort provided for the traveler. I may truly say we are going to return.[111]

So impressed was JR with Glacier National Park that he readily donated funds to construct a new trail from Granite Peak Chalet to a point overlooking a scenic region near Flat Top Mountain. The Rosenwald Trail turned out to be eighty miles long and was entirely constructed with JR's gift of $100.[112] It is also notable that among the many organizations JR supported was one whose goal was to make the Indiana Dunes a national park. As JR said in 1917: "Here is the opportunity to make a park very close to the center of the country's population."[113]

Harry Kersey: A View of JR from the Front Seat

A vivid picture of JR at this period comes from a somewhat unlikely source—not a famous business reporter or a colleague of the Sears president but JR's black chauffeur, Harry Kersey, a Canadian who went to work for JR in 1914 and has left a revealing memoir of his experiences.[114]

In April 1914, Harry Kersey was informed by the head of the Pierce Arrow Motor Car Company that the president of Sears, Roebuck needed a chauffeur. Kersey was given a letter of introduction and told to go see Julius Rosenwald. He duly went to Sears, and after a few minutes in JR's outer office, he heard his name called. "I stepped into a very plainly furnished office. At the desk sat a very stern looking gentleman with black hair and a mustache and wearing glasses. . . . He appeared to me to be about fifty years of age and weighing two hundred pounds. I greeted him with a good morning. He did not answer, but reached for my letter and card. He glanced at the letter, took a good look at the Pierce Arrow Company card, and said the letter was too long to read. He informed me he was a busy man and required the services of a willing worker and one who would not get angry and quit on account of hard work." Kersey informed JR that he would appreciate the chance to try. "Well," said JR, "the job pays $100 a month. Is that satisfactory?" Kersey said that it was, and JR told him to report for work the following Monday at the garage at JR's home.

After some initial minor mishaps, Kersey established a routine. JR would play tennis every morning at the private court on his grounds with a neighbor. Kersey would drive the friend home and pick JR up at his mother's home two blocks from 4901 Ellis Avenue. Then they would pick up Loeb and drive out to Sears.

The first few days, JR watched his new chauffeur carefully. One evening, on their way home, Kersey stopped at an intersection where two street cars were going in opposite directions. The northbound car was stopped, but Kersey started across the intersection anyway. JR shouted at him: "How do you know that that northbound car won't start? You can't see it." Kersey replied that he did not watch the actual street cars, he watched the trolley poles, which were clearly visible. JR said "Oh," and after that he trusted his new chauffeur's driving completely.

There was still a period of adjustment, however. Harry Kersey has left this picture of a furiously busy JR at work.

> I would receive a call at the [Sears] Garage to come right away for Mr. Rosenwald. I would park in front of the Sears, Roebuck Administration Building and Mr. Rosenwald would come running out of the building. There was a stairway with about twelve steps leading to the sidewalk; he would hit the top, middle, and bottom, run to the car, say where he wanted to go on the way past me as I was holding the door open, fall on the seat and away we would go. I would start out fast, thinking he was in a great hurry and he would soon shout, "Take it easy!" I would take him to a Loop office building; he would jump out before the car stopped and disappear through the doors. I would wait for him. Sometimes he would rush out of a building and run down the street. Often I could not get out of the place I was parking quickly enough so I would jump out and run after him to see where he went and then would come back and start the car and find another place to park where I had seen him enter a building. With all of Mr. Rosenwald's dashing here and there, shouting at me, short answers to anything I would ask him, he had a kind expression in his eyes and I really learned to like the man. I set out to study this man and to see if I could map out some way to help him. I found a willing helper in his secretary, a Miss Filer. I explained to [her] my difficulties in keeping up with him in the Loop. It was only the kindness of the police, who all knew and liked him, that I had not already lost him on several occasions. They would let me park anywhere, turn anywhere and help in any way possible. I suggested to Miss Filer that she give me a list each morning of his daily appointments; then I would know what he was going to do. That helped a great deal and I did not have to run after him.

Harry Kersey also describes JR's dislike of waste. He tells how JR requested his chauffeur to buy him some razor blades. "Naturally I thought he bought plenty of anything, and bought him a box of blades. He took a look at them and said: 'What do you think I would do with all those blades? First, I would use them up too fast and waste them, or probably lose track of them.' I had to take them back and bring three packages. 'And another thing,' he said. 'Suppose the price would go down.'"

As Harry Kersey's account makes clear, this was a busy time in JR's life. And starting in the winter of 1916, there was another factor which made JR's life even more hectic. World War I had broken out in Europe, and JR found himself dealing with its ramifications in the United States—not on the front lines but working for the government in a position of considerable importance.

5

World War I, 1916–1918

JR and the Early Years of the Great War

When the Great War broke out in Europe in August 1914, JR adhered to the neutral American position.[1] As he stated to a young lawyer, Leo Wormser, who solicited him on behalf of the German Red Cross: "I have taken the position from the start that I would do nothing which would help one side against the other in this great struggle, and that specific funds—be they French, German, or English—would receive no consideration whatsoever, and I have adhered strictly to that principle."[2] JR did, however, donate $2,500 to the German Red Cross. Although he was concerned about the situation of the Agricultural Experiment Station in Haifa, directed by his friend Aaron Aaronsohn, and he continued to send money in support, he turned resolutely against Aaronsohn when he learned in 1916 that the agronomist was working as a spy for the British. This meant that some of the financial aid JR was providing could be used to support the British war effort at a time when the United States was officially neutral. Angered by the news of Aaronsohn's activities, JR vowed to cut off his support.

At the same time that he was taking a position of studied neutrality, JR was becoming an advocate of American training and preparedness. He believed that the United States would have to enter the war sooner or later, and her soldiers had better be ready. Therefore, in 1916 he gave a two-year grant of $5,000 to the Universal Military Training System, a primitive ROTC for businessmen run by General Leonard Wood, who likewise stressed readying the country for a possible war. In making this grant, JR declared: "The need of defense is a subject on which my heart is very full. I fear that if the public continues in its present state of apathy toward means of defense and toward a higher national idealism, our children or our children's children will live to see a different form of government rule the United States. A people who prey upon a nation rather than work for that nation can expect no other end. This government will end in 25 years unless there is a strengthening of our physical and moral strength."[3] This apocalyptic vision was not universally shared by the advocates of preparedness, but it does indicate JR's zeal for this cause. Knowing of his attitude on military preparedness may well have caused President Woodrow Wilson's advisors to nominate JR to the Advisory Commission of the Council of National Defense.

Council of National Defense: The Call to Serve

Wilson was in a difficult position in 1916. He was running for reelection on the slogan "He Kept Us Out of War." At the same time, it was becoming clear that America had to be ready in the event that the country was forced into hostilities. The military appropriations bill that was making its way through Congress that summer contained an amendment calling for the creation of a Council of National Defense to be composed of cabinet secretaries chaired by Secretary of War Newton D. Baker. To aid the council in preparing for the possibility of war, there was to be an Advisory Commission, composed of seven prominent Americans. The bill passed Congress at the end of August, and the members of the Advisory Commission were named on October 11. JR was probably astonished to find his name on the list, for he had been working to elect Wilson's opponent, Charles Evans Hughes. His selection was all the more surprising because one of the members originally contemplated by Secretary Baker was vetoed by the president for being overly Republican.[4]

JR could not turn down this call to serve his country in such a prestigious capacity, and he assented to Wilson's request. Following his appointment, he received several congratulatory letters, but none was more thoughtful than the one from Felix Frankfurter, the famous jurist and future Supreme Court justice, who noted: "This Council is the only recognition we have thus far made that preparedness is not a question of ships and soldiers, but the concentrated forethought of the country towards the stimulation and mobilization of its powers, military, industrial, and above all human."[5] JR traveled to Washington, and on December 5 he hosted a dinner to make the acquaintance of his fellow commissioners.

They were an impressive group, representing various sectors of the economy. Daniel Willard, president of the Baltimore & Ohio Railroad, who was subsequently elected chairman; Hollis Godfrey, president of the Drexel Institute of Philadelphia, an engineer who had been interested in war preparedness for some time; Howard E. Coffin, president of the Society of Automotive Engineers, who was briefly the head of the Committee on Industrial Preparedness of the Naval Consulting Board, a precursor of the Advisory Commission put together by Edison and other scientists and engineers; Dr. Franklin H. Martin, a surgeon and director general of the American College of Surgeons, who had also been heavily involved in the preparedness movement; Bernard Baruch, a gifted financier and Wall Street investor, and Samuel Gompers, the English-born president of the American Federation of Labor. Describing this introductory meeting, Martin wrote in his autobiography: "Mr. Rosenwald, a prince of good fellows, was a genial host. He was of the type one loves instinctively, and in contrast to the usual culmination of such attractions, one's regard for him grew stronger from day to day."[6]

The following day, the commissioners met members of the Council of National Defense, the cabinet secretaries of war, interior, agriculture, commerce, labor, and the navy. Then the first joint meeting was held.

The council and the commission were in an anomalous position. The United States was still technically at peace as far as the war in Europe was concerned, and there was no certainty that the country would enter the conflict. Almost half of those present were "pacifists," opposed to military intervention. This was made clear when JR asked the members of the council if they favored universal military training. At this first meeting of the Advisory Commission and the Council of National Defense on December 6, 1916, a distinction was made between training and service, with the pacifists favoring the former but opposing the latter. JR then requested a vote on service from those present. With one council member absent, the group was evenly divided. Of the commissioners, only Samuel Gompers voted against universal military service.[7]

The issue of universal military service was one of JR's current passions. A few months later, his friend and unofficial public relations booster, H. H. Kohlsaat, wrote JR that the head of a national press association was claiming that it was JR who had convinced Secretary Baker of the necessity of universal service and that Baker had then won over the president.[8] Since Kohlsaat could be a sycophant, one need not take this statement too seriously; however, it is true that JR brought this subject up again in March 1917, saying: "In my opinion, the country is doomed unless we get something of the kind. . . . Compulsory service must come, and I am hopeful that Congress will see the necessity for it. . . . It is the hope of the country."[9] Although nothing was decided at that March meeting, Secretary Baker announced that he would immediately take up this issue with the president.

On December 6, 1916, the commissioners visited the White House, where the president greeted them cordially and spent half an hour chatting with them. Then they retired to the Willard Hotel, where they had their first meeting apart from the Council of National Defense. It was spent mostly on procedural and organizational questions.

The commissioners were not altogether clear about what precisely the purposes and objectives of the commission and the council were. According to the law creating the two bodies, the council had two tasks. One was to deal with transportation issues concerning mobilization and supplies. The second was to gather information on existing manufacturing and production capabilities and the possible adaptation of American industry to a war footing if that should become necessary. They were also to inform the leaders of American industry what role they were to play in the event of a national emergency. The role of the commissioners was not explicitly stated except that they were to be the "best specialists in their respective fields." It was made clear from the beginning that the commissioners were serving without pay. None of these issues concerning functions and duties was resolved at the December meetings or for several months thereafter. Before leaving Washington in December, the commissioners elected as their director Walter Gifford, a young engineer with AT&T who had worked closely with Howard Coffin on the Committee on Industrial Preparedness of the Naval Consulting Board. This committee had made some preliminary surveys of the current state of American industry, a task which the commissioners were presumably to continue.

Having agreed to meet once a month until further notice, the commissioners then adjourned.

1917—The Year in Washington

The commissioners gathered again in January for another series of meetings. A good deal of time was spent on procedural questions. It still was uncertain what their mission was. As Dr. Martin put it: "How much authority were we as Commissioners to assume? How much did the Council as a whole expect the Commission to do, if anything, in administering the work that it advised?"[10] The answers to these questions did not even begin to become apparent until the following month.

At a special meeting of the Advisory Commission on February 12, that body voted to form seven committees, each one headed by a commissioner. JR's was the Committee on Supplies, which was to include food and clothing. The formation of committees was approved by the council, and it was subsequently agreed that each committee could hire a staff and form subcommittees.

After a week of meetings, JR returned to Chicago and wrote to an old friend, Charles Eisenman, a retired manufacturer of children's apparel from Cleveland. JR invited Eisenman to be his assistant. In this letter he noted his frustration and his plans for the future: "We are beginning now to get down to business which has been very difficult up to the present. Of course the immediate probability of a declaration of war has caused greater activity in connection with this work." After praising the members of the council and the commission for their dedication and seriousness of purpose, he went on:

> The first plan we have in mind is to select not to exceed three men from each industry with which the government is likely to have important deals and have Secretary Baker invite them to come to Washington at a certain time. Either he or some member of the Cabinet and some member of the Commission will address them in a body, telling them of the plans the Council of Defense has in mind and requesting that they organize their respective industries in such a way so that if they are called upon to serve the government they will be ready to do so. This is just in the rough, and before the conference with the representatives of the industries it is ex-

pected that we will have the matter in definite shape as to what will be desired of them.[11]

He asked Eisenman to join him in Washington, indicating that he and the other commissioners had decided that the press of business required them to be on the scene. Eisenman accepted the offer.

The purpose of the Committee on Supplies was "to cooperate in an advisory capacity with the purchasing officers of the army and navy departments in working out problems of procurement and contracting."[12] Each new committee formed subcommittees, called cooperative committees. Those formed by JR and Eisenman were cotton goods, woolen manufactures, shoe and leather industries, knit goods, leather equipment, mattresses and pillows, and canned goods. The cooperative committees were to determine the needs of the manufacturers and the purchasing price for the items involved. Thus, in these committees, industrial leaders and government officials "cooperated" in the procurement of goods and supplies so that government would not have to fix prices unilaterally or take over key industries, actions that President Wilson wished to avoid at all costs. The irony is that Progressives of both parties in Congress viewed cooperation as collusion and would shortly accuse the industrialists of price fixing and violations of antitrust law.

In accordance with the plan outlined in his letter to Eisenman, JR and Eisenman would invite the leading figures in a given industry to Washington to set up a cooperative committee. Members would be addressed by someone on the council about their patriotic duty and the necessity of working together. The system that had formerly been in effect was that the Quartermaster Corps put out competitive bids for all supplies. But there was no time for that now, and the prices obtained through competitive bids were not always as low as they could have been due to the existence of middlemen and the growing certainty that war would be declared. Since prices were starting to rise rapidly, an attempt was made to set a fair price without having to go through a middleman. For example, the Committee on Shoe and Leather Industries would attempt to determine how much leather it would take to make a million pairs of boots. Then the members would calculate a price that would provide each manufacturer with a reasonable profit and that would be the price at which the army and navy would buy the boots. By eliminating the middleman, which JR felt was of paramount importance, he was essentially doing what he had done at Sears by taking over the entire manufacturing process of a given industry such as the construction of cars and houses and selling them. JR claimed in the press that by utilizing such practices he had organized the purchase of between three and four million boots and shoes and saved the government over $1.5 million.

Achievements such as these were trumpeted by JR in newspapers across the country, but it is uncertain how accurate these claims were. In his book on the War Industries Board, the de facto successor to the Advisory Commission, Robert Cuff claims that only Bernard Baruch was able to work effectively with industry. Although he admits that some of JR's cooperative committees were moderately successful, Cuff also points out that, in the case of shoes, for example, the government was still attempting to obtain a decent price for them in the summer of 1918.[13]

What is certain is that this negotiation of prices between the manufacturers and the government infuriated middlemen and their allies in Congress. The Democrats in Congress, who distrusted big business, had a perfect lever with which to attack capitalists working in government such as JR. It seemed fairly clear to congressional Democrats that by negotiating prices, these cooperative committees were going far beyond their mandates. They were created to advise the Committee on Supplies, which, in turn, was to advise the cabinet secretaries. Instead you had committees of leaders of a given industry regulating the prices in that industry. If this was not conflict of interest, then what was? JR argued that the committees were composed of patriotic businessmen who, at some cost to themselves, were making sacrifices in the interests of their country. They were not colluding to produce shoddy goods or enriching themselves at government expense by charging unreasonable prices. On the contrary, they were producing an enormous quantity of goods in a very short time for only a moderate profit. Such profits were necessary; if they were not available, the goods would not have been produced or the government would have had to take over industrial production, which no one wanted.

JR had a valid point. As congressional investigations later demonstrated, the businessmen he and Eisenman dealt with were, for the most part, not grasping tycoons but sincere, honest, and patriotic men. But the Sears president made the unfortunate mistake of issuing an intemperate and ill-considered blast at his enemies in Congress.

The Democrats on the Agriculture Committee sought to attach an amendment to an appropriations bill that would have barred any government agent from soliciting contracts in which he had a personal interest. This would have meant an end to the cooperative committee system because the members, though not paid, were still viewed as government agents. Back home for the July 4 weekend, JR gave an interview to the *Chicago Tribune* on the issue of the proposed amendment and stated: "This is very stupid. It is shortsighted. It is nonsensical and foolish. It means a return to the old slipshod days of unloading on the government—the days of rotten contracts in a time of national emergency."[14]

JR was praised for his words. He was, said a Commander Hancock speaking to the Illinois Manufacturers Association, "the most popular man in Washington. . . . When he has anything to say or do, he says or does it without any pussyfooting, and he has made one slogan famous in Washington: 'Gentlemen, this is no time to be polite.'"[15] But such words, as well as the July 3 interview with the *Chicago Tribune,* caused a furor in Congress where JR was denounced on the floor of the Senate. This may well have convinced President Wilson that JR was a loose cannon, not to be trusted in the political arena. When the War Industries Board was formed a few weeks later, Bernard Baruch was appointed to it, but JR was not. What might have been his slot was instead given to Robert S. Brookings, a retired woodworking and lumber company executive who was not about to roil the political waters.

In addition to speaking to the press, JR also cabled President Wilson urging him to do what he could to head off the amendment. In this plea, JR spoke to the reason for the Advisory Commission's existence: "It is vital that the cooperation that has already been established should be maintained; and furthermore, it is of the greatest importance that confidence exist between government and industry and that suspicion which has existed on the part of both be eliminated."[16] The Advisory Commission had been formed, in part, to create a healthy relationship between industry and government. Now this relationship was in danger of being eroded. Unfortunately, although Wilson may have agreed with JR, he was unwilling or unable to challenge the stalwarts of his own party on this issue, and so a watered-down version of this amendment ultimately did pass and was signed into law. The result of the law's passage was that, toward the end of 1917, some members of JR's cooperative committees resigned because they did not want to risk prosecution. JR wrote the others requesting their resignation and announcing the disbandment of the committees:

> To obviate the present embarrassing situation in which the members of the committee appointed by me or under my direction have been placed by being called upon to act both as government agents or advisors and also as the representatives of their respective industries, it has seemed wise to terminate the existence of your committee, and hence the tender of your resignation is requested.[17]

There were other frustrations inherent in the position in which JR found himself. The United States declared war on April 6, 1917, and a situation that had been merely theoretical now had to be dealt with immediately. Plans called for the arming, equipping, and provisioning of an army of a million men as soon as possible. Another half million troops were added later. As head of the Committee on Supplies, it was JR's task to deal with the provisioning and equipping of these men in conjunction with the Quartermaster Corps of the Army and Navy. The two Quartermaster Corps were in disarray. They were not used to filling such large orders in the short period of time that was necessary. Thus, it fell to JR's committee not only to obtain the necessary goods at a reasonable price but to ensure that they were of top quality and were produced quickly. This proved to be a difficult assignment, given the fact that the Advisory Commission and the committees had only been meeting since February. In May, JR was forced to confront the press with the preliminary results. He gave an interview to the *Chicago Tribune,* having just come from a conference with cotton manufacturers and members of the General Munitions Board, a precursor of the War Industries Board. The problem, he said, was that there was not enough cotton available immediately to make a sufficient number of good uniforms: "The trouble ahead of us right now is that we have no cloth in this country for manufacturing the thousands of standard grade uniforms that will be demanded. We are going about getting this cloth manufactured as rapidly as possible. Everything will come out all right in the end, but we may be forced to use inferior uniforms for the first 100,000 men or so."[18]

Another problem with the Committee on Supplies was that its scope was being whittled away, sometimes with the tacit consent of JR. When first created, the committee had had jurisdiction over food as well as supplies. In April, just after war had been declared, the commission, worried about the price of foodstuffs, proposed that a separate committee be formed to deal with the mobilization of food and that it be chaired by

Herbert Hoover, who had talked to the council and commission in February about his successful efforts in Belgium to coordinate emergency food relief. The future president had made a very favorable impression. In his memoir, Dr. Martin quotes JR as eagerly agreeing to the creation of a food mobilization committee, saying that he "had been thinking about some such scheme while lying awake in the night."[19] Thus the U.S. Office of Food Administration was created with Hoover at its head, and in October JR's committee lost part of its mandate when control over the purchase of foodstuffs was turned over to Hoover's committee. The cooperative committees were disbanded in November 1917. In January, General George Goethals was made quartermaster general and given charge of purchasing virtually all supplies. Little remained for the Committee on Supplies to do. Nevertheless, JR graciously acquiesced, praising Goethals and saying that his appointment would help greatly to eliminate red tape.

By the end of 1917, two issues relating to the Committee on Supplies greatly concerned JR. One was the question of waste. He believed that, if anything, he had been too successful. The government was buying up vast quantities of supplies, far more than even a million soldiers could use. No careful assessment had been made of what was needed. As he told Eisenman in November, "Not only is there much waste and expense in providing great excesses of the requirements, but the increase in cost both to the government and the civilian population is a matter to which we must give serious consideration and not go ahead blindly without being sufficiently informed as to the actual requirements."[20] And to the man who sent him an article on the subject of waste management, he wrote: "This matter was discussed at my dinner table yesterday."

The second issue troubling JR as 1917 ended was Congress and its distrust of businessmen. The Senate Military Affairs Committee investigating army contracts turned its fire on Charles Eisenman. The case involved the Base Sorting Plant in New York, which turned scrap wool ("shoddy") into uniforms. Eisenman was charged with spurning the cheaper offer of a Boston wool merchants association and instead siphoning business to the Base Sorting Plant, which, because it used shoddy, was believed to be making inferior uniforms as well as a huge profit. Eisenman defended himself as best he could. He said that the Base Sorting Plant had been created specifically to save the government money and had been successful in this endeavor. The new uniforms, he maintained, were entirely adequate. Moreover, the Base Sorting Plant was a government institution, and no one had made any profit from it.

JR was furious at this attack on his deputy. He prided himself on his integrity. On July 7 he wrote to Loeb and the Sears board of directors: "After giving this matter considerable thought, I reached the final decision that I would not receive a salary from the Company while I am actively in the work of the Council of National Defense."[21] He was, perhaps, almost overly careful in not involving Sears in military contracts so as to avoid even a hint of impropriety. He rightly saw the Senate attack on Eisenman as an attack on himself, although he was not asked to testify at the hearings and wisely kept his distance. He did, however, lash out at his Senate critics in the press, calling them "soreheads" and denouncing their charges as "lies."[22]

JR and Eisenman received loyal support from Secretary of War Baker, who testified on behalf of Eisenman. Speaking of the two men, Baker declared:

> Both of them are of unimpeachable integrity. . . . They gathered around them men who were expert in their business and asked them not to fix prices, but what the elements of cost were, what percentage labor bore to the aggregate product, and the cost of material etc., and what the overhead expenses were, and out of that this Committee undertook to arrive at prices, and Mr. Eisenman and Mr. Rosenwald were able to check up the Committee's recommendations and determine if they were fair recommendations.[23]

Eisenman was cleared of the charges by the Senate committee and by Quartermaster General Goethals, who visited the Base Sorting Plant with him in January and admitted that before going he had had serious doubts about the propriety of the operation. He wrote Eisenman: "I must confess that the information I had concerning the establishment gave me a strong impression that it was nothing short of a profiteering scheme, and that, while you were not directly connected with it, you were responsible for its establishment."[24] However, further investigation revealed this to be erroneous. Nothing untoward had occurred at the Base Sorting Plant. Although Eisenman was later assigned to Goethals's staff, his reputation had suffered a serious blow. JR must have felt great sorrow at the problems his friend had had thrust upon him.

What did JR accomplish in 1917, his only complete year of service in Washington? The press portrayed him as arriving at his office at 7:30 or 8 every morning and working late. It is true that Eisenman probably did the day-to-day work with the Committee on Supplies. JR was busy attending numerous meetings of the Advisory Commission and joint meetings with the Council of National Defense. And there was an endless series of meetings with members of the various cooperative committees: the shoe manufacturers, the meat packers, and the wool merchants; the meeting at which JR spoke before governors and state councils of national defense, etc. As at Sears, JR proved himself to be a good manager. For example, in September, he sent letters to the various camps where troops were being trained to determine whether supplies were arriving on time. The reports he received were encouraging: "The conditions with reference to supplies coming in and dispensing of same to the soldiers is excellent."[25] Probably the role that JR played best was that of court of last resort. This is illustrated by a case which also shows the confusion reigning at the beginning of the war between the Committee on Supplies and the purchasing departments of the army and navy.

In April, Sigmund Eisner came to see Eisenman and outlined a plan to make uniforms that would have resulted in tremendous savings in both time and money for the government. Eisenman was enthusiastic. At the very same time that he presented his bid to the Committee on Supplies, Eisner presented another plan to the army quartermaster in Philadelphia. The latter accepted the plan presented to him and signed the contract first. Only later was it revealed that this maneuver had cost the government $240,000. Eisenman, who did not like the fact that Eisner had gone behind the back of the Committee on Supplies, protested. Eisner responded that under the existing rules his actions had been perfectly fair and legal. At length, JR was brought in to mediate. He met Eisner, and the two men concluded that Eisner would have an accountant chosen by the government go over his books. If, in fact, it was determined that the government had lost money, Eisner was to repay it.[26]

It is undeniable that clothes and food were procured efficiently and at generally reasonable prices for a large army and navy between the declaration of war in April and the end of the year. Whether or not this can be directly attributed to JR and his committee is uncertain. He did take credit in the press for obtaining vast amounts of supplies at considerable savings to the government. He seems to have found the job initially rewarding and at times exhilarating. In May, he wrote Gussie: "One thing is very evident: that our being here (I mean the Commission) is having a fine effect on the country; they feel, or seem to, that if we are willing to devote our time and energy, others can do no less, and in that I think our usefulness is far-reaching."[27] In October, he wrote to his friend Jacob Schiff: "So far as my work here is concerned, while it is at times strenuous, it is also interesting."[28]

Nor was work the only activity. There were also the parties and dinners, a constant social whirl, which JR and later Gussie found enjoyable. Some of these events were connected to work, such as the state dinners at the White House or other events at which the members of the Advisory Commission were expected to be present; and there were other social functions, such as the annual Gridiron Dinner for the press corps, or the dinner at the home of Alexander Graham Bell where the guest list included numerous dignitaries.

One aspect of this year 1917 in Washington was not so pleasant. Shortly after JR moved to the capital full-time in early March, Gussie became ill—so ill that she required hospitalization. For JR this meant numerous short trips back to Chicago, one of which lasted only one day because he was summoned to the White House to meet the newly arrived delegates from Britain and France. JR's separation from Gussie ended in August when he leased a house in Washington and Gussie and the two youngest children joined him.

Growing Frustrations

The first seven months of 1918 were to be a time of increasing frustration for JR. The Committee on Supplies had been stripped of almost all its functions, and its staff had been taken over by other agencies. In June, the last vestiges of its authority were taken over by the War Industries Board. Relations between Goethals and JR, which had seemed to be going well in December, grew chilly, judging from the tone of Goethals's letters to JR. For example, when JR wrote the quartermaster about his concerns over waste, Goethals replied that, as JR had said, goods had been contracted for, but they had not been satisfactorily delivered, thereby creating an emergency.[29] JR did not reply to what could be construed as an implied criticism of his leadership.

The question of overpurchasing, oversupply, and waste was becoming an obsession with JR. At the end of January, he wrote Benedict Crowell, the assistant secretary of war:

> The items bought by the government at this time are of such magnitude that intensive study is justified in each particular case, and the conditions surrounding that case well considered; for example—the amount available, how rapidly can they be secured if needed, what is the likelihood of change in the article. This and other considerations should be given careful study before the quantity to be ordered is decided upon.[30]

At a joint meeting of the Advisory Commission and the Council of National Defense on February 4, 1918, "Commissioner Rosenwald discussed his duties as a member of the Commission and suggested various ways in which valuable service might be given, referring to the work done by his Committee in bringing to the attention of the Secretary of War and causing cancellation of proposed orders for excessive quantities of materials and supplies."[31] Still, no one was listening. Two weeks later, JR sent a brief memo to Bernard Baruch, his fellow commissioner and soon to be named head of the powerful War Industries Board: "The report for week ending 2/16/18 shows that up to 2/9, 2,175,000 overcoats have been delivered as well as 12,490,000 pairs of shoes delivered up to the same date. Surely it would seem that there would be overcoats and shoes enough for 1,500,000 men."[32]

JR began spending increasing amounts of time on other matters. As early as October 1917, Dr. Franklin Martin had made him an honorary member of the General Medical Board because he had been coming to so many meetings of that body.[33] He was becoming increasingly frustrated and dissatisfied with his position in Washington. The reorganization of the Quartermaster Corps and the naming of General Goethals had left him with almost nothing to do. No one was willing to listen to his warnings about overpurchasing supplies. Rumors of his impending resignation were circulating around Washington. One Chicago newspaper reported his resignation was imminent; another stated categorically that he would not resign. On March 1, he wrote to his children: "So far nothing has developed that would be worth my while remaining here very much longer." And he continued with a statement that showed that at least one Rosenwald found being in Washington at this time enjoyable: "I think I should be ready to go now if it were not on Mother's account. She thoroughly enjoys the life here. . . . She meets many interesting people, and is delighted the way she has been received and sought out when she happens to meet people whom she has met before in any kind of an assembly. We know, of course, how reserved she is and disinclined to push herself forward."[34] Indeed, Gussie was having a fine time. She had become heavily involved in the suffrage movement and had persuaded JR to contribute to this cause.[35]

JR's unhappiness at the turn of events could not be denied even if Gussie was thriving. In mid-March, he wrote to a friend: "The Supplies Committee have moved away from [my office] building, and although I manage to keep fairly busy, it is nothing like as interesting as it was."[36] Yet JR was in a difficult position. If he resigned, he would look like a quitter; moreover, leaving during a national emergency did not look proper. None of the other commissioners was in this position, although others were not altogether happy with their role. In desperation, JR wrote to the president. "At the joint meeting of the Council of National Defense and the Commission I advised the Council that since the reorganization of the Quartermaster's Department I have been practically marking time. I also indicated this to the Secretary of War who urged upon me, however, that there would be ample opportunity to be useful and that I await developments. . . . My services are at hand should you desire to use them."[37] Wilson replied with what amounted to a very polite brush-off: "I have realized that you must have felt recently that you and your associates were a bit thrown out of function, but I hope you realize that if that is true, it is largely because of the excellence of the work you did and the fact that it has come to a full fruitage. I shall keep your generous suggestion in mind and hope that if you have any thoughts of your own in the matter, you will not hesitate to let me know what they are."[38] Nothing had been resolved. JR remained in Washington and continued to attend Advisory Commission meetings.

There was another task JR performed, and it was a fitting one, given his dislike of waste in wartime. JR was to be the government's unofficial spokesman on the need for frugality in time of war. In an article he wrote and had published in the *Chicago Tribune* on May 26, and in subsequent interviews in other newspapers, JR laid out his plan for winning the war.[39]

First, everyone should save goods. This was an imperative that cut across class lines, from the palatial home of the superrich to the humblest tenement dwelling. The corollary of this was that everyone must give up luxuries. People who spent money on items that were not necessities were causing businesses to produce goods that were expendable. These goods were being made with capital and labor that should properly be going to the war effort. But on this point JR went overboard: he proposed in June that Christmas be scrapped for the duration of the war because buying Christmas gifts was tantamount to spending money on luxuries. He stated that he did not mind wearing an old pair of shoes or driving an outdated car. These kinds of products could be purchased after the war ended. He stressed, however, that necessities did have to be produced, both for the soldiers and for the civilian population.

The second contribution that citizens could make for the war effort was invest in Liberty Bonds to the greatest extent possible. This was a subject which JR knew well, for, in addition to buying them himself, he had made sure that both Sears and the newly formed employee pension system were heavily invested. He firmly believed that these government-backed bonds were as good as gold and that investing in them was the patriotic thing to do. By May 1918, two groups of Liberty Bonds had been issued. Sears and Sears employees had both purchased $1 million in each offering. JR had contributed $1 million of his own money, and Gussie had given $35,000. Both JR and Gussie spoke at rallies to drum up sales of Liberty Bonds. By the middle of 1919, JR, Sears, and Sears employees had invested $17,066,750 in Liberty Bonds.[40] Americans purchased almost $14 billion worth of such patriotic monetary instruments.

JR's article and interviews on savings and waste in wartime were essentially his last act as a member of the Advisory Commission. Still frustrated and demoralized, he had begun to devote more and more time to other interests. In March he journeyed to Tuskegee. As he wrote Lessing: "I am expecting to leave for Tuskegee Sunday night on account of a teachers' conference which will take place there next week, and inasmuch as I am contemplating so large an investment in rural schools during the next three years, I want to learn something and also indicate my interest in the people who will have charge of the schools."[41] In April he returned to Tuskegee to conduct a review of the Agriculture Department with board chairman Frank Trumbull and to attend a board meeting. By early June, he and Gussie had left Washington for Ravinia, their estate near Chicago, and he was working for Sears again while Albert Loeb was on vacation. As he wrote to Schiff: "After my long absence from business it seems rather strange to be even temporarily in the harness as I am supposed to be in the absence of our vice president, Mr. Loeb."[42] Yet his quandary remained.

He could not resign from the council and he could not rely on the president or the secretary of war to find him a more meaningful job. He would have to create his own.

Two letters arrived on JR's desk within days of each other at the end of June, and they provided the creative spark that JR needed. The first was from Thomas S. McClane, chairman of the Overseas Entertainment Section of the YMCA. He explained to JR that the YMCA had been put in charge of providing entertainment for the troops in France. He continued: "It is our purpose to send to France for two or three months representatives of American industry, who shall carry to the soldier the story of American ingenuity, the romance of business in all its fascinating ramifications." He asked JR to nominate someone from Sears who could deliver this message to the doughboys (as American soldiers of the time were called).[43] JR had the perfect candidate in mind—himself. Then came a letter from Herbert L. Pratt, vice president of Standard Oil. It deserves to be quoted in full because, as JR noted, "This letter was the cause of my going abroad":

> From personal experience within the last two months in several of the camps in France, it is my opinion that no better work can be done for the boys "overseas" than to give them a talk on a particular kind of business by a man who knows that business. America is the great business nation of the world and most of our boys were in one or another line before being drafted. As the most interesting thing to you yourself is a business chat, just so it is to the boys.
>
> Can't you go yourself or, failing that, send a substitute to tell the boys the story of your business and let them ask the thousand and one questions they will want to about its workings?[44]

It seems odd to think that the YMCA should have been put in charge of the entertainment of the troops. Clearly, no one was quite sure how to go about this. There was no USO. Nor was there time to mobilize popular young performers to go to France. The idea of soldiers listening raptly to speeches on American business may strike a twenty-first-century American as ludicrous.

For JR it was merely a question of obtaining the approval of Secretary Baker. By July 10, JR was back in Washington for that purpose. He was so sure of the response that he spent much of July assembling materials on the history of Sears, Roebuck & Co., particularly the early days. He also wrote to every governor and every senator asking each to provide him with a letter he could read aloud to the troops from his state. He did this, he told the members of the Commercial Club of Chicago after the war, because he thought "it might be more like a word from home than anything I might bring them."[45] Every politician naturally complied with JR's request.

Finally, on July 29, the expected letter from Secretary Baker arrived: "I want you to go to France, move about among our American troops, and avail yourself of every possibility which arises to address our boys on the conditions at home, and particularly on the opportunities of American life as you have observed them in your own successful business career." Baker asked him particularly to visit the supply units, in part because the soldiers in those units felt like second-class citizens since they were not in the front lines. "Your special opportunity or usefulness to them," Baker continued, "will be to take a message from home, pointing out how the country appreciates the service they are rendering, and how great the opportunity will be for them to build up business and professional careers at home when the menace of militarism has been removed from the world."[46]

As soon as it became known that JR was going to France, he was bombarded with letters. Most were like the one from former president William Howard Taft, who urged the Chicagoan to look up his son. But one, from his friend Emmett Scott, the late Booker T. Washington's assistant, who was now serving as a special assistant to Secretary Baker, was more important. It urged JR to carry his message of good cheer specifically to black troops.[47] This was one message JR heeded.

The Mission to France

On August 5, 1918, JR bid farewell to Gussie and his children and set off on the *Aquitania,* the second largest boat afloat, which was carrying 6,100 soldiers, including 500 officers. The crossing, which took a week, was uneventful. JR assured Loeb and his family that no one was really worried about torpedoes. At the appropriate time a fleet of escort ships met them and accompanied them to Liverpool. He stayed in England only a few days, all of them in London, getting his papers in order. It was there that he encountered Aaron Aaronsohn. The two men patched up their differences. It was the last time JR was to see the Israeli agronomist alive, for he perished the following year in an airplane accident.

By August 20, JR was in France. He spent several days paying courtesy calls and meeting the people who were to arrange his itinerary. He went to Pershing's headquarters, but the general was not there; however, he did receive a warm reception from Charles Dawes, one of Pershing's top aides, whom JR knew well. At Langres, behind the front lines, he encountered the son of a neighbor named Harris, who gave him a ride in a tank. As Lieutenant Harris tells the story:

> A general's car drove up. You can always tell them. . . . At a distance I recognized General Smith. . . . Accompanying him were two other men in khaki. One was a lieutenant, the general's aide, and the other was Mr. Rosenwald.
>
> . . . The General says, says he, "Lt. Harris . . . this is . . . " Not being a military guy, the aforesaid Mr. Rosenwald broke in—absolutely interrupted the General with "For God's sake, Harris. . . . How are you? Saw your folks not long ago and they are all fine. Why, General, he was one of the best men at the University." "He is one of our best men here, too. I come out to see him often here," quoth the General.
>
> This was beginning to get my goat, so I carried on with "Sir, is it your wish to have a tank maneuver for Mr. Rosenwald?" He said it was, so I got my best sergeant and told him to take the shell holes, trenches, and then hit for the woods about 300 meters away. Damned if it didn't go swell, just like a circus horse, and I felt like the trainer receiving the plaudits of the audience. I had an opportunity to ask Mr. Rosenwald how he liked it—that I had noticed his name in arrivals in Paris, how long he expected to be over. "Fine, yes, and 2 or 3 months." Just then, the tank hit a tree at the edge of the woods, went up on end and disappeared. "He's tipped over!" yelled Mr. R. I said we'll go over and see. We went. Tipped over hell! It was moving thru, riding over stumps, trees, wells and everything. Then it backed out just as easily. "The sight of a lifetime!" said Mr. J.R. and even the General got ecstatic.
>
> Then Langstreeth came up and I introduced him. Between us we got a suit of overalls—black with grease—and managed to get our guest into the critter without banging his head or cutting him up. He stood up, acting as a gunner, and the Sergeant gave him a ride over the course. When he got back he said it was a great experience and asked if he had taken the shell holes and trenches. He had, and altho he had a darn good driver who minimized every bump, I really believe he was a little "leery," and while bracing and holding on, he had forgotten to look out of the slits to see where he was going. But he got the sensation. "I'll write to your folks

at once and tell them I have seen you. Good luck and thank you, Lieutenant."[48]

At Chateau Thierry "where the first great [American] victory was won," JR got his first true taste of the war: hundreds of ruined homes, miles of troop transports. At Vinx, in a rubbish dump, he found a German helmet and decided to keep it as a souvenir. Later that day he visited Big Bertha, the huge German gun which had been captured. He even took cover during an air raid in a castle used by the U.S. military when there was an air raid warning, but no attacking planes materialized. He then returned to Paris and made final arrangements with the YMCA for his mission, which was to start three days later in Brest.

Something that bothered JR almost from the moment he embarked on the *Aquitania* was the question of his uniform. He was dressed in military fatigues and was treated as a VIP, but he had no insignia of rank. He worried that someone who didn't know who he was would wonder why this elderly "private" was getting so much special treatment. In Paris before setting out on his mission, he wrote his family: "So far I have no insignia and have been spending some time on that. Will probably have tomorrow an arm band of some description—probably of plain green, which will mean nothing in particular, or I can make it mean anything, as no one ever wore one like it."[49] Eventually, he decided to use his discomfort with the uniform as a way of opening his speech, and he would send the doughboys into howls of laughter at his description of his attempts to solve the insignia "disease." Ultimately, this led to one of the more amusing episodes of the trip. Toward the end of his mission, he found himself delayed by a day because he could not make arrangements to speak in camps where he had not previously been. "It so happened that the Secretary of War was to be here at 7:40 the following morning, so I decided to get up early enough and join in the reception committee and there were all kinds of starred and eagled and silver and gold leaf dignitaries in line waiting to greet him." As Secretary Baker went down the line, each officer would step forward, salute, and announce his name and rank. "There was I, a perfectly good uniform but no insignia. When I came up to him, I was standing between two Generals, and I said 'This is General Merchandise.' He roared and stopped to talk to me for a minute or two, complimenting the tailor and the belt maker, and saying how well I looked in soldier's clothes."[50]

Figure 13. "General Merchandise": JR in his World War I uniform. Courtesy of the Department of Special Collections, Regenstein Library, University of Chicago.

On August 29, JR began his speaking tour in Brest. "Well, I have made a start and it is gratifying. I spoke twice on Tuesday night at Camp *** . . . in a small hut holding *** and then in a large one holding about ***, and packed, not even standing room. My letters from the Governors and Senators made a great hit. Boys from each state called for the letters from their state, and it is pandemonium. So I read those from states having the largest representation . . . and every one gets applause. First talk to them awhile, 15 or 20 minutes. So far business has not been touched upon. After I got through, they crowded around me to shake hands. . . . I shook hands with everyone. Made a fuss over the Chicago boys."[51] Later, as he became more familiar with his role, he added a peroration that must have been notable even for such inspirational speeches at that time:

> I generally spend the last fifteen minutes to tell them what they must make of America when they return—a real nation, all belonging to one another. They are demonstrating in the army that men from all places have their faults and their virtues, but are all made of good stuff. It is the same way with nationalities. There should be no more prejudices against people from any country if they become Americans. I speak of civic matters and politics. I often show them what a disgrace it is to our country to treat the Negro as we do, and not give him a square deal, such as they like to have. I also tell them we must honor the men we elect to office, and not suspect them of improper motives if they are trying to serve the state or nation.[52]

It was typical of the man that he was eager to bring up these issues which no one else would mention and which were so important to him. The concern about prejudice was a subject he had felt compelled to speak out on since at least 1913 at the inauguration of the Wabash YMCA in Chicago. And clearly the issue of not suspecting public officials of improper motives reflected his recent experiences in Washington, from which he was still smarting.

These speeches were given in all types of locations and to different kinds of soldiers: at YMCA "huts," in field hospitals, to the support troops behind the lines, and, heeding the words of Emmett Scott, to the regiments of black troops. Sometimes the audience was racially integrated.

What was the reaction to these speeches? JR claimed he was a great success. "The treatment received everywhere is royal. I couldn't have believed it. Wherever I speak, the officers are pleased and enthusiastic, and say it does the men great good." He boasted in his letters home of the great crowds before which he spoke and the number of speeches he gave: "I doubt if anyone who has gone to Europe has talked to as many people in double the time," he wrote home. "I am very happy over the success of my undertaking so far. Much greater than I expected, and it is largely due to my reaching the boys in a personal and intimate attitude, and also bringing them word from their Governor and Senator. . . . It is inspiring work and I am very happy to be doing it. As a rule the audiences are very demonstrative."[53] JR was indeed a great success. He and Gussie received copies of letters that soldiers sent home which indicate that he was exceedingly popular, as this letter of Russell C. Gates, who heard JR in Issoudun, makes clear:

> After luncheon, I dropped in on the Y.M.[C.A.], there was a lecture going on and the place was packed. The enthusiastic cheering, whistling and clapping aroused my curiosity and I knew it must be something worth while to stir the fellows up so. I wedged in at the back of the hall. The speaker was a short, heavy man of middle age, and he was in officer's uniform, had iron gray hair, a ruddy face, a little flushed because of the effort to make himself heard over the whole assembly, and perhaps due also, in part, to the enthusiasm with which his remarks were received by the boys. As I listened, I was deeply impressed by what he was saying. He was an artist at touching just the right chord in the fellows, and he talked in such a personal way and so wholeheartedly, mixing in a few good stories now and then, that he took the boys by storm. I turned to a mechanic next to me and said "Who is he?"—"Damn fine. The fellows call him Rosy, he is a big bug from Chicago on the National Defense. He certainly is damn good." I stayed through to the end and joined in the three big cheers that were given him. It's the first time a speaker has been cheered in this camp since I've been here.[54]

Other eyewitnesses produced a slight note of caution, especially about JR's statements concerning blacks. Corporal H. R. Kern wrote his colleague at Sears: "This latter point started the Southerners off, but I believe they are beginning to see the Northern point of view."[55] After the war, in Senate testimony, James W. Laffity described how JR was almost lynched by white troops when he told black soldiers that they deserved a "square deal." Asked about this incident, JR told the *Kansas City Star:* "I often spoke of the good feeling that should exist between the members of the white and the colored races. But to the best of my knowledge, there never was any offense taken by the soldiers. As a matter of fact, they thought that was the proper spirit to show. I used to ask them from the platform, and they indicated that they agreed with me. Negro soldiers were willing to fight and willing to do any menial task asked of them. I never heard any opposition to my sentiments, although there may have been some Southern boys who didn't like to hear the Negroes praised."[56]

For JR, the high point of the trip occurred when he visited his friend Abel Davis, one of the founders of the Federated Orthodox Jewish Charities of Chicago, who was a lieutenant colonel serving at the St. Mihiel sector of the front. JR received a cable from Davis, inviting him to come and visit, and with his voice growing hoarse from speaking to large crowds up to five times a day, he decided to take advantage of this opportunity. On September 14 he drove through fields filled with barbed wire and was dropped four miles from Davis's position. Davis brought him to the first trenches he had ever seen. JR was fascinated. He wrote his family on September 15:

> I wish you could see the place where I am dictating this letter. . . . I am about ten feet underground in a very comfortable dugout where I slept last night in a room adjoining Colonel Abel Davis. . . . Today I spent the banner day of my trip. I have been over one of the most famous battlefields in France where the Colonel is now located. I saw through a glass the front lines of the enemy. I have walked miles and miles through trenches and tunnels, and one about five eighths of a mile long and as dark as pitch since it is about twenty feet below the ground and wet and muddy all the way through. Nevertheless, a wonderful construction. The guns are going all day long and I have seen any number of airplanes shot at from both sides of the line with antiaircraft guns. I had a lesson in the wearing of the gas mask. It is necessary to carry one here at all times, also wore a steel helmet on about a four hour tramp. In the towns around this place there is not a semblance of a building standing.

The next day, he wrote, he walked for hours through the trenches. Then there was a dinner with the military officers. "Abel did everything he could to make my visit pleasant and interesting even to ordering a bombing party by the enemy while we were at the General's house." Bombs exploded for two hours in the clear night air, but no damage was done, as far as could be determined. "They shoot at the planes but . . . never hit one. On the way home, we were going in the direction of the enemy and could see the various signals made by fireworks. What they signified of course we could not tell. I did not want to go to bed at all." Returning to Paris from the front, he stopped at General Pershing's headquarters a second time. JR had been given a letter of introduction to Pershing from his brother-in-law, Sig Eisendrath. This time the general was available and wanted to know all the details of JR's mission. "He is a wonderfully energetic person," JR concluded. "Full of 'pep.'"[57]

There is something mildly disconcerting about this picture of JR as a tourist at the front, reminiscent of the accounts of seventeenth-century warfare or the picture of Washington ladies riding out in their carriages to see the Battle of Bull Run during the Civil War. Yet any such ironies seemed to be lost on JR, who was clearly enthralled by what he was seeing. Of course, JR was not allowed to go to the most forward of the front lines, and by September 1918 Germany was fielding a tired and bedraggled army; the war would end less than two months later.

Following his excursion to the front, JR returned to his speaking tour behind the lines. He came down with a bad cold a few days later. Pneumonia was feared, and he was ordered confined to bed. Just when he appeared to be getting over the cold, another affliction struck him, this time in the foot. The soldiers called it "trench foot." By October 3, he could only get around on crutches. The next day he was on the train for Brest, and by October 6 he was on the ocean, returning home with 380 wounded men and the secretary of war. The return voyage was not nearly as pleasant as the trip out had been. At one point the dressing on his leg caught fire through "spontaneous combustion." His sheets and blankets burned, though he was not injured. The following day there was a flood in his cabin.[58] On October 13, ill and exhausted, Julius Rosenwald disembarked.

Despite the unfortunate conclusion, this had been a revivifying trip for JR. The frustration of the months in Washington was replaced by a tremendous feeling of optimism as a result of meeting the troops. He was happy to tell all who would listen how wonderful the "boys" in France were. As he said at the Commercial Club of Chicago upon his return: "There never was a finer set of men anywhere on the face of the globe than our boys who are in France. I could never make you understand how my affection for these fellows grew as I met them day by day. . . . I never saw them do a thing that was rowdyish . . . [and] in all the time I was abroad, I never saw one of them drunk."[59] For an abstemious drinker such as JR, who abhorred the inebriated, this was the highest form of praise. He marveled at the lack of complaints of any kind. Every soldier had been eager to do his job carefully and thoroughly. While JR's listeners might have marveled at this angelic picture of America's armed forces, much of it was deeply felt—it was not just oratorical effect. True, JR had an ulterior motive in making this address: He wanted to make sure that the returning troops were properly welcomed by those who had spent the war on the home front, and probably wished to ensure that his audience felt the doughboys were worthy of such a welcome. Nevertheless, it seems clear that the images of these eager and somewhat naive young men both moved JR and inspired him.

There are two interesting footnotes regarding the mission to France.

One story contends that JR took crates filled with Sears catalogs to France. His purpose in doing so was only indirectly to promote his company. Supposedly, his true objective was to distribute them to hospitals to let the wounded soldiers have something to remind them of home. According to an account by Secretary of War Baker, who visited France several months after the conclusion of hostilities, he stopped at a hospital to see how the patients were doing. In the course of the conversation, he asked what the men were reading. The nurse answered that works such as *Tom Sawyer* and *Huckleberry Finn* were much in demand. "However," she whispered, "if you really want to know what we have a waiting list for, it's the Sears catalog." The story of the catalogs is also mentioned in the unpublished memoirs of JR's son, William, who notes that his father was criticized for his action in taking them. The gesture of providing catalogs to the troops not merely as a marketing tool but as a means of providing the soldiers with a touch of home was smart business, but it also exemplifies the human and caring side of Sears's president.

Another interesting aspect of JR's mission to France is how well reported it was. He was a master of public relations. He roomed one night with a reporter for the *Chicago Tribune* who wrote the next day at considerable length about JR's trip to Big Bertha and his ride in the tank. He sought out a *New York Times* correspondent he knew in Paris. When he had a cold, U.S. newspapers reported that he had pneumonia. His family sent his letters to the press so that they would be excerpted in newspapers and magazines.

Back Home

JR returned to Chicago in mid-October 1918. The fifty-six-year-old philanthropist was not well, and despite a cheerful tone in letters to Jacob Schiff, he confided to Charles Eisenman that he had been ill for five weeks, confined most of that time to bed. In early December, he and Gussie checked into Johns Hopkins Hospital for a lengthy and thorough physical examination. Nothing significant was found to be wrong with either of them.

There was still one item left over from the war that occupied JR as 1918 came to a close: the reconstruction of Europe, words that were on many Americans' lips as the Great War ended. Toward the end of November, he received a letter from Jacob Schiff, reminding him of talks they had had at Schiff's home on Mt. Desert Island in 1916. At that time, they had discussed the possibility of establishing an American fund to help Europe rebuild from the ravages of the war. JR had suggested putting in $1 million, and Schiff had agreed to match that sum. The two men had then discussed obtaining additional large gifts from other wealthy Americans, but the talks had ended with no resolution. Now, with the war over, Schiff reminded JR of their conversation two years before: "It has occurred to me—and I have not discussed this with anyone else thus far—that it might be proper at this time for you and me to take the initiative and pledge $1 million each toward a fund of $500 million to be raised by the American people for purposes of restoration in Europe."[60] He went on to suggest that President Wilson be approached on this subject and, if Wilson approved, that he be asked to set up and head a commission for reconstruction.

JR, who had just seen the terrible devastation caused by four years of war in France, was immediately inspired by this idea. As soon as he received Schiff's letter, he cabled his reply, suggesting that he and others give five or ten times more than he had originally proposed because the problems in Europe were so critical. Without mentioning his illness, he added that he would be willing to go to Washington immediately and join with Schiff in an appeal to the president.[61] Schiff, somewhat taken aback, replied that he was not prepared to be as generous as his Chicago friend. The two men then conferred by phone and decided that because of JR's health and Wilson's imminent departure for Europe, it might be best to wait. JR then cabled Schiff again: "I consider what we have in mind of such great importance that, even in disobedience of the doctor's orders, and your own, I should have gone to Washington. I am willing to subordinate my personal welfare to serve in this great cause."[62] At the beginning of December, JR and Schiff met. Schiff summarized their conversation: "I hardly need dwell at length upon the necessity of assistance being extended to the people of France, Belgium, and other countries where such great havoc has been wrought by the war in order that these people may become reestablished in their former homes under conditions which shall assure their well-being and dignified existence hereafter, which can likely only be accomplished with adequate cooperation from the American people."[63] JR and Schiff agreed that a commission for the restoration of Europe should study the situation carefully to determine where the funds could best be applied. The total that they envisaged being collected was a minimum of $500 million, but both men were confident that the American people would willingly contribute the money if the case were adequately presented to them. Since Wilson had already left, they decided that their idea could be presented to him on his return. Two days later, JR wrote Schiff: "I have heard also from other sources that the French have an idea of floating a very large loan here for restoration purposes and our plan might have an unfavorable effect upon the floating of such a loan. Under any circumstances, I think it is wisest to await the return of the President, who will no doubt have some exact knowledge on the subject."[64] Thereafter, the subject was never brought up again, and so came to an end an idea that seems to prefigure the Marshall Plan and that appears to be naively based on the tremendous power of American goodwill and philanthropy.

The $10 Million Pledge

The power of American philanthropy was demonstrated in a remarkable outpouring of money, mainly Jewish, for the relief of Jewish war victims. This campaign was spearheaded by JR, who galvanized people into giving more than they ever had before for such a cause.

When the war first broke out in Europe, JR, though no Zionist, attended a rally at Temple Sinai on November 23, 1914, on behalf of Jewish residents of Palestine (which was pro-British) who were being hard-pressed by the Turks, allies of Germany. The main speaker was the eminent jurist Louis Brandeis. Rabbi Hirsch began the proceedings with an impassioned appeal, and pledges started flowing in. But JR had come with an idea of his own. "In his impulsive direct way, [he] fairly jumped onto the rostrum to point out to his hearers that single donations, however generous in size, would not meet the emergency, that 'tomorrow all that has been wrought in Palestine will again be faced with extinction unless we Jews make provision for the future.' He then called on his hearers to change their donations to monthly pledges, leading the way by a promise of $1,000 a month for the duration of the war and for one year thereafter."[65]

Despite this generous pledge, JR was decidedly ambiguous about contributing to a fund that was solely for Jewish war sufferers, and he differed with his colleagues on the American Jewish Committee on this issue. When Louis Marshall solicited him anyway for such a fund, he sent a check for $10,000, but insisted that the gift be anonymous because he had not changed his mind about the fund and was making his contribution solely out of deference to Marshall. "Making anonymous contributions is contrary to my policy," he wrote Marshall, "since I have always urged that, as a rule, the personality behind the gift is far more valuable than the gift itself, and should be known, but in this case, I can see no other means of accomplishing the desired end."[66] But by December 1915 he was advocating the creation of a $2 million fund to aid Jews in Eastern Europe. JR was one of four wealthy Jews to pledge $100,000 to this cause. Mass meetings in 1916 in which JR was involved led to tens of thousands of dollars being pledged to help Jewish victims of the war. It was clear that JR had changed his mind.

When 1917 opened, the leaders of the American Jewish Committee decided that the goal for the year for Jewish war victims should be $10 million. They feared that this would be a difficult sum to obtain, and it was suggested that the committee try to find someone willing to contribute a lead gift of $1 million. Jacob Billikopf, the fund-raiser from Kansas City, volunteered to travel to Washington to solicit JR. He arrived on the day of Wilson's second inauguration, and when he asked for JR at the Willard Hotel, he was told that the Chicagoan was at the festivities. So Billikopf waited all day, rehearsing his speech. The hour grew later and later, but Billikopf dared not leave for fear of missing his quarry. Around 11 P.M., JR finally came in, accompanied by several senators. Billikopf approached and asked to speak to JR in private. JR politely bade the senators good night. Then he drew Billikopf to a corner of the lobby, sat him down, and said, "Well, tell me all about it." As Billikopf describes the scene:

> I glanced up at him and my entire harangue, on which I had spent so much arduous toil and thought, evaporated; and I heard myself, to my own great surprise, telling him in the very simplest and unadorned style that a campaign for ten million dollars was about to be launched; that it needed some powerful dramatic stimulus to start it off effectively and to end it successfully; that the committee had determined that nothing but a great single gift would serve—and that he, transcendentally, was the man to make that gift. . . . I merely indicated in a matter of fact way . . . that the condition of the European Jews was growing increasingly worse and that a renewed effort on a much greater scale than had ever been tried must be initiated. He listened without comment while my appeal was gathering momentum. . . . As I concluded with my specific request—request for a round million—the earnestness of his expression deepened. He said merely, "Do you think it

will do any good?" I nodded, and was about to proceed with a highly colored forecast of the results of such a contribution, when he rose. "Very well," he said with a gentle kindness. "You may go back to New York and tell them that I'll do it."[67]

Like so many Julius Rosenwald gifts, this was in the form of a challenge grant: he would contribute $100,000 for every $1 million raised until he himself had contributed $1 million. In his letter announcing the challenge grant to Louis Marshall, he set a time limit of November 1, 1917.

The announcement of Rosenwald's challenge grant created a sensation. It was, newspapers across the land proclaimed, the largest gift ever given by an individual to a public charity. President Wilson sent JR the following telegram:

> Your contribution of $1 million to the $10 million fund for the relief of Jewish war sufferers serves democracy as well as humanity. The Russian Revolution has opened the door of freedom to an oppressed people, but unless they are given life and strength and courage, the opportunity of centuries will avail them little. It is to America that these starving millions look for aid, and out of our prosperity, fruit of free institutions, should spring a vast and ennobling generosity. Your gift lays an obligation even while it furnishes inspiration.[68]

Herbert Lehman, treasurer of the American Jewish Committee, in his letter of thanks, acknowledged the need for JR's gesture. People had become so inured to the horrors of the war that contributions to a fund for Jewish war sufferers had fallen off.[69]

A grand gesture, however, was not enough, no matter how much praise was bestowed on JR. The match had to be made, and committees were formed in cities across America to meet it. Attempts were made to find wealthy individuals willing to make a challenge of their own on a smaller scale. Full-page ads appeared in Jewish newspapers across the country with a picture of JR and the question: "Who will be the Julius Rosenwald of *your* community?" JR himself took part in the effort. On April 15, he was one of two honorees at a dinner in New York that raised over $2 million in pledges. "It was a great evening," he cabled Gussie. "Ovation quite embarrassing, but I think my offer is showing considerable effect."[70] To his host, Jacob Schiff, he wrote: "The results of that splendid meeting will be very far-reaching indeed."[71] On May 20, another massive gathering was held at Chicago's Temple Sinai. As the *Chicago Tribune* noted, "men cried, jurists whooped, merchants shouted." Jacob Schiff sent a telegram: "Would there were more Julius Rosenwalds in Chicago." Then JR rose to speak and stunned his audience by announcing that there was a new Rosenwald in Chicago, his second grandson, Richard Deutsch, who had just been born. He went on: "He is a most precocious young man. The first thing he suggested was a contribution to the fund. Being financially somewhat embarrassed, I lent him $500, which he hereby tenders to the fund." Then, to thunderous applause, he announced that he and Gussie would contribute an additional $150,000. Men began leaping up, shouting their pledges of $10,000. When the meeting ended after midnight, over $500,000 had been pledged.[72] Three days later, JR was in New York, and Billikopf persuaded him to engage in some face-to-face solicitations. He wrote Gussie: "[Billikopf] wanted me to see Adolph Lewisohn for the War Fund. . . . I did and got $10,000. He had persistently refused."[73]

The campaign appeared to be going fantastically well. By July 1, it was reported, over half the challenge had been met. Over one hundred cities had exceeded their goals. But then the momentum slowed down. By the end of October, when a meeting of 1,500 Jewish leaders occurred in New York, only $6 million had been raised. JR reluctantly agreed to extend the deadline to midnight on December 31. In a letter to Schiff, he described the atmosphere surrounding the last few days: "Mr. Billikopf telephoned all over the country at my suggestion to the effect that only money received by 12/31 would come under my offer. I have urged him to return home and endeavor to get in every dollar possible and to get the list of every unpaid amount throughout the country and solicit the subscriber direct from New York. He will tell you that I have been most concerned about getting in every available dollar."[74] JR almost broke with Schiff over the issue of pledges unpaid by December 31. He was willing to make certain exceptions, but in general he wanted the cash in hand.

The nation, and especially the Jewish community, watched the countdown to New Year's Eve 1918 with special interest. Articles appeared in newspapers of all kinds throughout the country. Would the match be made? The answer . . . was yes! This campaign was a great triumph for American Jews and for fund-raising in the United States.

At a dinner in New York on April 18, 1918, JR and Gussie were honored for their impressive contribution to the fund to aid the suffering of Jewish refugees in Europe. In his speech at that dinner, JR hinted that his gesture not only had assisted the Jewish cause but also had enabled the American Red Cross to meet its $100 million goal. He could claim this on the basis that donors to one cause would be inclined to contribute to another organization engaged in similar work.

Fund-raising for Jewish causes simply went on to new heights, an effort in which JR participated. In December 1918, after his return from France, JR attended a meeting in Chicago with Schiff at which it was agreed that the "Windy City" would attempt to raise $1 million out of a nationwide total of $15 million. The funds were to go to Jews in Poland, Russia, Turkey, Palestine, Galicia, Rumania, and other countries where mobs and soldiers were reported to be pillaging the homes of Jews and murdering thousands.[75] JR ended by donating $790,000 to this effort. Subsequent years saw campaigns with ever greater goals until the Depression. It is possible that JR's grand gesture in 1917 launched a whole new trend in both fund-raising and philanthropy.

Charitable Foundations

JR became involved with two charitable foundations in 1917—one belonging to another famous philanthropist, John D. Rockefeller, and the other his own creation. These facts were probably interconnected.

In January 1917, Julius Rosenwald was invited to join the board of directors of the Rockefeller Foundation. This was not surprising because the Chicago philanthropist had several ties to organizations with which Rockefeller was involved. One was the University of Chicago; moreover, his work on the black schools in the rural South had brought him in contact with the staff of the General Education Board. Abraham Flexner, one of the chief staff members of the Rockefeller Foundation, was one of JR's closest friends. It may have been Flexner who suggested that the board of the Rockefeller Foundation nominate JR. Finally, because of the YMCA and rural school projects, both highly publicized, JR was acquiring a national reputation as a philanthropist.

Charitable foundations were a new phenomenon on the American philanthropic scene. Only a handful of them existed. They were totally unregulated, and their purpose was, to some degree, still uncertain. The role of foundation board member was also in a state of flux. Thus JR had little to guide him when he accepted the Rockefeller Foundation's invitation in January 1917.

He was introduced at a meeting on May 23, 1917. "It was a fine experience," JR wrote Gussie, "and I must say my reception was most cordial. Mr. Rockefeller asked me to sit next to him at the meeting and later at luncheon."[76] A month later, he was called by Dr. George Vincent, the foundation's president. A special meeting was being summoned to determine how much money should be given to the Red Cross, which was conducting a $100 million campaign. "They greatly desire me to come," he wrote Gussie, "another evidence that 'all honors are honorous.'"[77] When the meeting was held two days later, JR was astonished at what occurred. "The odd part of the meeting was that Mr. John D. Rockefeller, Sr. was positively opposed to giving more than two and a half millions—although he was only expressing his personal view as a trustee—and he was unanimously voted down by the board which favored giving five millions."[78] One suspects that JR believed that, since it was John D. Rockefeller Sr. who had provided the funds to establish the foundation, his wishes would be deferred to. However, in later years, when the Julius Rosenwald Fund had a large board consisting primarily of nonfamily members, JR must have remembered this incident, for he did not try to impose his wishes concerning grants on his board.

Not much is known of JR's tenure as a Rockefeller Foundation trustee. He appears to have taken his duties seriously and attended meetings as frequently as his schedule would allow. He served on its board until just before his death in 1932.

A few months after being named to the Rockefeller Foundation board, on October 31, 1917, JR established the Julius Rosenwald Fund. His reasons for doing so are unclear, but they are probably related to his service on the Rockefeller board. This was one of the few instances when the generally efficient JR public relations machine broke down. Stories appeared in the press in Chicago and elsewhere that JR had established a foundation with a $1 million endowment in order to give money for the education of poor children. This was only partially true, and a new press release stated: "The Julius Rosenwald Fund is organized for the purpose of systematizing and perpetuating Mr. Rosenwald's charities. It will be used for philanthropic, charitable, or educational purposes. . . . The organization of definite plans for operating the Fund are in the preliminary stages only."[79] According to the original articles of incorporation in the State of Illinois, the stated purpose of the Rosenwald Fund was "the well-being of mankind,"[80] a mission so vague that it could be invoked to support whatever its donor wished. This was a common practice in the early days of foundation philanthropy. Once the Fund started operating, it was, initially, a conduit through which to funnel many of JR's charitable contributions. Eventually the Julius Rosenwald Fund focused largely on the rural schoolhouse construction program in the South. Only in 1928 was it transformed into an entity that operated apart from the wishes of its founder, with a paid professional staff and a board of family and nonfamily trustees. By that time JR had provided it with both a much larger endowment and a more focused mission.

A year after the creation of the Julius Rosenwald Fund, JR established the Sears, Roebuck Foundation. Although the company had made corporate contributions before 1918, this was an attempt to systematize them. The Sears, Roebuck Foundation may have been among the earliest corporate foundations in the country. It quickly became the largest corporate foundation then in existence.[81]

Looking back at the years 1916–18, JR must have been proud of his accomplishments. He had served as chairman of the Committee on Supplies of the Council of National Defense, his mission to France had been a triumph, his speeches had both entertained and enlightened the troops, and his spectacular gift to the campaign to aid Jewish war sufferers may have launched a whole new era in fund-raising. Finally, though his new foundation was still something of an unknown quantity, the seeds of its future greatness had been planted.

6

The Rescue of Sears and the Consolidation of Philanthropic Endeavors, 1919–1924

The Rescue of Sears

The mail-order business during and immediately after the war was excellent. At the end of 1918, Sears's net sales stood at $181,665,829, and net profits for the year were $12,704,064. At the end of the following year, net sales had risen to $238,982,584, and net profits were up by a third to $18,890,125. And the first six months of 1920 were just as spectacular. Retail prices kept rising, but customers bought as if the increases did not matter. The situation was reminiscent of the early days at Sears, with the company struggling to keep up with inventory. Lessing notified his father: "Business continues very big. Our listing has averaged $1 million a working day since October 1, and at that it is coming in faster than we can handle it. We are not in bad shape yet, but we will be if business continues to come in at this rate, until we can put through even more than we can now—1,848 orders every ten minutes."[1] Indeed, the company could not keep up with the demands of its customers. Tens of millions of dollars were returned to customers because the goods they had ordered were not in stock, a troubling situation that had arisen as early as 1917.[2] Virtually everything in the catalog was selling briskly, and extra catalogs of special items were mailed out and performed well. In a desperate attempt to build inventory, goods were ordered from suppliers at inflated prices because prices were rising steeply in every economic sector. As a result, inventory did rise dramatically, going from $42,685,776 at the end of 1919 to $105,071,243 at the end of the following year.[3] No corporate leader could foresee that this boom was not going to continue forever. JR planned a new satellite plant for Philadelphia to be headed by Lessing, who had worked his way up to a top management position in the company and whose business sense proved that all those nagging letters about money had not dampened his spirit or enthusiasm. It was Lessing who oversaw each detail of construction of the new facility, carefully reporting to his father every step of the way.[4]

The first few months of 1920 were skittish as far as both Sears's business and the national economy were concerned. It was difficult to read the signals. In May, with prices continuing to rise steeply, a consumers' "strike" developed. Some customers began boycotting companies whose prices they considered too high, although the number of such disgruntled people was never significant. For the first nine months of 1920, Sears's sales were $27,664,070 ahead of the same period the year before, a gain of 18 percent.[5] By the late summer, prices were beginning to fall. The downturn was a long, gradual decline.

By the very nature of its business, Sears was in a difficult position. Obtaining goods and printing and mailing a catalog takes time. The fall catalog with inflated prices was mailed at the very time when prices were trending downward. Thus few people ordered from it. The local retail store, smaller and more agile, could benefit because it could turn around and immediately reflect the drop in prices by slashing its own. Sears required several weeks to have the lowered prices reflected in the catalog and reach the public consciousness. The problem of declining prices affected producers who were also Sears's consumers; in the next eighteen months of 1920–21, farm income dropped dramatically. The price of wheat sank almost 60 percent, and corn fell from $2.17 to 59 cents.[6] So farmers could no longer afford Sears products.

These general economic problems were compounded by JR's ethical scruples. Even though enormous numbers of goods had been ordered at inflated prices to fill company warehouses in expectation that the boom would continue, JR refused to cancel any such orders once prices dipped. His motivation was partly the conviction that to break the contract was morally wrong and also his fear that Sears's credit would suffer.[7] The CEOs of other companies were not so scrupulous. Eventually the Sears president was forced to change this policy, but the alteration may have been too little, too late.

Finally, lax management practices occurred that cast doubt on whether a firm hand was truly running the organization. Orders for goods were initiated by unauthorized persons who wrote them on scraps of paper rather than the proper forms; some fairly high-level executives took an inordinate number of days off on the golf course, on the theory that business was so good that their presence was not needed.[8] JR was not one of those executives, but there is some question about his direct involvement in the management of Sears in 1919. Werner as well as Emmet and Jeuck imply that JR did not really return to his post at Sears until 1920.[9] But such an interpretation does not appear to square with the facts. In January 1919, JR was at Johns Hopkins, undergoing a thorough physical checkup, and at the end of the year, he was participating in the Second Industrial Conference, but he spent the remainder of 1919 at his desk in the Sears "plant," according to numerous letters and papers. Yet how could this talented corporate leader have allowed such shoddy practices to occur? It is possible that JR's health was more affected by his experience in France than he or anyone else would admit and that, though present at his desk, he was not fully engaged until 1920. For it is evident that in 1920, once JR became aware that a crisis was occurring, he and his colleagues acted decisively to repair the damage.

In the fall of 1920, as prices headed downward, JR convened an advisory committee consisting of persons from a variety of departments covering the entire company which met every morning to plan strategy.[10] Out of this group came the decision to obtain an immediate infusion of $50 million in cash. So Sears issued special gilt-edged securities in three nearly equal installments paying 7 percent interest. Although JR's bankers urged him to make these notes redeemable in ten years, he insisted that all the notes could be redeemed in three years. Sears took other measures to deal with the crisis. The fall catalog announced drastic reductions in prices, and this trend continued throughout 1921. Moreover, both Sears and its archrival, Montgomery Ward, took measures that neither mail-order house had done before: They started to appeal to urban and suburban dwellers with full-page ads in big-city newspapers, and "they began pushing sales over the counter through outlet stores."[11] Both of these measures were to constitute part of the marketing trend of the future, but few people realized this besides General Robert Wood, who had recently been hired by Montgomery Ward, and probably JR.

Price reductions, ads to urban dwellers, and outlet stores were designed to deal with the huge inventory backlog, which had to be eliminated at almost any price. JR also took steps to deal with mismanagement. He ordered all executives to arrive early and stay late—he himself set the example, sitting down at his desk at 8:00 A.M. and remaining there until late at night. Much to his regret, he cut the workforce between 10 and 30 percent, including reductions in management.[12] He ordered salary cuts and canceled his own salary until 1924. It had stood at $100,000 a year; when he reinstituted it, he reduced it to $60,000.

Sears stock continued dropping in 1921, and more drastic cost-cutting measures were taken. Operating expenses in that year were cut by $20 million. Factories that had been purchased to manufacture goods exclusively for Sears were now sold or closed. With dividends on common stock due in February, JR canceled the dividends and instead issued scrip bearing an interest rate of 6 percent and redeemable on August 15, 1922. Clearly he believed at that point that the crisis would be short-lived and that in eighteen months both Sears and the economy would rebound. JR was worried, however, that the small investor, especially employees who had invested in the profit-sharing plan, would be forced to sell the newly issued scrip to traders at a discount in order to obtain ready cash. Thus he announced that he would buy at par the scrip of anyone owning fifty shares or less who wanted to sell. Some employees had pledged their stock as collateral to banks in order to obtain loans. JR offered to guarantee these accounts to protect those employees from heavy losses. Such actions prefigured the steps he was to take in October 1929.[13]

Nevertheless, the economy continued its decline. Six million people became unemployed. Sears stock, which had been as high as $243 a share in the spring of 1920, sank to $54.50 in 1921. By the end of 1921, some 17,000 businesses had gone under. Rumors were circulating that Sears would be one of the next to go.

By November 1921, it was clear that Sears was facing a crisis. Sales had slumped to the point where only two of approximately fifty departments were doing more business in 1921 than they had the previous year. Sales of durable goods, once the backbone of the company, had slowed to a trickle because of the recession. Sears faced an operating loss of $16,435,468. Most worrisome of all, the dividends were due for the gilt-edged securities that the company had issued in 1920. These would have to be paid in December, and the sum needed was $559,188. It was Albert Loeb who suggested that JR make a large gift of his own money to the company and purchase the land on which the Sears plant stood. JR wrote his old friend Henry Goldman, president of Goldman Sachs, on January 3, 1922: "Albert suggested it a month or two ago and I had been debating it in my mind and had practically decided on it by December 1st."[14] He agreed to donate $5 million to the company in the form of 50,000 shares of Sears stock. It was stipulated that the stock was not to be sold at less than par ($100 a share) and that JR was to have the right to repurchase the stock at any time within three years at par. Since Sears stock was then selling for $60 a share, the idea that JR could only buy it back at $100 a share seemed like seriously misplaced optimism. With regard to the land on which the Homan Avenue plant stood, JR purchased it for $16 million with a first payment of $4 million in cash and Liberty Bonds. The remaining $12 million was secured with only a trust deed, which freed JR from personal liability.[15] The interest rate on this sum was 7 percent. The $4 million down payment was regarded as a loan, on which the company had to pay interest. As the *Chicago Tribune* noted: "In effect this means that, aside from the payment of interest on $4 million, the company will be able to use the property without charge."[16] The result of JR's actions was that Sears, instead of having a $16 million deficit, could end the year with a small surplus of $1,745,607. Moreover, the dividends on the gilt-edged securities could be paid on time.[17] By agreeing to Loeb's suggestion, JR had saved his company.

The announcement of the $5 million gift plus the purchase of the land, made at the end of December 1921, electrified the financial world. Most fulsome in its praise of JR's actions was the *Boston News Bureau* headed by C. W. Barron, founder of the publication that bears his name. In articles and editorials, Barron eloquently described what he regarded as JR's magnificent gesture. In an editorial on December 31, Barron hailed JR's actions as "business philanthropy" and added: "There is the broader lesson of the sort of trusteeship shown by the man whose commercial genius did so much for the almost romantic upbuilding of the concern known to thousands of farmer families. In that same sweep of country it has been the fashion for many to conceive of men of wealth and captains of industry as utterly selfish and as given to preying on the misfortune of others. Here is the chivalric answer!"[18] Other newspapers were equally enthusiastic.

A number of individuals wrote to JR expressing their delight and amazement at his rescue of Sears. JR's former colleague on the Council of National Defense, Bernard Baruch, wrote him: "I have seen the splendid thing you have done for your company. Truly you are a noble chap. But it is really characteristic of you."[19] Henry Goldman declared, "I am deeply impressed by this most unusual act [of yours]."[20] And Victor H. Munnecke of Armour & Co. noted: "The action taken by you . . . is to my mind the biggest thing that has been done for big business by any one individual in this country within my recollection. In addition to that, it is the biggest thing that has been done for fellow stockholders by a big man in their company and, I think, will give the stockholders of Sears, Roebuck & Co. more encouragement, coming just at this time, than anything else that could be done for them."[21] The raising of the morale of both stockholders and employees was considered of tremendous significance.

Evidently contemporaries believed that JR's actions were unusual, and perhaps they would be viewed similarly in our day. One can imagine a businessman of JR's stature writing off his losses, taking his millions and simply closing down the business. Thus this comment by Frederick Rawson, of the Union Trust Company, seems to speak most clearly to our own era: "It is unique in business annals and will stand out as the one great shining event in the business life of 1921. It goes beyond business activities, and will be referred to for all time as one of the sublime sacrifices and splendid examples of altruism and regard for those who cannot afford to take a loss. There was no moral reason why it should be done, which makes it the greater, and I am sure will prove an incentive to others to emulate your splendid precedent."[22]

Although others did not follow JR's example, his risky gesture turned out to be beneficial both for Sears and for himself. The economy was already starting to turn around, and the bull market of the "Roaring Twenties" would soon be under way. After extending the time in which he could buy back the 50,000 shares of Sears stock, JR repurchased the stock in 1926. By that time, Sears stock had risen to the point that the purchase price of $100 a share, which had seemed almost utopian in the depth of the 1921 recession, proved to be a bargain. Thus JR actually made money on the transaction, though he could have had no way of knowing that in

1921. With regard to the land purchase, Sears in 1931 offered to repay the $4 million and cancel the remaining $12 million debt within thirty days of JR's death or on December 31, 1936, whichever occurred later.[23]

There were some dissenting voices about the significance of JR's action. John Higgins, a vice president of Sears, was asked whether he thought the company had been in danger of going under eight years earlier. He replied: "We were all too busy rowing the boat to think." Asked about JR's actions at that time, Higgins replied that "JR's stock 'gift' in 1921 was essentially a paper transaction for bookkeeping purposes."[24] While it may have looked that way in retrospect, there is no denying that on December 31, 1921, JR's action appeared to be a true gamble. No one knew how long the recession would last or what its economic effects would be.

Even with the economic upturn, JR and his colleagues were very cautious about restoring the dividend on common stock, and they did not do so until 1924. In the great rivalry between the two Chicago mail-order houses, Sears and Ward, the latter came close to equaling Sears's net profit in 1922 and for the first time excelled in marketing. Even more interesting in terms of the future, Sears continued to advertise in big-city newspapers, and in 1923 opened a retail store in Chicago to sell its "ready cut houses."[25] Thus, even before General Wood was brought in and started retail stores in a non-crisis atmosphere, JR was already moving cautiously in that direction.

Although marketing had been the strong suit of Richard Sears, not JR, it was the latter's marketing ability that was stressed in a blizzard of stories about the Sears president and his company that began appearing in publications in the early postwar years. The public relations machine at Sears was being cranked into high gear. Numerous interviews with Sears's president appeared in magazines and newspapers, and some articles were purportedly authored by JR himself. An article entitled "What We Have Learned from 6,000,000 Customers" under JR's byline appeared in the *American Magazine* in July 1920, and Sears's president made many of the same points in an interview with the *New York Times* three years later. In both articles, Rosenwald claimed that America was becoming more homogeneous in its tastes. No longer should the farmer be considered a rube, for he and his family had the same kinds of taste and bought the same kinds of goods as the more sophisticated city dwellers. JR attributed this phenomenon to what he called "the three m's": magazines, movies, and motor cars. Rural people were increasingly subscribing to magazines and were reading not only the stories they contained but also the ads. Thus they saw the items that were considered fashionable and wanted them for themselves. These desires were reinforced by the movie industry, then in its infancy but already widespread. People of all social strata attended the cinema and could see how Hollywood portrayed the latest fashions—which these moviegoers could then go out and purchase.

Finally, JR argued, a trip to town was no longer an extraordinary occurrence for the farm family. They could easily drive there by car. While JR recognized that such shopping expeditions could benefit local retail stores, he argued that it still benefited Sears because if the local retailer did not have the goods that were wanted, the mail-order house, with its huge volume, certainly did. What JR failed to realize was that "motor cars" could be a two-edged sword, that the relative ease of automobile travel and the affordability of cars would make mail order more bothersome and ultimately cut into his business. Large retail stores carrying a wide range of goods were becoming increasingly popular in cities and towns. It was easier and faster for farmers to pick up the items they needed right away rather than go through the cumbersome process of ordering by mail and waiting for their purchases to arrive. Despite the experience with over-the-counter stores that Sears had had during the recent recession, it would fall to General Wood to impress upon JR the importance of turning Sears Roebuck from a purely mail-order company to one that was a mixture of mail-order and retail stores.

Almost every article and interview about JR and Sears emphasizes that the marketing of Sears was based on the bond of trust between seller and consumer. This is generally portrayed as a comparatively new concept, and it is always credited to Richard Sears. JR is usually mentioned in an entirely different context. The bond between seller and consumer is predicated on the notion that the seller will be entirely truthful in everything. In the case of Sears, the need for veracity underlines the importance of accurate catalog descriptions. Another aspect of the bond between seller and consumer was the guarantee—the notion that if the product was defective, or even if the customer did not like it for some reason, he or she could ship it back at Sears's expense and receive a refund. This was another way to build trust on the part of the consumer and to ensure that customers would remain loyal. JR and other Sears spokesmen emphasized in interviews that only a minute fraction of goods was ever returned. Finally there was the concept that the customer could be trusted—that certified checks were not required and that personal checks were perfectly acceptable. Again, the company took pains to point out that the number of bad checks or unpaid bills was infinitesimal. All of these elements of the bond between customer and company were cited as reasons for the phenomenal growth of Sears.

Intimately connected to this bond of trust between the mail-order store and its consumers was the concept that the customer, even though he or she was unseen (so different from the case of an over-the-counter store!), needed to be treated as a person. Thus hundreds of "girls" were employed to answer letters, and the publicity department enjoyed relating the stories of lonely farmers writing letters asking for wives, children requesting baby brothers or sisters, or people unwilling to make up their mind from the catalog descriptions, asking Mr. or Mrs. Sears to please pick out a nice hat and send it on. In short, as an article attributed to JR stated: "In dealing with the customer, we believe in the importance of the human and personal touch. The result is that our patrons are real people to us and we are real people to them. We feel as if we know them, how they are living, and what their ideals are."[26]

Another thing these articles and interviews were at pains to emphasize was the sheer size of Sears. Seven million customers in 1919 had grown to 8 million four years later, and JR boasted that, in fact, he was providing goods for approximately 32 million people, assuming a family of four and one order per household. The statistics were meant to impress, and they just roll off the pages of these publicity pieces. For example, the statistic most often cited was that the wallpaper factories of Sears turned out 20 million rolls a year, enough to circle the world four times. The catalogs, too, were a marvel. They were over 1,000 pages long, many of them in color. They contained over 100,000 separate articles of merchandise, weighed five pounds, and were shipped to customers absolutely free of charge. According to the *American Magazine* article, it cost the company $1 per copy to produce and mail.[27]

The flip side of the millions of satisfied customers was "humanizing the relationship between the firm and its employees."[28] The starting point for the bond between firm and employee was JR's notion that his employees did not work *for* him but *with* him. Mentioned in almost the next breath was the savings and profit sharing plan. By 1919, it was said, 96.7 percent of the eligible employees had become members of it, making Sears by far the most successful company to introduce profit sharing as part of the "welfare capitalism" movement.[29] Like the profit sharing plan, the anniversary plan, inaugurated in 1912, rewarded length of service. And by the 1920s, a number of employees had been with the company for twenty-five years. For such people, the anniversary checks, which only provided bonuses for up to ten years of employment, were not enough. What happened to someone who had been with Sears for twenty-five years can be seen in the case of Walker Lewis.

In 1896, Walker Lewis joined the still small Sears, Roebuck & Co. "at the bottom of the ladder." Through the years, by hard work and merit, he advanced until, in 1921, he was treasurer of the company. His father, C. T. Lewis, from Petersburg, Illinois, was invited to be present for the festivities marking Walker's twenty-fifth anniversary. He described the occasion in an article in the local newspaper. First there was a dinner hosted by the employees of the Treasurer's Department at the Sears YMCA. At the dinner, short informal speeches were interspersed with skits and songs. The following day, Walker and his family were invited to JR's office.

> After we were all seated in Mr. Rosenwald's private office, he turned to Walker's boys and said, in part: "Boys, you cannot now appreciate what your father has gone through. His experience is too big for you now, but some day I hope it may be your great joy." Turning to Walker he said: "Walker, you are a wonderful man, because of your influence which is great both in the house and out of it. Your own people are telling good things about you. Your own people—they listen to your good advice. You have played a big part in the character building of our firm. You are probably better known than any man in the house—more people mention your name than any other of the firm." Turning to me he said: "Your son is one of the big men we are proud of." I watched Mr. Rosenwald very closely. I could see he was giving vent to the feeling of his innermost soul in such beautiful language of love and high respect he completely overcame the father. . . . To know that you have a son working for a firm that so heartily appreciates his services certainly gives his parents a great uplift and carries them back twenty-five years when a homesick boy desired so much to come back home.[30]

C. T. Lewis evidently thought the occasion not only completely appropriate but very moving.

The profit sharing and anniversary plans, along with excellent recreational facilities and liberal sick days, made for relatively contented employees. There were no unions at Sears, presumably because the employees had the profit sharing plan. The long-term risks of striking and being terminated were too great.

Almost all the articles about JR created a mythical character. His history was retold, and although not exactly a Horatio Alger stereotype, it nevertheless showed that, from relatively humble beginnings, one could rise to become one of the wealthiest men in the world. Yet what especially surprised people was JR's often-quoted modesty: the concept that it was not his great brains or great skill that had brought him to this point, but luck. He had, he kept repeating, merely taken advantage of good opportunities. Many articles mentioned his philanthropy as well as his business acumen. JR's love of family, which was genuine, was thus added to the image of this business paragon. The author of "Satisfaction or Your Money Back" did not even meet JR, but he interviewed JR's associates to find out what kind of man the president of Sears was:

> He wears no jewelry or other marks of wealth, but he gives to charity $1,000,000 at one time. He works ten or twelve hours a day, setting a pace that few of his young employees can follow; the only thing that appeals to him more than work is a personal affection or a philanthropic duty. . . . He holds that employees require few written laws; their own sense of right should govern them; it is better to have a principle of right in man's heart than a rule of conduct in his head. Principles not rules are the guiding force of the company.[31]

JR emerged from the financial crisis of 1921 having learned some valuable lessons. One, which is noted in an article he purportedly wrote for the *Christian Science Monitor* in 1923, is that it is important to watch inventory: "It is a gigantic task . . . to buy sufficient quantities of merchandise of all kinds to supply the demands of all customers without having a large amount of surplus stock at the end of a season."[32]

Another lesson learned was that it was imperative to care for the welfare of his most loyal customers—the farmers. Part of Sears, Roebuck's problems in 1921 had stemmed from the drastic drop in farm incomes. JR determined to find some vehicle through Sears to help farmers, and in 1923 he created the Sears, Roebuck Agricultural Foundation. Just as he had popularized the agricultural extension movement in 1912, so this foundation was designed to provide farmers with information and aid them to do what they lacked the expertise to do themselves. Farmers could write in with questions and have them answered by a panel of experts. JR thought of this as a "mail-order county agent." A group of wheat growers in Kansas wanted to organize for the purposes of cooperative marketing, but lacked the expertise to begin. The Agricultural Foundation gave them funds to finance the organizing committee. It also offered $1,000 to the first five counties that would employ full-time paid leaders for farm boys' and girls' clubs. It was the Agricultural Foundation which launched radio station WLS in Chicago. The initials stood for "World's Largest Store." In the local country store, said JR, much important information sharing takes place around the stove in the back room. "The Agricultural Foundation," he went on, "is the stove in the rear of our store."[33] JR acknowledged that his reasons for starting the foundation were not altogether altruistic. He even admitted that Sears would gain good publicity because of the actions of the Foundation. In short, helping farmers help themselves, and improve their economic prospects, was simply good for Sears's business. It was an example of JR's view of philanthropy applied to business.

Revamping the Schools Project

The crisis at Sears was by no means the only problem that preoccupied JR in these years. A number of projects or programs which he had started earlier required either fine-tuning or complete revamping. Chief among these was the rural school building program that had begun with such promise in 1913.

Following Booker T. Washington's death in 1915, the school building program continued unabated. JR remained very enthusiastic. He was content to leave its administration in the hands of Tuskegee. Moreover, his government work consumed him for most of the two years following Washington's death.

In August 1917, a group of Negro state agents met with JR.[34] They decided that Tuskegee should continue to administer the Rosenwald school building program and that a committee of three state agents should meet with Dr. Robert Moton and Emmett Scott to draw up new guidelines that would be given to JR. The report of this group specified that JR would provide no more than $400 for a one-teacher school and $500 for a two-teacher school. Each one-teacher school had to have a classroom, a kitchen, a library, and a "manual training room." The report emphasized that JR would give only a small portion of the funds necessary to build each school and that the bulk of the funds still would be provided by state and local government and local residents of both races. Moreover, JR's money would be given only after all other funds had been appropriated or collected, and the school building would have to be completed and furnished within six months after reporting that it qualified for JR's aid. Tuskegee and the State Departments of Education were to decide each year on the number of schools to be built in each state. The type of building to be erected had to be approved by Tuskegee and, where appropriate, the state Education Department. In order to extend the school year from four to nine months, an additional $30 was to be given to participating schools by JR. It was envisaged that this agreement would last for three years. The budget for 1917–18 called for the construction of three hundred schools in ten Southern states. Besides the schoolhouses, it called for JR to pay the salaries of an assistant director for Clinton J. Calloway, who was overseeing the program, and a bookkeeper/stenographer. Finally, JR was to continue paying the full salary of a special rural school agent in Alabama (Booker T. Washington Jr.) and half the salary of assistant rural school agents (who were black) in the nine other Southern states. These county agents, who were actually called "Rosenwald agents," had existed since the summer of 1915. The total expected from JR in this 1917–18 budget for salaries, printing, travel, maps, charts, and photographs was $150,000.[35] JR approved this report with its budget and recommendations after asking the advice of his friend Abraham Flexner. The only change he made, at Flexner's suggestion, was an emphasis on the active participation of the county authorities. In other words, a school could not be built because the rural school agent and the local blacks wanted it. The local county government had to not only approve but become actively involved. Implicit in this arrangement, as it had been from the beginning, was the concept that every Rosenwald school was a public school.

For the next sixteen months, despite the war and a shortage of building supplies, the program continued operating, although the pace of construction was slowed. There were few changes, except for an emphasis on the consolidation of scattered and inefficient one-room schools so that one larger school serving several communities might be built in a county. Moreover, the community and county authorities were responsible for guaranteeing the completion of the building, and Calloway was responsible for ultimate oversight.[36]

On May 14, 1919, the first criticism of the Rosenwald school program surfaced, but it could have come years earlier.[37] As far back as 1915, James L. Sibley, the rural agent for Negroes in Alabama, had written to JR's assistant, William C. Graves:

> I believe it would greatly expedite matters in the erection of new schoolhouses through Mr. Rosenwald's assistance if he would allow about $250 to be used in the preparation and printing of plans to be followed in the various communities. We have arranged for some blueprints to be made at Tuskegee Institute and are now looking for some means to have them printed. If they could be put in a neat little folder with instructions to be sent to each community making application so they might be studied by interested parties, it would save a great deal of talking and visiting and unnecessary loss of time.[38]

Washington informed Graves later that month that he had had a conference with Sibley and "the matter has already been carried out to the satisfaction of all concerned."[39] A set of blueprints and plans was subsequently prepared and sent to those who wanted to build schools,[40] but there was little effective oversight from Tuskegee to ensure that the guidelines were being followed. Calloway did make occasional field trips and did criticize buildings he believed were not up to the program's standards, but the territory being covered now was so vast and the number of schools being constructed was so large that Calloway's efforts were insufficient.

Thus, four years after Sibley's note to Graves, Frank P. Bachman, superintendent of public instruction of North Carolina, wrote Abraham Flexner: "[T]he best results are not now being attained from the Rosenwald funds. First, because the Rural School Agents are not provided with an adequate number of suitable plans. Second, as the fund is now administered, it is not possible to do the best by the most aspiring communities; and, third, adequate provisions are not now made for the needed inspection of Rosenwald schoolhouses during the course of their erection."[41] A few days later, N. C. Newbold, the state agent for rural schools in North Carolina, sent Flexner additional details. Numerous schools were poorly constructed. They lacked adequate windows, doors and walls were in the wrong places, and adequate inspections were simply not being carried out. Flexner, in a soothing reply, promised that he would take the matter up with his colleague, Wallace Buttrick, chairman of the General Education Board, and with JR.[42]

Such a conversation took place in early June. Flexner and Buttrick suggested that JR hire Dr. Fletcher B. Dresslar, professor of hygiene and schoolhouse planning at George Peabody College for Teachers in Nashville, as a consultant. On June 18, Buttrick contacted Dr. Dresslar on behalf of JR. "He has conceived the idea of requesting you to make a survey of the way the work has been handled and of schoolhouses thus far erected." He urged Dresslar to go to Tuskegee and familiarize himself "not only with the schoolhouse plans, but with the entire procedure followed in obtaining local money, putting through the work of construction, and supervising the results."[43] Dresslar immediately accepted.

On July 1, Rosenwald and Flexner were at Tuskegee for a conference on the Rural Schoolhouse Program attended by three hundred teachers. While there, they met with Moton and Calloway and told them about Dresslar's assignment. Moton immediately saw the handwriting on the wall and wrote an anguished letter to Flexner regarding the "transfer of the Rosenwald Fund from Tuskegee Institute." He went on: "The moral effect on the whole Southern situation of having this Fund administered through a Negro school is very great in bringing about better race relations."[44] This had been the argument used so effectively by Washington to retain JR's interest. In this instance, it fell on deaf ears. Flexner replied that the matter was not in his hands but in JR's, and added: "I feel sure that Mr. Rosenwald is not going to do anything that does not by its soundness command the approval of all interested in the work."[45]

Even though the Dresslar mission was about to begin, Bachman continued to send Flexner additional evidence of shoddy workmanship. In forwarding Bachman's second letter to JR, Flexner made the telling statement: "I doubt if Major Moton quite takes in the situation."[46] Indeed, Moton was not very cooperative.

At the end of September, an audit, which was carried out independent of Dresslar, was completed. It confirmed JR's suspicions. The financial records at Tuskegee were in complete disarray. Flexner put the best face on the situation and provided what was to be the official line when he sent the audit to JR: "It seems quite clear that, as was natural and inevitable, the Rosenwald school activity has grown so rapidly that the accounting and control arrangements have hardly kept pace with it."[47]

Dresslar began his study of the construction of Rosenwald schools

Figure 14. (*Top*) Workers putting windows in a Rosenwald school in Gregg County, Texas. Since all schools were built before rural electrification, they all faced east-west and had huge windows for light. (*Bottom*) JR and an unidentified man at the dedication of the 4,000th Rosenwald school, the Barry O'Kelly High School in Wake County, North Carolina, 1928. Courtesy of the Jackson Davis Collection, University of Virginia Library.

around August 20. Conditions were often difficult. He wrote Flexner: "Thus far I have not had to employ an aviator to transport me, but several times I have sorely needed one to clear the mud. One day we stuck tight six different times. Fortunately, I can fix a Ford, even if I cannot run a typewriter."[48]

As Dresslar was performing his study, Flexner received other complaints. Leo Favrot, the state agent for Negro schools for Louisiana, one of the most intelligent and thoughtful of these officials, complained to Flexner of the poor administration of the program. He said that local peculiarities were not taken into account, and added: "I have for the past three years received approximately $40,000 for the building of Rosenwald schools in the state and I have never been checked up on in any way."[49] Other comments were of a more racist character. T. H. Harris, the Louisiana superintendent of public education, wrote Flexner: "I can fully appreciate the motives which prompted Mr. Rosenwald to select a group of Negroes to look after the administration of such funds as he might expend in the South on Negro school buildings. . . . [I]t was a very unwise thing to do." He added, "If the Negro committee continues to administer the funds, I predict that the Southern states will soon begin to withdraw."[50]

By January 31, 1920, the Dresslar report had been completed and sent to JR. It was scathing. Many schools were poorly constructed, a pamphlet of plans or architectural drawings had frequently not been made available, and there was not always accountability to or follow-up by Tuskegee.

In February 1920, JR decided that he would transfer management of the school building program to the Julius Rosenwald Fund and would hire one of the state agents for Negro schools to run the operation. His first choice was Leo Favrot. But Favrot declined, perhaps because, despite his earlier criticism of Tuskegee, he favored keeping the program there. So JR turned to S. L. Smith, the state agent for Tennessee. Smith, who had attended a one-room schoolhouse himself, had studied under Dresslar at Peabody and had been a state agent for Negro schools since 1914. Smith was considered an expert in school construction, and he had a thorough knowledge of black rural schools He accepted JR's offer.

JR had a difficult task, for he now had to inform the people of Tuskegee, including Washington's widow, Margaret, of his decision. Flexner posed the problem to JR in a letter at the end of April: "You know without my assuring you, that Dr. Buttrick and I want to do everything in our power to carry out your plans and wishes, but the situation to be dealt with is so complicated and delicate, involving Mrs. Washington's just pride, Major Moton's prestige, our own relationship to these good people at Tuskegee, and finally your attitude toward all concerned."[51] The meeting eventually occurred on May 13 in Buttrick's office. Moton's feelings were summed up in a letter to Buttrick: "I suppose [Mrs. Washington] felt as I did and as our Tuskegee people feel—somewhat as a mother does when she gives up her daughter to be married; while she knows it is the natural and proper thing for her daughter, yet as a whole they do not rejoice in giving them up, and sometimes weep."[52] Mrs. Washington also wrote Buttrick and could barely hide her bitterness. "I have always known how the men, with whom we have to deal, felt about having to ask a colored man for aid. This is natural, and I am enough of a Southerner to understand it, and also to appreciate it. He feels exactly about me as we feel about him; no sensible reason for this attitude of either of us, however, a natural prejudice, which only time, common sense, and the courage of a few people to trust us, and to be patient with the Southern white man, not giving over too quickly to his whims." She went on to say that what was important about JR's gift was that he showed enough confidence in blacks to give the school building program over to them in the first place.[53] In Mrs. Washington's eyes, JR had betrayed his own project by giving in to the racism of some of the program's critics. He had, in effect said, "Blacks are not competent enough to do this job." In JR's defense, it is likely that he would have looked at the matter differently. The people at Tuskegee had failed to perform satisfactorily, regardless of their color. There was no qualified black candidate not connected with Tuskegee who was available and could take over the project. Hence JR felt he had no choice but to turn the school building program over to a white man with the requisite amount of experience.

Smith, who began work in June 1920, did an excellent job managing the program. Moreover, as he admitted to JR a year after taking over, he was happier than he had ever been in his life. He said that he had been reluctant to accept the position because he had enjoyed being a state agent, but he liked working for the Rosenwald Fund even more.[54]

Under Smith's leadership, architectural plans were carefully drawn up and sent out to black community leaders who wished to build schools, there was a sufficient amount of follow-up activity, and buildings were inspected before the final piece of funding—the Rosenwald money—was paid out. The complaints that had plagued the program in 1919 vanished almost completely. Because of the size of the program, there was bound to be the occasional glitch, such as the Mississippi state agent who absconded with the funds, but these problems were kept to a minimum. And the program grew enormously. The vast majority of the more than 5,300 schools built as part of the Rosenwald program were constructed while Smith was in charge. JR left the entire management of the program in Smith's capable hands. He would review the yearly budget and approve it, or attend an occasional school opening; but once JR had started the program, then rescued it by picking the right man to ensure its success, he believed there was little more he had to do, and he could turn his energy to other projects.

Smith continued to delight in his position, feeling, correctly, that he was truly accomplishing an important task. Yet the administrator of the school building program also knew that the work he was engaged in could not be done without the collaboration of other foundations which had been working in the area of black education for years. As Smith wrote to Wallace Buttrick in June 1924, reflecting on his ten years of work in the field of black education: "What a wonderful change in the whole attitude toward Negro Education in this time! Not because I have been on this work has the change come, but because of the united efforts of all [of] us interested in Negro education guided by the wisdom of men like you and Dr. Dillard [director of the Jeanes and Slater Funds], who have ennobled the task and inspired us to put our whole souls into the work. The work of the General Education Board, the [Phelps] Stokes and Jeanes Fund, etc., has advanced Negro Education at least a quarter of a century: this is to say, the opportunities now enjoyed by the Negro children of today would have been denied them, and their children would no doubt have had poorer opportunities than are now afforded the Negro youth. I am still happy in the work on entering the duties of the second decade."[55]

The best description of S. L. Smith was written by Edwin Embree, his employer from 1928 through the mid-1930s:

> Mr. Smith was just the man for the job. He knew the South and he knew its people. Moreover, he had a gift for establishing friendly relations with people at all levels, even the most difficult and disagreeable, and of transferring his enthusiasm to community leaders. . . . Disarming, sincerely friendly, instinctively tactful, he refrained from raising unnecessary prob-

> lems, but managed, nevertheless, to point out glaring faults without giving offense. And because he was so generous in recognizing the finer qualities even of men who were base and reactionary, he encouraged them to be better than they were and obtained their support almost in spite of themselves. Negroes came to look on him as a personal symbol for Julius Rosenwald, and to love and trust the northern philanthropist they had not seen because of the kindly Southerner they knew.[56]

In many ways, the Rosenwald Fund's was the most progressive of all the foundation programs dealing with black education and garnered the most support in the black community. "According to Leo Favrot, the Rosenwald program stimulated unity, pride, and autonomous development in black communities. Rosenwald schools united people, 'regardless of denominational difference' around a 'common cause.' In this way they fostered a 'community spirit' among blacks. Rosenwald schools openly encouraged black self-help and autonomy."[57]

Renewing the Y Offer

In 1920, when JR was thinking about how to restructure the Rosenwald school program, he had to make another decision about a program he had started a decade earlier: the building of black YMCAs. The careful way in which this decision was arrived at demonstrates JR's method of proceeding as far as his philanthropy was concerned. It is also important to realize that at the very moment this and the school decision were taken, intimations were beginning that both Sears and the economy in general were in serious trouble.

Since JR had made his initial offer to the YMCA on December 30, 1910, thirteen YMCAs and one YWCA had been built or were under construction.[58] Although JR's original offer had only been for a five-year period, he was liberal about granting extensions. Still, by 1920, it was clear that the operation of this program needed to be evaluated.

The review process began with Graves asking for reports on the completed YMCAs from both William J. Parker, the business manager of the Chicago YMCA, and Jesse Moorland, the African American minister who had spearheaded the drive for black Ys. Among the questions asked were: Had the new Ys led to improved race relations between whites and blacks through cooperation in such areas as fund-raising? Were they financially self-sufficient? Did they serve as community centers as well as Ys? Both men were asked to be as objective as possible. In addition, letters were sent out to the white YMCA general secretaries in every city that had built a black Y, asking for an assessment. Finally, there was the question of whether there should be a new program or merely an extension of the old one. A number of smaller cities and suburban communities wanted to build black Ys. Could JR's offer be applied to them, and what would that mean?

The first to send in his report was Jesse Moorland. Because he had initiated the idea for this program, Moorland had a definite stake in making it appear successful, but he tried to be objective. He noted that "not very much progress has been made with educational work outside of practical talks and lectures, some class work, but it is yet negligible." Otherwise, Moorland was very positive. The Ys were serving as community centers, and almost all were financially self-sufficient. But his main point in favor of the Ys was one that resonates strongly in our own day: these buildings were truly important in terms of raising the level of black self-esteem. As Moorland says:

> Probably the inspiration which these buildings, including the building campaigns, have given to the various communities, has been worth more than we can estimate by any sort of tabulated report. It has blazed the way for many enterprises which are proving successful among the colored people. This building movement has taught many men how to promote secular business enterprises in the matter of establishing banks, building apartment houses, as well as churches and in some cases schools, putting their affairs on a better financial basis. Many of our prominent colored men regard this movement as the most outstanding evidence of progress among our people as anything that has been done in the last generation.[59]

Moorland also strongly supported the idea that the program should be extended to smaller communities.

Parker also favored the program's extension. He emphasized that the Ys were proving to be a school for black managerial talent, at least as far as leadership positions were concerned. Leading black businessmen and professional people in each city were willing to sit on the boards of the black YMCA and presumably engage in fund-raising, although not as much money was raised from blacks as had been hoped. As Parker tactfully put it: "They pledged in good faith, but overestimated their ability to pay."

Relations between black and white boards and upper-level staffs "seem to be very intimate and cordial." And these good relationships seemed to be percolating down to lower level staff, although Parker acknowledged that "progress in this direction is not as rapid as one wishes." There were other negatives which Parker noted. Some of the YMCAs were so well used that they were already too small. Physical education was nonexistent except as it related to boys. Membership in the completed Ys was greater than expected, and blacks seemed generally able to pay the relatively steep membership fee of $500 a year, but most blacks were not able or willing to make additional donations to general operating expenses. Parker concluded, "All these Associations give promise of being permanently successful enterprises. They have proved acceptable to both white and colored people, and while results have not been satisfactory in every respect there is a uniformly confident feeling among those who know the local situations intimately that steady progress is being made. . . . [T]he record made by these twelve Associations thus far may persuade you to reopen your original offer for a reasonable period."[60]

After receiving this report, Graves phoned Parker and asked him to name the cities that were asking about building new black Ys. Parker replied that there might be as many as ten, including such urban and suburban centers as Montclair, New Jersey, Los Angeles, and Detroit.[61]

On March 22, 1920, Graves summarized the reports of Moorland and Parker and added some editorial opinions of his own. Contrasting the approaches of the two men, Graves stated: "Mr. Parker, while sympathetic in his work, seeks to uncover actual conditions, good and bad. Dr. Moorland, while honest, tends to emphasize the good results. . . . Mr. Parker is a business man; Dr. Moorland, a promoter." Although the overall picture was undoubtedly quite favorable, there were some disturbing signs. One was the fact, deplored by Moorland, that the Wabash YMCA in Chicago was controlled by a white board because of factional fights and jealousies on the part of local blacks. Another was that the executive secretary of the Kansas City YMCA sought to use that institution "for DuBois propaganda and became insubordinate. He was dismissed."[62]

What happened in Kansas City is uncertain, but one can surmise that protests were raised about the YMCA being a segregated institution. Construction of the Detroit YMCA was delayed for at least four years for precisely this reason.

Graves does not make any recommendation with regard to an extension or modification of the YMCA building program. He notes that Parker and Moorland are in agreement that the 1910 offer should be extended, but that whereas Moorland believes the offer should be extended to smaller cities, Parker thinks this would be "impractical." Finally, he indicates that there is likely to be increased support for new buildings.

JR did not make up his mind based on Graves's memo. He asked for additional information from Parker and Moorland. Parker proposed a much more detailed outline of what each building should contain. "Moorland urged Rosenwald to support YMCAs where they were needed, not just where the local black population was willing and able to finance them."[63] He wanted smaller, less well-equipped buildings so that poorer communities in the South could also apply for JR's aid. Of the YMCAs built between 1910 and 1920, only three were in Southern cities: Washington, D.C., Baltimore, and Atlanta. Moorland thought this unfair and believed that JR's offer should be for $15,000 with a match of $35,000, an idea which JR dismissed out of hand.

JR began his second grant to the YMCA by reviewing the reasons for his 1910 offer. He said it had occurred to him that in the interests of black people and of the country as a whole, there should be buildings in the black community for men and boys devoted to education, recreation, and service. Since there were not enough wealthy blacks to build such buildings, "[i]t, therefore, seemed the duty of the White people to show interest in the welfare of these their neighbors by helping to supply this need." Gone was the argument of the kinship between blacks and Jews. Rather, this almost biblical statement declared, it was incumbent upon whites to aid blacks because they were neighbors.

Other reasons were stated as well, among them the belief that, despite the segregated nature of the facilities, the very act of cooperating on the financing of these buildings would bring the races together for more than a mere moment. Such cooperation between the races was especially important because of changing circumstances: both the black migration north and the race riots of 1919 in Chicago and other cities, to which JR merely alluded without being specific.

Not only circumstances but the terms of the offer had changed. JR's $25,000 was now contingent upon $125,000 being raised from both blacks and whites. Moreover, accepting Parker's plan, each new building must come equipped with: "(1) Separate quarters for men and boys; (2) Standard gymnasium; (3) Swimming pool; (4) Class and club rooms; (5)

Restaurant; and (6) not fewer than fifty dormitory rooms." Rosenwald's money would be granted only after L. Wilbur Messer, general secretary of the Chicago YMCA, had approved the plans and attested to the fact that $75,000 had been collected and spent on land, buildings, and equipment. Moreover, Messer was also required to certify that the building would be completed within six months of the receipt of JR's funds. Paradoxically, however, JR also seemed to agree with Moorland that smaller buildings should be built. He mentioned that he had been assured that there were requests from eleven cities, but these included smaller suburban towns such as Montclair and Orange, New Jersey. The letter closed with the hope that many other communities would apply.[64]

In the two years stipulated in the second YMCA offer, not one city met the required financial match.[65] The terms were simply too severe. JR granted extensions liberally, and black YMCAs continued to be built under the 1920 formula until after JR's death. In 1928, the entire program was absorbed by the Julius Rosenwald Fund. Eleven new YMCAs and one YWCA were built under the 1920 extension.[66] Twenty-four YMCAs and two YWCAs were built under the Rosenwald program at a cost of $5,815,969, of which JR and the Fund contributed $637,000. Blacks contributed $472,319, and other whites and white YMCAs contributed $4,490,893.

The YMCA/YWCA building program had an impact even beyond those constructed with JR's funds. As George Arthur, onetime head of the Wabash YMCA, stated in a book on the YMCAs: "Fifty other cities not able to meet Mr. Rosenwald's offer but inspired by his spirit have organized colored YMCA branches through the cooperative effort of white and colored people. One hundred and five student organizations have been organized throughout the United States and forty Associations in South Africa which are supervised by Negroes sent by North American Associations."[67] In addition to the YMCA in Washington, D.C., the Ys in Los Angeles and Buffalo were designed by black architects, and in the case of Los Angeles, the building was built largely by a black construction crew. Until the Depression was felt with full force, most of the new YMCAs were self-supporting, which had been one of JR's primary goals. Income came from the cafeterias and from the rental of dormitory rooms.

Overall, the YMCA program should be counted as a success. It probably did not fulfill JR's dream of bringing the races together. The new Ys were, after all, segregated, as DuBois and others noted. Fund-raising efforts may have brought the two races together briefly, but after the buildings were constructed, race relations returned to their unfortunate if familiar pattern. Yet it may be, as JR contended, that the act of coming together to fund the Ys brought blacks greater self-respect and more respect in the eyes of whites, some of whom doubted that blacks could ever raise the required sums of money.

The Chicago Urban League and the Chicago Commission on Race Relations

The volume of business and civic affairs with which JR was involved prevented him from devoting as much of his time and energies as he would have liked to many of the causes involving African Americans. Thanks to Graves, he did keep well informed, and despite minimal personal involvement, he was still able to play a vital role. This can be seen especially in the case of two organizations involving African Americans that converged during this period: the Urban League and the Chicago Commission on Race Relations.

In 1917, a relatively new black organization to which JR had begun contributing, the League on Urban Conditions among Negroes, sent an organizer, T. Arnold Hill, to Chicago. Hill soon became so successful there that he decided to stay on as the local executive director. This decision was taken at the very beginning of the great black migration to the North. Blacks were starting to arrive in Chicago in increasing numbers, hoping to acquire jobs at higher wages than they could find in the rural South, especially in the steel and meatpacking industries. The Chicago Chapter of the Urban League, as it was soon called, helped these recent arrivals to find housing and jobs. Graves held several meetings with Hill and eventually persuaded JR to pay one-third of the fledgling organization's first year budget of $3,000.

In December 1917, while JR was in Washington working on the war effort, Graves wrote him a memo about the Urban League: "I am satisfied that the organization is up and coming and doing a work of value to our community. It is bringing cooperation from scores of Negro civic and philanthropic organizations which have been working at cross purposes and with much jealousy. It has received the migrants from the South, has advised them, has helped them secure homes and has found work for them. It has been their constant friend and adviser. On the other hand, it has been of assistance to many employers whose forces have been reduced by employees volunteering and being drafted for military service. It has opened kinds of employment hitherto closed to Colored people." He went on to say that the Urban League was beginning to conduct a survey of black housing. Graves reminded JR of his previous contribution (twice as large as that of the next largest contributor) and stated a figure that he knew JR would like: 75 percent of the organization's donors were black, although their contributions amounted to only 10 percent of the organization's budget. Graves added that Jane Addams was joining the board and that he had decided to do so also "to inform myself for you and because of my deep interest in these problems and my desire to do what I can to help." He urged JR to again pay one-third of the Urban League's budget, which had now risen to $9,000, a proposition to which JR agreed. Graves concluded with this revealing statement: "Please do not confuse the Urban League with the Chicago Branch of the NAACP. I long ago ceased to have interest in this because of the state of almost chronic in- activity."[68]

Thus, although JR was not on the scene, his funding played a key role in helping to launch the Chicago Urban League. When, a year later, two board members and Arnold Hill wrote to thank him and to solicit the next gift, they were not just writing hyperbole when they noted: "We all feel that, but for your countenance and help, the substantial service our League has been able to render to our colored fellow-citizens would have been quite impossible."[69]

JR continued to support the organization with a $3,000 grant, which was 22 percent of the Urban League's budget in 1920. That support continued for several more years, in both decreasing amounts and a decreasing percentage of the agency's budget. However, in April 1920, JR told Graves to ask Albert Loeb to make a grant on behalf of Sears "in view of the League's service to our Company and to the people of Chicago." Loeb authorized $1,000.[70] JR's association with the Urban League helped the organization gain respect, and the Chicago philanthropist was willing to praise it to others. In November 1920, he wrote: "The Urban League in Chicago, under the guidance of Mr. Hill, has been helpful in acting as a sort of clearing house for more than 60 different colored charitable organizations. . . . Here under Mr. Hill's guidance, the Chicago Urban League has made a good name for itself for practical usefulness and reliability."[71] By this time, JR had come to know members of the Urban League's Board and staff very well. He was working with them on an important commission to which he had been named by Illinois governor Frank Lowden.

The summer of 1919 was a hot and contentious one. Relations between the races in Chicago were at their nadir. White soldiers returning home from the front found numerous blacks employed in the steel mills and packing houses. The migration from the South had caused the black population of Chicago to double in the previous three years, leading to incredible overcrowding in the city's "Black Belt" on the South Side. Gangs of racist white youths roamed the streets. The houses of blacks who dared to move into white areas were firebombed. It was in this incendiary atmosphere that on Sunday, July 27, 1919, a black teenager, swimming in Lake Michigan to escape the oppressive heat, was killed by a rock thrown by a gang of whites. Opposite a crowd of irate blacks, an angry mob of whites assembled. Soon shots were fired and the race riot of 1919 commenced. When it ended on July 30, thirty-eight people had been killed: twenty-three blacks and fifteen whites. Over five hundred people had been injured.[72] In the intervening three days, the city had been in chaos with armed gangs driving through the "Black Belt" shooting from their cars while black snipers protected their territory. Mobs in the city's Loop had dragged blacks from streetcars and beaten or murdered them. Mayor "Big Bill" Thompson had stationed police around the "Black Belt" in an attempt to cordon it off, and although Governor Lowden had called up the National Guard, it could not act unless the mayor requested it, something that, for days, Thompson refused to do, insisting that his police could contain the situation. Complicating everything was a transit strike. Racist policemen frequently arrested the black victims of mob violence rather than the perpetrators.

Finally, a group of prominent businessmen (which did not include JR) appealed to the mayor in the strongest terms to restore order; and Thompson himself could see that his police force was totally exhausted as well as ineffectual. Reluctantly, he asked for the deployment of the National Guard troops. As they left their armories, a heavy rain fell, breaking the heat wave and dispersing the rioters.

JR was heartsick at this violence, which went against everything he had undertaken for the previous nine years in terms of race relations. When Governor Lowden asked him to serve on a commission to deal with the riot, he accepted. According to one historian, JR was instrumental in helping to choose the other members of the commission, both directly and indirectly. The man to whom Lowden turned to set up the commission, and who ultimately chaired it, was Francis W. Shepherdson, a former University of Chicago professor, who served as Lowden's unofficial cabinet member for education. Shepherdson turned to JR, who suggested that, for the names of possible black members, he consult A. L. Jackson, director of the Wabash YMCA.[73] The commission that was formed contained a number of luminaries besides JR, including Robert S. Abbott, editor of the *Chicago Defender,* the influential black newspaper; George C. Hall, a physician at Provident Hospital, one of the strongest pillars of the black community; and Victor Lawson, editor of the *Chicago Daily News.*

Even before the commission's first meeting, JR worried about who would be the executive director, and he sent letters out to numerous friends, such as Abraham Flexner, asking for suggestions. Graves, who attended the first meeting in the absence of Julius Rosenwald, read out the voluminous list. The commission debated whether to have two executive secretaries, one white and one black, and finally decided to have an executive secretary (white) and an assistant executive secretary (black). The man ultimately chosen to head the commission, partly at the recommendation of JR, was Graham Romyn Taylor, the son of JR's friend Graham Taylor, who came highly recommended. The assistant secretary chosen was Charles S. Johnson, a graduate student at the University of Chicago in sociology who also performed research for the Chicago Urban League. When the leaders of the staff arrived in December, they came with thoroughly formulated plans of how the commission should conduct its business. As Graves reported to JR: "They presented a joint syllabus for proposed work which was a marvel. Dr. Shepherdson . . . said it was the finest thing of the kind he had ever seen."[74]

Six committees were created dealing with such subjects as housing, industry, racial clashes, crime and police, racial contact, and public opinion. This last committee dealt with such subjects as the role played by rumor in the riots (which was considerable) and the portrayal of different ethnic groups in the black and white press.[75] JR was placed on the housing and public opinion committees and was also named to the executive committee. A staff, mostly University of Chicago graduate students, did research, performed interviews in an early version of focus groups, and held hearings. Evidently commission members were urged to attend hearings of committees other than the ones they were on, for JR attended a meeting of the racial contacts committee.[76] The staff did the bulk of the work of researching and writing the report, and after they were hired in the early months of 1920, the commission met infrequently.

In addition to studying the past, the commission was also involved with what was happening around them. Racial tension remained high in the city. One organization that was notorious in fanning the flames of race was the Kenwood and Hyde Park Property Owners Association, which operated in the area near the University of Chicago where Rosenwald lived. This group published incendiary newsletters, held rousing meetings, and firebombed the homes of blacks who dared to move into the area. Commission members protested such activities and demanded that the authorities crack down on the Property Owners Association. They remained convinced that the embers of racial violence had not died down sufficiently and could flare up again at any moment. As late as August 1921 JR, Shepherdson, and another commission member were wiring then ex-governor Lowden to warn him of what they thought was the imminent return of racial strife.[77]

JR assisted in financing the commission. The governor absolutely refused to expend public funds to pay for it. JR lent the commission $600 just to start, but this was regarded as a loan and was speedily repaid. Although a committee of prominent businessmen was formed to obtain money for the commission, fund-raising was a constant battle, partly because Taylor and Johnson hired a staff of eighteen. Attempts to raise funds for the commission from blacks proved to be largely ineffectual. Eventually JR gave $2,000 (over $21,000 in 2005 dollars) to the cause.[78] Others provided lesser amounts.

The report was finished by the end of 1920. It was a sober scholarly document that influenced future scholarship on race relations but did little to address the political realities. Like most such reports, this document had no real effect whatsoever; after being delivered to Lowden's successor, the report was probably filed away in a drawer. In late 1922, the 700-page document was published under the title *The Negro in Chicago: A Study of Race Relations and a Race Riot.* According to Albert Waskow, the report influenced Gunnar Myrdal's seminal work, *An American Dilemma.* It is unlikely that many people read it aside from some students of sociology.

The Chicago Commission on Race Relations did have an impact on JR in two respects. When he freed himself from other obligations and began devoting time he could ill afford to the commission, he developed great respect for Charles S. Johnson.[79] Second was his admiration for Francis

Shepherdson. After Lowden left office in 1921, the former education aide was unemployed, so JR engaged him to work at his foundation. Unfortunately, Shepherdson's job at the Rosenwald Fund was ill-defined, and after two years he left in search of other opportunities.

At the height of the riots, Carl Sandburg, a reporter for the *Chicago News,* interviewed Julius Rosenwald. Citing the lack of decent housing for blacks and the importance of black workers, the Chicago philanthropist noted:

> They came here because we asked them to come, because they were needed for industrial service. There is no solution for the problem apparent now. That is all the more reason both sides must be fair. It will do no good to see red. With immigration restricted, it will be necessary for business to seek another source of labor supply. This exists in the colored population. When they settle here and become workers in the community, they have a right to a place to live amid conditions that insure health and sanitation. I know from experience that the Negroes are not anxious to invade white residence districts any more than white people are willing that they should come.[80]

Except for the allusion to "seeing red," a reference to the fact that some blamed the riots on "red" provocateurs, and the mention of blacks "invading" white areas, one could read the entire interview and not know that one of the most serious race riots in Chicago history was raging.

Two articles attributed to JR about the subject of blacks appeared during this period. One was published in a black newspaper, the *Chicago Broad Axe.* In this article, printed just two months before the outbreak of the riots, JR voiced the hope, optimistic as it turned out, that the experience of the World War would bring the races closer together. He wrote about his experiences in France and how he had seen and heard that black soldiers both performed bravely in battle and worked tirelessly behind the lines. On the home front, too, blacks had helped the cause by buying Liberty Bonds and by filling needed positions in American industry. In short, said JR: "Surely after the many demonstrations of patriotism both on the battlefield and at home, the white people of this country will be willing to accord the colored people a square deal by at least giving them a fair opportunity to earn a livelihood in accordance with their ability." JR also pointed out that blacks should be treated in the same fashion as whites because they acted in much the same way as whites: "The colored people as a rule are industrious and thrifty, and have come to appreciate their importance as a factor in the economic and financial world, as indicated by their prosperous business enterprises, their large holding in real estate, their management of banks, and their scrupulous handling of the millions of deposits entrusted to their care."[81] It is unfortunate that this article appeared in a black newspaper, for there were numerous whites in Chicago who should have heeded this message.

The second article attributed to JR on this subject was published in the prestigious *New York Times* six years later. Like the *Broad Axe* piece, this article was optimistic in tone. It dealt with the black migration to the North and, in addition to citing statistics, JR posited the theory that this shifting of populations was good for the country: "There is good ground for believing that the migration of the Negro will have a beneficial effect on the nation. It will be a good thing for the South because the colored population will be more evenly distributed over the entire country, and will lessen Southern fear, real or alleged, of race domination, and will thus remove an outstanding factor that has hampered that section's development." As for the North, JR repeated his assertion that, in most respects, blacks and whites were not so different: "The Negro's rise in the scale of occupations has given him a greater purchasing power, and a higher standard of living. To his credit it should be said that, for the most part, he tries sincerely to live up to his opportunities in the North. He is usually a law abiding citizen, buys his own home when possible, and gives his children the best schooling his income will permit."[82] It is significant that JR was willing to publish such views in a white newspaper with a large readership. These two articles contain JR's deeply held belief that blacks were inherently the equal of whites politically and economically and should be treated as such. This view set him apart from even the great majority of progressive Americans. In Chicago, only Jane Addams and the circle around her were known to hold similar views.[83]

Jewish Causes

The restructuring of the Rosenwald schools program and the fine-tuning of the YMCA program could be considered a revisiting of unfinished business by JR as far as his former charitable interests were concerned. There was one other area in which such a revisiting of an old issue occurred, and it was the one where he had begun his philanthropy: Chicago Jewish causes.

A division existed within the Jewish community of Chicago as well as other U.S. cities—the result of different origins, religious practices, and migration patterns. The East and South sides of the city were home to Jews of German origin, who had arrived in the United States earlier, and acquired wealth sooner than the later arrivals from Eastern Europe. The German Jews tended to be Reform, or more Americanized in their religious practices; the Eastern European Jews tended to be Orthodox, or more traditional in terms of their religious practices. Considerable distrust existed between the two communities. German Jews regarded their Eastern European brethren as interlopers who failed to adapt easily to America, believed in an outmoded form of Judaism, and were embarrassing because of their different language, customs, and practices. The Orthodox regarded the German Jews as betrayers of the Jewish religion who had assimilated American customs and values too readily. Tensions were often so great that the German Jews refused financial assistance to their Eastern European counterparts.

Following in the footsteps of Rabbi Hirsch, JR had tried to bridge the gap between the two communities. He had aided in the creation of the Federated Orthodox Jewish Charities, the charitable organization for Eastern European Jews. When the building he had donated that housed the offices of the Associated Jewish Charities had opened in 1915, JR had insisted that the offices of the Federated also be housed there. Because of the influence of JR and other enlightened leaders, such as Samuel Deutsch and James Davis, some of the antipathy between the two branches of Judaism began to break down. The war also helped with this process. Orthodox and Reformed Jews served together at the front and quickly realized that more united them as Jews than divided them. The Jewish relief campaigns also brought the two groups together; JR's $1 million challenge grant in 1917 was meant to have all Jews across America participate, as were subsequent relief efforts. The goal for which JR and the other leaders were striving was the unification of the two umbrella charitable groups, the Associated and the Federated. Not only would this serve as a symbol that Chicago Jews were one community, but it also would be more efficient and avoid duplication of effort.

This unification began in 1919, but the process took three years. The task was not an easy one, for despite a unity of purpose among the leadership, there was still considerable distrust among the rank and file. The Associated Jewish Charities was much larger and much better funded than the Federated Orthodox Jewish Charities. The former raised approximately $1 million a year and had a cash reserve of $500,000. The Federated collected about $250,000 per year and had no cash reserve. The Orthodox Jews feared that their organization would be absorbed into and dominated by the larger agency. Reformed Jews believed that the Federated would be a drag on their fund-raising. Finally, in late November 1922, agreement was reached. By a unanimous vote, the leaders of both organizations agreed to form the Jewish Charities of Chicago, the forerunner of the Jewish United Fund. The new organization was to be a partnership where both sides were treated equally. Both organizations agreed that they would "enter the union debt free, conform to approved methods of raising funds, and adhere to their budgets." Such strictures would appear to apply more to the Orthodox groups, but they agreed to them nevertheless.[84]

Once the decision had been taken to unify, the obvious person to lead the new organization was Julius Rosenwald. He was the honorary president of both the Associated and the Federated. He had worked long and hard for this moment. But he was, briefly, unsure about taking up this challenge. An editorial in the *Chicago Chronicle* entitled "It's Up to You, J. R." detailed why he was the best candidate and tried to persuade him to accept: "His leadership, his 'moral force,' and brilliant personal example has been a tremendous personal influence in both groups. There is perhaps no other man in Chicago whom both sides will accept each as its own, and certainly none whom both will trust as implicitly and follow as enthusiastically."[85] Although others had worked hard to bring about the union, Hyman L. Meites was not alone in thinking that JR deserved most of the credit: "In this historic achievement, Rosenwald's efforts are universally recognized as the decisive factor."[86]

JR did agree to accept the presidency of the Jewish Charities of Chicago for one year, starting January 1, 1923. His first goal was to raise $250,000 from new members. This was quickly accomplished.[87] Next, he turned to a campaign to raise $2.5 million, the largest campaign ever attempted by the Jewish community of Chicago. The money was to go toward three building projects: a training school for nurses of Michael Reese Hospital (the German Jewish hospital preeminent in the city) and two branches of the Chicago Hebrew Institute. All three building projects had been put on hold because of the war and the effort to raise funds for international Jewish relief. Now that the war was over and some of the worst problems were being dealt with effectively by other organizations, funds could be raised once again for Jewish concerns at home. Using the proven tactics of the old Associated, an army of 4,000 volunteers was mobilized, inspired, and dispatched to raise money. The result was a triumph for JR and the newly amalgamated organization, and $2,751,380 was raised.[88]

One other aspect of the Jewish Charities of Chicago pleased JR enormously and shows once again his penchant for good management. The Research Bureau was an important part of the newly formed organization. It was designed to go through every department of the agency and eliminate duplication. If a new Jewish charitable organization wished to become affiliated with the Jewish Charities of Chicago, that agency would have to prove that it was performing a function or operating in a geographical area that was unique. The Research Bureau decided whether a new Jewish charity was "needed in the community." This urge to eliminate all waste and duplication demonstrates that the Jewish Charities of Chicago was as well run as the Associated had been under JR's leadership fifteen years earlier.[89]

Some members of the Chicago Jewish community regarded the creation of the Jewish Charities of Chicago as Julius Rosenwald's greatest achievement. However, the amalgamation of the two agencies did not eliminate overnight the distrust that had built up over decades. Divisions lingered, but a giant step toward the unification of Chicago Jews had been taken.

With regard to national Jewish organizations, JR remained exceedingly active during these postwar years, although nothing he did had quite the impact of the 1917 campaign. He frequently traveled, raising money on behalf of causes such as the Joint Distribution Committee (JDC), which was spearheading the relief effort of European Jews. He also wrote an article for a Denver newspaper on the subject. The extent to which he was working on the 1919 fund-raising drive can be seen in this note sent by JR's secretary: "For the past ten days Mr. Rosenwald has been devoting his entire time to the Jewish Relief campaign and has given no attention whatever to his mail."[90] Thanks in part to his efforts, Chicago raised prodigious amounts of money for such causes as the JDC—and not just from Jews. In 1919, a decision was reached to ask non-Jews for support, since some of the funds raised would be used to assist non-Jews. Typical of what occurred at fund-raising functions were the events at a dinner at Chicago's Blackstone Hotel on October 24, 1919. Two hundred men present at the dinner pledged $871,000 in less than an hour, starting with JR's pledge of $250,000. Chicago's quota was $2 million. A few nights later at a mass meeting at Chicago's Medinah Temple, another large sum was raised. The *Chicago Herald* reported that two women who were unable to make pledges offered their gold rings.[91] The goal for the 1921–22 drive was decided at a meeting of four hundred national Jewish leaders chaired by JR. Despite the national recession, a goal of $14 million was agreed on. Chicago raised $1.8 million of this total. Part of the money was raised at an innovative event organized by chairman Jacob Loeb. Since most of the money was going to alleviate starvation in Eastern Europe, "several hundred wealthy Jews were invited to a banquet at the Drake Hotel. They found themselves in a dining hall dimly lighted by candles, where they were seated on bare benches at pine board tables without cloth, glass, or china, and, it proved, without food. This grim foodless banquet made a profound impression."[92]

JR made his mark in national Jewish circles in this period but not for something as impressive as the 1917 fund drive. He welcomed Prohibition when the temperance measure took effect in 1920.[93] Moreover, he feared that Jews who used real wine during liturgical services were not only skirting the law but also making Jews in general look disreputable, even though rabbis did have a dispensation from the government to use wine. Thus, JR scandalized his audience at a New York banquet in 1923 when he advocated the use of grape juice in Jewish services. The fact that this eccentric suggestion was part of a speech on antisemitism was lost in the furor. This particular idea was greeted with universal derision.

In fact, antisemitism was becoming an increasing personal problem for Rosenwald, although it had not been a major factor in his life before. Now, for the first time, he was publicly singled out for attack because of his religion. As part of a national wave of antisemitism, JR was denounced by name in Henry Ford's scurrilous newspaper, the *Dearborn Independent.* And when a fundamentalist preacher in North Carolina preached a series of sermons against him, JR was defended by a courageous newspaperman who published a series of articles claiming that the preacher's sermons were a tissue of lies. None of these scurrilous attacks slowed JR down, but he saw them as part of a large and dangerous movement directed against Jews in America. As he told his New York banquet hall audience in 1923: "The campaign of hatred waged against us daily and weekly, the tendency toward restrictions of the Jewish population at universities and elsewhere, and other similar symptoms of discrimination and ill-will, though they need not occasion despair, nevertheless must fill us with grave concern."[94]

School of Social Service Administration

Julius Rosenwald had been associated with Graham Taylor's Chicago School of Civics and Philanthropy as both a donor and a board member since 1910. He had served as a trustee of the University of Chicago since 1912. He now helped to bring about the marriage of these two institutions and worked quietly but persistently behind the scenes to guarantee the success of the union.

The Chicago School of Civics and Philanthropy had limped along from crisis to crisis for years. JR had been instrumental in efforts to save it, but they proved ineffective. The school was well respected, and its graduates were in great demand. During the war, enrollment had slowed to a trickle, but it increased in the summer of 1919, as the school offered an array of interesting courses that addressed some of the chief exigencies of the time. During the war years, attempts had been made to see if the school could affiliate with one of the universities in the Chicago area. Only the University of Chicago had evinced any willingness to consider such a move, but also indicated that the right time had not yet arrived.

In the summer of 1919, Graves warned Graham Taylor that JR was becoming disheartened by the constant crises, seeing them as a sign of mismanagement, and was unlikely to renew his contribution at the same level. Indeed, JR announced that he was going to halve his donation. The school was still trying to remain independent, but it needed to raise a considerable amount of money in a hurry. Attempts to rescue the school in February 1920 essentially failed.

Talks began behind the scenes to reopen discussions of a merger of the School of Civics and Philanthropy with the University of Chicago. These talks bore fruit. At a meeting of the University of Chicago board of trustees on August 4, 1920, JR, Graham Taylor, and Sophonisba Breckenridge, a gifted teacher and social worker and one of the pillars of the school, presented their proposal. They suggested that the Chicago School affiliate with the university, where it would be known as the School of Social Service Administration. The affiliation was to be on a trial basis for five years. A group of trustees of the school guaranteed the university an annual sum of $25,000 annually for the five years. If there was a shortfall in this payment, JR was one of several who guaranteed to make up the difference. JR was one of two people who offered $5,000 per year as part of the $25,000.[95] The university trustees accepted this offer.

JR's exact role in bringing about this merger is not known. He was not on the university committee appointed to consider the merger, but since he was a trustee of both institutions, and since he was highly respected by both sets of trustees, one suspects that his role must have been considerable.

Having worked to consummate this marriage, however, JR discovered that the road ahead was somewhat more rocky than he had imagined. The promised $25,000 per year proved more difficult to collect than anyone had foreseen. Of the $25,000, only $16,250 was collected and the shortfall was not being made up. The head of the new entity was Leon C. Marshall, who was already overburdened as dean of the School of Commerce and Administration (forerunner of the Business School). He knew nothing about social work, and by 1923 he was threatening to sabotage his new charge when the five-year trial period ended in 1925. On the other hand, enrollments had risen considerably, and more funds were being raised by tuition than had been forecast, so that by the second year the shortfall in contributions was not significant and the School was raising a total of $25,000 from both earned and contributed income.

In December 1923, JR received a letter from Ernest Freund, a professor at the University of Chicago Law School who had offered classes at the School of Civics and Philanthropy before the merger and who had continued to do so after 1920. Freund sketched for JR the problems the new School was facing, stressing particularly the lack of interest on the part of the dean. He suggested that Edith Abbott and Sophonisba Breckenridge, who were, in effect, managing the School, and who were most closely associated with it in the public mind, be given the opportunity to take over the administration formally.[96] JR went to see university president Ernest Burton and told him what Freund had written. The result was swift. Edith Abbott was named the dean of SSA on December 12.

JR and Graves also worked to raise support for the School so that its future with the University of Chicago could be ensured. JR used his influence to obtain grant money from the New York–based Laura Spelman Rockefeller Memorial as well as the Chicago-based Wieboldt Foundation.

Not only had JR helped bring about the creation of the School of Social Service Administration at the University of Chicago but he had worked to ensure that the social work school would succeed there. SSA remains today one of the most respected schools of social work in the country.

Family Affairs

In 1920, Marion and William both went off to college—she to Wellesley, he to MIT. "We are now living in our city home for the first time without any of our children with us and the house seems very large and empty," JR wrote to his German relatives in November of that year.[97] That same year, Lessing and his family moved to Philadelphia. He had spent the past two years overseeing the construction of the Sears plant there. Now he was to manage it. JR and Gussie were sorry to see Lessing and his family leave, but they frequently visited JR's country home at Ravinia in the summers. JR's daughter Edith, separated from her husband, moved to New York and became the owner of a children's clothing store.[98] In 1921 she met and married Edgar Stern, scion of a New Orleans family of cotton brokers.[99]

Adele, the second oldest daughter, was married to Armand Deutsch and was living in Chicago with her two sons, but the marriage was becoming increasingly strained and would end in divorce. After one year of college, Marion came home and announced that she intended to marry. JR sent her off to Europe, hoping that she would forget about her infatuation. But the journey had the opposite effect. Marion returned in September, and in October 1921 she wed Alfred K. Stern of Fargo, North Dakota. Stern, a charming and handsome fellow whom the members of the family called "Sir Al," did not seem to have any career goals in mind. His father-in-law gave him a job on the staff of the Julius Rosenwald Fund, and for a time he served as the Foundation's executive director.

JR was also concerned with his extended family, especially the German "cousins." He had worried about them during the war, though he could not easily contact them. The dividends on the shares of Sears stock JR had given them were frozen and did not start flowing again for several years because of the economic downturn in the United States. JR wrote to them frequently. Concerned about their welfare, he also asked people to visit them and report back to him. As the economic situation in Germany worsened, JR became increasingly concerned, not only for his relatives but for all Germans. When a fund drive was launched in Chicago for the relief of German children, he contributed $100,000. As he told his relative

Figure 15.
"Liebe Grossmutter," JR's mother, Augusta Hammerslough Rosenwald, with her first great-grandchild, Armand Deutsch, around 1914.

Simon Rosenwald: "My object in giving so large a sum was to create an interest throughout the whole country, and I think it has helped very much to do that."[100]

The two family events that significantly shaped this postwar period of JR's life were both deaths. His mother, Augusta Hammerslough Rosenwald, died on February 24, 1921, at the age of eighty-eight. Her death was not unexpected. Just four months earlier, JR wrote his German relatives: "Our dear Mother has now reached an age when we hesitate to separate ourselves from her by any great distance or for any great length of time."[101] Once her death occurred, it was actually a blessing, he told Mr. and Mrs. Gustav Rosenwald in Germany: "For a month, at least, her mind wandered a good deal of the time and when the sad day came it was a great relief for her and for us all."[102]

It is unfortunate that relatively little is known about JR's mother, though she was unquestionably one of the major influences on his life. Said someone who knew the family in Chicago in the 1880s: "Julius Rosenwald's Mother was sweet, lovable, philosophical, kind, possessed the keenest sense of humor, and was admired and loved by all who knew her."[103] Two qualities that she passed on to her son were a deep and abiding sense of the importance of family and a lack of ostentation. In 1910, when she was seventy-seven, she left an informal testament to her children. In it she wrote: "Please omit flowers positively. Only by those who are bound to me by love and affection. None from outsiders, as I do not like display. My good friends have always been kind and good to me. It needs no outlay or lavishness of money. Better spend on the living needy."[104] She also indicated that she was certain her children would look after each other, which definitely did occur. JR credited his mother with teaching him about the importance of charity. And Augusta Hammerslough Rosenwald was certainly inclined in that direction.

JR undoubtedly missed her greatly. The bond between mother and son was noted by numerous reporters who wrote about JR. They marveled that every day that he was in Chicago, he stopped to see her. And if he was out of town, he did not fail to telephone or wire her. All of the children knew her as Liebe Grossmutter (Dear Grandmother), and her portrait still hangs in her granddaughter Edith Stern's house in New Orleans, now a museum (LongueVue House and Gardens). Her birthdays were always grand celebrations, one of which was even captured on the new medium of film. Although she was not highly educated and appears to have thrived on gossip, she was kind and loving, and she may well have influenced her son so that he was not harsh and ruthless, as were some of his business and philanthropic contemporaries such as John D. Rockefeller Sr. and Andrew Carnegie.

If Augusta Rosenwald's death was sorrowfully anticipated, the demise of his brother Morris came as a great shock. Morris was two years younger than JR and seemingly in good health. He and his wife went on a vacation to Hawaii in 1923, and when he returned in August, he checked into a hospital with a disease that baffled his physicians. JR called it a poison in his blood. For six months he lingered on. JR consulted New York specialists, but it eventually became clear that there was no cure. Morris was the president of Lowenthal Securities, an investment house, and although not as successful as his older brother, he left an estate of approximately $3 million. Morris served as president of the Jewish Home Finding Society and was a director of the Municipal Voters' League. He appears to have been quieter and less flamboyant than JR.[105] The two brothers were very close emotionally and lived in houses only a few blocks apart.

In 1924, JR, Gussie, and their daughter Adele returned to Europe for the first time since the war. The Chicago Rosenwalds visited the family homestead in Bunde where JR's father had been born. There were joyful reunions with the German relatives who had survived the war and the resulting economic dislocation. Yet in the midst of the family gatherings, JR insisted on seeing some of the more depressing sides of German life. Having contributed $100,000 toward the relief of German children, he wanted to see how his money was being spent. He, Gussie, and Adele visited a Quaker "feeding office" in Berlin. Then they went to a creche (daycare center) for children under six connected to the Lutheran Hospital. JR noted that the children were "all under size about two years" but otherwise appeared to be healthy. Next they visited a tuberculosis clinic for children in the open air where the patients were fed and received medical treatment. Then it was on to a soup kitchen for mothers and children in one of the poorest areas of Berlin. The next day they asked to be taken to a hospital in the same district to examine outpatient services.[106]

JR journeyed to Washington for the Second Industrial Conference and for other political purposes. He and Gussie were present at President Harding's inauguration, and he was also in Marion, Ohio, for Harding's funeral. There were frequent journeys to New York for business or to attend meetings of the Rockefeller Foundation Board or the American Jewish Committee. Once Lessing moved to Philadelphia and Edith married Edgar Stern and moved to New Orleans, he and Gussie often traveled to see them and the grandchildren.

A verbal portrait of JR in this period comes from a rather unlikely (and not exactly impartial) source—his youngest daughter, Marion, who wrote an essay on her father for a senior high school English class in December 1920. She presents a warm and admiring picture:

> [Julius Rosenwald] possesses all the characteristics which go towards making friends. In spite of his success, he has retained to a large extent the simple, humane but practical outlook on life of the boy who peddled shoe buttons in Springfield. He has a fund of sympathy and understanding, which he draws on without reserve, and his ready wit and informal manners make him easy to approach and delightful in conversation . . . Mr. Rosenwald feels a kindly interest in every individual, not only men who have been recognized, but anyone who has a story to tell or work to do. If a man comes in by appointment to see him in his office, his conversation will probably run like this. "Good morning! Isn't this great weather we're

having? Sit down, do. Yes, that's my mother over there, the first lady of the land. That picture over there is my grandson, a fine youngster." He is never too busy to be pleasant and polite, and his tone is the same to everyone.

His family occupies a very large place in his affections. . . . His children know that no matter how occupied he is, he will always lend a sympathetic ear to their problems, and counsel them as best he may. He often reads aloud to them, mostly about Abraham Lincoln, whom he considers America's greatest man. His grandchildren, in fact any children, are his dearest friends. He stops to talk to all the babies he meets on the street, and I have never known one to be afraid of him, and all who know him proclaim him a wonderful playfellow. In fact, there is really no one great or small, black or white whom he will not greet as a brother, converse with as an equal, and advise as a father.[107]

Retirement from Sears

Although JR had been ill upon his return from France in 1918, he seemed to have recovered his health by the spring of 1919. Certainly through 1923, he appeared to be in good condition. He was able to climb mountains, hike three and a half miles, and play eighteen holes of golf. He wrote to friends and family members that he felt fine. But by mid-1924, his health had once again begun to deteriorate. And there were other serious problems. Albert Loeb, his right-hand man at Sears since the beginning of his involvement with the company, fell ill with heart trouble in 1922. JR worried about his longtime partner and assumed the extra burden of work. Loeb's recovery was long and slow. Then in April 1924, JR was stunned to learn that Loeb's son, Richard, who had been held up to Marion and William as a paragon of virtue, had been arrested along with his friend Nathan Leopold for the brutal kidnapping and murder of Bobby Franks. Albert Loeb never recovered from this blow and died six months later.

By the end of July 1924, JR knew that Loeb would never return to Sears. He would have to be replaced. Moreover, JR was sixty-two; he acknowledged his health was failing, and he wanted to devote more time to philanthropy. He began thinking seriously of retiring. On July 28, he wrote to Lessing, asking him to find an executive search firm that would suggest the "name[s] of 10 outstanding men among railroad vice presidents in the United States not over 50 years of age."[108] He asked that this be undertaken without delay.

Why did JR not decide to promote someone from within, which might have seemed the easier course? The answer was that Max Adler and Otto Doering, the two vice presidents who were likely candidates, were also nearing retirement age. Lessing, though he had done an excellent job managing the Philadelphia plant, was too young and inexperienced to assume the presidency. Moreover, JR wished to avoid any suggestion of nepotism. Werner suggests that JR was insistent on hiring a railroad man because of his association with Daniel Willard, president of the Baltimore and Ohio, with whom he had worked in Washington during the war.[109] He may also have been influenced by the biography of the railroad magnate William Baldwin, which had introduced him to African Americans. In short, he had determined that his successor would be a man with a wealth of business experience, such as the vice president of a railroad, and that he should be a relatively young man who could remain as the head of Sears for a considerable period of time.

Whether an executive search firm found Charles M. Kittle or whether JR knew him, the vice president of the Illinois Central Railroad had made a clear success of his business. JR entered into discussions with Kittle and offered him the post of president at the end of October.

Before the negotiations with Kittle had concluded, another candidate appeared. JR had met General Robert E. Wood in Washington during the war, when Wood worked in the Office of the Quartermaster. After the peace, this bright, aggressive young man had gone to work for Montgomery Ward, and despite the difficult economic times, he had had a positive impact on that company. He had, however, run afoul of Ward's president, possibly by suggesting that Ward begin establishing retail stores. By mid-October, Wood had left the company.

Wendell Endicott, a noted shoe manufacturer, knew both JR and Wood, for he sold his products to both Sears and Ward. He knew that Wood was looking for a job and that JR was looking for a successor. He suggested that the two men meet. Displaying the antisemitism that was to characterize his career, Wood was at first not enthusiastic about the possibility of working at Sears. He wrote to Endicott: "I fear I might find myself hampered by a lot of Jewish relatives, and life is too short to be surrounded by people that you do not like, no matter how much money you may be making." Endicott replied: "I have heard it from several sources that it has been pretty generally talked that Sears, Roebuck should get Gentile blood into the business."[110] This may have reassured Wood, for he did meet with JR and the meeting went well. It is likely that Wood told Rosenwald about his interest in opening retail stores and that JR, mindful of Sears's experience in 1921, decided that this approach deserved another try. JR could not offer Wood the presidency because by that time the position had already been offered to Kittle, who, JR knew, was almost ready to accept. However, he did offer Wood the position of vice president for factories and retail stores.

On October 18, Wood met with JR at Ravinia and said that he would accept the position. "I told him that I would leave the terms in his hands. He gave me the following: Salary, $40,000 a year; bonus on the same terms as the other officers of the Company, Mr. Adler and Mr. Doering. He also stated that he would make a personal arrangement with me by which he would turn over to me a minimum of one thousand shares of Sears, Roebuck stock on the basis of $100 per share, this minimum to be considerably increased if he could make the proper arrangements." This entire transaction was to be kept absolutely confidential.[111]

JR announced his retirement as president of Sears on October 24, but added that he was staying on as chairman of the board, a post he retained until his death. In practice, this meant that he would stay on in what was essentially an advisory capacity. Four days later, Charles Kittle and Robert Wood were formally elected to their positions and they began work on November 1. A new era at Sears had begun.

It was not, at first, easy going. Doering and Adler were resentful that they had been passed over, but their loyalty to JR kept them from resigning. Kittle, who had no experience in retailing, could be high-handed and rude. When Lessing was out of the country, Kittle summarily ordered the ground floor of the Philadelphia plant turned into a retail store. Lessing returned to find a fait accompli. He was furious.[112] Kittle even was rude to JR on occasion. Wood threw himself into his job, and the retail stores began to prosper. Wood was not sanguine about his prospects for advancement. He was three years older than Kittle, who, despite his rough start, seemed to Wood to be firmly entrenched. Little could Wood have known that a mere three years after his installation, Kittle would be dead and Wood would be the new Sears president.

The decision to retire from the presidency of Sears must have been painful for JR. Yet from a business standpoint it was the right decision. Peter Drucker, the noted economics writer who greatly admired JR, noted in his textbook on management: "[Julius Rosenwald] apparently realized that he did not want to run a giant company. He also knew that Sears could and should become one—and he knew the correct conclusions for himself." Drawing the generalization from JR's experience, he adds, "The top man who concludes that his company needs to grow but who also then realizes that he does not want to change himself and his behavior has, in conscience, only one line of action open to him. *He has to step aside.*"[113]

Drucker was correct. By naming General Wood vice president for Factories and Retail Stores, JR clearly indicated that he was willing to push Sears in a new direction. According to Emmet and Jeuck, he had been opposed to the idea of retail stores, although he had tried them in 1921. Even if JR initially had been opposed to retail stores, it is significant that he was willing to change his mind. Perhaps he was persuaded by what must have been a very forceful presentation by Wood. Or perhaps JR realized independently that the consumer market in America was changing and that Sears had to alter its marketing strategy—selling directly to consumers instead of relying on the mails. The move from mails to malls lay in the future, but the stage had been set by JR, the far-sighted businessman, who, as he had demonstrated so often in his life, saw the opportunity and took it by hiring Wood. Having guided Sears successfully through the economic shoals of the early 1920s, JR was willing to step down from his leadership position and leave it in the hands of capable younger men who possessed both good management experience and a sense of vision.

7

New Philanthropic Ventures, 1924–1928

With Charles Kittle and Robert Wood installed in the top executive posts at Sears, Julius Rosenwald could spend more time and energy on the causes that increasingly interested him. Some of these were old interests that now took on a much greater importance, such as the University of Chicago. Another was an old idea that he decided to act on because he had the time and the opportunity to move it forward: the Museum of Science and Industry. Still another cause that greatly attracted JR was a new venture, in some ways a variation on an old theme, since it dealt with an agronomist and Jews; yet it was indicative of JR's openness to new ideas that he could seize the concept of Jewish settlements in Russia and work tirelessly toward that end. JR was able to engage in these and other philanthropic enterprises because his fortune was growing steadily during the mid-1920s as an economic boom accelerated. Just before the stock market crash in October 1929, his fortune was estimated at $200 million (the equivalent of over $2 billion in 2005 dollars).

The Museum of Science and Industry[1]

The memory of an eight-year-old boy's wonder at and eager curiosity about science led JR to one of his most notable and enduring philanthropic achievements: the founding of the Museum of Science and Industry in Chicago.

Like many American museums, the idea for the Museum of Science and Industry originated in Europe.[2] During their 1911 trip, the Rosenwald family spent several weeks in Munich, and the two younger children, Marion and William, enjoyed a pleasure they had not known in Chicago. JR devoted one day each week to the wishes of each of the "babies"—he would go with them wherever they wanted. William always chose the Deutsches Museum, a newly established museum of science. It was a museum unlike any JR had ever seen. Youngsters were encouraged to push buttons and pull levers, to visit the coal mine, or to have their hands x-rayed, something that William particularly enjoyed.[3] After repeated visits, JR, impressed with his son's eager curiosity, wondered whether a similar museum could be built in Chicago. But the press of business and the intervention of other concerns, such as World War I and its aftermath, prevented him from taking any action.

In 1921, the president of the Commercial Club of Chicago, Samuel Insull, sent out a survey to members asking them for an opinion on the most worthwhile projects for the city in which the club should be engaged. JR replied:

> I have long felt that Chicago should have, as one of its most important institutions for public usefulness, a great Industrial Museum or Exhibition in which might be housed, for permanent display, machinery and working models illustrative of as many as possible of the mechanical processes of production and of manufacture.[4]

He noted that Chicago was the perfect site for such a museum, and that similar exhibits at the Columbian Exposition had drawn large crowds. JR offered to contribute $1 million toward the construction of such a museum if additional funds could be raised, but Insull did not follow up on the suggestion, and the idea lapsed for a time.[5]

Toward the end of 1925, JR began promoting the idea of an industrial museum to sympathetic members of the Commercial Club, and by December a committee had been formed to study the possibility. Among its members were some of Chicago's business leaders: Sewell Avery, president of the U.S. Gypsum Company as well as the Commercial Club, Frank Wetmore, chairman of the First National Bank, Charles Piez, president of the Link Belt Company, and Col. A. A. Sprague, the city's commissioner of public works. Perhaps the most important of the men to whom JR broached his idea was Leo Wormser, a young lawyer in the firm of JR's close friend, Lessing Rosenthal. It was Wormser who enabled JR to make his dream a reality.

JR had developed the perfect plan. He had chosen a site, and he knew exactly how the museum should be financed. In February 1894, almost all of the buildings that comprised the Columbian Exposition of 1893 had burned down in a spectacular fire. Among the few survivors of this conflagration was the Palace of Fine Arts, a huge Greek-style building complete with Caryatids, which had housed works of art from the contributing countries. Representatives from these countries had insisted that the building be made fireproof before they would contribute any sculpture or paintings. For some twenty-six years after the fire, the Palace of Fine Arts in Jackson Park on Chicago's South Side had housed the first exhibits of the Field Museum of Natural History until the permanent museum near Chicago's Grant Park opened in 1920. By 1922, the Palace of Fine Arts was visibly decaying.

The fate of the building lay in the hands of the South Park Commission, an administrative body appointed by the mayor to oversee the city's southern park lands (and the structures on those lands), including Jackson Park.[6] Unfortunately, the South Park commissioners were divided. In 1923, they voted 3-2 to raze the Palace of Fine Arts, but pressure mounted from all sides. The brother-in-law of Mayor "Big Bill" Thompson as well as the editor of the *Chicago Tribune* urged caution. Commissioner Edward J. Kelly, a rising Democratic star and future Chicago mayor, managed to hold off a second vote until a new member of the commission board could take his seat and vote with the preservationists. The commissioners then asked South Side voters to approve a $5 million bond issue, which they did in June 1924. The funds were to be used to restore the outside of the building and to convert the inside into a mixed-use structure.

Thus the site was readily available, as was the money to restore its exterior. The major problem was how the structure would be used after the restoration. In addition to a convention hall, Kelly and other supporters envisaged it housing "a school of industrial arts, a Women's Memorial Hall, a complex of centers devoted to athletics, art, and social activities, and a museum of architecture and sculpture."[7] JR was convinced that the entire building should be used solely for an industrial museum. He proposed to the Commercial Club committee and later to the South Park commissioners that he would contribute $3 million to install exhibits and pay for the upkeep of the museum.

The idea of founding an industrial museum in the United States did not originate with Julius Rosenwald. In 1914, the Museum of the Peaceful Arts was incorporated in New York City, but nothing was accomplished until 1924, when Henry R. Towne of Yale and Towne Lock Company died, leaving the museum a bequest of $3 million. The New York museum had prominent businessmen on its board, but it needed more money, and the board was having grave trouble finding a suitable site in Manhattan. A more ambitious plan was for a national museum of engineering and industry to be associated with the Smithsonian Institution. The champion of this idea was Samuel Insull, which perhaps explains why JR failed to receive a response to his 1921 letter to the Commercial Club. The National Museum was also having difficulty getting off the drawing board.

In the winter of 1926 JR traveled to Europe, a trip that was part vacation, part scouting expedition for the future museum, and part public relations.[8] The Chicago philanthropist and his son, William, visited industrial museums in Munich, Vienna, Paris, and London, but JR also stopped in to visit *Chicago Tribune* reporters stationed in Vienna and Paris. In a story from Vienna, JR explained his dream of an industrial museum to *Tribune* correspondent Floyd Gibbons:

> American inventive genius needs greater stimulation and room for development. . . . I would like every young growing mind in Chicago to be able to see working models, visualizing developments in machines and processes which have been built by the greatest industrial nation in the world. . . . America has thousands of these historical old models stored away in research laboratories of many of our great industries. These and specially built working models showing the insides of the workings and why the wheels go around should be assembled together and exhibited in a great museum in Chicago.[9]

From Vienna, JR and William went to Munich, where they visited a refurbished Deutsches Museum. William described his amazement at walking through ten miles of corridors and seeing such exhibits as a U-Boat, various kinds of mines, and rooms detailing such information as the development of the steam engine. "The greatest point about this museum," he wrote, "is that an accurate concise explanation of the apparatus is given in every instance."[10]

By June 1926, JR was back in the United States. Talks with the South Park commissioners continued, and the Commercial Club Committee was about to make a decision: to go forward with the project. On June 30, an important meeting of the committee occurred. Wormser was appointed counsel and an ex-officio member of the committee. The committee voted to accept the Palace of Fine Arts as a site. The South Park commissioners believed that the restoration of both the inside and the outside of the building could be completed with $3 million of the $5 million bond issue, a wildly optimistic forecast, as it turned out.

On August 18, Wormser stated: "Mr. Rosenwald will contribute a sum of not less than $3 million to the Museum Corporation, out of which sum there shall be paid the deficit, if any, of the cost of constructing the Museum after the proceeds of the bonds have been applied toward such construction, and the remainder of the said sum shall be used for the general purposes of the Museum Corporation."[11] It was further envisioned that industries would furnish exhibits to the new museum and, as no cost is mentioned, the tacit assumption was that these would be donations.[12] There was a precedent for such donations in Germany, for that was how the Deutsches Museum obtained exhibits. Thus the Chicago press reported that the full cost of the museum would be around $20 million: $5 million from the bond issue, $3 million from JR, and the remainder in in-kind contributions from interested corporations.

On August 16, a luncheon was held to formally announce that Julius Rosenwald would give $3 million toward the establishment of an industrial museum provided the South Park commissioners agreed to use the funds from the bond issue to renovate the Palace of Fine Arts. The press loved the announcement of the planned museum. Rosenwald had gotten the idea at Munich, said the *Chicago Journal,* that "America should have a similar 'popular university,' free to all[13] where the mysterious processes of industry will be made so plain that every child can understand and learn how the world makes, trades in, and transports its needs."[14] Even the staid *New York Times* in an editorial entitled "Chicago Does It First" reminded readers of the old rivalry between the First City and Second City and bemoaned the fact that while New York merely talked, Chicago had acted, thanks to JR.[15]

One unresolved issue was to be a source of considerable frustration to JR: the name of the museum. The future trustees of the museum worried about that issue as well. On July 21, Frank Wetmore wrote to Wormser:

> I am wondering . . . if arrangements are finally made with the South Park commissioners to occupy the Fine Arts Building, to call the Museum "The Rosenwald Industrial Museum." I favor this as a tribute to him who, in my opinion, exemplifies all the best qualities of citizenship. . . . From a remark that Julius made to me one day I believe he wants this museum to be a permanent monument to his name, and the wonderful amount of good that he has done entitles him to that honor.[16]

Wetmore could not have been more mistaken. While JR was on vacation in September, the newly constituted board met to consider the museum's name. Wormser wrote to JR that a decision was imminent: "No title will be sufficiently descriptive of an institution of such broad scope. We cannot make it comprehensive enough. Moreover, the public will always abbreviate the title and will, I think, refer to this as the Rosenwald Museum."[17]

JR cabled back: "Museum Science and Industry my preference. Cheerfully defer to majority opinions."[18] This was to prove a costly mistake. Wormser reported to JR:

> The group adopted as the corporate name "Rosenwald Industrial Museum." Your telegram was considered and appreciated. . . . There was unanimity of opinion about attaching your name to the museum, in recognition not only of the present gift but also of your munificence and civic leadership. I will not undertake to repeat all of the tributes that were paid to you; I know how modest you arc about these things.[19]

JR was most upset. On September 16 he wrote to Wormser, begging him to have the Rosenwald name removed. His reason was simple. "If I were contributing the building it might be a different matter, but as that is the greatest part of the investment it looks as tho I were getting a bargain."[20] Moreover, JR may have feared that if the museum bore his name, his family would be saddled with a financial obligation for it after his death.

Unfortunately, it was too late. The papers of incorporation had been signed and sent to Springfield. JR poured out his unhappiness to Wormser in a second cable on September 16:

> Although there is no hurry to make the change in the corporate name of the Museum and greatly as I appreciate the attitude of the Trustees for whom I have the profoundest respect and for many of them real affection, I must insist upon the removal of my name. My regret is the trouble it will cause you. I am sure it is in the best interests of the project. Permit me to assure you, there is not the slightest desire on my part to appear modest, that I make this decision. If I were not convinced that it will in the long run be prejudicial, I would have been delighted to have my name connected with it, as you may readily imagine. If no name is used, it will belong to the people the same as the Art Institute. The people supply the building and will be taxed to support it and then will be solicited to give exhibits and again others contribute money to memberships and special purposes. All will come easier and with better grace if it is the I[ndustrial] M[useum] of C[hicago]. My wife was the first to bring it to my notice and I at once agreed as it had been on my mind, although I had never mentioned it. Please, therefore, make it as easy as you can and see that the change is made *the sooner the better.*[21]

For the next three years, JR worked to bring about the name change. He was accustomed to being obeyed, and his explicit wishes had been willfully disregarded by those he considered his friends and associates.

The search for a museum director, which continued for almost two years, was another source of great frustration for JR. In July 1926, board member Charles Piez wrote to Wormser: "It was Mr. Rosenwald, I think, who suggested that we ought to secure quite promptly a man who could assist the general committee or the president of the corporation in a personal way to interest the industries and to fetch and carry."[22] On August 25, JR and Wormser discussed the necessity of an immediate search for a museum director. JR, however, was not satisfied that the search was moving fast enough. He finally contacted Samuel W. Stratton, the president of the Massachusetts Institute of Technology, but that led nowhere.[23]

By February 1927, the director had still not been selected. Wormser was annoyed. He had been devoting more and more time to the Museum, to the detriment of his legal work. He wrote to JR: "The need for an Executive Director is constantly presented to my mind. There are many things that ought to be done right now to further the project. They can only be done if we have a man employed for the purpose and so circumstanced that he devotes every bit of his time, thought and energy to this end."[24] JR agreed and replied to Wormser almost plaintively: "Hope it won't be long before we get a Director."[25]

Wormser eventually believed that the position should be advertised, and so did one of the candidates, *New York Times* science editor Waldemar Kaempffert, who wrote the copy for an advertisement in his publication that described the need for a multifaceted leader.[26] Although Kaempffert suggested several people for the position, he was nominating himself. That was not lost on Wormser, who was immediately impressed with the science writer. Kaempffert quickly became the leading candidate, but the courtship was agonizingly slow. Negotiations dragged on. In December 1927, JR invited Kaempffert to come to Chicago, but the issue of the museum director was still unsettled.

The agreement signed with the South Park commissioners in mid-August 1926 was not official. There were still a number of issues left hanging. They revolved around three points.

First was whether the Palace of Fine Arts was to be used exclusively as a museum. Part of the problem was that the bond issue passed by the South Side voters in 1924 had specified that the building could be used for a variety of purposes. That was clearly not what JR wanted, but others had different ideas, holding out for a convention hall or something else to share the museum space. Thus JR, Wormser, and members of the museum board had to convince the reluctant commissioners that the building could only be a museum and that there really was not enough space for anything else. A second point of contention was control. The museum board clearly wanted to control the museum, but Kelly, the ultimate politician, had other ideas. He wanted the commissioners to exercise control over the entire building, arguing that if the Palace of Fine Arts had multiple uses, only the commissioners could deal with those different aspects. Wormser argued that it would be very difficult to get corporate donations of exhibits to the Museum if the controlling agency was perceived to be a political body.[27] Finally, of course, was the question of money. The commissioners wanted to know what would happen if the museum cost more than had been originally supposed. Kelly wanted JR to agree to foot the bill for any overage, and JR did not object. The final arrangement was a compromise. The commissioners ultimately agreed that the building should be used only as a museum and that sole control should rest in the hands of the museum board. JR pledged to contribute whatever was necessary over and above the cost of the bond issue.

In 1927, before the final resolution of all these differences, in an attempt to solve the question of multiple uses, Rosenwald decided that it was essential to win over the South Park commissioners, so he invited them to travel to Europe at his expense in order to examine industrial museums there. Three commissioners took him up on his offer, and the European trip was a qualified success. The commissioners certainly took advantage of JR's generosity by bringing along their wives or children and by visiting places where there were no industrial museums, such as Rome and Switzerland. On the other hand, commissioner Louis Behan had the good taste to write Wormser, thanking JR for a valuable and worthwhile experience.[28] A final agreement between JR and the commissioners, however, did not result from the trip. Before leaving for Europe, Kelly had advised against a formal agreement as a political strategy. But once back on the shores of Lake Michigan, he proved elusive, and Wormser spent months trying to track him down to work out a deal.[29] One meeting that he had with Kelly was not encouraging. The wily commissioner "made it clear that the commission was strongly enthusiastic about proceeding with the Museum as the dominant factor of the Fine Arts Building, that they favored putting the building on a terrace, which would permit a forty-foot basement, and working out a landscaping treatment to the South of the Museum somewhat on the order of Versailles."[30] Clearly the trip to Europe had given Kelly a grandiose vision. Kelly also indicated on his return that, if the Museum were to rival or surpass the Deutsches Museum, it would cost $10 million, not $8 million.

By mid-September, an agreement between Wormser and the commissioners seemed to be drawing closer. But a final agreement between JR, the museum board, and the South Park commissioners was not signed until March 1929, and then only after JR had agreed to increase his contribution to $5 million.

The delays in signing an agreement with the commissioners were matched by delays on the part of the architect. Those and other causes for delay produced great frustration in Rosenwald, a man used to controlling situations and getting things done speedily. Architect Ernest R. Graham, whom the South Park commissioners had retained from the very beginning, was involved in most of the major public buildings of the era, including the Civic Opera House. At times JR believed that the dilatory Graham was more interested in Insull's Opera House than in his museum. While the intent of all concerned was to preserve the original 1893 structure, no one knew precisely how much of the building could be retained. There were also questions about a subterranean or basement story, which was essential for a coal mine. Graham proved as difficult to pin down as Kelly. Delays were blamed on draftsmen, and there were also problems with bids and subcontractors. As the months dragged on, JR and Wormser grew more and more exasperated. In July 1927, JR received a letter from Calvin W. Rice, a backer of the Museum of the Peaceful Arts in New York. "Hats off to the Rosenwald Museum!" wrote Rice, who enclosed a clipping which declared that a Russian tourist intending to visit the United States had indicated that among the first sights he wanted to see in America was Chicago's newest museum. JR replied: "I wish the so-called Rosenwald Museum was in such a condition that we could show it to this world-traveler. Unfortunately it is moving very, very slowly."[31]

Finally, there was the lawsuit. Most Chicagoans were delighted with the idea of the museum, but disgruntled lawyer William Furlong sued the commissioners because the original bond issue had called for a mixed-use building. The suit dragged on from one court to another for years.

In short, by the end of 1927, after nearly two years of work, some progress had been made on the museum, but much remained to be done, and the entire project was becoming a source of frustration to JR. A director still had not been hired, the name of the museum remained unchanged, an agreement with the South Park commissioners still had not been finalized, the architect appeared to be dragging his feet, and the lawsuit that seemed to have been won in 1926 had been appealed. JR very much wanted to see this project completed before he died, but the odds were not good.

The Russian Colonization Project

In 1925, JR returned from one of his periodic trips to Europe, and on the boat he encountered Felix Warburg, an investment banker related to the Schiffs by marriage, whom he had known for about ten years. Warburg also was chairman of the Joint Distribution Committee (JDC), the relief agency formed during World War I to assist European Jewry. JR was certainly familiar with "the Joint" (as it was known) but had not contributed to it in recent years. Warburg told JR about a project the JDC was involved in that definitely piqued Rosenwald's interest.

Following World War I, the newly installed Bolshevik government had freed Russian Jews from the strictures that had bound them to towns and villages ("shtetls") for centuries. Under the old regime, Jews could not own land, and Jewish occupations had been severely restricted. The vast majority were small tradesmen. Suddenly Jews found that they were permitted to own land and could choose whatever occupation they desired. But their financial condition was deplorable. And if they were interested in choosing agricultural production as a career, they knew nothing about farming. Enter Joseph Rosen, a Russian-born American agronomist who discovered that the Soviet government was willing to sell land cheaply or give it away to Jewish communities. The land was incredibly fertile in the "breadbasket" of Russia in the Crimea and the Ukraine. All that was needed, Rosen believed, was to persuade Jews to move from the shtetl to the land and teach them how to farm. The result would be productive agricultural settlements filled with happy and prosperous Jewish families.

In 1924, Rosen began a pilot program using $400,000 from the JDC. His goal was to settle 1,000 families in agricultural "colonies" not too dissimilar from the present-day kibbutz, the Israeli agricultural community run along socialist lines. Eventually, the amount of money given to Rosen was doubled and the number of families to engage in this experiment was quadrupled. Rosen estimated that 25,000 individuals had been assisted by this effort. He had just issued a glowing report of his activities and was preparing to formally present it at a meeting of the JDC in Philadelphia in September 1925. His goal was to solicit $9 million to be matched by a like sum from the Russian government. The funds would be used to acquire additional land in Ukraine and the Crimea on which to settle the additional "colonists."[32]

JR discussed Rosen's idea with Warburg and became quite excited. This was a scheme that merged a number of his interests. He certainly knew agronomists after his experience with Aaron Aaronsohn. Moreover, this was a plan that, for a relatively small amount of money, would help thousands of people and enable them, in a fairly short time, to become self-sufficient. Finally, JR was no Zionist. He did not favor Jews from around the world moving to Palestine to create a Jewish state. Here was a way to assist Jews by keeping them in their native land. All of these reasons for looking favorably on Rosen's project seemed to fit together into a neat package. He told Warburg that he would read the Rosen report, and that if he agreed with its findings, he would be prepared to contribute $1 million on a matching basis, much as he had done in the great campaign of 1917. Because of other commitments, Warburg agreed to put in a smaller sum, approximately $100,000.

On returning to Chicago, JR read the Rosen report and was tremendously impressed. He must have particularly liked Rosen's conclusion, which stated: "By concentrating our effort on one proposition we can accomplish with the same amount of money much greater results than by spreading over a variety of enterprises."[33] Here was still another reason for helping to finance what JR considered to be a brilliant plan. He wrote Warburg:

> En route I read Rosen's report and, assuming that his statements will all be borne out upon investigation, also that the attitude of the Russian government toward Jews and agriculture will continue, I consider this a rare opportunity for constructive work—an opportunity that comes once in a lifetime.[34]

At almost the same time that JR learned of the Rosen report from Warburg, he received word of it from Jacob Billikopf, who was just as enthusiastic as Warburg had been: "The more I study the colonization work, the more I am thrilled with its possibilities; the more I feel it is the most worth while plan yet conceived for relieving, in great part at least, the acute Jewish situation in Russia."[35] He urged JR to go to Philadelphia.

JR did attend the meeting, which was quite contentious. A number of Zionists were there, led by the charismatic Rabbi Stephen Wise, and they correctly saw the Russian colonization movement as a threat to their cause. On the second day of the conference, Rosen presented his report. As soon as he had finished, JR arose, declaring somewhat ingenuously that he had not planned to make a speech but had been moved to do so by Rosen's address; in fact, it is likely that JR attended the meeting with the sole objective of making this speech and proposing his offer. The speech is vintage Rosenwald and says a great deal about his philosophy of philanthropy, especially the notion that donating to a cause where there is no element of self-help will simply cause the recipient to become dependent upon charitable handouts.

> I am firmly convinced that Jews have never had an opportunity to do a real constructive piece of work for their co-religionists until this time; I have always felt that whatever they have done heretofore has been palliative. . . .

> I am willing no longer to give in any large measure for palliative relief. I believe that the people will always require assistance. This thing is going to continue. There will always be orphans and sick. There will always be poverty, but I believe those things have got to become local duties imposed upon the people who live in a community.
>
> We can't hope to provide funds for people who live all over this world who are poverty-stricken. Furthermore, I don't believe it is helpful in the long run to make people dependent upon charity. If we can put them in a position to help themselves, I am in heartiest accord with work of that nature. I am very anxious indeed to have this the primary motive in connection with any campaign that might be started in this country. I would deplore the failure of this movement which I am sure will result if we are going to mass everything and consider the so-called colonization work in connection with relief work. I am very much afraid that any movement along that line will fail.[36]

Following this echo of the conclusion of Rosen's report, JR made his offer. He would give $1 million if $9 million could be raised in three years to be devoted solely to Russian colonization.

JR's offer was ultimately accepted, although the committee that drafted the final resolution of the conference did not have an easy time. The Zionists (who wanted to scuttle the whole colonization movement) put up a stiff resistance. The final resolution merely announced that the JDC was launching a $15 million campaign, without specifying where the money was to go. JR called it "a pussyfoot compromise which did credit to neither group."[37]

In January 1926, JR sent Warburg the first installment of his pledge—stock worth approximately $75,000—even though the first $750,000 had not yet been raised.

JR gave no thought to Russian colonization while he was on a trip to Egypt and Europe, but upon returning in May, he became involved once more. In June, Billikopf wrote him complaining that more people were needed to get the word out convincingly. David Brown, the executive director of the JDC, and the lawyer James Rosenberg, who was soon to head the Russian Colonization project, were convincing speakers, but Billikopf wished there were more such men. The most persuasive orators, those who could make audiences open their pocketbooks most readily, were eyewitnesses, people who had been to the new Russian colonies and who could come back to deliver vivid reports on what they had seen. Billikopf proposed that JR pay for several noted rabbis and social workers to make this journey to the colonies and then have them go on a speaking tour of America. JR summarily rejected this plan.[38] Later it was suggested that JR himself go to Russia, an idea the Chicago philanthropist briefly toyed with but ultimately decided against for health reasons. Finally, in July JR suggested that his son, William, then in Europe, travel in his stead. William accepted with alacrity. Before William left, JR wrote to him: "Keep an open mind and do not permit what I have done to influence you, because I may have been wrong, and if so I am as anxious to know it as any one."[39]

The group traveling to Russia that William joined was headed by Sherwood Eddy, a writer and lecturer, and included academics, businessmen, and students. At the last moment, Billikopf decided to join the party. The purpose of the tour was to examine conditions in the new Soviet Union objectively and then report back to the American public.

JR received reports from three sources on the Eddy Mission about the Russian colonies. One came from William. In his unpublished memoirs, William describes a stop in Simferapol in the Crimea: "We drove through the barren landscape, stopping occasionally at a house that looked more like a tool shed. The wonderful weather precluded the need for much shelter. Hens ran around the house scratching for food. Dr. Rosen assured me that the settlers were delighted with their new lives and would build better homes as they prospered." William evidently found much of the trip rewarding. He cabled his parents:

> Tremendously impressed with colonies, especially Cherson district which grew half million bushels of wheat beyond personal needs, total salable produce worth $1 million. Despite fewer working cattle, Jews grew two times the weight/acre as neighboring Ukrainians, and Jews' poorest quality betters Ukrainians' best. Relations satisfactory. All colonists said even if conditions in towns improve materially they would remain on account of greater security and promising future. Average Agro-Joint investment, $250 per family. Convinced no other philanthropy could yield such returns. Work could be more than doubled at same efficiency within a year.[40]

Another member of the Eddy Mission who informed JR about the Russian colonies was Samuel Cahan, a professor of journalism at Syracuse University, whom William described in his memoirs as "a little energetic Russian Jew, always very much on the alert, always willing and pleasant,

[who] is kept frightfully busy interpreting." After returning to the United States, Cahan wrote at length to JR, recounting his observations on the colonies he had visited in the Crimea. He said they were a revelation. Although the first ones they saw were squalid and oppressive, it turned out that these were very recent colonies. The ones two or three years old were better off and even possessed some comforts. Cahan continued:

> Despite the dark side of the picture, I wish to tell you without reservation, and I think that your son will agree with me, that the Jewish colonization project is unparalleled by anything that was done for the Jews of Eastern Europe, and especially those of Russia, before. While we have seen poverty and suffering and privation, and all that which casts a gloom and oppresses the heart, we have seen a heroism that is new in our people; a determination that is sublime; a faith that is inspiring. . . . The achievements of the Jews in the colonies are extraordinary.

Cahan concluded that they had even visited a colony named after JR, and although the harvest there had not been quite what was expected, conditions were better than they had been. "Two years ago it was a desert overgrown with wild weeds, with a handful of Jews, naked, hungry, and tired, struggling to keep body and soul together. Now there are two rows of immaculately white little homes, with contented people living in them, and that colony is typical of many others we have seen, some of them that are in their fourth year of existence showing even signs of prosperity."[41]

All the Jews on the Eddy mission were very impressed with Rosen. Billikopf called him "a rare personality, one of the rarest I have ever met."[42]

JR was truly inspired by the accounts of the Russian colonies by William and others on the Eddy Mission. At a meeting of the JDC in Chicago in October, he made a further pledge for the Russian colonies, offering an additional $1 million provided Felix Warburg also put up $1 million and if an additional $3 million could be raised from other sources. This $5 million fund would be used to make loans to the Russian government for colonization. The payments would be made in 1927 and 1928 as the matching sums were raised, and if less than $5 million was collected, JR agreed to pay a proportionate share of the total.[43] This was on top of his pledge the previous year at the Philadelphia Convention. Nothing ever came of this initiative, as the matching funds never materialized.

A problem was developing, however, regarding the payment of that first pledge. From the beginning, JR had tied his initial $1 million pledge to the JDC's raising an additional $9 million for the same effort. One year after the Philadelphia Conference, the JDC found itself in an embarrassing position. It had allocated less money than previously planned to Russian colonization. If JR stood rigidly by his pledge, this would mean less of his pledge would be paid. Moreover, his pledge had been used to spark support in Jewish communities throughout the country.[44] If JR were to prove obstinate, and if this were to become known, it might result in less money collected from other sources.

Various attempts were made to persuade JR to change his mind about the conditions he had set for his pledge. He was asked to earmark his money for Russia in general and waive the requirement that it all had to go for colonization. He steadfastly refused, despite the appeals of Warburg and others. Finally, David Brown, director of the JDC, sent him a letter saying that the budget for 1928 had been set, but he would have trouble reaching it unless JR increased his gift. He intimated that the $15 million decided on at Philadelphia had been budgeted, but that anything over that sum which was collected would surely go to Russian colonization.[45] JR responded with a gift of stock worth between $70,000 and $75,000. Shortly before the new year, David Brown reported to Warburg that he had talked to JR, who had promised more funds in the coming year, and that he was convinced that another large pledge could be obtained from the Chicago philanthropist.[46]

The JDC continued to be wary of providing the information JR desired. Several times during the winter and spring of 1927, Graves wrote to JDC officials asking for a simple piece of information: "A statement showing the amount of money collected since the Philadelphia Conference, as a result of that Conference and (giving date sent and amount of each remittance) how much has been sent to Russia for colonization work only from such collections."[47] Either someone sent the required information or JR relented, because by April 13, JR had paid $224,000 of his original $1 million challenge.

In the summer of 1927, on his way back from Europe, JR once again encountered Felix Warburg, who was completing a trip around the world that included a visit to the Jewish colonies. JR's enthusiasm for this project revived as Warburg told him of the marvels that Rosen had brought about in the Crimea and Ukraine. As a result of this meeting, the two men realized that a new initiative was needed, especially since JR's offer of the previous year had led to nothing. They agreed that a major gift campaign should be launched, targeted to a relatively few wealthy donors, and that Herbert Hoover, who had worked with Rosen on Russian relief efforts earlier in the decade, should be enlisted to give his imprimatur to the Russian colonies. A party was held at the Warburg mansion on November 5, 1927. Those in attendance included many of the important figures in New York Jewish society: Herbert Lehman, a partner in the investment firm of Lehman Brothers; Alfred S. Ochs, publisher of the *New York Times;* Cyrus Sulzberger, head of the firm of Erlanger Blumgart & Co., a noted politician, and onetime chairman of the United Hebrew Charities of New York; Cyrus Adler, president of Dropsie College in Philadelphia; and Abraham and Bernard Flexner, brothers who were advisors to the Rockefellers.

At this dinner, JR delivered a speech in which he described how he had become involved in this project (oddly enough, he failed to mention Felix Warburg, his host) and how he had consulted his family once he had thought of making a fairly sizable commitment back in 1925.

> [I] told them that I thought it was the greatest opportunity that I had ever known to do a great thing for a large number of people, the most promising piece of work that had ever come to my notice, and, as good children, they all agreed that if I was interested to the extent that I was—and they also expressed themselves as believing that there was a good opportunity—they advised me to go ahead and contribute to it in a larger way than I had been accustomed to contribute to other things. I said to them at the time, "I am envious of anybody else that has a part in this."[48]

JR then made another challenge grant that demonstrated not only his commitment but his enthusiasm, for it assumed that this project would last another five years at least. He pledged to give $200,000 a year for five years if an additional $9 million could be raised. Felix Warburg pledged to put in $100,000 a year for five years. The Jewish Colonization Association, better known by the acronym of that name in Yiddish (ICA) or the Baron de Hirsch Fund, was thought to be willing to put in $3.5 million. This organization was interested in aiding Jewish agricultural colonies all over the world. It was further anticipated that the Russian government would match the $10 million fund being created and issue bonds as proof of that match to the American donors.

Following JR's address, Herbert Hoover spoke. At this point, only a year before his election as president, he was clearly a figure of international prominence. He said, "I do not know of a more important experiment in human engineering for generations. It has been proven to be founded on common sense, and while it is an idealistic scheme, the practical problems of sound and capable farming dominate the work."[49]

The JDC Philadelphia conference of 1925 had decided to raise $15 million but had refused to earmark formally any of this money for Russian colonization as distinct from relief work in other European countries or in Palestine. At this dinner, the JDC indicated that it was willing to take an important step, because the fund that was being created was to go entirely to Russian colonization efforts. In addition to the funds either pledged or hoped for from the ICA and the Russians, $5 million remained to be raised, but this goal was over a five-year period. The economy was booming, and it appeared that wealthy individuals might be able to supply the remainder of the campaign funds within the anticipated period. Nevertheless, this last issue was a source of serious concern to the JDC leaders.

As 1927 ended, several issues regarding the Jewish colonies in Russia remained to be settled. Rosen had returned to Russia and was in serious negotiations with the Soviet government about their contribution to the project in terms of land and money. The ICA portion of the match seemed in danger of falling through. James Rosenberg, the young lawyer who had been interested in this project for some years, was being pressured by Warburg to assume the chairmanship of the fund drive. He was reluctant to do this because he believed it would be essentially a full-time job and he did not have the means to give up his law practice.[50] He was also concerned about how many major donors could be attracted to this project. The main question that was posed to Rosen was: What was the absolute minimum that the Americans could provide that would be matched by Russia and still ensure the continuation of a successful program? A second question was: What was a realistic pledge period? Was it five years? Ten? Nor was it certain what the attitude of the Soviet government was, or whether the bonds that they would issue to American donors would be worth the paper they were written on.

As far as JR was concerned, the start of a very exciting program had been made. Despite the fact that he was never to visit Russia and see the colonies firsthand, his commitment to the Russian colonies was only to grow in the years ahead. In contrast to the Museum of Science and Industry, this appeared to be a project that would produce quick and highly visible results.

The University of Chicago

Between 1925 and 1928, JR's involvement in university activities greatly increased, and he became one of the university's most generous trustees during the first decades of the century.

JR's dealings with the university in this period began with the development campaign of 1925. Fund-raising on a broad scale by universities was a relatively new phenomenon in the 1920s. Increasing capital needs and costs meant that universities could no longer rely on the largess of deep-pocketed patrons, as the early University of Chicago had depended on John D. Rockefeller Sr. To organize and run university capital campaigns, a new profession had been created just after World War I, the fund-raising consultant. These firms were hired by university trustees to conduct needs assessments and to staff and run fund-raising campaigns, because on-site fund-raising or development offices were virtually nonexistent.[51] Since neighboring Northwestern University had conducted a successful capital campaign, president Ernest Burton and the newly elected young board president, Harold Swift, decided that it was time for the University of Chicago to embark on a similar venture. In 1924, a trustee committee, which included JR, was formed to pick a consulting firm. The respected East Coast firm of John Price Jones was selected, and an ambitious goal of $17.5 million was decided on.

As a trustee on the development committee, it was incumbent on JR to propose an important lead gift, and by December 1924, he knew what he would do. He agreed to pledge $1 million payable in three equal installments, starting in 1925. But because of his dislike of endowments, he added another provision that was to prove significant: Both income and some of the principal had to be expended annually until the principal was entirely exhausted.[52] Such a proposition was something revolutionary in higher education. To meet JR's terms, the university created what was called a "Suspense Account." The university agreed to spend between $75,000 and $100,000 a year from this fund, including principal. The money could be, and was, expended on whatever the university faculty or trustees wanted: research, equipment, travel, or buildings.

JR added to this fund from time to time, at one point giving it another

$1 million. He also used it as a vehicle for paying off many of his numerous additional gifts to the university. Although there was grumbling at the time that the gift was not solely endowment money, the university probably benefited during the Depression. The "Suspense Account" lasted for over ten years after JR's death in 1932 and was available in the lean years of the 1930s when the university was undoubtedly grateful for the funds it was obligated to expend. JR may have thought that he would be starting a trend in higher education funding. Unfortunately, no other philanthropist interested in higher education followed his example.

JR's formal pledge of $1 million was announced at an alumni dinner in March 1925 to kick off the capital campaign. It was by far the largest pledge of any trustee.

JR was directly and indirectly responsible for $3 million of the capital campaign total, because, in addition to his own $1 million pledge, he solicited others who collectively pledged $2 million. This fact was especially significant because the campaign was a failure. By September 1926 only $9,253,655 had been collected and the campaign had clearly run out of steam.[53] President Burton had died suddenly, and his successor was unfamiliar with capital campaign fund-raising and unwilling to attempt it. The campaign was called off.

About the same time as the capital campaign pledge, JR made a major donation to another component of the University of Chicago, the Oriental Institute. JR's interest in the work of its director, James Breasted, dates from 1918, when Breasted spoke at a Sunday morning service at Temple Sinai. Sensing that JR was intrigued, Breasted asked to see him, hoping that JR would agree to fund the extensive excavation work he was planning in Egypt. Breasted made a very convincing case. JR said he would consult Wallace Buttrick, director of the General Education Board, when the two men met at a Rockefeller Foundation Board meeting. Also at that meeting was the University of Chicago's president. The three men agreed that it was up to the university to take the lead in securing funds for Egyptian excavations, not Breasted. But JR clearly remained intrigued. A couple of months later, he proffered a proposal. "As you and I both know," he told Breasted over the phone, "the initiative in such a matter belongs with the president and with the university. Please explain to the president that if he approves, and desires to take up your plans, that I shall be interested to see how much it will cost, how much the university can contribute from the budget, and to see what I can do to help out."[54] No figure was mentioned, but the matter shortly became moot, because JR was preempted by John D. Rockefeller Jr., who eagerly provided much of the money Breasted needed. Breasted may not have been far off when he thanked JR in June 1919: "I am convinced the action of our Eastern friends [Rockefeller] was greatly influenced by the interest which you yourself showed in my work."[55]

Breasted was reluctant to give up on the man he regarded as his second major supporter, and he continued to press JR for additional funds. At first, JR was mildly interested. But eventually he turned Breasted down. "Valuable as the work you are undertaking is, and proud as anyone might be to be connected to it, I have come to the conclusion that I do not want to branch out into odd and end things in educational matters, giving a driblet here and a driblet there. In my opinion, the University should provide the funds, inasmuch as the expenses are being taken care of otherwise."[56]

Early in 1926, James Breasted had two visitors at Chicago House in Luxor. William Rosenwald, JR's youngest son, then age twenty-three, was extremely interested in what he saw, and reported to both of his parents. Shortly thereafter, JR himself arrived in the course of his second trip to Egypt. JR described his visit in a letter to the university's newly installed president, Max Mason: "We had five wonderful days at Luxor with Dr. Breasted as our guide and visited U. of C. House and the staff. They appear to be doing a remarkably fine job. I was so impressed that I was glad to have a small part in furthering their addition to their quarters. I am therefore enclosing my check for $30,000, the proceeds to be used for the purchase of additional land and to complete the building and furnishing of the addition, the plans of which were shown me."[57] Unfortunately, the building did not go smoothly. The Egyptian architect hired to oversee the construction was ill and omitted some critical structural items from the dome, so the entire dome had to be torn down and rebuilt. Breasted asked JR for an additional $7,500 for this, which he agreed to donate. The new Rosenwald Library of Chicago House was formally dedicated on March 15, 1927.

JR helped Breasted in other ways. For example, Sears donated some free furniture for Chicago House. The two men remained friends; Breasted dined at Ravinia and was invited to receptions hosted by JR. But when Breasted, who had a nagging streak in him, hounded JR about helping provide him with free mattresses for Chicago House, JR politely told him to stop.

At the end of 1927, JR made two generous contributions to two quite different branches of the University of Chicago. He had been associated with the Chicago Lying-In Hospital since 1909. He had helped the hospital in 1917, when this institution, which provided first-rate obstetric and gynecological care for poor women, moved to a newly constructed building. In 1927, the hospital was planning to move again. This time it not only was affiliating with the University of Chicago Hospitals but was planning to construct a new building adjacent to Billings Hospital on the university campus. Unfortunately, a bitter feud had developed between the hospital's chairwoman, Mrs. Janet Fairbank, and Dr. DeLee, the charismatic director of the hospital. The dispute involved money—the size of the projected hospital and the number of beds to be devoted to gynecology patients. Mrs. Fairbank believed that Dr. DeLee's requirements were excessive and that the hospital would end up being too expensive. Dr. DeLee convinced JR that there had to be a sufficient number of gynecology beds for teaching purposes. JR seems to have tried to act as a peacemaker. In December, he informed Mrs. Fairbank that he would contribute $250,000 subject to certain conditions, which he ultimately relaxed. For when he partially fulfilled his pledge in 1929, paying out $200,000, it was clear that the hospital and the university could not build the facility that had been contemplated.

In 1927, JR became involved in the construction of a new mathematics building, donating $250,000 of the approximately $1 million cost. More than that, he solicited the $250,000 gift that named the structure for his friend B. F. Eckhart.

Although JR was assiduous about being a trustee, giving generously, and soliciting others to donate, in this period, for the first time, he attempted to take a hand in setting policy—which was not the traditional role of a trustee. His attempt to have students pay for the full cost of their education, an effort that grew out of the capital campaign and was an issue the university took extremely seriously, was ultimately unsuccessful. The university had just embarked on its capital campaign, and the John Price Jones firm had just been engaged. John Price Jones himself interviewed JR and then reported back to the board chairman, Harold Swift. Swift then wrote the following anguished letter to President Burton:

> Mr. Rosenwald seems very keen on the thought that Colleges of the future are going to be financed by the payment on the part of the student of the actual cost of education, either during his College course or by deferred payments. He told Mr. John Price Jones when he was here a few weeks ago that he would give $1 million to any institution that would institute a plan which would require every student either to pay the total cost of his education or to sign some kind of document saying that he expected to do so eventually. He doesn't seem very keen that the document be legal or airtight but that it must recognize a responsibility on the part of the student and an obligation.

Jones then asked JR whether he would give the funds to the University of Chicago, and JR replied that he had mentioned it to other trustees but "had not stirred up much interest." Swift's memo went on to say that there was a serious danger that JR might give the $1 million to the University of Pennsylvania, whose president was more receptive to the idea. Since the Jones firm was also conducting a capital campaign for Penn, they found out about this. D. F. Duncan, the fund-raising consultant firm's employee covering the Chicago campaign, asked JR about Penn, and the Chicago philanthropist indicated he was ready to go ahead with that university. Swift went on to say that Duncan had called him "all of a flutter" to tell him that Chicago might lose $1 million if they were not careful. Swift concluded: "The suggestion appears rather radical; at the same time, I understand it is being very much discussed in educational circles." Swift then sought to examine how the University of Chicago could obtain this $1 million grant and how they could conduct an experiment to see if the scheme would work without getting in serious financial trouble.[58]

A meeting with JR and University of Chicago officials was held, at which JR raised his concerns about tuition. It was decided that the subject was so complex that a thorough study would have to be undertaken. Duncan then met with JR to discuss the matter of students being made responsible for their own tuition, and followed this up with a memo stating that it would be very difficult to agree on a policy "providing for the signing of a paper by matriculates." Duncan continued: "As I understand it, you are desirous of working out some plan whereby the students are brought to realize what is being given them by the University in excess of what they pay." He suggested the creation of a department of financial promotion whose function would be to educate all undergraduates about the financial status of the university and the obligation of a student to support his alma mater in later life. But the so-called department suddenly metamorphoses, in this planning document, into a series of chapel talks, pamphlets, and a promotional film made for the development campaign. It was to be a soft sell, designed to last all four years of a student's residence at the university, with the object of turning the student into a dedicated alumnus and donor.[59] Duncan had grasped the essence of JR's vision, but his solution was singularly unimaginative, as JR no doubt recognized, because no further action was taken.

One can see how this notion would appeal to JR's business sense. He was opposed to subsidies and felt that people should pay the true value of such important items as education. The impracticality of a student paying the true cost of his or her education is apparent to us today. Despite the high cost of tuition in the twenty-first century, no major research university can survive on tuition alone. Nor does the price of tuition reflect the true value of a student's education. These facts were as true in the 1920s as they are today, and they must have been brought home to JR, for no such experiment was ever attempted, either at the University of Pennsylvania or at Chicago.

JR's contributions to higher education in this period were not limited exclusively to the University of Chicago. Following a successful solicitation of JR to honor the birthday of Harvard's President Eliott, Judge Julian W. Mack pressed his close friend to make additional gifts to Mack's alma mater. He urged JR to support the work of noted legal scholar (and later Supreme Court Justice) Felix W. Frankfurter. Frankfurter himself wrote a wide-ranging letter to JR, apparently asking for the general support of the Law School, which seemed to link it to the future of American civilization.[60] This appeal was followed by a more concrete letter from Judge Mack asking that JR contribute to a fund for the publication of books emanating from Frankfurter's program in administrative law. JR agreed to donate $10,000 for this purpose, but ended in a semantic tussle over the wording of the gift which, like the possible $1 million to the University of Pennsylvania, exemplified his naiveté in academic matters. The problem with JR's original wording was that it implied that the gift was conditional on Frankfurter's remaining at Harvard. This would mean that a donor would have control over whether a professor stayed at a university or left. Such a notion is rightly anathema in academia. At the first hint of a problem, JR figuratively threw up his hands and declared that Judge Mack and the Harvard Law professors (including Frankfurter) should come to an agreement about acceptable wording.

Although he contributed to Harvard and the Massachusetts Institute of Technology, as well as supporting Professor Horace Kallen of the New School at the urging of Judge Mack, it is clear that JR's main interest in higher education in this period centered around the University of Chicago. Precisely what caused JR to take his duties as a trustee more seriously and to start pouring money into the university at this particular time is not certain. Probably his withdrawal as president of Sears enabled him to devote more time and energy to the university. Furthermore, he appears to have become very much involved in the capital campaign, and this tied him closer to the university and its administration. As he began to work more closely with men such as Harold Swift, the ties deepened. The very nature of the Suspense Account, with its mandatory disbursement of funds each year, meant that he was constantly informed about the numerous and varied uses to which his money was being put. And these reports, too, served to tie him closer to the operations and the future of the university. These ties were to continue and deepen in the years ahead.

Politics

Freedom from the top position at Sears enabled JR to become involved in politics once again, something he had not really done since the war years. Unfortunately, this foray into the political arena was to lead JR into one of the most foolish mistakes of his life, the Frank L. Smith affair.

In the Merriam mayoral campaign of 1911, JR had shown his zeal for "reform" politics and his distaste for machine-bred corruption. Thus his reaction to Smith can be understood. Frank L. Smith was a Republican from Dwight, Illinois, who had served various political bosses and who was elected to the U.S. House for one term from 1918 to 1920. He then aspired to higher office and ran an unsuccessful campaign to unseat the incumbent, Senator William B. McKinley. As a consolation prize, Illinois governor Len Small, a thoroughly corrupt machine politician, named Smith to be head of the state commerce commission, which, among other duties, was to regulate the utility industry.

Early in 1926, Frank Smith decided to run again for the Senate. Once again, he was pitted against McKinley. The campaign was a costly one.

McKinley, who was independently wealthy, spent his own money freely. Smith, who was not wealthy, waged a vigorous campaign and ultimately beat his opponent in the primary. Rumors began to circulate about where Smith had obtained his money.

Meanwhile, in Pennsylvania, another corrupt primary was occurring, and this one reached the ears of the U.S. Senate. A special Senate committee chaired by James A. Reed of Missouri was formed to investigate campaign corruption in Pennsylvania. On June 26, Senator Thaddeus H. Caraway of Arkansas appeared before the Reed Committee and delivered an oratorical bombshell. He accused Frank L. Smith of having received a substantial sum of money for his primary campaign in April from Samuel Insull, the CEO of Commonwealth Edison, one of the very utility companies that Smith, in his capacity as head of the Commerce Commission, was supposed to regulate.

The Reed Committee soon added Illinois to its agenda and came to Chicago in July for an initial round of hearings. They revealed either blatant corruption or total incompetence on the part of several political figures. Smith swore he had very little idea where his money was coming from. Insull read a carefully drafted statement skirting the truth and then refused to answer any questions on the advice of counsel, claiming that the committee lacked jurisdiction in the case. The campaign managers of both Smith and McKinley, it turned out, kept no records whatsoever. Eventually, Smith's campaign manager, Allan Moore, acknowledged that he had gone to see Insull on behalf of Smith in November 1925. Insull had stated that he did not think McKinley was a good senator and that he wanted to aid the Smith campaign. He then reached into his desk and produced an envelope containing $50,000 in cash, a token, he said, of his admiration for Frank Smith. In March 1926, Insull summoned Moore again and asked how the campaign was going. Moore replied that he was having a difficult time because McKinley was spreading the rumor that Insull was financing the Smith campaign, so people did not think it necessary to contribute. Insull said he definitely sympathized with this and produced another packet of $50,000. A couple of weeks later, shortly before the primary election, a further $25,000 was produced in a similar fashion. It later transpired that Smith had received five-figure sums from other people involved in utilities and that Insull, seeking to hedge his bets, had also contributed to the campaign of the Democratic candidate, George E. Brennan.

JR was shocked at the revelations of the Reed Committee and began floating the idea of naming an independent Republican to challenge Smith in the general election. A devoted Republican, JR feared that Smith's corruption might throw the election to Brennan. He decided that an effort should be made to induce Smith to withdraw on the grounds that, even if he won the general election, the Senate would not seat him—a move for which there was precedent in recent Illinois history.

In mid-August, President Calvin Coolidge summoned JR to the summer White House to discuss the business climate, especially as it related to farmers, a constituency JR knew because the bulk of Sears customers were part of the agricultural sector. JR decided that he would attempt to persuade the president to intervene to force Smith to withdraw or, at the very least, to deny him any support. Although politics was touched on in the meeting, JR and Coolidge agreed that the subject would not be mentioned when JR came before the press at the summer White House.

The campaign against Frank Smith was heating up. JR was active in moves to find a credible candidate who could run as an independent in the election. Following rejections by several possible candidates, the anti-Smith group turned to Hugh S. Magill, general secretary of the International Council of Religious Education. Magill had unimpeachable credentials as a reformer, but he faced stiff odds. His entry into the race was not announced until September 28, giving him barely a month to conduct a campaign against two well-financed opponents.

JR returned to Chicago from a trip on the day Magill's candidacy was announced and told the assembled press that he was delighted with the candidate but he was not "going to be the 'insulator' of the Magill race."[61] He and the other Magill backers agreed that only $25,000 should be spent on this campaign; JR announced that he was limiting his contribution to $5,000. The whole endeavor appeared to be something of a quixotic protest against the undue influence of money in politics, which has a most familiar ring in the early years of the twenty-first century.

Almost from the moment of his return to Chicago, JR sought to arrange a meeting with Frank L. Smith. At first, the senatorial candidate turned him down, but he finally agreed to see JR. This meeting, which was kept secret for five years, led JR to make one of the most unfortunate and ill-considered offers of his life.

The meeting, as reported by Smith to the *Chicago Tribune,* began with JR saying that even if Smith won, he would never be seated by the Senate.

Smith replied that no one could know what the future would bring. JR said that his information on Smith's probable disbarment came from the highest authority—presumably Calvin Coolidge. After Smith had dismissed this by attacking the Reed Committee investigation, JR made his proposal:

> After the meeting the other day, I went into an inner room to take a siesta upon orders from my doctor. While lying there thinking, I had a brainstorm. I thought to myself, "If I will give $500,000 to have Magill elected, why not give Frank Smith $500,000 and have him withdraw?"
>
> So I acted. No one knows what I am about to say to you except my wife, whose consent I had to get before I could make the offer; and no one else will know from me. If you will withdraw from the Senate race, I am here to offer you 10,000 shares of Sears, Roebuck stock whenever you sign your withdrawal notice. In a few months, that stock will be worth three quarters of a million dollars.

Smith was incredulous, but JR remained resolute, prophesying again that Smith would win the election, but would then not be seated. To his credit, Smith categorically refused the offer. Two years later, the two men ran into each other at the Republican National Convention in Kansas City. Again according to Smith's version of this encounter, JR said to him: "You are the first man I have known to refuse a million dollars" (which was what the proffered stock would have been worth by that time). Smith says he replied: "No, the woods are full of them, and most of them would have been less courteous in refusing you than I was."[62]

This is all Smith's account, and the only suspect piece of information is the notion that JR was willing to pay $500,000 to have Magill elected. This does not square with other statements JR made at the time. He testified before the Reed Committee that he had not given such a sum to the Magill campaign, and it is extremely unlikely that he would have committed perjury. So this detail of Smith's recollection may be faulty. But no one denied the basic fact that JR had offered Smith the stock. When this news broke in 1931, JR was gravely ill and could not respond. But other "unnamed sources" who were friends or family members acknowledged the basic truth of Smith's account.

What could have possessed JR to make such an injudicious move? According to these "authoritative sources," JR "attempted only what he thought would be the best thing for the people of Illinois—to save them from the shame of witnessing the rejection of a man they had elected to the Senate—and for that reason, he offered Smith what he considered reimbursement for the costs of the expensive primary battle he had been through and the heavy obligations already incurred for the election campaign, then well advanced."[63] Thus his motives were altruistic, if inexcusably naive. He thought he would be aiding the Republican Party, the people of Illinois, and even Smith himself. JR probably reasoned that if Smith were so corrupt as to have taken Insull's money, then he would surely jump at JR's offer, which at least was in a "good" cause. The fact that what he was proposing was illegal seems not to have occurred to him before the meeting—although Smith claims he brought the subject up during the meeting. This serious lapse of judgment is probably the greatest stain on an otherwise clean public, business, and personal record.

The rest of the Smith story is soon told. Everything that JR prophesied in his meeting with Smith proved to be correct. Smith was elected, handily defeating both his opponents. Then, before Congress reconvened in January 1927, incumbent Senator McKinley died. Governor Small named Smith to fill the month and a half of his predecessor's term (the new Congress reconvened in March) but the newly elected senator from Illinois never had the opportunity to serve. Proceedings to deny Smith his seat were begun immediately, and the entire process took a year. Finally, on January 19, 1928, the Senate, by more than a two-thirds majority, voted to bar the duly elected senator from Illinois. Smith tried to stage a comeback later that year, but he never was elected to office again.

JR's involvement with Smith was not over. In 1928, he contacted Magill and suggested that a book be written regarding the Smith case. Magill was not interested, so JR wrote to his friend Charles Merriam, the Progressive reform candidate he had championed in 1911, who was a professor of political science at the University of Chicago. Although Merriam also turned the project down, he suggested that one of his colleagues, Carroll H. Wooddy, might be interested. It was not until February 1929 that JR sat down with Merriam and Wooddy. Wooddy asked for a stipend of $5,000, which JR agreed to. But it took some time for the book to be researched and written. *The Case of Frank Smith* did not actually appear in print until the summer of 1931. JR ordered a thousand copies sent at his expense to friends and legislators.

It seems clear that Wooddy knew something of JR's meeting with Frank Smith, but not much is revealed in his account. "When the Colonel [Smith] came to Chicago to start his campaign after the primaries, Mr. Rosenwald arranged an interview with him and urged strongly that Smith abandon his candidacy on terms that would fully safeguard him from loss incurred by the effort and expense already invested in his campaign. . . . Smith, however, had by this time definitely made up his mind to fight to the end; all efforts to bring about his elimination from the campaign were fruitless."[64]

In fact, the publication of the Wooddy book enraged Smith and made him decide to go public with his version of the interview, which was presented to the press as an open letter to Wooddy.

JR's foray into politics in 1926 was no more of a success than his earlier venture in 1911 or his World War I experience in Washington. In this case, he learned that corrupt politicians value ambition more than amassing money. This was a lesson he should not have had to learn.

Black Education

JR's dealings with two black colleges demonstrates what he regarded as the good and the bad attributes of the principals of such institutions.

By 1925, JR had been on the board of Tuskegee for fourteen years. While his relationship with Booker T. Washington had been excellent, his relationship with Dr. Robert Moton was rocky. He did not much like Moton, who appears to have lacked the suaveness and self-assurance that Washington possessed. There is a note of servility in Moton's letters that would never have appeared in Washington's.[65] JR did not trust Moton's leadership, and he became increasingly concerned about the financial situation at Tuskegee. Werner suggests in his notes that the fact that JR was no longer "king" of Tuskegee rankled with him.[66] But JR was not such an egotist. He was also unhappy with his fellow board members. As he wrote to one in January 1926: "Personally I am of the opinion that for an institution having so large an endowment fund and spending the amount of money we do, Tuskegee has the weakest Board of Directors I know of."[67] He also wrote fellow trustee, George Foster Peabody: "[W]e must have some new members who will take an interest in the institution, otherwise, I fear the future of Tuskegee is not bright. I have never been entirely happy with our conduct of affairs there."[68]

In late 1924, a joint capital campaign was launched on behalf of both Tuskegee and Hampton Institute. JR was not enthusiastic about it, but participated nevertheless. He was instrumental in persuading the philanthropist George Eastman to make a truly significant multimillion dollar challenge grant to the campaign. He also solicited John D. Rockefeller Jr., who gave $1 million, and Arthur Lehman, a partner in the investment firm of Lehman Brothers. Moreover, JR pledged $100,000 toward the campaign, and later said that he would match all Chicago gifts dollar for dollar up to a second $100,000. Apparently because Moton made "an ass of himself" at a fund-raising cocktail party in Chicago, the second $100,000 was not fully raised.[69] In the end, JR paid $174,776 to the Hampton-Tuskegee capital campaign in 1926. It may be symptomatic of JR's feelings toward Tuskegee that, aside from his pledge to the Hampton-Tuskegee campaign, he gave very small amounts of money to the latter institution during those years, always under $1,000, and usually earmarked for something such as Christmas toys or supplementary gifts to faculty members. But he gave no money to the general operating funds of the institution.

Two things especially bothered JR about Tuskegee. One was that Moton and such other board members as Anson Phelps-Stokes believed that funds from Tuskegee should go to help small struggling private schools such as Snow Hill. In 1912, JR had been in favor of aiding such schools. But then he became involved in the Rosenwald School project. Now times and circumstances had changed. JR closely examined Tuskegee's budget and realized that the Institute was deeply in debt and that the debt was accumulating annually. To help schools such as Snow Hill while Tuskegee had serious problems of its own seemed to JR sheer folly. As he wrote to board president William Jay Scheiffelin: "Firstly, we should provide carefully for our own needs. We have always run the Institute with a considerable deficit. Secondly, considering the size of the institution, I know of none which is run with so inadequate a Board of Trustees, only a few are really seriously concerned with its affairs. Hampton seems to me to have a thoroughly well-organized, competent Board of Trustees and their affairs are in first-class shape."[70]

Poor financial management and Tuskegee feeder schools were not the only problems JR had with Tuskegee and with Moton. The Institute's principal worked so hard during the Hampton-Tuskegee capital campaign that his health suffered. He spent weeks in Johns Hopkins Hospital, and finally persuaded the trustees that he needed a complete rest and that he should take his wife and daughter on a cruise around the world. JR was initially sympathetic, but when he learned that the trustees were paying for the daughter's trip, he exploded. The episode shows a side of JR that is not very attractive. Moton's daughter had just graduated from Tuskegee and been accepted at the Oberlin Conservatory. She was probably bright and talented. But to JR, this was a boondoggle. He felt that Catherine Moton should stay at home and take care of her younger siblings, and he believed that sending her on a cruise set a thoroughly bad example. He voiced his displeasure not only to his fellow trustees but also to Moton, who apologized for the whole incident but said the cruise could not be called off. Despite his repeated threats to leave the board, JR never did so, and he was nominally still a member when he died.

In contrast to Tuskegee, which he considered an inefficient institution, JR admired two other black colleges with which he had been involved, Fisk and Howard Universities. He was not on the board of either, but he had contributed financially to both of them, and he remained interested in their welfare. Both universities acquired new presidents during this period. JR attended the inauguration of Thomas E. Jones as president of Fisk in 1926 and was on very friendly terms with Mordechai Johnson, president of Howard. He had lobbied quietly behind the scenes for Jones's election at Fisk, and as he wrote of a visit to the university in 1927, "I am to a degree responsible for his being there."[71] In 1928 he gave approximately $25,000 to Fisk, and in 1927 he gave two gifts of $25,000 each to the Howard Medical School. He also supported the research of Howard's noted marine biologist E. E. Just.

During his trip to Nashville for the inauguration of Thomas E. Jones as the new president of Fisk, JR gave an interview to the *Nashville Tennessean.* He expressed optimism on the progress of race relations in both the South and the North. He cited the example of the Commission on Interracial Cooperation, headed by W. W. Alexander. "This committee is arranging meetings between representatives of both races," he said. "In this way the two races are getting to know each other better. And when you know a man, you understand him. That is the way we must solve this problem, through knowledge and understanding on the part of both races." He also cited the example of the Union League Club of Chicago. Ten years ago, JR maintained, the members of that club would go a mile out of their way to avoid the black community. Now they invited black speakers to their meetings and "they go into Negro communities and study conditions with a view to improving conditions, because they realize that if conditions are bad in the Negro communities, the surrounding white communities will suffer."[72] Although such a viewpoint was slightly naive and exceedingly optimistic, it did reflect JR's view of black-white relations at that time.

Health and Travel

Health and travel seemed to dominate JR's personal life during the mid-1920s, and the two were often connected. JR and Gussie took many trips during this period for health reasons, but there were other factors as well.

There were several reasons why JR retired as president of Sears in 1924, but one of them was health. Prior to resigning, JR had been keeping up a frenetic pace. He had heart problems, and when he visited the summer White House in 1926, he fell ill; it was reported that he had suffered a heart attack, although this proved to be a false rumor. In 1925, he was examined by specialists at the Rockefeller Institute, who urged him to slow down, take frequent vacations, and have an office only at home rather than at the Sears plant; the last injunction he resolutely refused to accept.[73] Earlier that year, he had told several of his fellow Tuskegee board members that he could not do much on the board for health reasons. "[I]f I follow my doctor's advice," he wrote Challis Austin, "I shall have to resign from the Board. They are insisting that I withdraw from all activities which give me any concern whatsoever and my family demands that I follow these instructions."[74] Perhaps this was merely a manifestation of JR's disenchantment with the Tuskegee board. However, Austin was one of the people he most respected on that board, and it is hard to believe he would mislead him.

In March 1927, when the family was vacationing in Santa Barbara, California, chauffeur Harry Kersey noted that both JR and Gussie were unwell. "I noticed Mr. Rosenwald was not playing golf. I overheard a chance remark one day while at the hospital where I went daily for medicines for Mrs. Rosenwald that Mr. Rosenwald was suffering from a dangerous malady called Paget's disease of the bone that had formed in his shoulder. I had noticed him several times getting in the car release his hold on the door and step back, his expression showing that he was in pain."[75] Elsewhere, Kersey mentions how JR seemed to be shrinking in size, an effect of Paget's. Photographs of this period also show a marked change from the man of robust health of 1912. However, one should not suppose that JR was ill throughout this period. In November 1925, he wrote to Sears's agent in Berlin: "Am feeling very well indeed, although, as you may imagine, am extremely busy."[76]

Partly for health reasons, partly because he was no longer the president of Sears, Rosenwald took numerous trips during this period. Trips to Europe occurred yearly. One in early 1926 took JR and Gussie to Egypt, southern Italy, Rome, Florence, Vienna, Munich, and Paris. This was the trip during which JR visited Professor Breasted in Luxor. William accompanied him to science museums in Vienna, Munich, and Paris. In Vienna, he stood in a bread line and witnessed the European Depression firsthand. It was not until May that he and Gussie returned to the United States.

In the winter of 1927, JR and Gussie traveled to Santa Barbara, California, where they stayed for six weeks. Gussie, who was ill much of the trip, describes the beauty of the location and excursions that they made to the homes of friends who lived in the mountains nearby. JR wrote his children: "Lazy is a mild term for my attitude these days—neglect everything except reading, sleeping, eating, talking too much, very little writing. . . . We are unaccountably and increasingly popular and are taking advantage of it before the mistake is discovered. Even our friends are benefiting through the mistake."[77] By June they were back in England for the wedding of their daughter, Adele, who had divorced Armand Deutsch and married noted child psychiatrist David Levy. While in London, they met a number of dignitaries, including Lord and Lady Astor and Charles Lindbergh, who had just arrived in the British capital following his historic flight. JR wrote his sister, Selma: "[W]e were invited to the Ambassador's home to meet Lindbergh. Gussie was too tired, and much to my regret missed a red letter event. Only about 100 people were there, but they were the 'Creme de mints.' . . . I had several nice chats with Lindbergh."[78]

There were frequent journeys to visit children and grandchildren in New York, Philadelphia, and New Orleans, in addition to trips to Washington on political business, such as the inauguration of Coolidge (for which Herbert Hoover provided the tickets) in 1925 or a trip in February 1927 when JR had lunch with Coolidge at the White House.[79]

When he was in Chicago, Rosenwald was kept quite busy. A fragment of JR's date book for October and November 1926 has been preserved by the faithful William Graves with the notation: "The attached gives an indication of Mr. R.'s activities during each day."[80] There are cultural ac-

Figure 16. JR and Gussie (*center*) on the boardwalk in Atlantic City, 1928. Woman on left unidentified.

tivities (the opening night of the symphony, an opera), social occasions ("November 13—Mr. and Mrs. John Stuart presenting the Misses Stuart at the Casino Club"), luncheons (to meet Admiral Byrd or New York mayor Jimmy Walker), and an endless round of meetings, some for civic organizations (Commission appointed by the mayor on Home Rule, Chicago Crime Commission), educational institutions (the University of Chicago board of trustees), and social service agencies (the Marks Nathan Home, the Jewish Home Finding Society). There are several meetings of the Union League Club Committee on Race Relations. What is truly odd about this list is what is omitted. This was the period when JR was working hard to defeat Frank Smith, but the only hint of politics occurs after the election. This was also the period when intense activity was occurring concerning the Museum of Science and Industry, but only one meeting is listed that could have taken place with that on the agenda. Nor is there much mention of the Joint Distribution Committee, except for the national meeting that took place in Chicago in October. In short, if one factors in the organizations and causes that primarily concerned JR during this period, as well as the numerous meetings of other organizations and the travel, one realizes that JR was, for the most part, as busy as he had ever been. This impression is confirmed by a list of the organizations with which JR was connected in 1927. He was a vice president of five—all but one (the Boy Scouts, Chicago Council) Jewish. He was a trustee of fourteen others, ranging from the Rockefeller Foundation to the Art Institute of Chicago, and a director of nine others, ranging from the Jewish Home Finding Society of Chicago to the Chicago Grand Opera Company. And that does not include the six organizations where JR was a member of the executive committee.[81] No doubt the Chicago philanthropist spread himself too thin and allowed his name to be used too widely. He could not possibly give a decent amount of time to every organization. However, the schedule and this list confirm that he cared about a great number of causes and organizations and sought, when possible, to attend their meetings.

The Julius Rosenwald Fund

The Julius Rosenwald Fund had been established in 1917, and at first it had had essentially no staff, except for William Graves. In 1920, S. L. Smith had been hired to run the Rosenwald School program from Nashville. Between 1921 and 1923, Francis Shepherdson was employed to direct the foundation. He was replaced around 1925 by Alfred K. Stern, the husband of JR's daughter Marion. Stern was a young man with no experience in running anything, let alone a multimillion dollar foundation. He was affable and hardworking, but it became obvious to JR that he would need to hire a person who had professional experience with foundations.

In November 1925, probably at a Rockefeller Foundation Board meeting, JR consulted his friend Abraham Flexner about the future direction of the Julius Rosenwald Fund. Flexner suggested that JR continue to concentrate on the field of black education in which his name was becoming widely known. He then outlined a program in education (broadly conceived) that sounds remarkably like that of the General Education Board, urging JR to cover all areas of black education including high school and to deal with health matters affecting blacks. Finally, he suggested that the YMCA program be continued and that other social centers might be funded as well. Flexner concluded with a brief discussion of staff:

> The extent to which the foregoing program could be carried out would depend upon the resources of the fund and the constructive capacity of the director. If the scheme should be fully developed, it would require an organization consisting of a Board of Trustees interested in Negro education and in general education, a director who would have general oversight and perhaps carry on one division himself, and such assistants as might be required to take charge of the specialized activities, as they are entered upon.[82]

In fact, many of these ideas were eventually incorporated in the reorganized Rosenwald Fund, but JR did not immediately take up Flexner's suggestions. Nothing was done for another two years. Then Flexner sent JR an article he had written on foundations, and this sparked JR's renewed interest in dealing with his own. In a letter of mid-October 1927, JR set forth the job description as he envisaged it, in the broadest possible terms: "The fact that money is available often causes one to overlook many of the pitfalls which you point out. After reading the documents I feel even more the need of having someone who can keep me straight, and when you have the time (which I know is a rare commodity), please remember I want the best man I can get to enable me to use my money wisely."[83] The two men discussed this the next day in New York. Flexner recommended someone whom JR duly interviewed, but the Chicago philanthropist did not think him suitable for the position, possibly believing him to be overly academic. In any case, he now had his own candidate in mind.

JR met Edwin Embree the day he attended his first board meeting at the Rockefeller Foundation. The two men became better acquainted during World War I when JR was in Paris. JR was staying at the Ritz Hotel and discovered that Embree was in town staying at a less elegant hotel that, however, had one great advantage over the Ritz: it had cheese. It seems the French government had banned the consumption of cheese at luxury hotels, and JR had a great fondness for French cheese. So he and Embree struck a deal: he would go to Embree's hotel for lunch and have cheese, and Embree would have a lavish cheeseless supper at the Ritz with JR.[84] After the war, the two men remained on good terms and saw each other at board meetings of the Rockefeller Foundation. Eventually, Embree was named director of the Division of Studies, specializing in health issues, including nursing education. In 1927 he was made a vice president of the Rockefeller Foundation. But there were problems. As he wrote to his friend, the author Clarence Day:

> I had been getting increasingly dissatisfied with what seemed to me formalistic attitudes, professional viewpoints and bureaucratic tendencies in the Foundation. I kept wanting to do new things, to try out fresh ways of helping, instead of going on doing over and over, however well, types of work the benefits of which had already been thoroughly established. It seemed to me that the only justification for foundations lay in making social experiments, in launching courageously upon imaginative enterprises, in a word, in doing the kind of thing which other governmental or private agencies or individuals were not likely to do, and which, therefore, were the unique opportunity for these new, large, untrammeled funds.[85]

According to Embree, JR had similar reservations about the Rockefeller Foundation. Thus, after an early November board meeting, the two men talked and began exploring the possibility of Embree's coming to Chicago to direct the Julius Rosenwald Fund. JR invited Embree to the dinner for Rosen given by Felix Warburg on November 5. Embree attended and was most impressed. He wrote JR: "In this back-to-the-soil project in Russia you have evidently hit upon one of those rare proposals which combine immediate relief with far-reaching results. Those who made the early plans and who supported the work in the beginning must take great satisfaction in having started something really worthwhile."[86] At this point JR consulted Flexner again, and Flexner, who had worked with Embree for years at the Rockefeller Foundation, gave him a hearty endorsement.

Embree came to Chicago for an interview after Thanksgiving and the visit was highly successful. JR offered him both more money and more freedom than he had enjoyed at the Rockefeller Foundation. Embree was delighted. He wrote Clarence Day: "Well, just as I was most dissatisfied, Mr. Julius Rosenwald came along and offered me a fairly free hand in directing his giving. He has a foundation, and, in addition, wants to give away a number of millions directly. He wants to give wisely, but he is untrammeled by tradition, willing and anxious to do just the kind of creative things that Mr. Rockefeller, Sr. started two or three or four decades ago."[87] Yet Embree's exuberance was also tinged with doubt. He felt that he was taking a momentous step, and he feared that he would be walking away from the prestige of the Rockefeller Foundation to—who knew what? He even told JR in his letter of acceptance that he was leaving Rockefeller with mixed emotions after eleven years. But he added: "On the other hand, I look forward eagerly to the association with you. I believe we can do some good things: it will be a joy to work with you and for you. I hope you are as sincerely happy in thinking of the new connection as I am."[88] JR was indeed. He wrote back: "I was so pleased with [your letter] that I took it down to read to Mrs. Rosenwald who said 'that has a ring of genuine sincerity.'"[89]

After consulting with George E. Vincent, president of the Rockefeller Foundation, Embree informed JR that he could start work on January 1, 1928. An announcement was made to the press, and praise of the appointment came to both men. E. F. Keppel, president of the Carnegie Corporation, wrote JR that he had the highest regard for the "qualities of Embree's head and heart."[90] And Henry Jaggelon of the Carnegie Endowment for International Peace wrote Embree: "Mr. Rosenwald is a rare man with whom to work, and you will have much useful happy work ahead."[91]

A new chapter of JR's philanthropy was about to open that was to place greater emphasis on the foundation and professional grant making. The three years preceding Embree's arrival had shown JR to be heavily engaged in a number of useful and innovative projects. JR was not about to lose his enthusiasm for these ongoing endeavors, but his grant making was to become more systematic and focused under the experienced eye of Edwin Embree.

8

The Julius Rosenwald Fund, Hoover, and the Depression, 1928–1930

The Julius Rosenwald Fund under Embree

As Edwin Embree settled into his new position, he had much to do. He had been hired to take the Rosenwald Fund in new directions. The board had to be enlarged by adding people from outside the family to provide it with greater expertise and objectivity. There were old programs that Embree needed to become acquainted with and perhaps refine and new programs to consider.

A difficulty Embree faced was that, for most of the first two and a half months after his arrival, JR was not available to give direction. Because of Gussie's fragile health, JR and his wife spent February and much of March 1928 in Palm Beach, Florida. Embree decided to take advantage of JR's absence to travel to the East and South. This trip had several purposes. One was to learn as much as possible about the programs JR was currently funding, both through the foundation and as a private individual. With S. L. Smith, manager of the Rosenwald schools program, and Alfred K. Stern, his predecessor as the foundation's director, Embree toured some of the Rosenwald schools. He also wanted to maintain close ties with his former colleagues at the various Rockefeller philanthropies. Many of them were working in areas similar to the Rosenwald Fund or in areas in which Embree hoped the Fund would become engaged. Yet he, as well as JR, clearly wanted the Fund to break new ground in the philanthropic world, not just follow in the wake of the larger foundations, funding what was currently fashionable.

One of Embree's main goals was to develop a series of clear program areas in which the foundation would operate. Up to 1928, the Rosenwald Fund had been mainly concerned with the school building program. Other Rosenwald Fund grants were earmarked for various causes JR had supported previously as an individual. One of Embree's tasks was to make a clear separation between JR's giving as an individual and the work of the foundation. This required a certain amount of tact. As he explained to JR: "You may feel that . . . gifts outside the school building program should continue to be cared for by your personal contributions. Something, I imagine, could be said on either side of that question, and I am sure we all shall be ready to follow your judgment."[1]

In shaping the future of the Fund, Embree wanted to build on the achievements of the past. Following his trip to the South, he praised the school building program effusively: "The change in Negro schools during the past seven years is almost unbelievable. It is an illustration of the effectiveness of programs as contrasted with sporadic contributions." Using the school building program as a starting point, Embree recommended giving aid to those colleges which trained black teachers—no longer just Tuskegee and Hampton but also the agricultural and mechanical (A&M) schools and such institutions of higher education as Howard, Fisk, and Meharry. Training teachers for primary and secondary schools was important, he wrote, but it was also vital to train the teachers of teachers at a higher educational level. Embree even suggested that two small denominational colleges in New Orleans combine to form one "excellent institute, upon which ultimately could be built a medical school."[2] The Fund was to take up this suggestion and become deeply involved in the future Dillard University.

Another area that had interested JR and that Embree saw as an excellent opportunity to make a significant difference was medicine, not in the realm of pure research but in the field of public policy. Medical care needed to be made affordable for the middle class and the poor, and it was crucial that underserved communities have better access to it. Almost no one in philanthropy or government seemed to care about the health care needs of African Americans. The Rockefeller foundations were interested in curing disease, but no foundation was working seriously on the matters

Figure 17. Edwin Embree, president of the Rosenwald Fund, making a presentation. Courtesy of Franklin Library, Fisk University.

Embree was proposing. Black hospitals were, for the most part, deplorable. There was a shortage of black doctors, which JR had tried to alleviate in the early 1920s with a program suggested by Abraham Flexner that ran for a couple of years and then was taken over by the General Education Board. There was also a serious shortage of competent black nurses, although the Fund had already begun such a program on a small scale in 1926 focusing on public health. Following a Rockefeller sponsored program, it called for paying one-quarter of the salary of a public health nurse for five years. The remainder of the salary was provided by state and local government. While this initiative had taken place only in Tennessee, Embree expanded it to cover six other Southern states.[3]

Another idea on Embree's agenda was even more unconventional. When he had been hired, it had been understood that the Fund would not seek to operate in foreign countries.[4] However, Embree wanted to build on the success of the Rosenwald schools in the South and, with the cooperation of the Mexican government, begin constructing Rosenwald schools in that neighboring country. The time for this seemed right; there had been a change of government in Mexico, and the new regime appeared to be receptive to the idea. The new Rosenwald Fund president, whose idea of helping Mexicans was decades ahead of its time, proposed that the Fund move cautiously, gathering data and consulting with officials of both the U.S. and Mexican governments. JR was intrigued by this idea and cabled Embree: "I am favorably inclined toward investigating and securing data on Mexican schools."[5] The idea was proposed to the trustees of the Fund, who endorsed it in principle. There was even talk that JR might visit Mexico. But this project never came to fruition because the Mexican government was not really interested.

Embree was concerned not only about the directions of the Rosenwald Fund's policy but also about the form the revised Fund would take. He and JR had agreed that the board of trustees, which had consisted solely of family members, would be enlarged and that persons outside the family would serve on it. Embree hoped that Raymond B. Fosdick of the Rockefeller Foundation would agree to join the board. Fosdick was approved, but he politely declined the honor. Embree also suggested Harold Swift, whom JR knew from his position as chairman of the University of Chicago board of trustees. Swift accepted. A second outsider was Frank L. Sulzberger, the vice president of the Enterprise Paint Manufacturing Company and an important figure on the board of the Jewish Charities of

Chicago. In addition to Embree and JR, the other board members were Lessing Rosenwald, JR's eldest daughter, Adele, and Edgar B. Stern of New Orleans, husband of JR's daughter Edith. Harry W. Chase, president of the University of North Carolina, agreed to serve in the position that Fosdick had declined.

Beyond formalities, the first real meeting of the reconstituted board took place at the end of April. Embree, with JR's consent, planned a two-day meeting. The first day, April 29, was to be a retreat for discussion and reflection. Embree invited a number of experts to be present, such as Dr. Michael Davis, director of the New York Dispensary, a pay-clinic which Embree hoped to emulate in Chicago. He also hoped that Davis would join the Rosenwald Fund staff as a consultant, which indeed occurred later the following year. Also invited was Jackson Davis, a staff member of the General Education Board, and others with expertise in fields which Embree wished to discuss. Other family members were also invited, including Gussie, Edith, and Marion Stern, JR's youngest daughter. The meeting on April 30 was to be strictly a business meeting in which the board members voted on grant proposals.

Embree prepared carefully for both meetings. He sent all board members a thick docket of materials. The first day was essentially to discuss philosophy and the direction in which the foundation should go. Embree presented his board with a brief history of the foundation to date, talked of other foundations, especially the Rockefeller and Carnegie philanthropies, and laid out a series of fields in which the newly reconstituted Rosenwald Fund might be engaged. These included such areas as "material necessities and comforts," dealing with subjects like food production; health; education (in which the Fund was already involved); social sciences, and "expression, the fine arts, and religion." Here Embree proposed a concept that he called "development of promising individuals and support of creative workers." In a sense, JR had done this already by supporting Dr. E. E. Just, the Howard University marine biologist, and Embree advocated the continued financing of Dr. Just. He suggested fellowships for "men or women who may be entering one or more of the fields in which we take special interest."[6] It is likely that this was the origin of the important fellowship program that was to help dozens of prominent black (and some white) artists, writers, scholars, and teachers. Finally, Embree put forward three distinct proposals: schools for Mexico, pay health clinics and a program for black medical care in the rural South, and an extension of the rural education program to include grants to black A&M colleges and industrial schools. As a result of this first meeting, the board did decide to go in certain directions. They turned down the idea of a health program designed for Southern rural blacks, although they later voted money for black schools of nursing, and awarded fellowships to black physicians to study at elite eastern medical schools if they would agree to return to the rural South to practice. Such a program was similar to the one JR had funded in 1920.

The first formal meeting of the board took place on April 30, and JR started the proceedings with a bombshell. He announced in a letter to the trustees that he was giving the Fund an additional 200,000 shares of Sears stock, worth approximately $2 million. This would bring the total assets of the Fund up to $20 million, making it one of the top ten foundations in the country. Although it paled before the Rockefeller and Carnegie philanthropies, this was still a formidable amount of money. In the next year and a half, while the nation's economic boom lasted, these assets more than doubled. The rest of JR's announcement reflected his philosophy of philanthropy, which he had held since 1912 and which he was shortly to articulate to a much wider audience. In his letter of April 30, he explained his actions and philosophy as follows:

> My experience is that trustees controlling large funds are not only desirous of conserving principal but often favor adding to it from surplus income. I am not in sympathy with this policy of perpetuating endowment and believe that more good can be accomplished by expending funds as trustees find opportunities for constructive work than by storing a large sum of money for long periods of time. By adopting the policy of using the Fund within this generation, we may avoid these tendencies toward bureaucracy and a formal or perfunctory attitude toward the work which almost invariably develops in organizations which prolong their existences indefinitely. Coming generations can be relied upon to provide for their own needs as they arise.

JR concluded by stipulating that the Fund would be required to spend all of both principal and interest within twenty-five years of his death, thereby going out of existence.[7]

News of JR's gift and the twenty-five-year time limit was released to the press and published across the country. One other fact also was added to the news release: JR (age sixty-six) and Embree (age forty-five) had decided that no trustee except themselves could serve on the foundation's board for more than six consecutive years. These steps were taken to reduce the risks of "bureaucracy."

Articles and editorials appeared in papers all over the United States, including the *New York Times* and the *Christian Science Monitor.* The *Chicago Tribune* opined: "It is to be hoped that [Julius Rosenwald's] example will be followed by other men of wealth who expect to make the world a better place to live in."[8] Individuals wrote letters of enthusiastic support. Bernard Sunny, a fellow University of Chicago trustee, told JR that he had "read of the additional contribution to the Rosenwald Trust [*sic*] in tonight's newspaper." He went on: "The Trust is not to be an everlasting loafing place for smug and complacent trustees."[9] Because foundations were a relatively new aspect of American philanthropy, many of JR's ideas, including term limits for trustees, were considered to be novel by contemporaries.

The remainder of the April 30 meeting consisted of voting for grant appropriations. Most were to previous programs or to those already under discussion. For example, $410,000 was voted as the Rosenwald Fund's share of school construction costs estimated to be incurred during the 1928–29 fiscal year. In the next couple of years, this program was amended in various small ways. It was decided to phase out the building of one-room schools, as communities no longer desired to erect such small structures, and a small bonus was given if school districts agreed to use bricks instead of wood as construction materials. The school library program was expanded. A list of appropriate books had been drawn up by a librarian at Hampton Institute. The Fund agreed to pay one-third the cost of each library, or $120 per school, plus the cost of shipping the books. State and local sources of funding, such as school boards, were expected to pay the other two-thirds of the costs of the libraries. Up to $14,470 was expected to be expended on this effort.

In 1927, schools in Louisiana had designated February 27 as Rosenwald School Day and had used the occasion as a fund-raiser for the schools. A total of $20,000 was raised at 150 schools throughout the state. Other states also were beginning to utilize this practice, which was precisely the sort of self-help effort that delighted JR. The Fund offered $100 per state to aid in the promotion and expenses of Rosenwald Days. Oddly enough, the docket to the April 30 meeting states: "It is understood that Mr. Rosenwald did not care to have his name used in connection with these programs."[10] This was one injunction that was totally ignored. The schools had been and continued to be known generically as Rosenwald schools, although each building had its own name, usually the place where it was located. JR had not objected earlier to the generic name. Rosenwald Days continued to be used by Rosenwald schools as fund-raising events throughout the South well into the 1930s.

Funding in new areas was voted up to a certain amount with the understanding that the situation would be studied and that the executive committee would authorize the expenditure of funds if a worthwhile proposal was submitted. Thus it was decided that $40,000 would be authorized to look into the possibility of building urban vocational high schools in black communities in the South. It was ultimately decided to go into this area, and five such high schools were constructed using Rosenwald Fund money. Funds were also appropriated to study aiding A&M schools, other black colleges, and black teacher training institutions.

The sum of $10,000 was set aside for studies on pay clinics, and up to $50,000 was to be expended to study the funding of black hospitals and the training of black public health nurses, other fields with which the Fund ultimately became involved. Up to $2,500 was authorized to investigate the possibility of the Mexican schools.

To run the Nashville office, $22,255 was authorized, and it was decided to hire an assistant to aid S. L. Smith. The Chicago office was more expensive. The staff was increased, and $34,770 was budgeted there. This latter sum represented two-thirds of the total. The other third of the staff salaries was paid by JR because the staff was aiding him on philanthropic projects unconnected to the foundation. At its November meeting, after additional staff was hired, the total budget of running the Chicago office of the Fund was increased to $69,196, of which JR paid one-third, $21,082.

Several new staff were hired, including a comptroller and assistant comptroller, secretaries, and two program officers. One of these program officers was George R. Arthur, hired as associate for Negro welfare. Arthur, who had served for the previous ten years as executive secretary of the Wabash YMCA, was probably the first African American hired as a program officer of a major foundation. He served ably in that capacity until 1934. In 1929, Dr. Michael Davis became director for medical services.

By the end of 1928, the staff of the Fund was essentially established, although a couple of additional people in the financial department were hired in the next two years. The board also expanded in 1928 from nine to eleven members. One new member was Dr. Franklin McLean, the chief of the medical clinics at the University of Chicago. A second was Beardsley Ruml, president of the Laura Spelman Rockefeller Memorial, one of the numerous Rockefeller philanthropies. With Ruml's election, Embree was able to fulfill his dream of having one of his former colleagues elected to the Fund's board. Ruml exemplified the close relationship that developed between the Rockefeller philanthropies and the Fund. For example, in a discussion of the wisdom of providing fellowships for young Southern blacks to study at Northern universities, Embree included the following in the docket for the May 11, 1929, meeting:

> Since the General Education Board is providing a limited number of fellowships for the training of teachers in Negro colleges and universities, a division of labor in this general field has been tentatively worked out by the officers of the board and of the Fund. According to this arrangement, the officers of the General Education Board will continue to grant fellowships for the training of teachers in the liberal arts, sciences, and education, and the Fund will limit its scholarship and fellowship appointments to:
> a) Medical and nursing personnel
> b) Teachers of vocational or industrial subjects
> c) Librarians and teachers in other specialties, such as music
> d) Individuals of unusual promise who desire to study at Northern colleges or abroad.[11]

This relationship between the Rockefeller philanthropies and the Fund was to grow even closer in the future.

After the April 30, 1928, meeting, the broad outlines of the directions in which the Fund would go—black education, medical care for blacks, making health care affordable for average Americans—was largely set, with three exceptions. One, implied by the foregoing but not explicitly stated, was the general area of race relations. At the November 30, 1928, meeting, a grant was given to the Urban League, and "it was suggested that the Fund rather than Mr. Rosenwald personally act upon further appeals from this agency."[12] Another grant went to the NAACP Legal Defense Fund. In December 1928, a ten-year grant of $50,000 was voted to the Commission on Interracial Cooperation based in Atlanta, and its head, Will Alexander, later joined the Fund's board.[13] As its name implies, the commission sought to foster cooperation between blacks and whites.

Given the prevailing prejudice in the South at that time, it was a progressive organization, but it cannot be said that the commission pressed boldly for racial equality.

Another area that the Fund entered after the April 1928 meeting was one of considerable interest to Embree: the social sciences. Embree was a great believer in the Social Science Research Council, an academic organization that vigorously pursued research in its chosen area and received several grants from the Rosenwald Fund. Also favored was the New School for Social Research, which JR had funded in response to pleas from Judge Julian W. Mack. Starting in 1922, JR donated $500 a year toward the salary of Horace Kallen, a professor at the New School whose work Mack admired.

The funding of scholarships and fellowships, which was to become the principal area for which the Fund became known, started slowly. There were two subjects under this heading that needed discussion and resolution. One was the provision of scholarships to Southern black undergraduates in various fields who wanted to study at Northern universities or colleges. In the meeting of November 30, 1928, the officers urged that these be grants rather than loans and that they be for black students with leadership potential. "In discussion, the trustees expressed themselves as desiring to give a trial to the proposal in a limited number of cases, it being understood that, for the present, the officers would vote upon such candidates as came to their attention without any public announcement and without any formal committee of award or recommendation."[14] This issue was later resolved by the accommodation with the General Education Board described above. Fellowships were also set aside for training black nurses and Urban League leaders. In 1929, these fellowships were lumped together, and $50,000 was appropriated for this purpose. Other fellowship categories, such as the training of librarians, were later added.

A second category in which awards were suggested was for "individuals of exceptional promise." Embree clearly thought the Fund could develop a niche here: "Other American foundations are too large and too formal in their organization to attempt this kind of thing. The Julius Rosenwald Fund is still relatively free and flexible; it might perform a unique service by supporting certain individuals during their creative periods."[15] When this issue was brought before the board, the trustees said they were interested "while recognizing the difficulty of selecting 'potential genius.'" They asked that interesting cases be brought before them.[16] They did agree to continue to support the work of E. E. Just. But when asked to support the work of a white physician on the faculty of Harvard Medical School who specialized in the nervous disorders of children, the trustees demurred and asked for further study. This was not because Dr. Bronson Crothers was white, for it had been determined that these pre-MacArthur "genius" awards should be given regardless of race. Dr. Crothers eventually did obtain a grant, although under the rubric of Social Science research rather than genius. But a white assistant professor of philosophy at Harvard was granted $2,000 a year for five years by the Fund's executive committee in their meeting of October 20, 1929.

In the docket for the trustee meeting of May 11, 1929, Embree returned to the theme of "Negro creative workers." The genesis of this idea came from the writers James Weldon Johnson and Charles Johnson, who proposed it to Dr. Anson Phelps-Stokes, a leading white philanthropist interested in blacks and race relations. Phelps-Stokes passed the concept on to Embree. The reasoning behind these awards was explained by Embree in a letter to JR:

> Attention was called by several writers, including James Weldon Johnson and Charles Johnson, to the recent brilliant work of Negroes in music, literature, and the arts and to the effect this was having in making people realize that the Negro was capable of creative work of as high a quality as anyone else. The Johnsons seem to feel that this expression in the arts is about the only thing that has made a favorable impression in the North to counteract, in part, the offense which so many Northerners have taken at the Southern migration of large numbers of Negroes into Northern cities. James Weldon Johnson thinks something should be done to make it possible for these writers and musicians more properly to prepare themselves for their work and to enable them to devote some time to this work without too great difficulty and distraction.[17]

"Because of our interest in Negroes," Embree wrote in the docket for that meeting, "we might properly give particular attention to outstanding individuals in this group, especially those showing unusual ability in the arts."[18] In fact, the executive committee had earlier embraced this idea and voted a $5,000 fellowship to James Weldon Johnson so he could "devote himself to a year of literary work." In 1929, sculptor Augusta Savage was given funds to study in France. Savage was supported for a second year (1930) and the same year saw the award of a fellowship to another young black artist, a singer who was embarking on her career, Marian Anderson. The fellowship program, the most famous part of the Fund, had been well and truly launched.

In September 1929, the Fund responded to a request from the U.S. Public Health Service to fund a joint project in Mississippi dealing with syphilis among the black population, which was known to be pervasive. The Rockefeller philanthropies had sought to eliminate ringworm from Southern whites, but no philanthropy had looked into the problem of venereal disease among Southern blacks. Although modern drugs now used to treat this disease were not known in 1929, there were relatively inexpensive cures available, yet they were not widely known. The program in Mississippi, which was supposed to be a pilot, was to set up clinics and try to educate poor rural blacks about syphilis. In November 1929, the board voted to expand this pilot project to several other Southern states. Clinics were established and some effective work was done, but the situation was difficult and touchy. The cure was painful and required several visits. People with the disease thought that it came from "bad blood," and little was done to disabuse them of this notion or explain the true nature of the disease. The Fund concluded its part of the program in 1932 on the grounds that the government was not doing enough to take it over. Although no one at the Fund knew it, this was the beginning of the infamous Tuskegee experiment in which a group of men who had syphilis were treated with placebos and deliberately misinformed so that doctors could study the progress of the disease. Fortunately for the reputation of the Rosenwald Fund, by the time this experiment was under way, the foundation had ceased to support it.[19]

The syphilis work exemplifies one aspect of the grants made by the Fund: the importance of what might be called public-private partnership. This had been a factor in the schoolhouse construction program, for JR expected that state and local government would play a significant role in meeting the match established by him and later by the Fund. Almost 50 percent of the cost of building a Rosenwald school was required to be contributed by state and local governments. But this same idea of government partnership was carried over to other programs, from school libraries to the syphilis work. In a sense, the Fund granted money to these pilot programs to demonstrate what could be accomplished through such a partnership. If these programs were successful, it was expected that the state or some other government agency would take over their funding and administer them. This notion, that the purpose of philanthropy was to stimulate social change which would then be taken up by government, was one of the distinguishing features of the Julius Rosenwald Fund throughout its existence.

To what extent was JR involved in the reorganized Fund? He was now chairman of the Fund, no longer president or chief administrative officer, for that post was held by Embree. He was on the executive committee, and he attended most meetings of both the executive committee and the full board. To some extent, these meetings were probably based around his schedule. Minutes of the board meetings are sparse, but when they do indicate someone introducing a topic, it is not JR. When JR was in Chicago, he and Embree probably saw each other frequently. When JR was out of town, Embree or Alfred K. Stern, second in command on the Fund's staff, would send him memos concerning Fund business. Sometimes he would scribble notes in the margins or at the top of these memos. For example, in December 1929, Embree wrote him

> We are getting ahead in the program of Negro Health. This goes more slowly because there is less to build on, but we are already cooperating actively with four Negro hospitals and are making possible intensive venereal disease programs and are supporting a general study of Negro health and medical services. . . . This very practical survey of just what is happening to Negroes and what should be done to improve conditions may be one of the best things we are doing.

At the top of the page, JR wrote: "Would it be possible to establish special venereal disease clinics in some of the Negro hospitals in large cities, Baltimore, Philadelphia . . . ?" There was also a question about Provident Hospital, the black institution in Chicago.[20] Thus, while JR was far from being disengaged, this was not exactly the kind of "hands-on" philanthropy he had become involved with earlier. Nor is his pulling back so surprising. Embree was hired precisely to take over the leadership function, the active role in managing the foundation effectively. JR was growing old, and he could not devote himself to his myriad philanthropic pursuits with the intensity he had formerly enjoyed. As far as the foundation was concerned, he let others control it. He agreed to the new areas in which the Fund was involved, but he did not try to control the Fund or exert pressure on Embree or other members of the board. He was kept informed and involved, but he did not manage the foundation, and this was doubtless the way he wanted it.

JR's Philosophy of Philanthropy

Following the publicity surrounding his additional contribution to the Fund, JR was asked to write articles explaining his ideas on philanthropy. He accepted two of these offers in magazines with entirely different audiences: one was the *Saturday Evening Post,* with a large and popular readership; the other was the *Atlantic Monthly,* appealing more to intellectuals.

Not since Andrew Carnegie espoused his "Gospel of Wealth" had a major American philanthropist seriously set out to explain his philosophy of giving.[21] JR used these articles to propound ideas he had been developing and speaking on for the past twenty years, principally his dislike of endowments, which he called "perpetuities."

The *Saturday Evening Post* article appeared on January 5, 1929. Although JR's name is on the article, the byline reads "As told to Elias Tobenkin." Perhaps because of its desire to appeal to a mass audience, the article, in many respects, presents the concepts of its author more clearly than the more scholarly *Atlantic Monthly* essay; the tone is more personal, and it includes more of JR's ideas on philanthropy.

The article begins with what JR calls "intimate personal details": he was forty years old when he first started giving away large sums of money, and he had been surprised to find himself in the class of multimillionaire. He also said that he did not dream of his fortune; his dreams, as is true of everyone, were of his youth. This clever device is utilized to make JR sound like an ordinary man, the friendly old fellow next door. JR candidly admits that he uses these "intimate personal details" in order to supply "a background for the views which I hold concerning fortunes and their social and philanthropic uses."

The almost folksy tone struck at the beginning of the article recurs throughout the essay. Also present are the clever memorable phrases that did embody JR's philosophy: "I can testify that it is nearly always easier to make $1,000,000 honestly than to dispose of it wisely," or "My credo with regard to rich men is that they are neither better nor worse than all other humans and that they contribute to greatness or mediocrity, strength of character or weakness in exactly the same proportion as persons in all other walks of life do."[22]

Following the personal details, JR proceeded directly to the concept that he had been espousing for years, that contributed money, whether in the form of foundations or gifts to organizations such as universities, should not be confined by restrictions, especially those that made mandatory only the spending of interest, not principal. Tying up money in this fashion, perhaps for centuries, he argued, was an act of folly for two reasons: it implied a lack of confidence in the future; and it would "inject the great fortunes of the day into the affairs of the nation five hundred or a thousand years hence." With the rapid changes that were occurring in every aspect of life, no one could predict what the United States would be like in five hundred years, and it was likely that the concerns of today would be completely superseded by other concerns in the far distant future. "These views," JR continued, "are not mere intellectual speculation with me. They are the basis of the program for public welfare for which I stand sponsor and which provides for the spending of a sum, in round figures, both capital and interest, of at least seventy-five million dollars." Where JR came up with this figure is not known. The foundation held $20 million, and his personal fortune was nearing its zenith before the stock market crash that would occur less than a year after this article was published. Presumably, JR imagined that this was a reasonable calculation of what he and the foundation were likely to give away during his lifetime and during the twenty-five years after his death.

Then follows one of the truly striking philosophical aspects of this article. In one sentence JR sums up the history of philanthropy over the last thirty years, which he views as a shift from "a metaphysical to a social basis." In other words, philanthropy has moved solidly in the direction of helping mankind alleviate social problems or, as JR states later: "Modern philanthropy searches out the sore spots of civilization and tries to make them whole." This has led to advances in medicine, the near elimination of hookworm and yellow fever by the Rockefeller charities. And "the yeast of social vision" sparked by people like Carnegie and Mrs. Russell Sage has led to studies on international peace and understanding or unemployment. In fact, philanthropy has taken on some of the trappings of government, "the unofficial administrators of public welfare on a mass scale." With the optimism of his generation, JR saw no problem in this.

The ideals of philanthropy were not all that had changed. So had the techniques of philanthropy. In a phrase that seems strikingly contemporary, JR noted that "benevolence today has become altogether too huge an undertaking to be conducted otherwise than on business lines. . . . Opportunities for philanthropic investment are subjected to careful scrutiny by individual donors or governing boards." Among the items that should be examined are ideas that are obsolete, and here JR reverts to his theme about the absurdity of tying up money for yesterday's causes. He provides numerous examples. One is of a charity founded to alleviate a problem that no longer exists, the fund established by Brian Mullanphy to aid travelers on their way west. The fund had been established when the main mode of transportation westward was covered wagon. Travelers were often stranded in St. Louis attempting vainly to assemble the necessary equipment and supplies for the journey. Mullanphy did not foresee the coming of the railroad. Thus thousands of dollars were simply sitting unused in a vault and could not be spent legally because of the terms under which the charity had been established. In England, this problem had been addressed, but not in the United States.

To solve this problem, JR proposes remedies, something he does not do in the *Atlantic* article that appeared several months later. The first solution he suggests is to amend laws so that the strictures on these obsolete charities can be changed. The second is to change the public's attitude toward the future establishment of endowments, which was what this article was designed to do. Beyond merely writing articles, JR sought to persuade wealthy individuals to adopt his viewpoint. In June 1929, he spent a day in Rochester with George Eastman, expounding his views in hopes that Eastman would agree with him. This visit proved to be successful.

Next, JR provides some of the principles that guide his philanthropy. One is timeliness, which he calls "one of the basic prerequisites of worthwhile philanthropy." Timeliness ties in with the idea that each generation should donate its money to the projects that are of concern to its members. This concept was what JR was trying to instill in his fellow philanthropists in 1912, when he gave away $687,500. The second principle that JR enunciates is also one that he had long believed, that "people do not value that which is given to them. I have tried to veer my philanthropies around to basic rather than palliative measures. I am a great believer in the influence of one man upon other men for good or bad, and I give not only with the idea of stimulating others to giving, but to proper giving." In other words, JR believes that his example and reputation, and the fact that his gifts are challenge grants, will stimulate others to support the same causes he believes in. He concludes his article with three examples of his challenge grants, although one, the Museum of Science and Industry, was a challenge that was never taken up. The first is the Rosenwald schools, where, oddly enough, he does not mention Booker T. Washington in his brief description but is somewhat modest. "I can claim for myself—and that in small part only—the initiative for the building of these schools. The credit for the operation goes back to the people, both white and colored, who have cooperated with me."

The second example of matching grants is the Museum of Science and Industry, where JR's $3 million was supplemented by the $5 million bond issue and, he expected, would be augmented by much additional money. He estimated that funds and in-kind assistance would come from "corporations, firms, and individuals who will provide many of the exhibits."

The final example of a Rosenwald-style challenge is the Jewish agricultural colonies in the Crimea and Ukraine. JR emphasizes that his pledge is conditional upon an equal amount being raised from other sources, as well as funds coming from the Soviet government.

Shortly after the newspaper stories appeared about the changes at the Julius Rosenwald Fund in May 1928, the Chicago philanthropist received a letter from Ellery Sedgwick, editor of the *Atlantic Monthly.* Expressing approval for JR's actions with regard to the Fund, Sedgwick asked if he would write an article "on your conception of the general policies which should govern the large charitable foundations. As they increase in number, it is of enlarging importance to Americans that their purposes and policies be outlined and delineated."[23] JR agreed to undertake the project. But he did not write the actual article, which was ghost-written. Most of the historical work that appeared both in the *Atlantic* and the *Saturday Evening Post* articles was doubtless done by Embree and others. Several drafts of the *Atlantic* article were written, but with no draft quite satisfying JR or his associates, Embree turned to William G. Rice, editor of the *Mining Gazette* in Houghton, Michigan. Rice had written speeches that JR had delivered on behalf of Herbert Hoover in the 1928 campaign, and he may have had a hand in the *Saturday Evening Post* article. JR evidently liked Rice's writing, which seemed to capture his own style. What was wanted, as Embree wrote one of JR's correspondents, was "a style easily read and one that would interest busy men of wealth who often do not take very much time for reading."[24] Rice's draft proved to be the one that was actually submitted to Sedgwick early in 1929. Whoever wrote the article, JR claimed it as his, for it doubtless expressed his ideas in a clear and forceful style. "The Principles of Public Giving" appeared in the May 1929 issue of the *Atlantic,* and JR sent numerous copies to friends and acquaintances throughout the country.

The *Atlantic* essay was far more scholarly than the *Post* article. The number of examples of foolish endowments was amplified. Benjamin Franklin joined Bryan Mullanphy as an example of someone who had established a charitable fund without thinking of the consequences. Franklin had set up endowed funds in both Boston and Philadelphia to aid "artificers not over the age of twenty-five who have served their apprenticeship." Now the class of people Franklin had wanted to aid no longer existed.

There is little in this article that goes beyond the material presented in the *Post* essay other than a forceful statement of JR's position: "I am opposed to gifts in perpetuity for any purpose. I do not advocate profligate spending of principal. . . . I advocate the gift which provides that the trustees may spend a small portion of the capital—say, not to exceed 5 or 10 per cent—in any one year in addition to the income if, in their judgment, there is good use at hand for the additional sums."[25]

JR provides personal examples of his adherence to this philosophy. He describes the "Suspense Account" fund he established at the University of Chicago, and he publishes the letter he sent to the trustees of his foundation regarding its reorganization. He then cites another personal experience. When he was active on the Tuskegee board before Booker T. Washington's death, he persuaded board chairman Seth Low to write to Andrew Carnegie to request a change in the rules regarding the endowment money that the steel magnate had given the school. According to the letter Low received from Carnegie's secretary, the Pittsburgh philanthropist was happy to consider changing the terms of the endowment so that some of the principal could be spent. JR's point was not only that someone of the stature of Carnegie agreed with him but also that most trustees were too timid and should not be afraid to ask enlightened donors to change the terms of their endowment grants. He reiterated the view that donors of tightly restricted endowments were essentially insulting their trustees, displaying a lack of confidence in those trustees to manage the funds wisely.

JR received a great deal of mail as a result of his *Atlantic* article. Almost all the correspondents agreed with JR's position. Friends from JR's distant past, such as his former business partner, Mo Newborg, suddenly surfaced. Abraham Flexner wrote a letter filled with praise. The presidents of Harvard, Yale, and Princeton all wrote. George Eastman noted his approval. George Vincent, president of the Rockefeller Foundation, and Henry Pritchett, president of the Carnegie Foundation for the Advancement of Teaching, wrote approvingly. JR replied to almost every letter, often noting that he had received much correspondence about his article, but that the writer's letter was the best he had seen.

Some people wrote that JR's article had induced them to change the terms of a gift they were contemplating. From the tone of these letters, it would seem that the article was the talk of clubs and boardrooms, and that may have been the case. Amidst the flood of praise, there were some notes of criticism. Harvard president A. Lawrence Lowell said correctly that he was not as certain as JR that future generations could be relied upon to be as generous as contemporaries.[26] A gentleman named Bernhard Osterlonk had a truly excellent point, touching on the motivation of the donor. What, he asked, if the donor was not as enlightened as JR? "Of necessity you ignore the large group of givers to whom the gift is secondary to the creation of a sort of monument to themselves, a monument to their philanthropy. To them, the endowments, which they hope will be in perpetuity associated with their names, are the chief attraction. I fear that your lucid reasoning and wealth of illustration will have little effect on them."[27] There was no effective answer to this argument.

A couple of months after the *Atlantic* article appeared, Ellery Sedgwick invited Rosenwald to write a follow-up. JR agreed to this, noting that he wanted to approach the subject from a different angle and wished to quote from some of the numerous letters he had received agreeing with his position.[28] Although JR promised the article for the autumn of 1929, it was not finished until almost a year later, and it appeared in the December 1930 issue under the title "The Trend Away from Perpetuities." There was not much new in this article, which was probably stitched together by Embree. Basically it was designed to demonstrate that JR's one-man crusade against endowments was having an effect. Not only did prominent people in the philanthropic world agree with him, but numerous people were changing their wills or creating foundations in ways that complied with JR's suggestions. The entire article comes across as self-serving. It did not generate the volume of mail that the first essay did, for it broke no new ground.

Perhaps it is only fair to ask: Did JR's crusade meet with any success or have any impact? In the short term, there seems to have been a brief flurry of activity. Various wealthy donors changed the terms of their contributions to make them more flexible and include the use of principal as well as income. These included George Eastman, Edward Filene, and Robert Brookings, founder of the Brookings Institution. John D. Rockefeller Sr. was persuaded to change the terms of his endowment to the University of Chicago in a similar fashion. Long term, however, it must be admitted that, although JR's arguments are convincing, they have not been adopted by many people. Endowments are generally not set up in a flexible manner, and they are as avidly sought after by nonprofits as they ever were in JR's day. Part of the reason for this may be that, since the Depression and the changes in the banking industry and the stock market that resulted, endowment money invested in securities is no longer the risky proposition that it seemed to be, even in 1929. As for foundations spending themselves out of existence, Martin Morse Wooster is correct that JR has had some imitators, notably Maurice Falk, founder of a Pittsburgh company that smelted copper and other metals.[29] The Maurice and Laura Falk Foundation intentionally went out of existence in 1965. In 1969 in a famous debate in Congress on tax reform, Representative Wright Patman and Senator Albert Gore Sr. "proposed that the life span of new foundations be limited to twenty-five years beyond the donor's death," an exact reflection of JR's idea. Although this suggestion was not adopted, foundations such as the Aaron Diamond Foundation of New York, the Lucille Markey Foundation of California, the Field Foundation of New York, and others have recently ceased to exist due to the expressed wishes of their founders. Moreover, in a 1996 book, *Inside American Philanthropy,* foundation expert Waldemar Nielsen provides a modern endorsement of JR's views. In words that Rosenwald would have welcomed, Nielsen states that "time is not the friend of foundation vigor and effectiveness. In fact with the passing of years, decay and stagnation are quite common, if not epidemic."[30] Nevertheless, considering the number of foundations being created, it is clear that those who choose to follow the path of consciously setting a time limit to their own foundation are the exception rather than the rule. Most donors, unlike JR, wish to perpetuate their name or that of their family. Unfortunately, JR's crusade against endowments has had little real impact.

The Conrad Hubert Estate

Among the letters JR received complimenting him on the first *Atlantic* article was one from Thomas Cochran, a partner in J. P. Morgan & Co.:

> [The *Atlantic* article] is one of the most constructive contributions to the subject I have ever read, and should be productive of much good. It has changed my conception of how I ought to handle a substantial gift that I am planning to make in the near future. Thus, I am indebted to you.[31]

JR was delighted with this and wrote a polite and friendly reply. Six weeks later, another letter arrived from Cochran, and it contained a most unusual and interesting proposition.

In March 1928, a wealthy inventor had died while on a trip to France. Conrad Hubert had emigrated from Russia to America as a penniless Jewish boy. He had held a succession of odd jobs, but he was an inveterate tinkerer, and among the items he invented was the electric flashlight. He started and ran several businesses based on this and other inventions, and when he died at the age of seventy-seven, he left an estate worth over $6 million. A portion of the estate was left to friends and relatives, but the great bulk of it was left to a foundation—which Hubert wanted dispersed as rapidly as possible. According to the terms of the will, Bankers Life, which was in charge of the estate, was to form a committee of three men, and this committee, in turn, was to select three prominent Americans to distribute the money quickly and effectively. The three prominent men chosen for this task were former president Calvin Coolidge, former New York governor and defeated presidential candidate Alfred E. Smith, and Julius Rosenwald. In his letter, written on behalf of the committee that had chosen the three donors, Cochran noted that Coolidge had accepted this honor precisely because the Chicago philanthropist had been nominated to be on the committee with him.[32]

Rosenwald responded with alacrity, thanking Cochran for the great honor that had been bestowed on him. However, he realized the task before him involved both responsibility and pleasure. Here was the opportunity to carry out the wishes of a man who certainly did not believe in creating an endowed foundation. On the other hand, as Werner points out, "The Conrad Hubert will was an example of just the kind of philanthropic carelessness to which Rosenwald was ordinarily opposed."[33]

JR was the only member of the three-man committee to have any experience with philanthropy. At the first meeting of the group in July, Smith proposed that some of the money be spent to tear down some New York tenements and build new, improved housing, forming a for-profit entity that would increase the amount of money available. The lawyers managing the estate vetoed that idea. JR then proposed that many of the grants be challenge grants, so that Hubert's millions could, in fact, help generate additional funds for the institutions involved. As the Chicago philanthropist wrote to Coolidge, "My experience has time and again proved that through stimulating the interest of the public in behalf of the cause, that cause is even more benefited indirectly than by all the money which it receives directly. As I stated at the meeting, after a person has once given to a worthy object, he is likely to continue his interest, making additional gifts during his lifetime, and also, frequently, leaving bequests in its favor."[34] The challenge grant idea was accepted by Smith and Coolidge, and the vast majority of the estate's funds were given in that form.

The committee met monthly from July through September. There were pressures to expedite the process of allocating the money. All three were busy men who did not want to prolong the distribution of the funds. Moreover, although attempts were made to keep the entire project secret, a story appeared in the *New York Times* of October 17, 1929. While much of the money had already been assigned by that time, the lawyers managing the estate were being besieged with proposals and were clearly anxious to have the whole process concluded.

In the end, it is fairly obvious from the list of recipients that most, if not all, of the money was disbursed through the polite equivalent of horse trading—"I'll support your cause if you'll support mine." Alfred E. Smith wanted to back building projects that would benefit New York City, such as the New York Foundling Asylum. Coolidge was interested in traditional organizations such as the Boy Scouts, the Girl Scouts, and the American Red Cross. Embree suggested several organizations to JR, who passed the names on to the committee. For example, at the end of September, he wrote to JR: "Don't you think the committee should consider the life and background of the man whose money you are donating?" Embree suggested that, since Hubert had been an immigrant, the committee might provide a grant to the International Migration Service.[35] This suggestion was accepted by the committee, which granted it $50,000. Altogether, a number of organizations in which JR was interested received money through the Hubert estate. Provident Hospital, the African American health care institution that was in the process of affiliating with the University of Chicago, received a challenge grant of $500,000 if it could raise $1 million. Howard University obtained $200,000. The School of Social Service Administration at the University of Chicago received $250,000. And, since JR was the only Jew on the committee, it seems clear that grants to the Jewish Mental Health Association and the Hebrew Theological Seminary, each for $250,000, were inspired by him, as was a $175,000 one-for-one matching grant to the YMHA of New York. It is also likely that a $250,000 grant to the National Committee for Mental Hygiene was inspired by Embree and JR.

JR never commented on his role in disbursing the grants of the Hubert estate, but one suspects that he did not find the horse trading aspects of it particularly edifying. Altogether, some $6.5 million was distributed to twenty-three organizations in the course of approximately five meetings.[36] There was no attempt at reporting or oversight. These were onetime grants, which must have dropped like manna from heaven on the organizations that received them. This was not carefully planned philanthropy in action.

The Harmon Foundation

Julius Rosenwald had dealings with one more foundation during this period, and this encounter was less onerous and more rewarding than his dealings with the Hubert Estate.

In the autumn of 1927, JR, who had received a number of crank letters, received one that was quite bizarre but that nevertheless delighted him. This missive, which purported to come from "Jedidiah Tingle," was addressed to "Dear Julius," and concluded: "I don't know which to admire most—your work for the Negroes in the South, or your disinterested service to the country through the development and financial rehabilitation of Sears, Roebuck & Co. I suppose my confusion comes from the fact that I evaluate constructive business so highly, and philanthropy with suspicion."[37] JR responded immediately, saying he was delighted to have Tingle's endorsement of his work, and then added this truly revealing paragraph:

> To be honest with you, I am so intent on finding useful things to do that I do not have time to think of how good or bad the things are that I have done. I am getting along now in years, age 65, where I begin to realize how little time there is left in which I can be of use, and while it may seem immodest, I can truthfully say that the only real worries I have in life are to find methods of using money in such a way that I believe it will justify

> itself and do more good than harm. You are right in saying that the opportunities which do present themselves must be sifted.[38]

The correspondence went on in this vein for several more weeks, with "Tingle" advocating a strange plan involving awards for good behavior to young students on which he wanted JR to advise him. When JR realized that "Tingle" was a nom de plume, he asked the newly hired Embree to find out who this curious person was. Embree, who certainly knew the foundation world intimately, made some discreet inquiries and reported to JR that "Tingle" was almost certainly William E. Harmon, "the man who has established the Harmon Foundation, which has done some interesting work in furnishing loans to students on a business basis. Their record in this matter is excellent."[39] There the matter rested. What JR did not realize was that he was shortly to hear from "Tingle" under his true name.

The William Harmon Foundation had decided to present an award for the person or persons who had done the most to further race relations in the United States. While the correspondence between "Tingle" and JR was under way, nominations for this award were being sought. An elaborate system had been established by the Harmon Foundation to evaluate the nominees, with forms for sponsors to fill out. The jury that made the awards consisted of two clergymen, the president of North Carolina College for Women, R. R. Moton, principal of Tuskegee, and Samuel McCune Lindsay of Columbia University.[40] Rosenwald was nominated by Will W. Alexander, director of the Commission on Interracial Cooperation, and by Albon L. Holsey, secretary to Moton. Seventeen other people were nominated, including James Harvey Dillard, the retired head of the Jeanes and Slater Funds, and Moton. Letters of reference in praise of Rosenwald came from William Jay Schieffelen, who had served on the board of Tuskegee with JR for years; Charles Whitney Gilkey, a Chicago minister who had served on the University of Chicago board with JR; and N. C. Newbold of the North Carolina Department of Education, who had known JR for years through the Rosenwald schools.

These assessments of JR were completely frank and honest, totally secret from the nominee, who had no idea that he was even being considered for an award. What did these people think of JR? Gilkey wrote: "I know of no one whose influence on race relations, both between whites and Negroes, and between Jews and Christians, has actually been so wide and deep." In answer to the question "Why do you endorse this candidate?" Newbold wrote, "Because he is genuinely interested in the cause of humanity and his genuine desire to do what he is doing in a quiet unassuming way." Schieffelen wrote: "He has charm, remarkable sympathy for Negroes, and wonderful sagacity and generosity in helping them."[41]

For the jury, it eventually came down to a question of whether to provide an award solely to Rosenwald or to present JR with a special award and give a second award to someone else. The jury chose this route, selecting Dillard as the other recipient.

The executive director of the Harmon Foundation informed JR of this honor in January 1928. He was to receive the "special award of a gold medal in recognition of the national importance of your work in promoting better school buildings for colored school children in the South, and YMCA buildings for colored men in various cities."[42] JR telegraphed his gratitude, but owing to Gussie's illness, he could not attend the ceremony to accept the medal in person.

The awards ceremony took place on March 18, 1928, at the First Congregational Church in Washington, D.C. The medal was presented in absentia to JR by Supreme Court Justice Harlan Stone. Before the ceremony, Rosenwald received a letter from Harmon, now writing under his own name: "I heartily agree with [the judges'] decision that no program of recognition of service rendered the cause of race relations would be adequate without taking into account the length and breadth in place and in time of your effective and farseeing method of helping others to help themselves."[43] JR replied from Palm Beach with characteristic modesty: "No tribute I have ever received has given me the genuine satisfaction which this award has. It was so entirely unexpected and to my mind undeserved, compared with what I regarded had been done by others. To have been included at the same time as Dr. Dillard was a special distinction also."[44]

The Museum of Science and Industry: Part II

As the year 1928 began, JR was annoyed by a number of problems regarding the Museum of Science and Industry that had not been solved: an executive director had still not been hired, the issue of the name change had still not been formally settled, and there were continuing differences with the architect and the South Park commissioners. Some of these issues were resolved or were on their way to solution when the Great Depression began.

The leading candidate for executive director, Waldemar Kaempffert, finally came to Chicago for an interview in January 1928. Wormser reported that the science editor had come to his offices to see him and was now doing some "positive thinking." Wormser added: "There are some financial factors which will also be influential."[45]

Finally, at the end of February, Kaempffert ceased playing Hamlet and set forth his conditions. They were steep. He sought a salary of $20,000, he wanted absolute control over the hiring of curators, and he insisted that after only a few months in Chicago he be enabled to go to Europe for an extended visit to study the Vienna and Munich museums. JR wrote to Wormser: "Whatever the committee [of the board, chosen to hire a museum director] decides will be entirely satisfactory to me. I would be in favor of accepting his proposition and the conditions he suggests—they all seem reasonable to me. . . . I like the enthusiasm he manifests for the job and the evident grasp of the needs. The salary matter seems to me entirely fair for a start. It will give an opportunity for increase when we get under way."[46] The committee voted for Kaempffert on March 14. Although he did not take up his official duties until July 1, an executive director had at last been found.

The issue of a name change from the Rosenwald Museum to the Museum of Science and Industry also was finally resolved, although it took a bit longer. JR reminded Wormser repeatedly to change the museum's name, and once Kaempffert was named director of the museum, he was similarly hounded. In October 1928, the director wrote to JR, Sewell Avery, the board chairman, and Wormser: "I discovered in talking this matter over with Mr. Simms, director of the Field Museum, that the name 'FIELD' has been a great handicap. There seems to be a feeling that the Field Museum exists for the glorification of the Field family. As a result, Mr. Stanley Field must exert all the influence that he can to convince possible donors of its real purpose."[47]

Here was another strong argument to add to those JR had been propounding for years. He did not want his family saddled with the responsibility of funding the museum far into the future. Thus he eagerly replied to Kaempffert: "As you know, I have always contended that my name in the title of the Museum would be a handicap."[48]

It was not until July 3, 1929, that the board finally voted to change the name. The solution was a compromise. The new name would be "Museum of Science and Industry (Founded by Julius Rosenwald)." A press release issued three days later quoted JR:

> From the very inception of this public project in 1926, I insisted that it should not be named after me, and I have now finally convinced the board of trustees that this is to the best interests of the Museum. The Museum belongs to the people of Chicago and the nation. Whatever I contributed toward founding the Museum has been in the firm belief that it will play a useful part in our educational, industrial, and scientific life. I hope the Museum will enlist the interest and aid of the entire country.[49]

The press was ecstatic at this act of what they regarded as self-effacement. The encomiums culminated in an editorial in the *New York Times* that stated: "Mr. Rosenwald regards himself primarily as an instrument for carrying out an idea in visual education new to this country. Thus he sets a new example in philanthropy."[50] The idea of a donor insisting that his name be taken *off* a building was indeed something unique in philanthropy.

In the long run, this seemingly trivial issue was important, and JR was proved correct. For decades, Chicagoans referred to it as the "Rosenwald Museum," but the Museum of Science and Industry is a national institution whose name should not be attached to any individual or family. The vast majority of people who visit the museum today have never heard of Julius Rosenwald and have no idea who founded the institution—which is probably the way JR wanted it.

The architect, Ernest R. Graham, who was busily working on other civic projects, was also a source of lingering frustration. By February 1928, JR was counseling patience, and everything seemed to be settled by mid-April. Kaempffert was on board, and according to South Park commissioner Michael Igoe, bids would be opened for the reconstruction on May 15, and specifications were being printed. Graham had finished his paperwork, and all was ready to go. In two years, perhaps, said Igoe, the museum would be finished and open.[51] But that proved to be wildly optimistic. On May 16, bids from five construction firms were opened, but all were rejected as too high. Not until June 19, 1929, was the bid finally assigned to the lowest bidder, W. C. Wieboldt & Co.[52]

The problem with the bids plunged the museum into yet another crisis. Because the bids were so high, the trustees asked the architect to go over the specifications yet again to see where costs could be cut. Graham finally suggested that the outside be finished in terra cotta rather than limestone, which would save approximately $300,000, and he persuaded commission president Edward J. Kelly to agree with him. This created an absolute storm of protest. Said commissioner Igoe: "No woman could be persuaded to accept an imitation pearl if she could afford the genuine."[53] To end the dispute, JR agreed, in his settlement with the South Park Commissioners, to bear the costs of construction if these exceeded the $5 million limit allowed by the bonds.

By October 1930, the exterior of the building was 90 percent complete. Bids for work on the interior then had to be sent out. That proved to be just as cumbersome a process as the exterior bids had been, and everything was further complicated by the Depression. Wormser was warning JR that the museum could not realistically be completed until January 1933.

Another source of frustration for JR was the lawsuit brought by disgruntled South Side resident William E. Furlong. The Illinois Supreme Court had dismissed the case in 1927. But Furlong was incredibly persistent. The suit proceeded from court to court and dragged on for years. It was not until October 30, 1930, that the Supreme Court turned down Furlong for a third time and he finally disappeared. In the meantime, his lawsuits had caused considerable turmoil.

Had he lost, JR would have had to pay a great deal more to have the Museum constructed. The commissioners, fearful of losing, repeatedly asked Rosenwald for financial guarantees, but in the end, when Furlong lost, they proved to be moot. In light of all the other factors causing delay, it is not certain how much Furlong's litigation served to lengthen the time until the Museum was completed. Unquestionably, the suits created an air of uncertainty.

The Depression had a mixed effect on the Museum of Science and Industry. It certainly had an effect on JR and the way in which he made his gift to the museum. The Depression undoubtedly had a hand in slowing down the opening of the Museum. But for the Museum it was not an unmitigated disaster. The prices of certain materials fell, which was good news for an increasingly cost-conscious board. Wormser wrote JR in August 1930: "The decline in the cost of materials and generally in the cost of construction will work a favorable result. It is probable that on the present Wieboldt contract you will not be called on for anything above

$30,000. . . . Indeed it is possible that on final accounting there may be a refund to you."[54]

The Depression also had the paradoxical effect of essentially eliminating the competition. While the other planned industrial museums (including one by Henry Ford) were conducting feasibility studies, the Museum of Science and Industry was laying the groundwork for future exhibits and preparing the building it was to inhabit. With such a head start and the generous backing of JR, the Chicago museum was better able to withstand the shock of the Depression than its counterparts in other cities.

Before December 31, 1929, JR had spent somewhat in excess of $150,000 on the museum.[55] By that date, he had decided to donate a large block of Sears stock. What role the stock market crash in October of that year may have had in that decision is unknown. Nevertheless, the value of Sears was beginning to fall. When he made his original stock gifts, JR offered to guarantee the value of the dividend—that is, if the stock fell and the dividend was smaller than when the stock had originally been donated, he would make up the difference. Thus, on December 29, 1929, 40,000 shares of Sears stock were presented to the museum. And, true to his word, almost a year later, JR gave the Museum $48,480, the difference in the value of the dividend on the 40,000 shares.[56]

To a great extent, the building had been a source of considerable anxiety to JR. The issue of the name change, the lengthy search for Kaempffert, the lawsuit, the wooing of the commissioners, the slowness of the architect, and the onslaught of the Depression—all proved personally troublesome or slowed down the work and the eventual opening of the Museum. But not everything involving the Museum was a source of frustration. Even without a building, a considerable amount could be done in terms of starting collections and planning exhibits. Kaempffert proved to be a man of considerable vision, and although his expensive tastes clashed with trustees who were becoming increasingly parsimonious in a period of economic downturn, he did accomplish a good deal and hired curators who proved their worth. That the development of the museum progressed as far as it did by 1930, despite the setbacks, owes much to Waldemar Kaempffert's leadership.

Kaempffert did have a clear, if somewhat grandiose, image of what he wanted the Museum of Science and Industry to be. In an article published in *Scientific Monthly* in June 1929, he set forth his vision of the new mu-

Figure 18. The Museum of Science and Industry under construction in June 1930. Photo courtesy of David Phillips, Chicago.

seum. It would, he maintained, be both better than and different from the Deutsches Museum, on which he lavished praise. He wanted to show both the history and the social and cultural implications of science and technology. For example, there would not merely be an Otis elevator in which people could ride; the elevator would lead to an examination of skyscrapers in cities such as New York and Chicago. That in turn would lead to a study of the effects of transportation and public health on large numbers of people crowded into the comparatively small space of large office buildings. The history of rail transportation would be examined with one long "train" consisting of different cars. The first car would be similar to one of the earliest trains of England in the 1840s. It would rumble and shake to simulate the difficult roadbeds of that era, and out the window, one would see a long painting of an 1840s English city flow past. The next car would be a somewhat more modern one. The final car would be a Pullman with a picture of contemporary Chicago flying past the window at accelerated speed.

Kaempffert envisioned a number of halls, but one that would be unique to the museum in Chicago would represent the most modern inventions. He names two striking examples: a Channel tunnel between England and France, and television, the concept of which he understood in 1929 immediately after Vladimir Zworikin had demonstrated the first TV set. A decade would elapse before the development of the first network broadcast. Above all, he viewed the museum as an educational tool, a place where people who knew little about science could learn the rudiments of the world around them. In the past, he said, even people who were not artisans could know something of what artisans did. But science, increasingly conducted in large laboratories, has become mysterious. People had no idea what went on in those new corporate workspaces. The museum would attempt to break down such barriers.[57]

As soon as the founding of the museum was announced, people began sending JR ideas for what to put in it. One man suggested a planetarium like that in the Deutsches Museum, which was under serious consideration for some time until Max Adler, JR's brother-in-law, built the Adler Planetarium in Chicago. JR and the trustees began to look for things that they could collect. Kaempffert took a very active role in this process.

Instead of going after existing exhibits, the Museum solicited exhibits from well-known scientists and inventors. The most interesting instance of this involved Orville Wright. The Wright brothers' celebrated airplane could have gone to the Smithsonian. But because that institution was in the hands of Samuel Pierpoint Langley, who claimed to have flown the first plane, Wright had sworn that the Smithsonian would never have the plane he had flown at Kitty Hawk, and he had given the plane to the South Kensington Museum in London. It was the aim of Wormser, Rosenwald, and Kaempffert to acquire it for the Museum of Science and Industry. An editorial in the *Chicago Tribune* suggested that the new museum should attempt to obtain Wright's plane.[58] Three days later, JR wrote Wormser: "We will have to get busy."[59] But nothing was done on that score for months. Rosenwald might have met Wright at a dinner at which they were both honored at the end of November, and Wormser even went to visit the famous aviator. Unfortunately, nothing came of all these maneuvers. The airplane remained in London until after Wright's death.

In addition to providing a sense of vision and building up a collection of exhibits, Kaempffert also hired a staff of five curators, all of whom were able and scholarly men. They worked effectively whenever Kaempffert was away, and they helped greatly in the task of amassing and organizing the museum's collections.

The trouble with Kaempffert was that his ideas were too grandiose and too expensive. To see his plans materialize, Kaempffert was willing to spend a considerable amount of money, and he did not seem to realize that there was an urgent need for economy because of the Depression. He planned to increase the curatorial staff to over sixty. The trustees, to whom he submitted his goals, were dismayed, and they formed a series of committees designed to rein in the director who had once had a free hand. As the end of 1930 approached, Kaempffert had to make a critical decision: whether to stay or go.

The Russian Colonies

JR had been enthusiastic since 1926 about the idea of settling Russian Jews on agricultural land in the Ukraine and the Crimea. He had already pledged $2 million toward this effort. On January 16, 1928, he came to a momentous decision. James N. Rosenberg, the young lawyer who had just made up his mind to head the effort, described the scene. A luncheon had been called at the offices of Felix Warburg. JR informed Rosenberg that he wished to meet with him privately beforehand. The two men chatted amiably about mundane things. Then, as Rosenberg later recalled:

> I said to myself, listening to the words that came from his lips: "Have my ears suddenly deceived me? Can I no longer hear? Is it true that he just said as if he were mentioning a matter of the slightest consequence, that he is increasing his subscription from $2 million to $5 million for this agricultural work?" It was in that kind of completely casual way that he dropped the remark. "I somehow think," said he, "that we ought to make this undertaking a little larger. We have been talking about a $5 million undertaking. I think I would like to make my own subscription $5 million instead of $2 million if everyone else will raise his subscription. Do you think our other friends would object to my making a little enlargement of

> the program and suggesting that they also increase their share?" . . . Someone might object. That was about the apologetic manner in which he made the proposal.[60]

At the luncheon that followed, JR repeated his offer, but he made the conditions more explicit. This, too, was to be a challenge grant and would be fulfilled only if an additional $5 million were raised from other sources.

Oddly enough, Rosenberg, Felix Warburg, and other leaders of Agro-Joint (as the movement to aid Russian colonists in the Crimea and Ukraine was known at that time) did not announce this astonishing news immediately. Instead, they waited two months, trying to find the perfect public relations opportunity.

Part of this effort was to obtain an endorsement of JR's pledge from Herbert Hoover, who had already endorsed the Russian colony idea at a private party for potential donors in November 1927. It was believed that an endorsement of JR's action by the influential politician would stimulate others to contribute. The letter the presidential candidate did write states that Lewis Strauss, Hoover's chief aide, had informed him of JR's $5 million pledge. He continued:

> That is indeed a princely benefaction, and I believe I know something of the great heart and the willing hand with which it is given. The dedication of that wealth to make it possible for a people who have been starving as petty tradesmen to return to their ancient calling and become producers of the necessities of life from the soil is a great experiment of human engineering, and you and I, who have watched together the fruition of so many enterprises born of a realization that the welfare of other human beings is the concern of all of us, can entertain no misgivings for its ultimate success.[61]

JR, who may not have realized that this letter was originally intended for public relations purposes, was delighted, and replied: "[Your letter] is especially prized coming from one who stands head and shoulders above any other human being in the preservation of human life. It is a high honor indeed to have my name coupled with yours as you have been kind enough to do."[62] Even with the Hoover letter in hand, the right moment to publicize the $5 million pledge did not seem to present itself, so in mid-March, fearful that the news would leak, Rosenberg informed the press of JR's offer. There were articles and editorials in papers across the country, and almost all were highly favorable. However, there was at least one discordant note from the pro-Zionist press, which disliked the Russian colonization movement because it was designed to keep Russian Jews on the land in Russia rather than encourage them to emigrate to Palestine. The *Chicago Chronicle,* a Jewish newspaper, wrote with amazing prescience: "[O]f what use is there to settle thousands of Jews upon fertile land, to make that land into a garden, when the first result will be the envy of the neighboring muzhik [non-Jewish peasant] and the second result his active hostility?" The editorial went on: "No man has the right to juggle the destiny of a people without first comprehending his entire responsibility." The editorial concluded by urging JR to reconsider his large pledge.[63] Felix Warburg, complaining about this piece, snapped: "I have stopped worrying about these idiotic little people that bark against the moon."[64]

JR said nothing about the editorial in the *Chicago Chronicle,* but the issue of Zionism continued to haunt him. An interview with Dr. S. N. Melamed that appeared in *The Day* in July 1928 had the author calling his interviewee a blatant anti-Zionist, despite JR's statement that he was merely a "non-Zionist."[65] In the Melamed interview and in private letters, Rosenwald repeated his opposition to Jewish colonization of Palestine. He had been there, and had seen for himself that the land could not support large numbers of Jewish immigrants. If they did come, they would find it very difficult to make a living and would essentially depend on charity. In Russia, on the other hand, the colonists were being settled on fertile land, they would not have to learn a new language or new customs, and in a remarkably short time they would become self-sufficient. Since the alternative of Russia existed, the emigration of Jews to Palestine seemed ridiculous. Nevertheless, JR did support certain causes in the future Israel and certain Zionists. When a fund was started for Gussie's friend Henrietta Szold, the founder of Hadassah, the women's Zionist organization, JR contributed to it generously. In 1930, this known "non-Zionist" even attended a Zionist rally in New York. The press mistakenly reported that JR had changed his mind about Zionism, but as he stated to a skeptical Judge Mack, who had heard this news in London:

> My attending so important an event as the Zionist protest meeting ought not to cause you the slightest surprise. You know I have always been interested in everything that pertains to the movement and to Palestine, even though I could not agree with the theories on which Zionism is

> based, nor the sentimental phases of the Palestinian movement, which probably marks me as lacking in idealism or far too practical. Furthermore, I have always felt that the experiment is fraught with the greatest danger, and I think I have frequently expressed to you my belief that the more successful the experiment is from the Jewish standpoint, the more dangerous it is.[66]

Fund-raising for the Russian colonies project remained difficult, largely because the Joint Distribution Committee (JDC) leaders had decided to target a relatively few wealthy donors rather than launch a broad appeal from the wider public, which would antagonize Zionist opposition to their plans. Thus, even after the announcement of JR's $5 million pledge, Rosenberg would occasionally report to JR that he was becoming greatly discouraged. In September 1928, Rosenberg, desperate over the slow pace of fund-raising, wrote Hoover and reminded the presidential candidate about JR's challenge grant. Saying that only $2 million of the $5 million challenge had been raised, he asked Hoover's advice. The candidate replied that, if it was amenable to JR, his letter commending JR could be released to the press. This was done.[67] Perhaps in response to the press coverage of Hoover's letter, some wealthy Jews did start coming forward, and the whole program was given a huge boost when, in October 1928, John D. Rockefeller Jr. announced that he was contributing $500,000 in one lump sum in honor of JR and Felix Warburg.

Beneath the prevailing optimism, however, there were occasional nuances of doubt about the future of the agricultural colonies. A new entity was created, the American Society for Jewish Farm Settlements in Russia. This was to be used for the Rosenwald challenge grant and to facilitate payment of bonds that the Russian government was issuing to American donors as surety for its involvement in the colonization project. The problem was that, according to Embree, JR refused to sign the agreement detailing his $5 million pledge without a provision that, should the work be discontinued for some reason, he would no longer have to keep making payments to this project, nor would his heirs. Needless to say, this caused considerable consternation at JDC headquarters. The issue apparently turned on distrust of the Soviet government. Eventually, a clause was inserted into the contract to the effect that if the Soviet government "materially failed in the performance of its obligations," JR would no longer have to abide by his pledge. With this clause in place, JR signed the pledge agreement in May 1929. It called for semiannual payments by JR of $312,500 until November 1, 1935, because Rosen had insisted that the whole campaign be telescoped into eight years instead of ten, and JR had agreed to this. Moreover, as of July 1929, the Soviet government was providing interest on the bonds it had issued.

In the autumn of 1929, just before the stock market plummeted, a new side to the Russian program was proposed, and JR was so intrigued that he almost seemed to lose interest in the agricultural settlements and devote himself to this new effort. At a dinner at the home of JDC treasurer Paul Baerwald, JR heard Rosen speak on this new plan. What, asked Rosen, is to be done with the Russian Jews who either cannot or do not want to become farmers? They cannot starve. Most had been petty tradesmen under the Old Regime. But there was only a very limited need for shoemakers and shopkeepers. Jobs were available in the manufacturing sector. Jews would have to learn new trades. He proposed training urban Jews for factory employment and setting up textile mills and workshops and "establishments for the manufacture of raw materials." There was a desperate need for this, and the Soviet government seemed willing to back such a project. Rosen called for an initial program of $3 million over three years. With uncharacteristic exuberance, JR immediately announced that he would participate at the same level as before; he would give five-eighths of the total.[68]

By the end of 1929, JR was involved in funding two Russian projects led by Rosen, one agricultural and the other industrial.

Rosen must not have been an easy person to deal with. He spent money with some abandon, although there is never any suggestion that he was not scrupulously honest. However, the agricultural program was chronically short of funds, and JR was constantly being asked to send in his money. In the spring of 1930, Rosen insisted that the last really good portion of agricultural land in the Crimea was available for Jewish settlements, but he needed the money immediately for tractors and to give initial help to Jews who were arriving in large numbers. He suggested that donors give an advance on their 1934–35 pledge payments. JR consented to this, and half of his payment, $312,500, was sent in several installments in April after receiving repeated but polite letters dunning him for the amount. By the end of 1930, more money was required, and JR proposed that the interest on the Russian government bonds, which was still being paid to him, should be plowed back into the enterprise.

The JDC leaders were only too happy to accept this suggestion and use it as an example that others could follow. By the end of 1930, JR had paid out $1,845,800 of his $5 million pledge.[69]

The industrial project encountered rocky going and showed another side of Rosen's personality: that he was willing to seize an opportunity and go off on his own without prior approval from his board in New York. First, the stock market crash made it immediately apparent that there was no way Dr. Rosen could have $1 million for this enterprise in 1930. He would have to be content with half that amount. Then in February 1930 the JDC leaders were informed that negotiations with the Russian government were going badly. The whole project would have to be put on hold. Then the entire situation changed. In the summer of 1930, Rosen cabled from Moscow that negotiations were going so well that he wanted everyone's entire three-year pledge immediately. He also said that the Russian government wanted to forego payment on bonds issued for this project for the present. This announcement did not meet with approval in the JDC offices in New York, nor was JR enthusiastic, although he continued to express his great interest in the project and continued assuring his friends at the JDC that he would go along with whatever they wanted. Some money was needed up front, however, to purchase machinery that would launch the project. By the end of 1930, it was agreed that Rosen would be sent $250,000 for the industrial project, and an additional $50,000 would be used by the JDC office as overhead. JR agreed to this. Just before the end of December 1930, he sent treasurer Paul Baerwald stock that was later sold for $285,247 for the industrial project.

Despite his flaws, Rosen was a truly charismatic personality who was able, up to a point, to charm his American backers and persuade an increasingly antisemitic Soviet government of the wisdom of his plans. JR was completely won over by this man, much as he had been by Aaron Aaronsohn in the 1910s.

The University of Chicago

JR continued his very active involvement with the University of Chicago on several fronts. The "Suspense Account" that he had established as part of the 1926 capital campaign continued to grow as he added to it, even as the university was spending it down. However, grateful as the university staff doubtless was for JR's many contributions, they also must have thought him rather a nuisance, for he applied his doctrine not only to his own fund but to others as well. When the son of noted trial lawyer John P. Wilson donated an endowment to the Law School in his father's name, JR sought to persuade John P. Wilson Jr. to change the terms of the endowment so that some of the principal would be spent each year.[70] And when he gave $50,000 to an endowment fund in honor of his late friend Samuel Deutsch, JR insisted that the fund be similar to his Suspense Account. This meant obtaining the approval of all the other donors to the endowment fund.

JR was involved in one more large building project for the University of Chicago—the erection of men's dormitories on the southern part of the campus, a complex known today as Burton-Judson Courts. The first approach on this matter was made by Harold Swift in August 1927. Describing the project in grandiloquent terms, he urged JR to consider this for the greater glory of Chicago as well as the university. But in the midst of the flowery verbiage, he provided the hook that was ultimately to persuade JR to go along with the dormitory construction: "A gift of dormitories is a continually living gift to the University because of the revenue it brings in, which can be used for any purpose most needed." There was no immediate reply, but Swift was persistent, for he met with Edwin Embree in January 1928, and at Embree's request he sent a detailed description of the number of dormitory rooms available for University of Chicago students.[71] This document led to a meeting with JR that included Swift, university president Max Mason, and others. They presented JR with an elaborate plan for the construction of dormitories, but the philanthropist protested that it was too much for him to consider. Swift then asked if he could present a more modest proposal, and JR agreed. In a letter recapitulating that meeting, Swift made his case for the dormitories: "We house only 700 students, less than 10% of our whole student body. I know of no University or College with so bad a record."[72] Following a meeting in July 1928 with Swift and JR, acting president Frederic Woodward reported to Embree: "Ever since our conversation on the subject I have been trying to acquire information as to the return which may be expected from an investment in dormitories." Unfortunately, the report was not all that promising. After examining the situation at various Ivy League schools, it appeared that such a return was 2.5 percent or less.[73] After thinking the matter over several more months, JR wrote his fellow trustees that he would agree to pay 40 percent of the cost of building the dormitories if the trustees would agree to pay the remaining 60 percent out of university reserves. It was assumed that both men's and women's dorms would be constructed. JR specified that he would not go over $2 million and that the buildings had to be finished by January 1, 1931. His motive for agreeing to this proposition was simple. "It is my hope that the return on the amount invested by the University will exceed the average income now being received from the endowment fund."[74] Needless to say, university officials were delighted. The secretary of the board wrote JR in thanks: "During the seventeen years in which I served as Cashier of the University, I was faced continually with the difficulty of trying to provide suitable rooms for students desiring to enter the University. In the light of that experience, I can well testify that the University has lost countless numbers of students of the most desirable type because of our inability to assure the parents of proper housing for their sons or daughters."[75]

Because of the onset of the Depression, this project proceeded more slowly than planned. JR was asked to push his deadline back, and he readily consented. By the end of 1930, the contract for building the men's dorm had been let, and it was assumed that the building would be ready for occupancy in time for the 1931–32 academic year. The women's dorm, for which there was a greater need (since some male students were housed in fraternities, and there were no sororities) was to be built later. JR's share of the cost of the men's dorm was estimated to be $685,000.

The range of initiatives with which JR was involved at the University of Chicago is truly impressive. At the end of July 1929, one of Embree's assistants prepared for JR a memo consisting of all his outstanding pledges to the university. The list was large and varied:

Dormitories	Up to $2 million
Nurses' Homes	$500,000
Eckhart Hall	$250,000
Chicago Lying-In Hospital	$250,000
School of Social Service Administration	$10,000 for general operating expenses
School of Social Service Administration	$5,000 to publish 2 textbooks
Medical Library	Up to $5,000 a year for 3 years
Scholarships for public school students	$1,000
Nursery School	$500[76]

And this does not take into account the Suspense Account, which, as of November 20, 1929, had in it $2,670,273.[77] JR used the Suspense Account to pay off his pledges. He also urged the university to invest some of the money in stocks somewhat more risky than usual, guaranteeing that if the price of the stock dropped, he would make up the difference, as he had done with the museum, a move which cost him a large sum of money after the stock market crash of 1929. Although Embree wrote to interim president Woodward that JR "would prefer from time to time to continue to consider regular gifts, rather than to give assistance to special activities," in fact, JR gave to those parts of the university that interested him or for which an advocate made a compelling case.[78]

The most extraordinary interrelationship between JR and the University of Chicago was the massive gift that never materialized. It was an attempt by JR, unwittingly, to meddle in academic policy, and it demonstrates once again that this brilliant businessman could be incredibly naive when it came to subjects outside his area of expertise.

In 1928, the university's fourth president, Max Mason, had resigned under a cloud of scandal, and after a lengthy search Robert Maynard Hutchins was named as the new president. Hutchins was the youngest holder of such an office in any major research university in the country at that time. JR welcomed Hutchins with a warm note on his arrival.[79] Soon Mr. and Mrs. Hutchins were invited to the Rosenwald country estate in Highland Park, Illinois. In the course of the conversation, JR seems to have floated the idea of giving the university an unrestricted grant of $5 million. Both interest and principal were to be expended in fifteen years. JR's one reservation was that he would henceforth be considered "a $5 million man." Hutchins must have left Ravinia with dollar signs dancing before his eyes. He sat down and wrote JR a masterful letter about what a gift of $5 million would mean to the university. Evidently, Hutchins was contemplating another $15 million capital campaign, and JR's was to be the lead gift. But Hutchins's letter went much further. It would be unfortunate, he said, if JR were embarrassed by the size of the gift, but it would certainly be embarrassment in a good cause. He continued:

> The following purposes would be attained by this gift:
> (1) The public and the Rockefeller group would be educated to the necessity of giving the University money *for general purposes;*
> (2) The public and the Rockefeller group would be educated to the necessity of gifts to working capital instead of perpetual endowment;

(3) An impression could be made on the City of Chicago which could not be equaled in any other way;
(4) The University would be able to begin the establishment of a respectable standard of living, to meet competition for the best men, and to attempt to regain the relative financial position it occupied at the close of President Harper's administration.

"My sole interest," Hutchins added, "is in bringing the best men in the world to the University of Chicago [to serve on the faculty] and keeping them here." If the university did not obtain this money, he warned, it would sink into mediocrity. It was this last point which seems to have really elicited JR's attention.[80]

JR was impressed. "If this is a fair example of your ability to make out a good case, all I can say is that the University is in good hands. I do not know that I ever saw a clearer or a more concise statement than this letter contains."[81] But he refused to commit himself. Hutchins then applied some gentle pressure. Several proposals regarding the university were up for consideration before the General Education Board at its November meeting. If JR would commit himself, the university would ask for a $5 million matching grant for general operating support.[82] JR refused to be rushed. But he did agree to have lunch with Hutchins. The two men met on October 10, 1929. According to Hutchins's account of the meeting,

> [JR] said he would put up money to eliminate from the staff men of any age or rank who we felt were not first-class and would also furnish money to bring in men who were. He repeated this several times. He said that he thought that the Rockefeller boards would come in on this basis. He said that the impression upon the City of Chicago which would be made by my scheme amounted to very little because five million dollars was very little. He said the Rockefeller boards would not be impressed by that sum of money. His recommendation was that I should take into my confidence some of the leading men on the staff and get their advice as to the people who should be appointed. I told him I would see whether such a plan was feasible. He wanted me not to do so unless my judgment accorded with his own.[83]

JR was not trying to decide which faculty members were second-rate and should be replaced or what criteria should be used to judge them. That was to be left up to the university. But the fact that Hutchins was willing to even consider such a proceeding is extraordinary. No wonder the memo describing this conversation was labeled "excessively confidential." If word of it had ever leaked out, Hutchins might have faced serious problems from his own faculty. In fact, it is uncertain how seriously Hutchins took this initiative. He did report back to JR on October 30 that he had consulted six trusted men and received reports on various departments. "I have also asked these gentlemen to suggest the names of people who should be brought here to replace second-rate men and have asked them to indicate the probable cost of the replacements." He concluded that, in accordance with JR's suggestion, they were proceeding carefully but were nevertheless planning to tell the General Education Board that major changes, including some economies, would be effectuated by the university, and that they hoped the GEB would match JR's gift.[84]

The fact that JR was interested in such a scheme shows his naiveté in matters dealing with academic politics, but this is not surprising. Doubtless, he was applying the principles of business to academia. If you have second-rate people, get rid of them. Moreover, he evidently believed that tenure was a mistake. In July 1930, he wrote the same thing to Abraham Flexner, saying that the best academics were bought off by research institutes, leaving only the mediocre with lifetime appointments. He concluded his letter to Flexner: "This policy, it seems to me, ought to be hit hard, and where inferior men are in these positions, they should be bought off and the practice of life tenure discontinued."[85] Had Hutchins's plan been carried out, the consequences in terms of academic freedom might have been severe. In any event, nothing came of this initiative. Most likely the Depression intervened. Almost a year later, Hutchins reported after a meeting with Embree that JR would not give $5 million now but might give $1 million for five years if the Rockefeller boards acted in some unspecified way, presumably by making a large grant to the university.[86] That did not happen because of JR's illness and subsequent death.

Michigan Boulevard Garden Apartments

During this period, JR made an important contribution in a new area with which he had dealt briefly before, but he now involved himself in a major way: housing. In a sense, this was part of his ongoing quest to make life easier for the "average man," the person from the middle class or lower middle class who could not borrow money easily, could not find a decent place to live, and could not afford adequate health care. The foundation was now dealing with the last part of this triad. JR's interest in the first part goes back to 1913.

It was that year that he met Arthur J. Morris, an economist who was establishing a series of new banks, patterned after similar institutions that had started in Germany and spread to other European countries during the second half of the nineteenth century. These banks were willing to loan small amounts to persons of modest means at very low rates of interest. They were useful for farmers and small tradesmen. The banks required no collateral but only the signature of a fellow worker or a relative who could vouch for the potential borrower's good standing. It was discovered, just as it has been rediscovered in recent years in experiences with micro-lending, that the rate of default on these small loans was almost zero.

Morris set up a test bank in Norfolk, Virginia, in 1912. It did well. He soon established a series of others, generally in medium-sized cities around the country, and was engaged in opening one in New York. It was at this period that Morris met Julius Rosenwald, who was very interested in the plan but, in typical fashion, did not want to commit himself immediately. Thus he asked a friend, Grainger Farwell, who had formerly been involved in the banking business in Chicago, to investigate Morris Plan Banks. Farwell did a thorough job, traveling frequently to cities where banks were being established. JR accompanied him on occasion. Convinced by Farwell's study and his own observation that this was a good idea, JR agreed to help establish a Chicago Morris Plan Bank.[87] He also was willing to become a board member of the New York bank, although he resigned after six months. In January 1914, JR announced to a correspondent for the *New York Times* that he would back a Morris Plan Bank in Chicago and hoped that it would be the first in a chain of Chicago banks. He declared that this was his attempt to combat loan sharks in America and added that this was not a philanthropic enterprise but a strictly business proposition. The bank was capitalized at $1 million, and JR put in one-tenth of that sum, assuring Morris and others that he would add more if necessary. The bank opened in April 1917, and though it did not spawn offshoots, as JR had hoped, it did do very well. In the first five months of its operation, the bank made loans to 3,927 individuals involving $571,580. Loans ranged from $10 to $3,000.[88] By 1928, the bank was loaning about $10.5 million to 45,000 Chicagoans, and there were 108 Morris Plan

Banks across the country, although JR was only involved in the one in Chicago.[89] Unfortunately, the Depression wiped them out.

By 1926, JR was steering the Chicago Morris Plan Bank in the direction of housing. Secretary of Commerce Herbert Hoover called JR's attention to the issue of second mortgages. Many people near the bottom rungs of the economic ladder were desperate. If they owned their own homes through a mortgage and needed immediate cash, there was virtually no way they could obtain a second mortgage. Because of the class of people seeking them, such second mortgages were considered extremely risky. Banks would only agree to issue them at extremely high rates of interest, because of the risk associated with the borrower and because if the borrower defaulted, the holder of the first mortgage would have to be paid in full before the holder of the second mortgage could obtain anything. Knowing that the customers of Morris Plan Banks included some of the same individuals who were seeking second mortgages, Hoover proposed that JR, through the Morris Plan Bank, create a fund to issue such mortgages. After talking to the commerce secretary, JR, as an experiment, placed $1 million with the Chicago Morris Plan Bank to determine "whether reasonable rates could be charged with a business return on the investment." Starting in 1926, 1,440 loans were made for a total of $2.6 million. In 1928, Embree pronounced the experiment a success, although he acknowledged that the bank was being very conservative about the type of customers to whom it granted second mortgages. Interest rates were the prevailing rate of 6 percent, but the commission rates were lower, and they continued to go down slightly. By the fall of 1928, JR was earning a net return of about 8 percent. Embree noted that the Rosenwald Trust established at the Morris Plan Bank had managed to reduce second mortgage loans throughout the city. "Other mortgage concerns now quote the same rate as the Rosenwald Trust."[90] This apparently successful experiment may well have been a revolutionary change in banking practices.

Rosenwald had become involved in a housing venture for the lower middle class several years earlier, although he was not as enthusiastic about it as he was about the Morris Plan Bank. The Chicago Housing Association was formed by JR's friend, Benjamin Rosenthal, in 1919.

The end of the war and the race riots of 1919 had demonstrated that there was a great lack of affordable housing in Chicago for both blacks and whites. Rosenthal, a real estate developer, decided to do something about this housing crisis. He was convinced that low-cost housing could be built and sold at moderate prices and that reasonable mortgage rates could be offered to working families. Part of his plan was to sell to people of various nationalities, especially lower middle-class immigrants, thus helping to tear down some of the ethnic ghettos into which Chicago was being divided. Rosenthal anticipated forming a corporation capitalized at $1 million and building 250 homes, which would be sold for around $3,500 each. He wanted Rosenwald to be one of the major investors in this undertaking.

JR had his misgivings, but he liked Rosenthal and wanted to help him. He told him he did not think this was sound as a business proposition but that if Rosenthal himself managed the project he would become an investor.[91] Ultimately, JR, Rosenthal, J. Ogden Armour, and Swift & Co. each put $100,000 into the Chicago Housing Association. William Wrigley Jr. and several others invested $50,000 apiece.

Rosenthal purchased a forty-acre site between 87th and 89th Streets and State and Wabash on Chicago's South Side. He envisioned selling some of the lots to businesses. Most of the houses that Rosenthal constructed were detached, made of brick or stucco, two stories high, with full basements. Each house contained five rooms. There was ample space for residents to plant gardens. He built 175 homes at an average cost of $6,000 and sold them for a minimum of $4,200 with mortgages at very reasonable interest rates. Yet JR felt that the Chicago Housing Association was mixing business and philanthropy, which he opposed. He explained in a letter to E. J. Buffington, president of the Illinois Steel Company, who had expressed interest in investing in the possible expansion of the project: "About two months ago I went out to see the 175 houses which are now being built and the lay-out seems very good. However, so much of the material was purchased at special prices, based on the philanthropic appeal, and the business lots which were sold were largely disposed of (if I am not mistaken) on the same basis, so that even if this attempt should work out well, it would not necessarily indicate that the next one would also."[92]

There were other problems with the Chicago Housing Association. The site was too far from public transportation and from the jobs of those Rosenthal was hoping to attract. Moreover, some of the new purchasers defaulted on their payments, so the houses had to be repossessed and rented out.[93] Half the original settlers had moved away by 1930, some to more upscale communities.[94] No further units were ever built. JR received only a small return from this investment. However, this experience did not totally sour him on the idea of subsidized housing for working people.

In December 1916, what must have seemed an astonishing story appeared in the *Chicago News.* Headlined "Apartments De Luxe for Negroes Plan; Innovation in Chicago Is Projected with Backing of Julius Rosenwald," the story explained that a site for an all-black apartment building had already been purchased at 32nd and Vernon Avenue. The sixty-apartment structure with gardens, a courtyard, and a fountain would be finished by May 1, 1917. Rents would be modest, but the investment was expected to earn approximately $18,000 per year. The article went on to explain that this was not a new idea. Dr. George C. Hall and A. L. Jackson, president and secretary of the Wabash YMCA, had gone to Cincinnati to examine the prototype, a very simple apartment building where rents were as low as $1 a month. The projected building in Chicago would be grander and rents would be slightly higher, but it was hoped that this would be the beginning of a new trend in Chicago housing for African Americans.[95]

This structure was not constructed at that time. JR envisioned making it a for-profit venture, but he realized that to make a 5 percent rate of return, he would have to charge rents far higher than any middle-class blacks could afford.[96] But JR did not forget this idea.

Several factors may have come together to influence JR in resuscitating his plan. In 1926, when he was in Vienna looking at the science museum, among other things, he visited a housing project there. Shops and other businesses were incorporated as part of the apartment building, which was built around a spacious courtyard. In 1927, JR's son-in-law, Alfred K. Stern, whose main job was working for the Julius Rosenwald Fund, became secretary of the Chicago Housing Commission, a purely advisory body created by the mayor and the city council in the summer of 1926. The commission, composed of realtors, businessmen, and social workers, only lasted one year, but it accomplished an important task: it changed Illinois law to allow builders of housing projects to construct their dwellings on improved land instead of only on vacant land.[97] Stern, well aware of the crisis in black housing, tried to nudge his father-in-law toward constructing an apartment building for blacks. But JR was keenly sensitive to this issue. As he told an interviewer, each day when Harry Kersey drove him to the Sears plant on Homan Avenue, he "was obliged to pass miles of ancient buildings, many of them erected shortly after the great fire [of 1871]. These were the homes of tens of thousands of his fellow citizens. They were not pleasant or wholesome places in which to live or bring up a family."[98] By July 1928, JR announced that he was engaged in planning the Michigan Boulevard Garden Apartments.

JR's nephew, Ernest A. Grunsfeld Jr., was hired as architect. He designed a group of five-story buildings encompassing almost an entire city block. Stores were on the ground floor of one side of the complex. There were to be 421 apartments varying in size from three to five rooms. In the center was a courtyard with a fountain and well-kept lawns and gardens. It was designed to resemble one of the quadrangles of the nearby University of Chicago. The structures were to be made of dark brick with terra cotta doorways into the courtyard.[99] The two drawbacks in the design were that the ceilings were only eight feet high and there were no elevators; all the apartments were walkups.[100] The site chosen for this development was in the heart of a thriving area of black Chicago known as Bronzeville. The Michigan Boulevard Garden Apartments encompassed the area between 47th and 46th Streets and between Michigan and Wabash Avenues. Nearby were jazz clubs, hotels, and other black-owned businesses. The Wabash YMCA and Provident Hospital were in the neighborhood, as was a branch of the public library that JR had had built in honor of his and Booker T. Washington's friend Dr. George C. Hall. There was good transportation with an elevated train stop two blocks away. The mistakes of the Chicago Housing Association were not going to be repeated.

Construction began in October 1928. Alfred K. Stern was put in charge of the project. JR was involved, and when he was in town, he attended meetings that dealt with such issues as the amount to be charged for rent. When JR was away, Stern kept him thoroughly informed.

There were several problems. One that has a contemporary ring was that, once construction began, there were protests that black construction workers had not been employed. Stern looked into this rumor and reported to JR: "We found that a large number of Negro laborers had been hired from the beginning, as well as eight out of sixty carpenters."[101] Then there were problems persuading businesses to rent the stores. The Kresge Company, for instance, indicated they were not interested; the obvious, though unstated reason, was that they would not locate in a black area.

When the building was completed, it contained a Sears store, a Walgreen's, an A&P, a bank, and a number of black-owned businesses, including a candy store and a millinery shop.

Rents were set at moderate levels depending on the size of apartment. A three-room apartment was $42.13 a month, with four- and five-room apartments renting for $50.73 and $58.09, respectively. Applicants were carefully screened by the newly hired management staff headed by Robert Taylor, son of a Tuskegee vice president, who later would become the chairman of the Chicago Housing Authority. Nevertheless, there was some difficulty in renting all the apartments. The fact that the last apartments were not completed until October 1929, only a few weeks before the onset of the Depression, may have been a cause.

Stern met with representatives from a similar housing project for whites that was being erected on the North Side and was sponsored by Marshall Field. George Richardson, who was in charge of the Field project, gave Stern advice, such as the importance of having a nicely furnished model apartment available for viewing. Stern and George Arthur obtained other ideas from similar apartment complexes for blacks that had been built in New York.

The Michigan Boulevard Garden Apartments were built at a total cost of $2.7 million. JR was the only investor; he made it very clear that the construction of these buildings was not an act of philanthropy but a business venture. As Embree noted: "It is intended to demonstrate that good, modern, healthful living quarters can be provided at rents within the means of the group for which they are intended, and also provide a return of 6% or more on the funds invested. Even if a business return cannot be earned, this project will at least demonstrate how far private capital can go in improving housing conditions."[102] Moreover, JR believed that economies of scale and economic construction and maintenance costs would help the investment.[103] There was another unstated reason behind the construction of these buildings: to show to a skeptical white world that middle-class blacks could live in comfortable and attractive surroundings and take excellent care of them. To this end, a small reduction in rent was accorded to those who kept their apartments in perfect condition.

Although the Michigan Boulevard Garden Apartments did yield a 5.59 percent rate of return on the original investment in 1930, the Depression ensured that the complex would not achieve the aim of its founder. By 1937, Stern was asserting: "Private industry cannot provide decent modern low-cost housing. Municipal, state, and federal governments must house those who cannot afford to pay the present scale of rents."[104] Rents were lowered after protests in the depth of the Depression, but even under these new conditions, many residents could not afford them and had to take in boarders to make ends meet.[105] This outcome also guaranteed that the Michigan Boulevard Garden Apartments would not be emulated.

For the people who lived there, the apartment complex, which residents called "The Rosenwald," was a godsend. The apartments were not spacious, but they were clean and nicely furnished. The residents were middle-class blacks. One of the first to move in was George Arthur. Other residents included post office workers, Pullman conductors, and some doctors and lawyers. The boxer Joe Louis and the poet Gwendolyn Brooks lived in the complex. There were numerous activities available, especially for children. Two nursery schools were on the premises, one of which was founded by JR's daughter, Marion. There were ballet classes, a Boy Scout troop, and star-gazing classes on summer evenings. One resident who lived there as a child said, "The grounds were so well tended that I grew up without knowing what a weed was."[106]

The relationship between the Julius Rosenwald Fund and the Michigan Boulevard Garden Apartments remained close, even though the money for the housing complex did not come from the Fund. Alfred K. Stern explained: "Although there is an independent board of directors for this project, the officers of the Rosenwald Fund give general supervision and direction to the management."[107]

Like the Rosenwald schools, the Michigan Boulevard Garden Apartments has been criticized by modern historians because it was segregated. Philpott stops just short of calling JR a racist. But as in the case of the schools, JR wanted results, and he knew full well the prejudices of his day. Philpott also provides ample evidence that the vast majority of white Chicagoans in 1929 would never have countenanced an integrated housing project.[108] If JR wanted decent housing for African Americans, he knew that it would have to be segregated. That does not mean that he liked segregation. On the contrary, he was working to bring about an accommodation between the races.

All three of these ventures of JR—the Morris Plan Banks, the Chicago Housing Association, and the Michigan Boulevard Garden Apartments—were innovative investments that were expected to yield a low rate of return and were designed to make a philanthropic point, even if they were not, strictly speaking, philanthropies. Today they would be called "program-related investments" (PRIs), and these are becoming increasingly common in the philanthropic world. In the 1920s, they were regarded as truly new and unusual.

Herbert Hoover

Julius Rosenwald was not fortunate when it came to politics. He had worked hard for the Merriam mayoral campaign in Chicago in 1911, only to see it fail. The presidential candidates he had backed in 1912 and 1916 had been defeated. Although he supported the presidential races of Harding and Coolidge, he did not campaign actively for them, and although he met Coolidge on occasion and visited the summer White House in 1926, he and Coolidge were not close friends. His campaign against Senator Frank Smith also had been a disappointment. But in Herbert Hoover JR found not only a presidential candidate he could support but a friend.

There was much in Hoover's ideas about American government and society that must have appealed to JR. The two men were cut from the same Progressive cloth. Both men believed in what Joan Huff Wilson calls "cooperative individualism," that individuals working together, starting at the grassroots level, could accomplish more and be more effective than a strong centralized government. Hoover also believed that business should work more closely with government and that businessmen should be enlightened through education to become advocates of social responsibility. In this sense, JR must have been almost a paradigm of Hoover's vision of an American capitalist.[109]

JR had worked with Hoover during World War I, and served with him in the Second Industrial Conference of 1919; the two men had become friends. In 1921, JR had donated $50,000 to Hoover's fund for the relief of European children and had made an eloquent speech on behalf of that cause. The two men continued to see each other occasionally and to correspond about a range of issues. At the Coolidge inaugural in 1925, JR and Gussie had stayed with the Hoovers.[110]

When Hoover was nominated in 1928, JR was delighted. After hearing the candidate's acceptance speech on the radio, a euphoric JR wired him: "Your acceptance address will take its place in history among the most statesmanlike documents. Every thinking person is ennobled by its ideals.

Because of it, every American is prouder of his citizenship today than he was yesterday."[111] Hoover graciously replied: "I am deeply grateful for your telegram. Your many years of friendship has been a fine part of this success."[112]

JR threw himself into the presidential race in a manner he had not done since 1912. He gave $50,000 to the campaign, making him one of the largest donors in the country. Unlike the campaign of 2004, it is likely that JR contributed such a sum not because of some expected return or because of access to the president but because he genuinely liked and believed in the candidate. He felt Hoover was the best man for the job.

In addition to donating money, JR wrote what we would today call an "op-ed" piece for the *Chicago Daily News.* In this article, JR began by stating that he favored Hoover because of the candidate's stand on Prohibition, a subject in which he fervently believed. But he used Hoover's uncompromising stance on this controversial issue to demonstrate that the Republican candidate was a man of principle, a thoughtful, deliberate man who gathered the facts before making a judgment. JR then examined Hoover's career and achievements. Stating that he knew Hoover in various capacities, he continued:

> From this personal acquaintance, and from my observation of his activities, I have come to know his deep sympathies for those in distress, and his ability to meet and solve great national problems. His record as an administrator in relief work during the dark days of the World War is a story of humanitarian achievement known the world over. . . . His contribution during the last seven years, as a member of President Coolidge's cabinet, to the stabilizing and upbuilding of industry, the welfare of the workers, and the solution of the many vexed problems of state that came under his jurisdiction exceeds estimate or due appreciation.[113]

Even Gussie, though seriously ill, contributed to the campaign, supposedly writing from her sick bed a short article entitled "Why I Am for Hoover," which also played on the Prohibition theme.[114]

JR used a medium new for him to promote his favored candidate: radio. He delivered a half-hour radio address promoting Hoover, using some very florid language. His main point was that the Republican candidate possessed the requisite leadership qualities. JR's peroration ably summed up his speech:

> I am for that leader because of his unblemished character, his great executive and administrative ability (tried in the crucible of many emergencies), because of his temperament and training, because of his profound understanding of the problems that demand solution, and finally because of his broad humanitarianism and deep concern for the well-being of his fellow citizens.[115]

Rosenwald was very pleased with this speech and wrote his German relatives: "I spoke Saturday for one half-hour in behalf of Mr. Hoover and received messages from many parts of the country—2,000 miles apart."[116]

Almost immediately upon Hoover's election, rumors started flying that Julius Rosenwald would be offered the cabinet post of secretary of commerce. An issue of *Time* magazine from November 1928 first mentioned the possibility, and the rumors continued into February 1929, when the *Washington Times* listed the likely choices for the cabinet, which included JR.[117] This was not entirely rumor. Walter Heineman, treasurer of the Republican National committee branch based in Chicago, did write the president-elect: "Mr. Rosenwald's fitness is unquestioned, and his appointment would be intensely gratifying to us in the Middle West."[118] But there were also dissenting voices. Jason Rogers of Kansas City wrote Hoover: "In the present confused situation regarding processes for marketing manufactured products, many business men whom I have met feel that it would not be desirable that a mere buyer and seller of goods who is now making matters difficult for independent retailers and reducing manufacturing to the sweat shop basis of goods made primarily for price, be placed in such an important post."[119]

Was JR ever seriously under consideration? The answer may never be known, although there is an unsigned and undated telegram in Hoover's papers with this remark: "Understand there is a revival of interest in Rosenwald and have heard that he would like some place with you."[120] However, JR wrote to one of the German relatives: "The newspaper talk about my having a cabinet position is all nonsense. There is not the slightest likelihood of such a thing being offered me, and I would not accept it if it were."[121] JR was never remotely interested in such a position. He was over sixty-six years old and not in good health. Under no circumstances would he have been interested in occupying such a demanding high pressure post. Moreover, his one stint of government service during World

War I had not been particularly happy. He was content to remain merely the president's friend.

Due to his friendship with Hoover, JR engaged in some discreet lobbying, suggesting friends for various government positions. He also sought to block an appointment, writing to one of Hoover's top transition aides that if "The Chief" was seriously considering the appointment of Silas Strawn, "not to commit himself until I can speak with him."[122] Strawn was a Republican National Committee functionary whom JR found objectionable.

It was to be expected that JR and Gussie would attend Hoover's inauguration. For part of the festivities, they were joined by their daughter, Adele. JR described the events surrounding the great day. They were assigned an aide, "a prominent citizen—a banker," and a special car, "a brand-new Cadillac with 'official' on the windshield which had the right of way everywhere." They attended parties with prominent dignitaries. On the morning of the inauguration, JR first went to the Lincoln Memorial, then was joined by Gussie at the last session of the Senate presided over by the lame duck vice president. Unfortunately, they did not get to see the swearing in or hear Hoover's inaugural address because it was raining hard.

> We drove to the White House for a buffet luncheon—quite elaborate—probably two hundred persons; then, an hour later, went to the president's reviewing stand. We met no end of interesting people—the old and new cabinet and the leading people in official life, and other important people in all walks of life. The Hoovers and family dined upstairs. It poured all day from noon on, and so the parade lost much of its attractiveness. I took Gussie home at four, pretty tired after five hours of exhilarating experiences. I returned, and Adele and I remained for the reception which took place after the parade. President and Mrs. Hoover greeted the guests who came back for a second feed after shaking hands. Later hundreds, or perhaps thousands, came and were received. They were still coming strong when we left. We were all in, and glad to remain at home and miss the Charity Ball.[123]

Following Hoover's inauguration, relations between the president and JR remained cordial. Hoover named the Chicago philanthropist to the Commission on Law Observance and Enforcement, one of those voluntary committees he saw as an important corollary of government. JR did not attend any meetings of this body. In July 1930, Hoover wrote JR as follows about the Commission: "[T]he backing which you have given me contributed materially to my ability to carry through on this end."[124] This clearly implies that JR gave some funds to the commission, but it is not clear how much.

He seems to have contributed other funds to the government. In July 1929, JR received a letter from one of Hoover's aides, who reminded the former Sears president that about a month earlier, when JR had stayed overnight at the White House, he had "honored me with a call to my little office. We were both congratulating the country upon having as president a man of such wide social vision and humane spirit, and if I recall your parting words correctly, they were, in effect, 'If I can ever help you to help the president in forwarding his plans for social programs, call on me—and I shall not mind if it costs me some money, either.'" The aide went on to suggest two possible funding opportunities, both conferences Hoover wished to hold: one on the home, the other on the health and protection of children. Each conference would cost about $1 million.[125] JR did not contribute to either conference. However, in November 1929, he did provide $100,000 through the Interior Department in support of the National Advisory Commission on Education.[126]

On June 6, 1929, while attending a meeting of the Mount Rushmore Commission, on which he served, JR spent the night as Hoover's guest at the White House. Unlike the first time he stayed in the presidential mansion, under Taft, there was no lyrical letter home describing the visit.

The one time JR tried to use his influence in a somewhat unusual direction occurred in December 1929. He wrote to Hoover at the suggestion of his son-in-law, Edgar Stern. The wording of the letter makes it seem likely that it was drafted by Embree. The writer argues that if black employment were increased, blacks would prove to be a good market for white retailers and everyone would benefit.

> The problem of opening this market more fully would involve the increase of standards of consumption and the development of higher earning power. The measures to be adopted are many, but three stand out conspicuously. First, educational programs should be accelerated, with particular reference to the elimination of illiteracy and the promotion of suitable vocational training. Second, health activities should be restudied to make sure that

> this group of people, whose conditions of life are in many ways different from those of whites, are receiving the aid in the elimination of disease that is desirable for their health and for the protection of the rest of the population. Third, the improvement of opportunities for employment should be made the serious concern of the government and such agencies as chambers of commerce and farm boards. No case can be made for employing an inefficient black man in preference to a more efficient white, but when employment can be given to the colored man on a sound basis, the national welfare and prosperity is promoted since, on the whole, the opportunities for employment for the Negro are much more restricted than for the white.

The letter concluded: "It seems to me that the Federal Government and business agencies could be helpful in urging this point of view from time to time when educational, health, and employment programs are under consideration." The president, who had integrated the Commerce Department when he was secretary and had favored his wife's inviting a black woman to the White House, replied with a polite note that said in part: "As usual you are most wise in your suggestions."[127] Nothing whatsoever came of this initiative, probably because of the onset of the Depression a month earlier.

JR, Sears, and the Depression

After naming Charles M. Kittle as president of Sears in 1924, JR had stepped back from the company. He attended board meetings in his capacity as chairman, but he left the day-to-day management of the company to Kittle, Wood, and the old guard of Otto Doering and Max Adler. Then, on January 2, 1928, Kittle suddenly died.

It was clear that the choice of a successor was up to JR. There were four contenders for the top post: Otto Doering and Max Adler, who were angered at having been passed over in 1924 but who had remained out of loyalty to JR; Lessing Rosenwald, who had been passed over in 1924 on the grounds that he was too young and inexperienced; and General Robert E. Wood. For a week there was fierce jockeying for position. Wood wrote his close friend Endicott: "The situation is unchanged here. Nothing has been decided. JR has on his best poker face. As a matter of fact I do not think he has made up his mind." He went on to describe how Adler had gone to JR to propose that Doering be named president and that an executive committee consisting of Adler, Doering, and Wood run the company for two years, after which JR could pick either Lessing or Wood as president. Wood said he could serve under such an arrangement, but it did not appeal to JR, who doubtless did not want to be faced with another choice in two years.[128]

Lessing was a different matter. JR's son felt that he had earned his stripes and was qualified for the top position. He had done a successful job running the Philadelphia plant. But he was Julius Rosenwald's son, and JR was the last person to agree to any kind of dynasty. According to Emmet and Jeuck, it was Gussie who stepped into the breach and averted a family crisis. Lessing had declared that if he were not chosen as president, he would resign. The young man went to see his mother, who was in the hospital recovering from an operation. Gussie told her son that, on the face of it, Lessing probably did deserve the presidency. But he had moved to Philadelphia precisely to get out from under his father's influence. If he obtained the top slot, it would simply assuage his pride. As long as JR was alive, people would say that he had obtained the job because he was the boss's son.[129]

For JR, the choice came down to two candidates: Doering and Wood. In a sense, however, there was not much choice. Doering was near retirement age and wealthy. He represented the old guard. Wood was young, dynamic, and ambitious, and his retail stores were proving to be a tremendous success. On January 11, 1928, JR announced his decision. General Robert E. Wood would be the next president of Sears. Doering and Adler promptly resigned. Lessing stayed on and was promoted to senior vice president, but he continued living in Philadelphia. Family harmony had been preserved, and Sears was apparently in good hands.

JR was ambivalent about the tremendous economic boom of the late 1920s. On the one hand he wrote someone who asked his opinion on "the outlook for a continuation of prosperity": "I have no hesitancy in expressing the opinion that the outlook for business between now and the new year is as bright as at any time during the past several seasons. This view is based almost entirely upon the experience of our own company. While we anticipate no boom, we are preparing for a normal healthy increase. This applies generally throughout the whole country."[130] On the other hand, as JR wrote to the German relatives: "It seems to me, although the business is good, the price [of Sears stock] is higher than is warranted by that condition. Many people no doubt are discounting the future value, and in that they are probably not mistaken."[131] The former Sears president was clearly nervous, and he persuaded Wood to rein in the number of retail stores he was planning to open. As a result, when the stock market crashed, Sears was in a much better position than its rival, Montgomery Ward, which had adopted the opening of retail stores with excessive enthusiasm.[132] JR's wariness rings true, for it squares with the fact that in the cases of Hull House, the University of Chicago, the Museum of Science and Industry, and other institutions, he urged their leaders to buy Sears stock but then guaranteed that if the market suddenly went down, he would make up the difference between the purchase price and the lower devalued price. Since many Americans at the time thought the market would never go down, this skepticism was healthy, if costly, to JR, who honored all these promises.

When economic disaster occurred on October 29, 1929, Lessing was in Los Angeles. Realizing the scope of the meltdown, he made an impulsive decision without consulting his father or General Wood. Some employees, he knew, who had borrowed on margin to buy stocks would be wiped out financially. Lessing "wired all stores to see that deserving employees who might possibly be in financial difficulty due to market conditions be taken care of."[133]

JR, informed of his son's decision, knew Lessing had done the right thing and immediately set to work. John Higgins, a Sears vice president, was charged with obtaining the necessary information from worried employees about their stock purchases. After going over their accounts with Higgins, many employees realized that their financial situation was not as dire as they had supposed. A slightly exaggerated newspaper account describes the scene:

> Negro laborers, frightened factory girls, important-looking executives with tense lips and nervous white-collared office men—they flowed yesterday into the office of John Higgins, vice president of Sears, Roebuck & Co. . . . Practically all of them had bought on margin when prices were high. Most of them had faced the prospect of losing their all—security against sickness or other emergency, nest eggs for future homes, the hope of future financial independence—until Mr. Rosenwald's offer. But all walked out of the vice president's office with the knowledge that their stocks had been saved. In each case, Mr. Higgins jotted down the name of the employee, of stock and of broker, and added them to the scores of other names of men and women saved from disaster.[134]

Once Higgins had the information, it was JR's task to phone the broker to guarantee the loan the employee had borrowed to purchase the stock. The story is taken up by Embree, who wrote this in the Fund's report for 1931–33:

> [JR] had been ill; nevertheless, he was at the office promptly at 8:30 on that memorable Blue Thursday of late October. As thunders and lightenings [*sic*] began to threaten the financial structure of America, he placed two telephones before him, squared himself at his desk, opened the three doors to his office and began to "do business." . . . He sold many securities and also bought thousands of shares. In the course of one attempt to get an order through to a broker, the report came back that the telephone exchange for the whole LaSalle Street [Chicago's financial district] section had suddenly gone out of order; he burst into a gale of laughter at the absurdity of such an accident on such a day. He made not less than a hundred separate decisions in this one day, many of them of momentous implication. . . . He saved hundreds of persons from immediate bankruptcy. He saw his own fortune in the collapse which culminated this day reduced by a hundred million dollars. He saw his business and his personal affairs plunging inevitably into the most troubled waters. It was one of the happiest days of his life.[135]

In a nation desperate for good news, word of what JR was doing was broken by the *Chicago Herald and Examiner.* Its headline read, "Rosenwald Aids Workers Caught in Stock Market; Sears Roebuck Head Arranges to Furnish Collateral for Brokers."[136] The story was picked up by the Associated Press and reported across the country. Soon scattered executives such as energy magnate Samuel Insull were following JR's example. The price of Sears stock rose $10 a share, and the market looked as if it might stabilize. Letters of support and appreciation poured in from all sides. Comedian Eddie Cantor telegraphed JR to say: "Understand you are protecting your employees on their margin accounts. Can you use a bright industrious boy in your office? I am ready to start at the bottom." JR replied: "Please come at once. Have a job awaiting you. Will meet you at station."[137] Other missives were more serious. Henrietta Szold wrote: "Such acts demonstrate that moral heights can be reached in our condemned commercial era as in the eras glorified by historians. When I read of it, I was proud of the right to call myself your friend."[138] JR was slightly embarrassed by what he considered adulation. He wrote to Homer Guck, editor of the *Chicago Herald and Examiner:*

> Your great scoop in regard to my action for employees will, judging by my mail, probably make me president of the United States. Such an avalanche of messages from all over the country and letters and telegrams galore! They are extremely embarrassing to me because the importance of the action was exaggerated far beyond its desserts. On a number of previous occasions I have followed the same course, but this seems to have been an aggravated condition, involving a great many more people. I never gave a thought to the idea of it becoming public. I do think this, however, that judging by what countless people have told me, the publicity did help to establish confidence. Whether this is true or not can never be proven.[139]

JR guaranteed $7 million in loans. A trusteeship was created by two Sears officers who borrowed the $7 million from the Chase National Bank on their note, which was guaranteed by JR, and these funds were used to pay off the brokers and other banks.[140] However, those assisted did not get off scot free. JR sent a memo that those who had been guaranteed were not to receive any stock or cash dividends against their accounts in the profit sharing plan.[141] Nevertheless, this noble gesture, initiated by Lessing, had saved three hundred Sears employees from financial ruin and had reassured countless others who had gone over their accounts with Higgins.

JR did one other public act in response to Wall Street's debacle. He tried to reassure the country in a newsreel. Early in 1929, at the request of Fox Movietone, he had made a newsreel about philanthropy. His performance was vintage JR. He said in part: "I have always believed that most large fortunes are made by men of mediocre ability who tumbled into a lucky opportunity and could not help but get rich, and in most cases others given the same chance would have done far better with it. Hard work and attention to business are necessary, but they rarely result in achieving a large fortune. Do not be fooled into believing that because a man is rich, he is necessarily smart. There is ample proof to the contrary."[142] JR received a great deal of mail in praise of this statement, and the Fox Movietone producers evidently thought they had a true winner on their hands. Thus, immediately after the disaster of October 29, JR was again approached by Fox Movietone. He agreed to do another newsreel, and it appeared in theaters on October 31, 1929. A tape of it survives. There is JR, looking frail and speaking in a thin high voice:

> I am a great believer in America. On Wall Street recently, large paper profits were wiped out. Millions of mine were, but that is no reason why I

> should lose confidence in the greatest country in the world. Without any special effort, our October business was the largest of any month in our history comprising thirty-five years. The country is sound at the core. Nothing risked, nothing gained. But always remember that where chance for gain is large, there is a proportionate chance for loss. A government bond is Uncle Sam's promise to pay and is absolutely safe, but the chance for a large profit is nil. If you want to buy stocks, get advice from reliable sources. If you don't get it, don't buy. Tom, Dick, or Harry's tips are dangerous, but common stocks of reputable companies are risks worth taking. They are investments in America's future.[143]

There were no floods of congratulatory letters following that optimistic pronouncement as the economy worsened.

Marriage and Death

In February 1928, the youngest of JR and Gussie's children, 25-year-old William, was married. He had ended a stay abroad with a visit to Argentina and had fallen in love with Renee Scharf, the daughter of a Viennese portrait painter who had moved to Argentina a few years previously. The young couple were married in a simple ceremony in Chicago, and following a honeymoon in Europe, they settled in Philadelphia, where William went to work in the Sears plant under his brother. It is notable that, with the exception of Marion, whose husband, Alfred K. Stern, worked for the Rosenwald Fund, JR's children sought to leave Chicago and remove themselves from the influence of their loving but domineering parents.

In 1926, Gussie became ill but seemed to recover. Then in October 1927, her condition took a decided turn for the worse and she entered a hospital in Chicago. The diagnosis was cancer, and she underwent several operations. Her recovery was long and slow, and it was for her health that she and JR went to Florida after William's wedding. There she continued to progress back to health. JR remained optimistic and frequently informed the German relatives of developments. By late summer he did not have good news: "My birthday was not a festive occasion this year due to my dear Gussie's being in the hospital and, of course, in every family celebration, she is the principal attraction. She returned home today after two weeks in the hospital, but it looks very much as though she will be compelled, some time during the next few weeks, to return there for another operation. The doctors give us assurances that there is no cause for worry, but nevertheless, it does give us much concern."[144] The reports to the German relatives continued. Gussie was able to get up and walk a bit, and occasionally she was able to go out. In January 1929, JR wrote that she had attended the opera but was unable to stay through the whole performance. At the end of February, she was able to travel to Philadelphia to see William and Lessing and their families. Then she and JR went on to Hoover's inauguration. It must have been a supreme effort for her to make it through even that portion of the festivities she attended. Yet she returned to Chicago seemingly in reasonably good health. Now it was JR who grew ill with a bad cold, and he was urged to go to Phoenix for his health. His stay there was brief. At the end of April, Gussie's health deteriorated markedly. By May 23, she was dead.

Gussie was a strong personality and one who had an important effect on JR. Their marriage had lasted thirty-nine years. During that time, despite the occasional frustrations inherent in any successful marriage, there had never been even a hint of any major disagreement. Husband and wife truly loved and respected each other and valued each other's thoughts and opinions.

To what extent Gussie had influenced JR in his philanthropy cannot be determined. He always claimed that it was the two Augustas in his life, his mother and his wife, who had been the greatest influence on his philanthropy. However, although the two women did not put any roadblocks in the way of JR's philanthropy, they did not lead it. Gussie had her own philanthropic causes and interests. She was a believer in the suffragettes, if not an overly flamboyant one, and she did persuade her husband to donate to that cause. She was on the national board of the Girl Scouts of America and was not just a figurehead in that organization. She became close to many of JR's important female friends, such as Henrietta Szold and Jane Addams; it is likely that she was closer to Szold than her husband was. Gussie made her own way through the philanthropic world. When she accompanied her husband on the train trips to Tuskegee, trips that continued long after Booker T. Washington's death, she was lionized and admired by the students and staff. She also had her own opinions on issues of the day. It is likely that she was far more attracted to Zionism than was JR. However, she never sought to change her husband's view on that or any other important issue about which he, too, felt strongly.

Gussie was devoted to the arts. JR enjoyed the theater and tolerated opera because his wife loved it. She also appreciated the fine arts more than her husband. She was very fond of nature, and with the aid of landscape architect Jens Jensen, she made the gardens at Ravinia into a showplace that must have been extraordinary. The house at Ravinia even had a small working farm, which she also loved.

She clearly inspired intense devotion. Less than a month before her death, her son-in-law Edgar Stern wrote her what he called, only half-jokingly, "a love letter." Saying that the old mother-in-law jokes did not apply, he continued: "Mother darling, I not only love you dearly but admire you so much that if I undertake to itemize your qualities I shall have you blushing red and my wife going green with jealousy, were it not that you may tell her in confidence that I think she has inherited much of your delicate refinement, your variety of mental interests, your social grace, and your sterling spirit. I shall never cease to be grateful that your blood flows in the veins of my children."[145]

Yet Gussie could be difficult to work for, as was her husband. Harry Kersey, the chauffeur, describes how one day she discharged him—he was not even sure of the reason—"whether I was too long in getting there or did not look any too happy when I did get there." It took JR to smooth things over and rehire the chauffeur, who had reluctantly packed his bags and prepared to leave. "Mr. Rosenwald called me to the house on Friday morning and gave me a lecture, and said that the children and family all liked me and would I like to remain."[146]

Gussie's funeral was strictly private. Only members of the family were present. JR had the simple casket placed under the portrait of his mother and made a few brief remarks, beginning with how devoted the two Augustas had been to each other. Then, after talking about her love of family, he went on:

> She loved her home and her garden, but hers was not a selfish pleasure in them. She wanted her family and her friends to enjoy them with her. She was always ambitious, and insisted that things about her should be done as perfectly as possible—an ideal which she always wanted her children to hold with her, for she was never satisfied with mediocre achievement. She wanted no thanks for any kind act, always saying that the satisfaction was in the doing, and a deed once done should be forgotten. Without her inspiration and encouragement, which was constant, my own life would have lacked much of the joy which has come to me.[147]

Letters of condolence arrived from all over the country—in fact, all over the world. President Hoover wrote: "I want you to know I have been so fondly thinking of you in these recent days. I only wish I were near to offer a helping hand and a word of true sympathy and understanding. All that is best within me goes out to you, my good friend."[148] There were hundreds of letters from people whose lives Gussie and JR had touched and who wanted to make their feelings known.

JR was stoic in his bereavement. As he explained to the German relatives, the last year and a half of Gussie's life had been neither happy nor comfortable, and her death could be viewed as a release for her and a relief for the family. JR's feelings were best expressed in a letter to the Bunde relatives about three weeks after Gussie's death: "My children have surrounded me with the desire to take every care possible from my mind and heart. We have all determined not to dwell upon the sad event, but to make our homes and those who have occasion to enter them as happy as the circumstances will permit. We all agree that there is nothing to be gained by speaking of our misfortune to others and that we shall all live our normal lives, making them as useful as we know how."[149] The notion that it made sense to carry on with life and not give way to grief is exemplified by the fact that only two weeks after the funeral, JR was in Washington attending a meeting of the Mount Rushmore Commission and staying at the White House.

Just six months after Gussie's death, JR was contemplating remarriage—or at least he was planning a trip for two to Egypt in late January. Shortly after the beginning of the new year (1930), he traveled to New York for the final meeting with Alfred E. Smith and Coolidge to dispose of the Hubert estate. On January 8, he married Adelaide Goodkind (known as "Addie"), Lessing's mother-in-law. The new Mrs. Julius Rosenwald was the widow of Benjamin Goodkind, a St. Paul, Minnesota, merchant who had died in 1919. Benjamin's brother, Maurice, had been Gussie's chief physician, and was a close friend of JR. Addie had moved to Chicago after her husband's death. The marriage was not necessarily a love match. JR was lonely, and evidently he felt this marriage would be a good solution. His children, who had continued visiting him in a constant stream after their mother's death, were probably delighted. After the wedding, the couple set sail on their honeymoon.

No diaries were kept of this trip. By the end of January, the newlyweds

Figure 19. JR and Addie on their honeymoon, January 1930. Courtesy of the Department of Special Collections, Regenstein Library, University of Chicago.

were in Egypt. There was the obligatory and now familiar trip down the Nile to Luxor, where they viewed Chicago House and its new Rosenwald Library. By mid-March they were in Paris where, according to a newspaper account, JR performed one of his acts of totally impulsive generosity. He and Addie attended a concert at which one of the performers was a young Russian cellist, Ria Garburova. After the concert, JR asked her to play a solo, but she refused, saying her cello was not good enough. JR discovered that she had her heart set on a 1703 cello costing $8,000, so he bought it for her and arranged for her to come to the United States for a concert tour.[150]

By April, JR and Addie were back in the Chicago area. During the summer of 1930, JR wrote to the German relatives that he had never felt so well. However, the heart problems that had plagued him since 1926 returned, and late in the autumn of that year he was once again seriously ill. As he recovered, his doctors urged him to travel to a warm climate where he could relax, and so, in mid-December, he and Addie departed for a winter stay in Honolulu.

Before they left, however, they moved out of the house at 4901 Ellis  Avenue. Now that all the children had grown and left home, there was no need for the large mansion. Perhaps it was too painful for JR to stay there after Gussie's death. He and Addie settled in an apartment in the Drake Hotel on the northern portion of Michigan Avenue.

The trip to Hawaii was to be the last one that JR would make. And the apartment on upper Michigan Avenue was to be his place of confinement for much of the last year of his life.

9

Final Year and Postmortem, 1931–1948

Illness and the Depression were the two overriding constants of JR's final year. He fought against the first, but ultimately lost. The Depression was beyond even his powers of optimism to combat.

When JR and Addie departed for Hawaii December 16, 1930, the Chicago philanthropist was not a well man. Doctors were worried about his heart and a "racing pulse." He tired very easily. A sensible man with regard to his own health, JR realized that complete rest was essential for his recovery. As he wrote his children from the boat, "I have given myself up completely to mental and physical recuperation."[1] And Addie, determined that her husband not grow worse, was a strict disciplinarian; JR said of her, "She waits upon me until I rebel."

During the first month in Hawaii, JR was essentially confined to the hotel. "Our life here is ideal and I can truthfully say that I have staged a fine comeback, although I am still taking very good care not to overdo. In fact, [we] have done little else but spend an hour on the beach in front of the hotel in the sun, having our meals in our room and resting a lot, reading and playing 'poker patience'—at the latter I'm a big loser. Addie is a shark at it. . . . I have a massage every day from a young lady of about 50."[2] Edwin Embree owned a house in Honolulu. His wife and daughter

Figure 20. An elderly JR.

were there and were very solicitous, but for the first month the Rosenwalds refused all invitations.

This regimen of enforced leisure had the desired effect. JR's health began to improve. Addie reported to JR's daughters: "You would be delighted if you could see how glad he is to do as he is told, and what willing cooperation he gives. He is as cheerful and happy as possible and feels and looks well and his appetite is excellent."[3] Gradually, JR and Addie began accepting invitations, and by the end of their stay they were participating in the island's busy social life: dinner with the governor, concerts, attending the opening of the Hawaiian legislature. JR and Addie were invited to a luau (Addie disliked the food) and even a Japanese wedding. Finally they had to reciprocate, first with a small party of ten for tea, and later with a lavish reception at the hotel for one hundred guests. They also engaged in tourist activities—an excursion in a glass-bottomed boat, an airplane trip to other islands (Addie enjoyed it, JR was nervous). But what made the greatest impression on JR was the Royal Hawaiian School at Panalu. JR described it in a letter to his children: "This morning was a thriller. We visited the Royal School—only mixed races—Japanese, Chinese, Philipinos, etc.—1,350—a glorified Tuskegee. . . . They have special exercises on Fridays. I shall try to go every week."[4] To Embree, who knew the school well, he wrote: "The place teems with interesting people and activities, a veritable beehive of civic and educational movements and all of superior quality, even the Salvation Army work. We cannot tear ourselves away."[5]

JR and Addie enjoyed Honolulu so much that they prolonged their stay a week. Before they returned to the mainland, Addie wrote the children: "Dad is so well and looks better than he has in a long while." But in a later letter she admitted: "He rather dreads getting back to the stress of things."[6] The couple returned to Chicago in mid-March. On March 21, JR was back at his office.[7] Almost immediately after that date, he became gravely ill again.

For at least a month after the onset of his second illness, JR was not involved in any of his numerous philanthropic projects. He was confined to his bed, flat on his back. Evidently word went out that no disturbing news was to be told to him, for W. Rufus Abbott, chairman of the board of the Museum of Science and Industry, wrote Leo Wormser: "I have not written to JR because of your statement that only pleasing things were to be communicated."[8] Very gradually, JR was able to receive such visitors as Embree and begin to resume his activities on a very small scale.

JR, Embree, and the Fund, 1931

While JR was in Hawaii, Embree sent him frequent memos telling him what was taking place at the Fund offices and bringing up subjects about which he felt JR should be informed. But it seems clear that Embree did not want to overburden the Fund's founder with material. In one of the earlier memos, Embree wrote: "I cannot say that we do not need you, but

I am increasingly convinced that you ought not to wear yourself out in daily routine, and that you could be of more help to all the causes in which you are interested if you would leave the detailed operations to us and hold yourself for consultation and decision on important matters. Whether in Hawaii or Chicago, I believe occasional, leisurely conferences on important matters will be much more helpful than the grueling routine in the office. You have done more than your share of that already in your lifetime. But your counsel and decision on important matters is of the greatest value. We are not bothering you with details of the daily work."[9] Was this a way of implying that JR was micromanaging the Fund when he was in Chicago? Given Embree's temperament, that seems unlikely. Moreover, JR did not see these remarks as any sort of criticism. In his reply, which spoke mostly of the people he was meeting and his activities in Hawaii, he told Embree: "Thank you for the good advice. I'll try to follow it. Mrs. Rosenwald blesses you for sending it."[10]

Typical of the sort of subject Embree discussed in his letters was that of industrial schools. He had initially been interested in building industrial high schools for blacks in urban areas of the South, and he had persuaded the Fund's trustees to vote for the construction of five. In *The Education of Blacks in the South,* James D. Anderson devotes a chapter to these schools in which he excoriates the Fund for seeking to prepare black high school students for menial jobs.[11] What Anderson neglects to say is that by 1931, Embree had become totally disillusioned with the concept of the industrial high schools. In words which Anderson would probably have heartily endorsed, Embree wrote JR: "My own guess is that the thing to do is give students good fundamental general education and then let them learn the tricks of their trades on the job. It does not take much education to train a carpenter or a plasterer or auto mechanic, if the man has some sense to begin with. I believe that the duty of the schools is to give this fundamental 'sense,' and to leave the applications of it to work on the job or to some sort of apprenticeship. . . . [B]eyond the experiments to which we are already committed, I do not want to see the Fund make further contributions—or persuade cities to put more of their own funds—into this very uncertain field."[12] JR fully agreed with Embree, but he looked at it from the cost-benefit viewpoint, as he noted in a letter sent two weeks later: "I am in full accord with your views on industrial education. Theoretically it sounds fine, but I am concerned that the results do not justify the cost, either in rural schools or in high schools. This may not apply to domestic science and that might be given further trial."[13] Despite the last sentence, JR was perfectly content to see the Fund end its grants to black vocational high schools, which Embree, as late as October 18, was calling "a very questionable movement." Overall, only five industrial high schools were built by the Fund at a total cost of $202,708, a small fraction of the more than $20 million expended by the foundation.[14] The only one of the five schools which Embree took any pride in was the one in New Orleans which was associated with an apprenticeship program.

In April, JR slowly began to recover, but he was unable to attend board or executive committee meetings of the Fund. However, that did not mean he was uninterested in the Fund or in other aspects of his philanthropy. Embree sent him memos several times a week, on which JR would scribble brief notes, and he would visit his employer approximately once a week.

Several issues particularly interested Embree and JR during this period of illness and slow partial recovery. One was the issue of what to do with the school building initiative. JR had at one time set a goal of assisting five thousand schools. By mid-1931, that goal had been surpassed. Embree was eager to end the program. But JR obviously felt strongly about it, and Embree was diplomatic in the way he broached the subject of termination: "I think it may be that in the reasonably near future we may wish to discontinue further general building of school houses. I think probably we should now give the same kind of attention to trying to improve the teaching inside these and other Negro schools." Embree should not have been so nervous, for JR wrote on this memo: "I am greatly pleased with the idea of the plan at hand for the Negro schools."[15]

In late 1930, the Fund's trustees authorized a study to be conducted on the quality of the education offered in Rosenwald schools. One of the two men who conducted the study was Horace Mann Bond, a young black education specialist who had received one of the early Rosenwald fellowships.[16] The study carried out by Bond and his colleague was scathing. The teaching that occurred in many Rosenwald schools was, at best, mediocre. In addition to ending the school building program and providing money for teacher training programs, Embree also hoped to strengthen county governments in the South so that more money could be placed at the disposal of black schools and some effort could be made to lessen the appalling disparity between the amounts spent on black and white education. The Fund's trustees acquiesced in these changes. Thus the school building program, which had been curtailed in 1930, was ended in 1932. In his book on the Fund, Embree described the reason for terminating the school building program as follows: "[The trustees and officers of the Fund] felt that this particular demonstration had served its purpose of stimulating interest and must be discontinued in order that the Southern states should not rely too heavily on outside aid, and thus be delayed in assuming full responsibility for the schools of this section as an integral part of public provisions for the education of all the people."[17]

Having vacated 4901 Ellis Avenue for an apartment at the Drake Hotel, JR tried to sell the huge house, but because it was the beginning of the Depression, there were no buyers. In May 1931, Embree first suggested that JR consider donating the house to the foundation. It would, he said, save $4,000 a year in taxes, the house could easily be transformed into a beautiful office, and it was much better located than the Sears plant where the foundation's offices then were. Embree preferred to be close to the University of Chicago. JR was not taken with the idea. He scrawled at the bottom of the memo: "Something to think about—but at first thought, does not appeal to me."[18] Over six months later, with JR now seriously ill again, Embree returned to the idea. In a carefully worded memo, he advanced three reasons why this made sense. In addition to the two reasons already cited, taxes and location, he added a third. "If real estate values rose again, the Fund could sell the house and put the profit in its assets."[19] There was no reply to this, but among the papers in JR's room at his death was a note in his handwriting that said: "Tell Mr. E[mbree] about the house."[20] The Fund offices did move there in 1932 following some renovations and remained there until the foundation went out of existence in 1948.

The other item in this final note was actually not carried out, and it was another issue that Embree had been quietly pressing. JR continued to give considerable sums of money away not through the foundation but as an individual. There were pledges that he had made as far back as 1928, and, as with so many Rosenwald gifts, they were challenge grants that required other funds to be raised before JR's money could be sent. These pledges ranged from $2,188,000 for the Russian colonization movement to $3,000 for the International School of Geneva. The total of the pledges amounted to $4,315,250. Embree, who realized that JR was dying, looked at these obligations, at the declining stocks that were JR's fortune, and wondered how the estate was going to honor these pledges.

He suggested that JR place them all under the foundation and provide the Fund with $5 million in non-Sears stock to cover these pledges. JR failed to reply to this suggestion.

The main subject of conversation between Embree and Julius Rosenwald during this last year of JR's life was the American economic downturn and its effect on the Fund. All of the Fund's assets were in Sears stock, and Embree watched in some alarm as the price of Sears stock, which had been considered one of the most solid of all investments before October 1929, continued its precipitous downward spiral. In 1929, before the October crash, the stock had been selling for $190 a share. On the day of JR's death, January 6, 1932, it was selling for $32 a share.[21]

Embree frequently attempted to reassure JR that the Fund was making the right moves in responding to the Depression. In early April, for example, he wrote that he had terminated one staff member "as we are not engaged in an excessive number of new projects." He added: "People always seem surprised when a foundation tries to maintain the same kind of efficiency as a business house—including the keeping down of unnecessary personnel and other overhead charges. But it seems to me that no other course is justified." To which JR replied: "If we are not as efficient and careful, it is, in my mind, a reflection on the officers. *It is a business.*"[22] A month later, Embree reported on the board meeting that had taken place without JR: "Hearty agreement to proceeding slowly with no new commitments at this time. Everyone felt that we should make sure we could carry out our established programs before we embark on any new enterprises. I think we are not in danger of becoming perfunctory or ultraconservative." JR scrawled in the margin "OK."[23]

In August, with the value of Sears stock continuing to slide, Embree wrote an extensive memo on how the Fund was coping with the deteriorating economic situation. In June he had announced the elimination of three staff positions. Now, he said, the Fund was trying to do with one dollar what it had formerly done with three. Moreover, "while we are making much smaller cash appropriations, we are making very large cash payments on commitments made two and three years ago. And we are giving the most active scrutiny to every payment and using our gifts to try to improve the management and accomplishment of every one of our beneficiaries." He continued: "I have been trying to exert every effort to improve, to make more aggressive and more strategic the efforts of this Fund. . . . Our task is different from what it was two years ago; but it is harder, more exciting and more interesting than ever. We want to keep our work economical and efficient, but this is no time to let up or lie down." And in a passage whose slightly purple prose marks it as vintage Embree, he added, "The Julius Rosenwald Fund is an astonishingly active yeast, and it is so recognized very widely throughout the country. It is the more significant at this time when the other foundations seem to be becoming more and more conventional and perfunctory. Whether our total appropriations are two million dollars or two hundred thousand dollars, we will be serviceable only if we keep the pot boiling."[24]

On October 18, as the economic situation continued to worsen, JR urged the Fund's president to consider cutting additional staff. Embree politely disagreed. In a memo he diplomatically stated the areas in which the two agreed: (1) At their November meeting, the trustees must "face squarely our present financial condition and must keep our new commitments at the very minimum," and (2) Every economy that could be made in the administration of the Fund should be made as long as the Fund's effectiveness is not threatened. But here agreement ended. The payroll was just "a drop in the bucket." "As our appropriations diminish, the importance of the influence of the staff must increase if we are to continue to be effective. I agree that we should economize so that our office will continue to be a model of efficiency, but to economize to the point of hampering our active influence would be the worst possible policy at this time." He agreed to cut six minor staff positions, but that was as far as he would go.[25]

Embree's final idea before JR's death for how the Fund could deal with the Depression was the interesting notion that the Julius Rosenwald Fund should combine with two smaller foundations, the Falk Fund of Pittsburgh and the Laura Spelman Rockefeller Memorial (a Rockefeller offshoot headed by Rosenwald Fund trustee Beardsley Ruml). The other two funds had been approached, Embree reported, and were interested. "Each agrees that the results would be beneficial to each of these groups, and might start an important movement which would make these foundations not merely useful enterprises but great social forces."[26] This union of the three foundations never occurred, but one wonders what the history of philanthropy would have been like if it had.

Despite occasional bursts of optimism in his memos to JR, Embree must have seen the death of the Fund's founder coming. Two of Embree's memos of this period seem almost like valedictory statements. His memo of August 21 concludes with this paragraph:

> The chief reason I find the atmosphere so stimulating here and the yeast more active in your Fund than in other foundations is because you are so aggressive, so open-minded and so courageous. (Confidentially, I think you have some shortcomings, especially that you are often unreasonable. But you are a marvelous person.) You are the least timid rich man I have ever known. This makes it easy for all of us to keep plunging ahead and trying to do things—because we know that you are not afraid to stand by even if it means taking criticism from stupid or selfishly interested persons.[27]

And in the memo of November 27, one of his last, he summed up what he believed Julius Rosenwald meant in terms of philanthropy:

> You have done so much already, not only in individual gifts, but in the principles of giving you have established, that I am most eager for you to make at least one or two more contributions to the general principles of philanthropy. The conspicuous and important ideas for which you have stood seem to me to be these. 1. A personal interest by the donor in all the activities to which he contributes. The old saying "The gift without the giver is bare" has been applied to certain wealthy philanthropists. It has certainly never applied to you. 2. Helping to give a start to new ideas. This seems to me to be the essence of all real philanthropy. . . . The creative thing is to give new projects and new social forces a chance to prove themselves. This takes imagination and courage. One of the things I have always admired most in you has been your willingness to sponsor new things, to take criticism and even abuse for supporting them. Rich men too often become timid and conventional. . . . 3. The theory that trust funds should not be held in perpetuity, but should be currently used as they are needed.[28]

The Museum of Science and Industry—Part III

One of JR's main projects outside of the foundation was the Museum of Science and Industry. By the end of 1930, museum director Waldemar Kaempffert, smarting at what he considered the board's distrust in him, reluctantly came to a decision. To the amazement of Leo Wormser, he announced that he was resigning to return to his post at the *New York Times.* The official version given in his letter of resignation was that he could not get along with the organizational structure.[29] Wormser reported to JR a month after the fact:

> The Kaempffert problem has naturally given us great concern. On Friday evening, January 2, he came to me with the news of his retirement. He was visibly distressed. That he had not slept well for several weeks was noticeable in every line of his face and in every word he uttered. He was not only unnerved, but angry—angry, I thought, not only because of what had caused him to act, but angry also because of the action he had taken. I was confronted with a tense man and a tense situation. . . .
>
> It strikes me that in the development of a project of this character there are two stages. The first is the period of the dreamer who must have the vision and imagination to philosophize about the project. In this period we were most fortunate. Kaempffert has not only imaginative vision but also the power to relate the dreams to others. By the written and the spoken word, he made the concept of the Museum articulate. His articles in the press and magazines told the story of our dreams as it had never been told. His addresses to clubs, trade organizations, and other groups, and his more peaceful talks with leaders in the fields of science and industry, vividly portrayed a project not easy by words to describe. The second period, as I conceive it, is to project the dreams into reality.[30]

Wormser's valedictory of Kaempffert was right on target.

JR's reaction to Kaempffert's resignation was a terse cable: "Resignation most unfortunate. Without knowing circumstances hopeful reconsideration possible."[31] But when it was clear that it was not possible, he avoided becoming involved in the search for Kaempffert's successor. Wormser and Rufus Abbott informed him periodically about the search and the final selection of Otto Kreusser, General Motors Company's department head in charge of proving grounds.[32]

After the onset of JR's illness, Wormser's letters to JR tried to strike a note of cheerfulness that somehow rings hollow, especially since progress on building the museum had slowed.

Yet JR, though ill, had not forgotten his brainchild. He was certainly alert enough to give additional gifts of stock to the museum made necessary by the Depression. He was seriously concerned about the financial future of the institution, as was Abbott, who poured out his concern when JR rallied in mid-June.

JR's solution to the apparent money woes of the museum was that others should contribute to it. Aside from the bond issue, he had provided virtually all the money to date. He firmly believed that the museum should acquire members who would give it gifts, presumably yearly. The question was how to start a membership organization. He thought the solution was to go back to the museum's origin in the Commercial Club. He wrote to Abbott: "I certainly had no such idea that the Club members should be taxed for the support of the Museum. What I meant was, that they formulate a plan and have a committee to bring the plan to the public for support by contribution, memberships of various kinds, by will, etc. I might be willing to match contributions from the public up to one million dollars, and later do the same again. This might create interest in the Museum. It might apply to certain kinds of membership."[33]

The board of trustees had appointed a membership committee in May 1930. Its task was "to consider what classification of membership the Museum should have, the fee incident to each class of membership and at what time members should be enlisted."[34] This committee had met, but had concluded that memberships at that time were not the way to go. In response to JR's offer of a $1 million match, Abbott noted: "It was very generous of you to offer." Abbott then explained the museum's financial state: "Of your original contribution of $3,000,000 we have used up approximately $250,000, in addition to the dividends and other returns received from the Sears, Roebuck stock. . . . The Trustees are more concerned with the cost of the first five years of operation of the Museum, up until the end of . . . 1937, and it was upon that particular item that I concentrated my remarks to you during our recent interview. . . . [Expenses are estimated at] $600,000 per annum to be met under some plan yet to be devised."[35]

JR's condition worsened after receipt of that letter, but his final gift of 20,000 shares of Sears stock on October 12 can be seen as a partial response. Yet he refused to completely give up on the idea of memberships. In mid-July, he sent Wormser a note in response to a copy of the Chicago Zoological Society annual report that the lawyer had sent him: "This membership list, though small, indicates the difference between trying and not trying. If they have secured $9,000—we should. Located as our building is, and considering its beauty and other fine points, we should easily get $90,000 in the same time. If not, why not?"[36]

One cannot help but sympathize with JR. The museum may have been his idea, but he rightly felt that others should make some effort and share some of the burden. At the same time, Abbott and the trustees also had a point. There was, as yet, nothing tangible to show except a group of exhibits and a half-finished building. Without something more concrete, it would be hard to peddle memberships. Above all, it was the middle of the

Depression and most people did not have money to contribute, even to such a grand design as the Museum of Science and Industry.

It was one of the few tragedies of Julius Rosenwald's life that he did not live to see the opening of the museum he had founded. The first part of the building opened on June 19, 1933, as part of the Century of Progress World's Fair. Only the coal mine and several smaller exhibits were ready. The building was still in a state of renovation and construction, and visitors had to pick their way through the work site. Although the Museum and the Century of Progress Exposition cooperated, the museum attracted far less attention than fan dancer Sally Rand.[37] The formal opening of the entire museum, including the west wing, occurred on March 2, 1938.

Nor was JR's hope that others would contribute to supporting the museum fulfilled until more than a decade after his death. JR, his estate, and the Rosenwald Family Association contributed $11 million to the museum between 1926 and the early 1940s.[38] By contrast, total cash gifts to the museum from all other sources up to 1944 amounted to just $15,000.[39] JR's gift to Chicago was one of the most munificent donations to found a museum ever given by an individual up to that time. It remains a true testament to the vision and leadership of Julius Rosenwald.

Russian Colonies and the University of Chicago

JR's concerns about the Museum of Science and Industry were matched by worries about the other two charitable organizations he cared about most deeply. One was the Russian colonies, where his affairs were managed almost entirely by his staff and Lessing. The other was the University of Chicago. In both cases, Embree and JR sought to extricate the Chicago philanthropist from challenge grant pledges that, because of the Depression, were going nowhere.

No charitable organization was prospering during the Depression, and the Russian colonies project was no exception. It was chronically short of funds. Moreover, chinks were becoming apparent in the image of this supposedly perfect organization. For one thing, it developed that the bonds issued to big donors by the Soviet government were largely worthless, a fact hardly surprising today, but one that must have come as a shock to people in 1931. The bonds were called "Certificates of Beneficial Interest," and although they ostensibly yielded 5 percent interest, they could not be traded or sold. They were to be held by the American Society for Jewish Farm Settlements, Inc. (as the Agro-Joint Program was now called), and the leaders of that organization indicated that any attempt to alter this arrangement would have serious implications as far as relations with the Soviet government were concerned and perhaps also relations with the settlers.[40]

In addition to the farm settlements, JR was involved with industrial projects in Russia, also organized by Dr. Rosen. But it was becoming clear that the Depression had taken a significant toll on this attempt to build Jewish factories, and in December Embree sought to deliver JR from this obligation. At the very end of December, Paul Baerwald, treasurer of the Joint Distribution Committee, admitted to Nathan Levin, JR's financial manager, that the industrial project was at an end.[41]

In fact, JR did not concern himself greatly with the Russian colonies toward the very end of his life. It was Lessing who authorized the dispatch of $175,000 in November in response to the importunate pleas of the American Society. Lessing followed this up with another check for $103,324 in December.

JR was more involved with the University of Chicago, although Embree sought to free him from some ambiguous pledges. Unlike the Russian colonies, this was done with the complete approval of the ailing JR. The two items Embree and JR were most concerned about were the nurses' home and money for the Lying-In Hospital.

In 1929, JR had promised Franklin McLean, director of the University Clinics, that he would contribute to the building of a dormitory for nurses at the hospital through a challenge grant. But the Depression had ruined the chances of the challenge ever being met. For that reason, Embree told university president Robert Hutchins that the philanthropist considered this pledge null and void.

With the Lying-In Hospital, JR had promised a grant of $250,000 if a gynecological unit were built. When this condition was not met, he agreed to donate $200,000 and said he would consider contributing the additional $50,000. Embree pointed out that no follow-up had come from this suggestion, and therefore JR regarded his obligation to the Lying-In Hospital as ended.[42]

Sears

After the assistance he gave to approximately three hundred employees who had suffered badly from the stock market crash of October 1929, JR did not participate actively in Sears affairs. General Wood consulted him on personnel and policy matters[43] and kept him informed of developments at the company, sending him periodic comparison figures on profits and sales. After JR became seriously ill, General Wood sent him a letter in May suggesting that JR resign as chairman of the board in favor of Lessing. This idea had been discussed with Lessing, who apparently had agreed to it. "The whole plan," General Wood wrote his predecessor, "is predicated on your health. It seems to me that if you are to have a number of useful and happy years ahead of you, you must rid yourself of every kind of business problem, not alone those connected with Sears Roebuck & Co., but those connected with your personal affairs. . . . [I]f you do not, you might be taken from us at any time."[44] Wood advanced several reasons for this proposal beyond the state of JR's health: (1) Lessing would need the time to handle JR's personal affairs, and he could not do that and still function effectively as vice president. (2) It would be better for the company and for Lessing if he did not live in Philadelphia. (3) Lessing's position would go unfilled, thereby saving the company money, something which would be a decided benefit given economic conditions.

Although Lessing evidently spoke to his father about assuming the position of chairman, JR refused to agree to this plan. Instead, mindful of the need for Sears to save money in the midst of Depression, he sent the following note to General Wood: "Altho I voluntarily reduced the rent of the property which I own, which is occupied by the Company, by $80,000 per annum from July 1, 1931, I now desire to reduce my compensation as Chairman from $50,000 per annum to $5,000 until such time as the Company's profits again reach at least $25 million. This reduction to date from October 1, 1931. The loyalty and devotion which you and the members of your staff—officers many without official title—have given the Company during these trying times seem to dictate this action."[45] In characteristic fashion, JR was thinking not of himself but of the Company he had done so much to build. General Wood tried to see Rosenwald on October 27 to thank him personally for his generous action, but was advised by JR's physicians that the visit was inadvisable.

Illness

JR fell seriously ill about the third week of March. In April he gradually began to improve, and around May 1 he was moved from the Drake Towers to Ravinia. Addie, however, was dissatisfied with the medical care that JR was receiving. There were reports that Dr. Goodkind, brother of her late husband, was incompetent. She sought the advice of Dr. Franklin McLean, head of the University of Chicago Hospital and Clinics and JR's close friend. In a lengthy memo possibly written for University of Chicago president Robert Hutchins, McLean describes in detail the hurried conferences and secret consultations that occurred in the month of June.[46] Various doctors were called in from New York to consult on the case, including David Levy, a child psychiatrist married to JR's daughter Adele, and Robert Levy (no relation), a noted heart specialist. The upshot of all the discussions, phone calls, luncheons at the Drake, was that the two physicians who had been in charge of JR's case since March were fired. Dr. Robert Levy was put in charge of the case. Since Levy lived in New York, Dr. Louis Leiter, a heart and kidney specialist at the University of Chicago, was on twenty-four-hour call. Also in attendance was a trained nurse. While some questioned the massive doses of digitalis that Dr. Levy prescribed, JR seemed to improve steadily. The patient himself reported in mid-July: "I am still flat on my back after four months, but with every comfort such a condition should have. Dr. Robert Levy . . . was here today and assures me that I am making definite progress and that 'It won't be long now' before I will be permitted more liberty. I fortunately haven't an ache or a pain and if my patience holds out will soon be about again under restrictions."[47] At the same time Addie was writing JR's longtime friend Abraham Flexner: "Mr. Rosenwald has been kept in bed entirely for three weeks now, and spends every minute of the day and night on his outdoor porch where he lies in comfort, and continues to be the cheery philosophical soul that helps me so much through all these long months of illness."[48]

Progress continued. On September 7, McLean wrote Adele: "Mr. Rosenwald has obviously improved a great deal during the past month. He is not only free from symptoms, but is stronger in every way. During the past week he has been a little discouraged that his progress was not even more rapid, but I believe Dr. Levy's talk with him will help reconcile him to what is necessarily a slow rate of improvement." McLean even went on to suggest that JR might spend the winter in the warmer climate of California.[49]

In late November or early December, JR took a definite turn for the worse. The family realized that the end was near, and they gathered in Chicago. Edith described the situation: "These are sad days but we must keep in mind our blessing in having Father free of pain. The doctors say he could have suffered agony, and both his body and mind seem to be quietly and gradually seeking the long rest. He was so tired of this fight that none of us could wish to see it prolonged with such meager reward. He is as beautiful a person as ever, and his waking hours are filled with love for all of us and thoughts outside of himself. He is a great man, whose example and spirit will live on forever."[50] Julius Rosenwald died at his home in Ravinia at 2:55 P.M. on January 6, 1932. According to his doctor, the cause of death was hardening of the arteries complicated by heart and kidney ailments.

JR requested that his funeral be extremely simple. Only close family members were present. He was buried in Rosehill Cemetery in Chicago under the simplest plaque imaginable. All it says is "Julius Rosenwald, 1862–1932." An imposing mausoleum would have been totally out of character.

In Memoriam

Julius Rosenwald's death was announced on the front page of the *New York Times,* and there were banner headlines in the Chicago papers. Tributes poured in from around the world. Friend and opponent alike tried to find the right words to sum up the life and spirit of this man who had been such an important force in both business and philanthropy in early twentieth-century America. Judge Julian W. Mack, who disagreed with JR over the issue of Zionism, was both sorrowful and laudatory: "He was one of the dearest friends I ever had. My personal grief is great . . . but it is nothing to the loss to the community of one of the finest men this country has ever produced, a nobleman in every sense of the word. What he gave in money was great, but what I admired of him was what he gave of himself. His entire life was devoted to unselfish deeds, to constructive thinking in the interest of humanity." There were few tributes from African Americans printed in the white owned press of that day, but there was one eloquent statement from Walter White, secretary of the NAACP: "No name is more revered and deeply loved among American Negroes than that of Julius Rosenwald, and I know of no one whose passing is more sincerely mourned. This feeling . . . is born of the fact that Julius Rosenwald, in his individual contributions and through the Julius Rosenwald Fund, did more than merely give money. The spirit in which these gifts were made was not that of patronizing charity, but of help towards promoting the rights and welfare of men."[51]

Graham Taylor took up this theme in an essay published in Paul Kellogg's *Survey Graphic,* a magazine JR had supported for years: "When asked why his interest and gifts were so large in promoting the welfare and progress of the Negro race, he said it was because he was interested in America and did not see how it could go forward if its Negro people were left behind." Taylor also said in a statement that seemed to truly reflect the character of JR and which was echoed in many of the other tributes: "He was so genuinely friendly, as soon to make acquaintances his own friends. This genuineness characterized his personality and carried his whole manhood into every relationship of life."[52]

Memorial services for JR were held across the country. One of the first was at Temple Sinai in Chicago, the congregation that the late philanthropist had belonged to since the mid-1890s. The speaker was Rabbi Louis L. Mann, who had succeeded Emil Hirsch, JR's mentor. In a lengthy eulogy, Mann made these points:

> Julius Rosenwald, the man! His personality was unique; he was innately modest, genuinely unselfish, deeply human. We see in his character a paradox, if not a combination of seething contradictions. He had a great strength of will, yet a loving tenderness; a penetrating intelligence combined with an abounding sympathy; unyielding conviction with greatness of understanding; a broad vision of the future with an intensely practical understanding of the present; a great talent for business and a genius for philanthropy; a non-university man who spent fortunes to establish and help universities; one who gave something better than all his money—himself. He gave himself with selfless modesty and self-effacing humility.

And Mann added: "He frequently disarmed those who disagreed with him because of the singleness of his purpose, because of his whole-souled integrity and because of his rugged simplicity—and often because of the naiveté of his humor."[53]

The most unusual memorial service took place in New York on March 27. It was broadcast nationwide over the National Broadcasting Company network, of which JR had been a director. The program was produced by the Joint Distribution Committee, and the first speaker was President Hoover, who noted once again that the Russian colonies project was a great work of "social engineering," but added, speaking of JR: "I remember how, guided by his keen intellect and great heart, he directed his wealth into those channels which inspiration and study convinced him were for the best service of his fellow men. I further recall that where there were no channels, he surveyed and dug them, recognizing no barriers of creed or race."[54] This was Hoover the civil engineer speaking. New York lieutenant governor Herbert Lehman called JR "a real statesman of philanthropic and communal activities" and noted: "Few men justly earn and retain the reputation for uprightness and rugged honesty that was Julius Rosenwald's."[55]

Perhaps the most extraordinary tribute to JR came from the pen of W. E. B. DuBois, who wrote this editorial in the NAACP's magazine *Crisis:*

> The death of Julius Rosenwald brings to an end a career remarkable especially for its significance to American Negroes. As a Jew, Julius Rosenwald did not have to be initiated into the methods of race prejudice, and his philanthropic work was a crushing arraignment of the American white Christians. Knowing that the YMCA discriminated grossly against Negroes, Rosenwald calmly offered to help pay for Negro Association buildings. To this end, he gave large sums, and few people had the wit to smile at his slap in the face of white Christianity. Seeing again that the white South did not propose to build decent schoolhouses for most colored children, Rosenwald again offered to help pay for such schoolhouses, provided they were real schoolhouses and on modern lines. The South accepted his gift effusively, and never even to this day has apparently grasped the failure of democracy which permitted an individual of a despised race to do for the sovereign states of a great nation that which they had neither the decency nor justice to do for themselves. Beyond this, Rosenwald reached out toward public libraries and hospitals, and endowed a great fund to carry on his work after his death. He was a great man. But he was no mere philanthropist. He was, rather, the subtle stinging critic of our racial democracy.[56]

This suggests the possibility that DuBois, who was named a Rosenwald Fellow in 1931, and Booker T. Washington might have agreed that the type of primary education which JR had helped make available for African Americans was something that was definitely important and worthwhile. DuBois may have recognized that, although the Rosenwald schools taught little girls sewing and little boys shop, they also taught the "three R's" successfully.

JR's death affected many people, from the rural black schoolchild, who had only a dim idea of who the fatherly-looking white man in the photograph on the school wall was, to the president of the United States.

The Economic Dilemma

The months immediately following Julius Rosenwald's death saw the depths of the Great Depression, and that economic cataclysm had a significant impact on both the settlement of JR's estate and the fate of the Rosenwald Fund.

Between 1923 and 1928, the average annual price of Sears stock on the New York Stock Exchange rose from $20.23 per share to $125.32 per share.[57] By September 1929, just before the stock market crash, Sears stock was selling for approximately $190 a share. JR and others believed that Sears stock was almost as safe as a government bond. Moreover, it paid a good dividend, $2.50 per share of common stock from 1927 to 1932. Because he possessed a fortune with a net worth estimated at $200 million in September 1929, JR was lavish in his pledges. As a result of his belief in the value of Sears stock, JR had all the assets of his foundation consist of Sears. Sixty percent of his personal fortune also was held in Sears stock, though he had diversified the remainder. Then came the fall of the stock market. At the time of JR's death, Sears was selling for $32 a share. By the end of June 1932, the stock was selling for just $10 a share.[58] This plunge in the price of Sears stock had huge implications both for the Estate and for the Rosenwald Fund.

The Estate

JR's will, dated December 19, 1931, was an exceedingly simple one-page document. It consisted of four main provisions: (1) All debts were to be paid off as soon after death as convenient. (2) A newly created foundation, the Rosenwald Family Association, was to be given "so much of his Estate as, together with gifts made during his lifetime, would amount to $11 million."[59] The Museum of Science and Industry was specifically mentioned, but the amount to be contributed to it was left to the discretion of JR's children, all of whom were members of the Family Association. (3) The remainder of the estate was to be divided in equal parts among the five children. Addie received no bequest. According to press reports at the time of JR's death, he had signed a prenuptial agreement which stipulated that she would receive $1 million upon his death but would waive all other claims to his estate.[60] (4) Lessing and Marion were named executors, but Marion dropped out of this role in May, leaving Lessing as the sole executor. He faced a daunting task.

There were estate taxes to be paid; the banks to which JR had guaranteed the accounts of the Sears employees he had rescued in October 1929 had to be dealt with; and the estate was obligated to pay the pledges of numerous charitable organizations to which JR had promised money, ranging from the Jewish farm settlements in Russia to the city of Berlin for a dental clinic, to the University of Chicago. Because of the Depression, all these charities were suffering significant financial loss and thus were eager to obtain the promised funds immediately.

Lessing's first action was to engage a large group of assistants. There were two legal firms, an accounting firm, and others. As his chief assistant he chose Nathan W. Levin, whom his father had hired as an accountant for the foundation in 1929. Levin proved to be extremely competent in dealing with the numerous thorny problems that arose. It took four and a half years to settle the estate, and administrative costs came to $800,000.

At the time of JR's death, the estate had a net value of $17,415,450, with assets of $48,621,616 and liabilities of a staggering $31,206,166. Approximately two-thirds of these liabilities were owed to six institutions:

First National Bank of Chicago	$2,360,000
Continental Illinois National Bank and Trust Company	4,038,975
Chase National Bank	7,825,000
Museum of Science and Industry	5,000,000
University of Chicago	900,943
Sangamon Corporation	770,091
TOTAL	$20,895,009

Except for the Sangamon Corporation, an investment company whose entire stock was owned by JR's three oldest children, "the liabilities were incurred for the purpose of obtaining funds to pay philanthropic commitments, guarantees of indebtedness of philanthropic organizations, business associates and employees of Sears Roebuck & Co., or for direct contributions to philanthropic organizations, payable in the future."[61] This sum included the note to Chase National Bank that JR had guaranteed to rescue the three hundred Sears employees, loans to Embree and General Wood, and aid to numerous charitable organizations.

The percentage of the estate's assets in Sears stock lost 70 percent of its value from the time of JR's death to the end of June 1932. That portion of the estate in diversified stocks also continued to decline. Two facts became clear to Lessing and his advisors. One was that, if the downward economic spiral continued, the estate would be insolvent and many groups and individuals would get nothing. The other was that if there were an attempt to liquidate the estate, the effect of selling such a large amount of Sears stock would further depress the price of that stock.

Thus the estate's lawyers, with the consent of the six major creditors, negotiated a historic "Standstill Agreement," which was signed on May 11, 1932, and it bound the parties not to press the estate for payment. A party could opt out after giving ninety days' notice, but it was clearly in the interest of all the parties to sit tight. It was assumed that eventually the bottom of the market decline would be reached, and then the stock would begin increasing in value. Lessing and the lawyers guaranteed that a payment plan would be worked out once the stock did rise. This agreement was accepted by the probate court, presided over by Judge (and future Illinois governor) Henry Horner, who had known JR and was probably sympathetic to the plight of the estate, though there is no implication that he did anything unethical in concurring with the Standstill Agreement.

For the next four years, payments were worked out with the six parties to the agreement, beginning with the University of Chicago. After negotiations, the university settled for a cash payment of $375,000 on November 16, 1932. The museum took longer, but eventually the amount owed it was paid partly by the Rosenwald Family Association (as specified in JR's will) and partly by the estate. Since the Sangamon Corporation consisted of JR's children, an agreement was easily reached. It took somewhat longer to deal with the banks, but by 1936, when the price of Sears stock had risen to around $44 a share, arrangements were worked out with all of them.

One of the other major creditors was the American Society for Jewish Farm Settlement, which continued to needle the estate and JR's heirs for payments. At the time of JR's death, they were owed over $2 million. They were ultimately paid by the Rosenwald Family Association, which gave back to the organization the bonds that had been issued to JR by the Soviet government and that, unfortunately, were worthless.

Besides the Standstill Agreement, the other notable accomplishment of those working for the estate was the raising of much needed cash through the sale back to Sears of a large block of its capital common stock. The genesis of this arrangement was the purchase by JR of the land on which the Sears plant stood for $16 million in 1921. In 1931, General Wood worked out an agreement with JR to repurchase the land after JR's death. Lessing, eager to obtain cash so as to begin settling tax obligations and other claims, sought a modification of the agreement with Wood. Under the new agreement, Sears would purchase 188,235 shares of its capital common stock for $4 million cash. The estate then had the option to buy back this block of stock by December 31, 1936, for $4 million plus an additional sum that was an adjustment of other payments. By December 1936, the value of that block of stock had risen to $11 million. Needless to say, Lessing took advantage of the opportunity.

The fact that the Standstill Agreement was worked out and adhered to without a problem is remarkable, as was the perfectly legal transaction with Sears. The other fascinating aspect of the settlement of the estate is that it took place in broad daylight. Random articles would appear occasionally in the *New York Times* or the *Chicago Tribune* containing the latest news of what was happening with the estate of Julius Rosenwald. This is probably what Henry Horner wanted, and Lessing was only too happy to comply. The estate had nothing to hide.

The Rosenwald Family Association

Created on December 28, 1931, just days before JR's death, this organization, which was essentially a foundation, was designed to give away $11 million according to the terms of JR's will. At the time of the association's creation, JR transferred assets worth $3.2 million to the newly formed charity. These included 2,000 shares of Sears and over $2 million worth of Soviet bonds from the Jewish agricultural colonies project. Eventually, once the estate was settled, some $9 million in addition was placed in the hands of the association. Like the rest of the estate, the

Rosenwald Family Association benefited from the upturn in the economy and the consequent price rise of Sears stock and the fact that the Standstill Agreement had held up.

The most important task performed by the Rosenwald Family Association was paying off the obligations incurred to many of JR's major creditors which were charitable organizations, including the Museum of Science and Industry and the American Society for Jewish Farm Settlements to whom it gave back the bonds. Other charitable organizations to whom JR had made smaller pledges were also satisfied. Additional funds were then distributed to charitable groups in which the children were interested. Perhaps the most remarkable untold story of how some of the Rosenwald Family Association money was spent was the rescue of close to one hundred Rosenwald and Nusbaum family members from Nazi Germany just before and during World War II. A social worker, Max Perlman, was hired to manage their departure from Europe and to ease their transition to American life. Thus Perlman helped find jobs for those able to work and ensured that schooling was available for the children. While not perhaps on the scale of a Schindler's List rescue, this act by the Family Association nevertheless saved numerous German family members from the concentration camps and the gas chambers and enabled them to lead useful lives as American citizens.

The Rosenwald Family Association lasted until around 1950. By December 31, 1947, it had given away $11,323,890 and still had $1,130,274 left over. In 1944, the five children each decided to form their own foundation and to spend the Rosenwald Family Association out of existence, a concept of which JR would have highly approved. Approximately $3.6 million of the Association's assets were distributed in almost equal shares of around $700,000 apiece to these foundations. It is interesting to note that each of the five foundations of JR's children was also self-liquidating, which was precisely what JR had envisioned.

The Rescue of the Fund

After JR's death, with the Depression worsening, Embree and the board and staff of the Julius Rosenwald Fund watched in horror as their assets, all in Sears stock, melted away. Convinced that the stock price would soon rise, the board decided not to sell the stock at the prevailing depreciated prices. But then how were they to pay the millions of dollars of pledges that JR had made? In desperation, they took out a $1.2 million loan from the First National Bank of Chicago. But the interest on that loan was considerable, and with the grants they had already approved added to that, it was clear that the Rosenwald Fund was in deep trouble.

Embree decided to appeal to his colleagues in the foundation world. Because the foundation had several projects involving libraries in Southern states, he approached the Carnegie Corporation, which had an extensive library program but was not much in evidence in the South. The president of the corporation, Henry Pritchett, had known and admired JR. Thus Embree's plea for assistance proved to be relatively easy. The Carnegie Corporation, without engaging in extensive investigations, granted $200,000 to the Rosenwald Fund to help it pay for these library projects. At the same time, Embree went back to his former employers, the Rockefellers, hat in hand.

In mid-May, Embree called on his old friend Raymond Fosdick, a longtime Rockefeller advisor. Embree followed his conversation up with a letter, signed by him and Lessing, who was chairman of the foundation. They were unabashedly honest about the problem. "The economic debacle has swiftly changed our financial position, so that the astonishing situation has arisen in which the commitments on our books actually exceed the current market value of our capital assets." They were also honest about the bank loan, stating that First National was not calling in the loan, but had asked them not to sell any of their assets at greatly deflated prices. "We seem to be confronted, therefore, with the alternative either of failing to pay a number of our pledges as they fall due, or of selling our capital securities in the present distressed market, or both." They asked the Rockefeller charities to "underwrite current payments of our obligations for a brief period in any amount you feel proper." However, they suggested $500,000 on the grounds that the General Education Board and the Rosenwald Fund were supporting a number of similar projects.[62]

The reaction to this letter was not cordial. The Rockefeller officers felt that the Rosenwald Fund should never have placed itself in such a situation. They were especially scornful of the bank loan. Thomas Debevoise, the lawyer for the Rockefeller charities, said that he "was not certain but thinks there is considerable responsibility resting upon the Rosenwald Trustees for their failure to sell their stock before it reached present levels."[63]

Debevoise quickly dismissed the idea of any kind of underwriting or loan. That was said to be impossible for legal reasons. Unlike the Carnegie Corporation, the Rockefeller charities never even considered an outright gift.

Embree returned at the beginning of June and was forced to undergo a thoroughly humiliating experience. He was asked to go over every single pledge, to see if there were ways to extend some without doing undue harm to the recipient, and attempting to take responsibility for others. At the same time, the Rockefeller officers were making their own lists based on the involvement of the General Education Board in the project or institution under discussion. On June 3, the matter was brought before the executive committee of the General Education Board; it was agreed that up to $200,000 could be applied to assisting the Rosenwald Fund. Interestingly enough, this news was kept from Embree when he talked with Max Mason, the GEB's president.[64] As Mason described it to his colleague Trevor Arnett: "I called Embree to New York following the meeting [of the GEB executive committee] and he went over their commitments in detail furnishing us thereby with a list of pledges which the Rosenwald Fund is unable to meet. This was in no sense a conference between two boards to save one, but was merely information from Embree to save our time."[65]

The system of payments that was worked out was designed to maximize the humiliation of the Rosenwald Fund. Embree was to inform approximately fourteen grantee organizations that the Rosenwald Fund would be unable to meet its obligation. This was to be followed by a visit to the charitable organization by Jackson Davis, a staff member of the GEB, to evaluate the situation. The organization was then informed that they could apply to the GEB for some or all of the pledged funds, but this proposal would have to go through the usual channels and procedures. If the funds were granted by the GEB, and the Rosenwald Fund later found itself able to make good on its pledge, it was to remit the money to the organization, and the recipient organization was to pay back the GEB. This legal sleight-of-hand was clearly to avoid any hint that this money was a loan. With his back to the wall, Embree agreed to these terms.

At the end of June, another plea for help arrived at the offices of the General Education Board. S. L. Smith, the Rosenwald Fund's staff member in charge of the school building program, sent a plaintive letter to Jackson Davis. The Fund had been counting on a dividend from its Sears stock to pay for the obligations incurred under the school building program, which, though formally ended, still had a number of pledges outstanding that Smith felt obligated to honor. With the price of Sears stock still sinking, it was clear that these dividends, due the beginning of August, would not be forthcoming, since Sears had suspended payment of dividends. As Smith wrote: "It will be extremely embarrassing to all concerned if we cannot pay for these schoolhouses, and will affect Negro education in many communities." Davis replied that it was most unlikely that the GEB would do anything in this matter except on the formal request of the state superintendent of education.[66] Smith kept up the pressure. Each of the schools to which the Fund owed money was in an area that had never had a black primary school before. His initial estimate of the need was $35,000. Eventually Jackson Davis acceded, and the actual situation concerning the Rosenwald Fund and the schools was quantified and clarified. Money was needed for forty schools, shops, and teachers' homes in fifteen states. The total amount came to $45,900.[67] Complicated procedures were worked out. Since the money from the Rosenwald Fund was the last piece in the funding puzzle for each school, Smith first had to check that all the Rosenwald Fund regulations concerning the building—the structure, the materials, and the funding—had been met. Smith was then to inform the state superintendents of education of this fact, and then tell them that, unfortunately, the Fund could not pay them at this time, but that they could formally apply to the GEB for the funds. The money for this was to come out of the $200,000 voted by the GEB on June 3. Unlike the deal worked out with Embree, there was to be no repayment of this money. It was to be, in essence, a grant from the General Education Board, based on the fact that the GEB, like the Rosenwald Fund, had as its mission the furtherance of black education in the South.

A few days after the meeting at which the GEB formally agreed to assist with the school building program, a letter was received at the GEB offices from John D. Rockefeller Jr.'s secretary. Her employer had received two letters from black universities thanking him for making good on the pledge of the Rosenwald Fund. John D. Jr. wanted to know what in the world was going on.[68] It seems curious that the GEB staff had failed to inform the Rockefeller family of the actions they had taken with regard to the Rosenwald Fund. However, an explanation was soon forthcoming. Thomas Appleget, a member of the GEB staff, wrote Rockefeller's secretary that the rapid fall in the price of shares of Sears stock "has created a serious situation in many institutions in which the General Education Board was interested with the Rosenwald Fund and in which the General Education Board had already made considerable investments."[69]

Embree returned in the fall, and at its November meeting the board of the Rosenwald Fund passed a resolution formally thanking the GEB for its assistance.

In the spring of 1934, the Rosenwald Fund was finally able to pay back its obligations to the GEB (by paying the institutions and having them repay the GEB), and a general accounting was made. It turned out the GEB had given money for Rosenwald Fund projects over the $200,000 limit it had set. A total of $69,119 was repaid to five institutions, ranging from $29,472 to Fayetteville, North Carolina, State Normal School (for buildings) to $3,450 to Flint-Goodridge Hospital in New Orleans (part of the new Dillard University) for special teaching services. Items that did not have to be repaid amounted to $74,161: $47,175 was for the completion of Rosenwald school buildings, and $26,986 was for the support of vocational shop supervisors in Southern states, a long-standing program of the Rosenwald Fund for which S. L. Smith had sought funding. A third category was payments the GEB made in the form of emergency grants, "the effect of which was not to relieve the Julius Rosenwald Fund of obligations but simply to postpone the time of payment of the Fund's pledges by one or more years." The original appropriations were retained on the Rosenwald Fund's books. The total here amounted to $113,793 to six institutions: four black colleges or universities, George Peabody College for Teachers (a white institution in Nashville), and the University of Chicago clinics. The grand total of GEB assistance came to $257,074.[70] Thanks to the General Education Board and the Carnegie Corporation, the Rosenwald Fund was saved, but certainly in the case of the GEB, Embree had been forced to undergo a truly humiliating experience. The papers of the GEB reveal an atmosphere in which a conscious effort was made to keep this example of inter-foundation cooperation largely secret. In their book on the Fund, Embree and Waxman are silent on this episode in the chapter dealing with the Fund's history. Only in the chapter entitled "How the Fund Operated" is there this curious, rather elliptical description of the events just described:

> A serious problem came with the financial crisis during the depression. Pledges to institutions made when the market was high, fell due when

> Sears stock, representing all the Fund's assets, had dropped to a fraction of its former value. In careful financial arrangements to meet this crisis, sister foundations helped generously. The General Education Board gave a number of emergency grants to Negro schools and colleges, thus making possible postponement of payment on the Fund's current pledges without hardship to the institutions concerned. The Carnegie Corporation, long interested in library service, appropriated a total of two hundred thousand dollars in 1932 and 1933 to support the program of library extension in southern counties. By agreement with the beneficiaries, interest rather than capital was paid on larger pledges, and payment for current expenses were spread over a longer period than originally planned. These measures enabled the Fund to meet all its pledges and to continue active work for another sixteen years.[71]

The virtual bankruptcy of the Fund was not alluded to, nor was the true nature of the arrangements with the General Education Board described.

Investment in People

The Rosenwald Fund was the first foundation to go out of existence voluntarily in accordance with the expressed wishes of its founder. Thus the book by Embree and Waxman was the first such account of the history and accomplishments of a liquidated foundation in American history. Both this slim volume and the Fund itself deserve appraisal. 

The most notable aspect of Embree and Waxman's book, *Investment in People,* is its candor and objectivity. This becomes apparent even in the first chapter, which is a very balanced discussion of JR—warts and all. "He was not a man of erudition," say the authors, and then in a passage which sounds somewhat like Embree's last memos to JR, they continue:

> It would be a mistake to leave the impression that Julius Rosenwald was a saint. His own modesty would have been outraged by such a suggestion. His faults and idiosyncrasies and a certain unpredictability which bewildered his associates were part of the humanness of the man. Those who worked with him remembered sudden quick tempers, unpleasant interviews at which they were thoroughly berated for real or fancied faults. But they remember, too, that he never played the role of the big executive, that anyone in the huge plant from stock boys to department heads could walk into his office and talk to him at any time. They remember that he refused

to pay them more than the market wages, that he vehemently disapproved gambling on the market.[72]

This evenhandedness continues to be displayed throughout the book. With a candor rare in such reports, Embree freely admits that the Rosenwald Fund had its disappointments as well as its successes. For example, in the section dealing with the schools, Embree, after pointing to the program's many successes, gives this critique in words with which James Anderson, a modern-day critic of the Fund, would surely agree: "In spite of interest, effort, and substantial progress, Negro children in 1932 were not yet receiving anywhere near their share of school money. The trustees and officers of the Fund recognized the continued inadequacies of provisions for Negro schools."[73] The reasons for failure lay outside the Fund, but Embree was disappointed that the Fund had not had a greater influence on the social climate. The same theme reappears in the chapter dealing with race relations. The Fund put a considerable amount of money and effort into this area, particularly after JR's death. Among other programs, they helped fund many of the NAACP cases that resulted in *Brown v. Board of Education of Topeka.* But in 1948 that decision had not been rendered, and although Embree saw some progress in race relations, it was not as great as he would have liked. Even in the chapter on the fellowships granted to black artists and intellectuals, which consists mostly of case studies of success stories and a detailed description of how the selection process worked, Embree presents a nuanced picture. "There were, of course, failures of judgment. There were fellows, both white and Negro, whose achievement fell far short of their promise, whose careers have not justified the faith and confidence placed in them. But their number has been relatively small."[74]

In examining the history of the Julius Rosenwald Fund, its impact and its reflection of the ideals of its founder are both important. Much of the funding the foundation carried out represented a form of public-private partnership that was not unique to the era but that is not seen much today, at a time when government itself is often distrusted and the funds for government to take over privately started programs are often lacking. This is a point stressed by Judith Sealander in her monograph *Private Wealth and Public Life.* JR and others involved in philanthropy in the early twentieth century believed fervently that if they could create a successful program, government would take it over eventually. One way of ensuring the governmental adoption of a project was to make government entities stakeholders initially through challenge grants. JR's interest in this type of cooperation with government goes back at least to 1913 with his imaginative use of corporate philanthropy: Sears's funding of agricultural extension agents in the Midwest. This program was indeed adopted by the Agriculture Department only a few years later. Other examples, such as the Chicago dental clinics in schools, were not so successful, with the Chicago city government failing to fulfill its expected side of the arrangement. But such failures did not dampen JR's belief that government should participate in and take over successful projects. As Sealander proves, he was not alone in this belief. The president of the Russell Sage Foundation, the Rockefellers, and others subscribed to similar ideas. But JR's faith in these partnerships imbued his philanthropy and was carried on by Embree until the Fund's end in 1948.

Another notable aspect of both the Fund and JR is that they were not afraid to become involved in important issues that no one else would touch. A perfect example of this is their decision to deal with the subject of making health care affordable to all Americans. In so doing, they incurred the wrath of the American Medical Association but remained undeterred. In the process, they emphasized a new field, medical economics, and tried to arrive at solutions to questions posed in that discipline. Out of a conference held in the mid-1930s under the auspices of the Rosenwald Fund emerged the organization that became Blue Cross–Blue Shield. That the Fund did not succeed in this area is clear, for the issue of affordable health care still confronts us with as great a sense of urgency as it did in the 1930s and 1940s.

Another controversial area that the Julius Rosenwald Fund entered to a greater degree than other American foundations is the field of race relations, and here the influence of the Fund was certainly wide-ranging, if not entirely successful. The Fund surely was a pathbreaker here, too, if not a lone voice. The Rosenwald Fund was the most progressive philanthropy working in this area. The General Education Board and such foundations as the Phelps-Stokes Fund did a great deal. Their role cannot be minimized. But in terms of leadership, of actively supporting the most progressive of the black and white organizations working for better race relations, the Rosenwald Fund was clearly of paramount importance. JR and Embree truly did come to see racial equality as the ultimate goal. This was not achieved by the time the Fund ended, but the accomplishments of the

Fund were still considerable. In the field of education, Embree estimated that by 1932, "15,000 teachers were giving instruction to 650,000 colored children in Rosenwald-sponsored schools in every Negro county in the South . . . The number of buildings aided by the Fund exceeded the total number of schools of every sort which existed for Negroes in the Southern states at the beginning of the Fund's program."[75]

If one realizes that the number of children attending Rosenwald schools at any one time doubtless increased in the succeeding thirty years, it becomes clear that generations of black children numbering in the millions obtained their only chance of a decent education at a Rosenwald school. The civil rights movement and the coming of desegregation meant that almost all of these schools (which had become physically inferior by the 1960s) were forced to close. Schools in the South were consolidated, and black children were enabled to attend better equipped schools. But interviews with alumni(ae) reveal that many of those who attended Rosenwald schools remembered them fondly. In many cases, the good basic education they had received in those schools had provided them with the opportunity to advance to careers and positions in society that had been impossible for their grandfathers and grandmothers. This is why there is a revival of interest and an effort to preserve these school buildings, which form an important part of the black heritage. Some have been torn down. Others have been remodeled into homes or stores. A few still survive as schools. In 2002, all surviving Rosenwald schools as a generic group were placed on the list of eleven most endangered structures by the National Trust for Historic Preservation. Partly as a result of this designation, surviving school buildings are being refurbished and transformed into senior centers, community centers, and tourist attractions as museums of black culture of the 1920s and 1930s.

Nor were the schools the only notable achievement of JR and the Fund. The Fund sponsored important programs that trained teachers for Rosenwald schools. It created busing programs so that black children in those rural areas could travel to and from school. The rural libraries started by the Fund were designed to break down racial barriers: they provided books to blacks and whites alike. In terms of medical care, the Fund pioneered in trying to bring to blacks some equalization of what was provided to white Americans, not only aiding such black hospitals as Provident in Chicago and Flint-Goodridge in New Orleans but also supporting the training of black doctors and black nurses.

The fellowship program provided money and recognition to almost every significant black artist and thinker of the 1930s and 1940s. A partial list of the best known reveals the astonishing breadth of this program: Marian Anderson, Augusta Savage, Catherine Dunham, John Hope Franklin, Jacob Lawrence, Zora Neale Hurston, Ralph Bunche, Langston Hughes, W. E. B. DuBois, and Ralph Ellison (who wrote *The Invisible Man* on a Rosenwald fellowship). Southern whites were also aided by Rosenwald fellowships, notably C. Vann Woodward and Ralph McGill. This fellowship program was truly unique in its day and gave a start to many people who otherwise might have labored in obscurity—black and white. Not every Rosenwald fellow became famous, but the number of people who used the award to embark on their careers is remarkable.

Finally, the foundation supported efforts to bring about racial equality. It would be absurd to say that without the Rosenwald Fund, the civil rights movement would not have happened. But it is certainly true that the Rosenwald Fund was in the vanguard of philanthropies contributing to racial justice. It might even be true that, by helping to advance the cause of civil rights, the Fund helped ensure that the civil rights movement would obtain the attention it deserved. This was probably JR's and the Fund's greatest legacy.

Conclusion

In his pathbreaking book *The Search for Order, 1877–1920,* Robert H. Wiebe describes the advent of a new American middle class around 1900. The men and women who made up this group were characterized by their optimism, their professionalism, their desire to impose order through bureaucracy. They were politically astute and worked in their communities for the reform of local government, wishing it to run smoothly and efficiently and be accountable to the people. In terms of national politics, they tended to be Republican, and their idol was Theodore Roosevelt. Moreover, they had a strong sense of the importance of a national government, as opposed to the localism that had been prevalent earlier. They believed in the power of education and in the gathering of relevant data to solve seemingly intractable problems. These, according to Wiebe, were the Progressives.

Julius Rosenwald fits snugly into this picture. He was born into the middle class, and although he attained great wealth, he retained the values and outlook of his social upbringing. He could be pragmatic, but he also was very much the optimist, in terms of both his business and his philanthropy. Moreover, he was forward-looking in both realms. For example, when he retired from the presidency of Sears in 1924, he knew the direction in which the company had to go; that is why he hired General Wood as vice president and later chose him as president. In terms of philanthropy, he envisioned a society where private initiative and government worked hand in hand.

As president of Sears, he was clearly conscious of his professional status, which is, in part, why the company flourished under his leadership. A thorough knowledge of retailing on a mass scale also led to his brief success working with the Council of National Security during World War I. While JR railed against bureaucracy in philanthropy, he meant a particular type of bureaucracy that did not look to the future but was stultifying, satisfied with the status quo and its own perpetuation. His great accomplishment at Sears was to systematize and bring order out of chaos through the creation of a bureaucracy that was effective but not rigid. In terms of philanthropy, JR recognized that he and William Graves could not handle the enormous burden of importunate requests and that professionalism and a staff were needed in his foundation, too. That is why he reorganized the foundation in 1928 and hired Edwin Embree, a professional foundation officer, to run it.

JR was definitely involved in local politics, particularly the Merriam campaign for mayor of Chicago in 1911. His concern for the Bureau of Public Efficiency over which he presided in the 1910s indicates that he was wholly in favor of honest and transparent government. It was his aversion to corruption that led him to make his unfortunate offer to Senatorial candidate Frank Smith. Moreover, JR served on various ad hoc commissions, from the Chicago Vice Commission in 1910 to the body that investigated the city's race riots of 1919. In national politics he was a devoted Republican, supporting every candidate of that party from Taft to Coolidge. He was truly elated by the election of his friend Herbert Hoover, another Progressive, many of whose ideas and ideals he shared. One of these ideas was that government should be supported by experts who served on appointed committees outside the purview of Congress and who gathered and analyzed data to deal with issues of national importance. JR contributed funds to one of these bodies.

Although Julius Rosenwald never completed high school, a fact that troubled him all his life, he was a fervent believer in the importance of education as a means of advancement. Thus he viewed education as the path that could take African Americans out of the poverty and racial quagmire they faced in the South, and he was willing to contribute to educational institutions of all kinds from the University of Chicago and Harvard to teaching hospitals and medical schools for blacks. Another aspect of Wiebe's middle-class Progressives was an admiration for social sciences, including social work. JR was led to social work through his friendship with Jane Addams and Minnie Low, and from there to his support of the School of Civics and Philanthropy and such organizations as the Social Science Research Council to which the Rosenwald Fund made numerous contributions after 1928.

In short, Julius Rosenwald was clearly a Progressive, which is why Kathleen D. McCarthy places him squarely in that movement in her book *Noblesse Oblige.*

How have historians judged Julius Rosenwald as a businessman and as a philanthropist? Boris Emmet and John E. Jeuck, the historians of Sears, Roebuck, are perhaps the most harsh in examining JR's role. The "Rosenwald era," they assert, "was essentially one of great gains, consolidation, and conservation." The main achievement of the period 1908 to 1924 was "better control of operating costs."[1] Otherwise, they view JR mainly as a naysayer. They claim that he was initially opposed to the profit sharing plan, the rescue of the company in 1921, and the introduction of retail stores. He consolidated the achievements of Richard Sears and aided the integrity and good name of the company by eliminating patent medicines from the catalog and opening the testing laboratory. The impression of JR that emerges from their book is that he was a man who essentially lacked vision and drive. While it is certainly true that JR lacked the ruthless streak that existed in the business practices of men like Rockefeller and Carnegie, it is also true that JR was no mere conservator.

JR was not an original thinker in the business realm. But he accepted and adopted the ideas of others, and as CEO he made the vital decisions that enabled Sears to remain in the forefront of the retail industry. In so doing, JR displayed keen judgment and sharp business sense.

Other historians and business experts are far more laudatory of JR's achievements. The noted business writer Peter Drucker unfairly dismisses Richard Sears as "a shrewd speculator." It was not Sears but Julius Rosenwald who made the company into "a business enterprise," says Drucker. He adds: "[Rosenwald] built the productive human organization, and gave management people a maximum of authority and full responsibility for results. . . . [He] is the father not only of Sears, Roebuck but of the distribution revolution which has changed the world economy in the twentieth century and which is so vital a factor in economic growth."[2]

Drucker's is the most extravagant claim made for JR's legacy, and it appears to be unfair to both Richard Sears and Otto Doering, the architect of the famous scheduling system.

Raymond D. Smith and William P. Darrow, authors of an article on the rise of Sears, Roebuck & Co., would seem to agree with Drucker in some respects. "Julius Rosenwald," they write, "was a visionary in terms of management, process and administration. In particular, he was ahead of his time in terms of his approaches to organization and employee relations. . . . Rosenwald was the chief strategist who took Sears into the 20th century and laid the foundation for the growth that followed." Smith and Darrow then explain JR's merchandising creed: "(1) Sell honest merchandise for less and people will buy, and (2) Never waiver in your commitment to maintaining quality." But JR's greatest achievement in business, according to these authors, is "logical incrementalism," which they define as "avoiding overcommitment and non-retractable blunders." This, they say, "describes the cautious yet simultaneously thoughtful approaches implemented during Mr. Rosenwald's tenure."[3]

One of the sources cited by Smith and Darrow is a more recent history of Sears by Gordon L. Weil. His assessment of JR is thoughtful and balanced. Summing up JR's presidency, he writes:

> [H]e believed in his business . . . and was determined to adapt it to changing conditions and make it work. He was able to bring out the best in his subordinates and to make sure that new ideas were put into effect. . . . He understood his business and the nature of competition completely. . . . He was the model of the modern corporate manager. But he was more than that. He was honest and he demanded honesty. He believed that fair management of a private company could bring benefit to society as a whole. He realized that business was not everything in life and devoted himself to extraordinary philanthropy with as much zeal as he ran Sears. Above all, Julius Rosenwald saw himself as a trustee.[4]

An additional assessment of JR comes from a study of mass marketing in America that uses the history of Sears, Roebuck as a case study. Richard S. Tedlow examines what he calls "traits" of JR which served him well through the trials of his business life. The first was "his intense sanity and grip on reality." Second, "unlike Sears, Rosenwald was a systematizer and institution builder." Tedlow acknowledges the importance of Otto Doering, but Doering reported to JR even when Richard Sears was president, and it was JR who understood and insisted upon the creation of an orderly and efficient system for sending out orders, a system which Doering created. Third, "because Rosenwald understood the needs of the company, he was able to modulate his strategy in the face of different circumstances." A fourth trait was JR's "ability to withstand severe interpersonal conflict in the service of his company's goals and of his own." Finally, "in addition to Rosenwald's level headedness and personal toughness that helped him emerge as a great leader of the firm was the high standard of conduct to which he held his firm and himself."[5]

Tedlow has high praise for General Wood and says that the decision to move into retail stores "took judgment and courage." But he appears to recognize that JR shares the responsibility for making this choice when he refers to the "Rosenwald-Wood decision."[6] Those who laud General Wood sometimes forget who hired him, knowing exactly what his agenda was with regard to retail stores. As the article JR wrote on the effect of movies and automobiles on American consumers makes clear, he was far more willing to countenance the move to stores than Emmet and Jeuck believe.

Three aspects of JR's career at Sears stand out. One noted by almost all historians and commentators is his honesty and integrity. There was always a whiff of the carny about Richard Sears that JR lacked. Hence his decision to eliminate patent medicines from the catalog and his creation of the testing laboratory. Another striking example of JR's integrity was his refusal to cancel contracts in light of the recession of 1920–21, even though his competitors were not so scrupulous. Such a decision may have endangered the company in the short run, but after JR's bailout of the firm, it probably helped Sears, Roebuck's reputation, at least among suppliers.

A second notable aspect of JR's tenure at Sears is his deep concern for the company and its employees. JR took heat for the wages he paid his lowliest female workers, but such wages were the going rate in the retail industry at the time. However, as a Progressive business leader, JR was in the forefront of the welfare capitalism movement, which created numerous amenities for workers. This stance was taken not because he feared labor unions but because JR believed that contented workers would perform better. The profit sharing plan was eagerly accepted by JR, and it brought real benefits to those who participated in it, including the lowest paid employees. JR's rescue of the company in 1921 and his bailout of the three hundred Sears employees who were in serious danger of bankruptcy in the autumn of 1929 are clear testaments to the concern that JR felt for Sears and its workers.

Finally, JR understood his company and the business environment in which he operated. He knew in 1908 that he was right about the future of mail order and how Sears, Roebuck should market itself and that Richard Sears's views on these subjects were incorrect. And he knew in 1924 that the shift to retail stores had to be made, even as he realized that he was not the person who could best make this move.

Julius Rosenwald was a Progressive not only in terms of politics and business but also in terms of philanthropy. As Kathleen McCarthy notes, "Progressive spokesmen demanded social justice. . . . Rather than helping the few, social justice would improve the urban environment as a whole." And she continues in a sentence that has striking relevance to JR: "Rather than constructing eternal monuments, the new philanthropy was to be 'of a disappearing nature,' experimenting with untried techniques, promoting the passage of socially-oriented laws, and subsequently passing on to new causes."[7] JR's dislike of perpetual named foundations does not merely stem from his Progressive beliefs—it is more deeply rooted and more carefully developed. Yet it does appear to fit within the pattern that McCarthy describes. She also believes that pragmatism and the use of experts to serve as a buffer between donor and recipient characterized progressive philanthropy. JR initially asked scattered experts such as Booker T. Washington or Abraham Flexner for advice, and he employed an assistant, William Graves, whose job was, in part, to obtain information on potential grantee organizations. It was not until 1928 that JR hired Embree and a staff essentially to take over the administration of the foundation, although he by no means withdrew from his philanthropic endeavors.

In an accurate and thoughtful statement, McCarthy sums up JR's "philanthropic credo" as "prevention, deinstitutionalization, and flexibility."[8] Examples of all three words are not hard to find. An instance of prevention would be the Rosenwald schools, designed to prevent Southern black children in rural areas from being deprived of an education; the crusade against orphanages on behalf of the Home Finding Society is a perfect example of deinstitutionalization; and the extreme flexibility of JR's programs can be seen in his gift to the University of Chicago, the "Suspense Account," where the only stipulation was that principal as well as interest be spent in a given year.

Two works of historical scholarship place JR in the context of his age by comparing him to the other titans of philanthropy, John D. Rockefeller and Andrew Carnegie. In his book *Inside American Philanthropy,* Waldemar Nielsen explicitly compares and contrasts these men in his chapter "Three Giants of the Past."

John D. Rockefeller Sr. was "a strategic or executive donor, not a hands-on or meddling type." Somewhat like JR, he was "in business as in philanthropy attentive, methodical and decisive." In a phrase that sounds remarkably similar to JR's speech to the Joint Distribution Committee in 1926 about the Russian colonies project, Nielsen says that Rockefeller saw the main task of philanthropy as attacking the root causes of distress, not merely alleviating symptoms. This was the new philanthropy, which dealt not with persons but with issues.[9]

Andrew Carnegie, according to Nielsen, "was the most generous of this great threesome, and was an extremist in every sense—extreme in work, extreme in abilities and self-confidence, extreme in ambitions, extreme in his boosterism for everything in which he was involved." Like JR, Carnegie published his ideas about philanthropy in a widely read magazine article, and JR would have agreed with many of Carnegie's concepts. Carnegie believed that it was the duty of a rich man not to leave his wealth to his family but to spend it while alive. The wealthy individual should live unostentatiously, should provide a moderate amount for his heirs, and regard the bulk of his fortune as a public trust—with the man of wealth administering this money "in the manner which, in his judgment, is best calculated to provide the most beneficial results for the community."[10] JR did not share the paternalistic aspects of Carnegie's ideas, although he did believe in living unostentatiously, and he strongly believed that each generation should create its own philanthropy. But Carnegie did not carry his ideas far enough, for he did not, in fact, give the bulk of his fortune away in one generation. He donated it to a group of foundations, some devoted to very specific causes, such as the advancement of education, which were intended to last forever. By making his foundation self-liquidating, Julius Rosenwald departed from the example set by Andrew Carnegie.

In distinguishing among his three heroes, Nielsen says that Julius Rosenwald was "the most committed to making American democracy work and to the struggle against racial and religious intolerance." By focusing on JR's commitment to American democracy, Nielsen refers to his emphasis on assisting African Americans, which Rosenwald did view in terms of blacks taking their rightful place in America. Other characteristics of JR's philanthropy, according to Nielsen, is that it "was down-to-earth, flexible, compassionate, and people- rather than institution-centered. Its spirit was personal and hopeful." Summing up his thumbnail sketch of JR, Neilsen says: "He was a humanitarian and a believer in democracy. His generosity was based on a solid and clear set of principles and convictions. At home and abroad, he sought to be a social healer, a conciliator, a unifier." Neilsen's characterization of JR appears to capture well the essence of JR and his philanthropy.[11]

Judith Sealander describes "scientific philanthropy" and calls Julius Rosenwald one of its chief architects. She even defines scientific philanthropy with a quote from JR: "I made my money in retail trade—but when it comes to philanthropy I am predictably a wholesaler." This referred to dealing in big concepts and big plans, not the gift to alleviate an individual's plight, which JR called a "palliative." Sealander believes that scientific philanthropy arose from two sources. One was religion, specifically the "Social Gospel" which held that "true godliness required that believers actively combat society's problems." To heal the world was indeed one of the main tenets of Rabbi Emil Hirsch, who had so greatly influenced JR. The second origin of scientific philanthropy was system, the kind of order that JR brought to the management of Sears and to his foundation.[12]

Assessing the impact of scientific philanthropy, Sealander shows that it had an effect on three broad areas: education, medicine, and social sciences. In medicine, scientific philanthropy went to the root of such diseases as hookworm and pellagra and sought to eliminate them. It also revolutionized American medical education, something JR contributed to with his lead gift to the University of Chicago medical school. In terms of social science, it fostered an entire discipline, and its practitioners believed that the accumulation and analysis of data would enable them to solve problems. Here, too, JR under Embree's influence contributed via the Rosenwald Fund to organizations such as the Social Science Research Council. In terms of education, the picture is somewhat mixed. While scientific philanthropy led to important changes in curricula in higher education, its effect on public education was not impressive, and here Sealander specifically cites JR and his goal to improve race relations in America. There were certainly some achievements. "By 1930, more than half a million black children studied in clean, comfortable one- to six-room schoolhouses. The creation of a network of modern schools where none had previously existed was a momentous achievement." However, ultimately, JR was not successful. "He wanted the Rosenwald schools to create a revolution in public funding for education, to 'shame' public officials into spending equal, even if separate, amounts for the education of black and white people. That big idea did not have even a remote chance of acceptance in early twentieth-century America; it would be decades before equal funding for education would even become stated policy, much less a reality. Julius Rosenwald's hopes for race relations were decades ahead of those shared by most of his fellow citizens."[13]

This notion that JR was a visionary, decades ahead of his time when it comes to race relations, appears entirely accurate and serves to counter the criticism that he was somehow a racist because he was willing to accept the system of "separate but equal" rather than fight against it. The failure was not JR's because he accepted the "system"; rather, it was that of his fellow citizens who could not accept his vision of a society characterized by true racial equality.

There are two additional aspects of Rosenwald's philanthropy that are worth noting. One is that it was, as Nielsen suggests, "hands-on." When JR first became involved in a project, he did not merely accept the idea, write the checks, and hand the project over to someone else to run, as John D. Rockefeller did. JR became actively involved, offering suggestions and even fund-raising from others. His early involvement with both Tuskegee and the Rosenwald schools program demonstrates this.

Second was his desire to help what might be viewed as the underdog, the persecuted, whether it was the African American sharecropper in the rural South or the newly emancipated Jew in Soviet Russia.

Finally, it is important to note that both in business and philanthropy, JR seldom acted alone. In business he formed a coherent management team that consisted of himself, Albert Loeb, Otto Doering, and Max Adler. They ran Sears, although the ultimate decisions were made by JR. In philanthropy, JR also liked to work with others. That is why so many of his donations were in the form of challenge grants. He preferred public-private partnerships, a fact clearly demonstrated by the Rosenwald schools. Even in the case of the Museum of Science and Industry, he did not wish to be the sole individual contributor, and he continued to hope that others would step forward to help build and equip the innovative museum.

What is Julius Rosenwald's legacy, and what meaning does his life have for our era? In terms of business, his probity and concern for his employees certainly stands in marked contrast to the behavior exhibited by the CEOs of such major corporations as Enron. One cannot imagine Kenneth Lay, the CEO of Enron, giving his company millions of dollars of his own money to save it from serious financial difficulties. Nor can one imagine many contemporary business leaders staking their own money to save three hundred employees from financial ruin. Many corporate leaders of our day seem more interested in their bonuses and "golden parachutes" than in the welfare of their employees. In the case of the 1921 crisis, JR found that doing the "right thing" was financially beneficial as well.

In philanthropy, too, JR speaks to our day. JR was interested in funding projects not because they were popular or risk-free but because he believed in them. Such contemporary philanthropists as George Soros appear to operate on similar principles. Moreover, philanthropists today are increasingly thinking not of perpetuating their names with foundations that will last forever but of donating their money while they are still alive so that they can witness the fruits of their beneficence. The concept that each generation should give away its own money speaks to the differences that clearly do exist between generations. Thus a younger generation need not feel hobbled by the constraints of its forebearers to support causes in which they have no interest. Such a flexible concept may make it easier to interest younger generations in philanthropy. It is true that for a wealthy individual to donate a fortune while he or she is alive presupposes that the individual has the time, the wisdom, and the inclination to take such a step. It was one of JR's favorite aphorisms that it is far more difficult to contribute money wisely than to make it in the first place. Nevertheless, if Julius Rosenwald's ideas on philanthropy can stimulate greater numbers of wealthy young people to donate their funds to the causes they believe in, that will be one more reason why Julius Rosenwald's life, his example, and his ideas are still valuable today.

Notes

AJA	American Jewish Archives, Cincinnati
CHS	Chicago Historical Society
GEB	General Education Board
JDCA	Joint Distribution Committee Archives
JRFA	Julius Rosenwald Fund Archives, Fisk University
LC	Library of Congress
LV	LongueVue House and Gardens
MSI	Museum of Science and Industry, Chicago
RAC	Rockefeller Archive Center
UCL	University of Chicago Library

1. Youth and First Business Ventures, 1862–1895

1. M. R. Werner, *Julius Rosenwald: The Life of a Practical Humanitarian* (New York: Harper, 1939), 3–4.

2. Hasia R. Diner, *A Time for Gathering: The Second Migration* (Baltimore: Johns Hopkins University Press, 1992), 66–73.

3. Werner, *Rosenwald,* 6

4. Ibid., 8.

5. UCL, JR Papers, box 48, folder 7 (Werner Notes), Mrs. Samuel Rosenwald to Mrs. Bendix Rosenwald, February 15, 1872 (original in German).

6. UCL, JR Papers, box 48, folder 7 (Werner Notes), Samuel Rosenwald to his family in Bunde, February 15, 1872 (original in German). Quoted in Werner, *Rosenwald,* 11.

7. Dun Papers, Harvard Business School Library, Department of Special Collections, Sangamon County, Illinois, vol. 200, 646.

8. Part of a short autobiography written by JR in 1927. UCL, JR Papers, box 48, folder 7 (Werner Notes).

9. Werner, *Rosenwald,* 10.

10. American Jewish Archives, Cincinnati, "Address of Mr. Julius Rosenwald at the Euclid Avenue Temple, Friday evening, November 26, 1920, speaking in behalf of Hebrew Union College."

11. UCL, JR Papers, box 48, folder 7 (Werner Notes), Augusta Rosenwald to Frau Elise Rosenwald, P.S. by Samuel Rosenwald, June 23, 1881 (original in German). See Diner, *A Time for Gathering,* 169–200. The postscript by Samuel Rosenwald is cited by Diner on 228.

12. UCL, JR Papers, box 48, folder 7 (Werner Notes).

13. For a fascinating description of New York in this period, see Edwin G. Burrows and Mike Wallace, *Gotham: A History of New York City to 1898* (New York: Oxford University Press, 1998).

14. UCL, JR Papers, box 48, folder 7 (Werner Notes).

15. Ibid.

16. Dun Papers, Harvard Business School Library, Department of Special Collections, New York City, vol. 205, 900 (a) 24.

17. UCL, JR Papers, box 48, folder 7.

18. UCL, JR Papers, scrapbook 5, 12, postcard from JR to Aaron Hammerslough, October 12, 1881. "Business," said JR, "is dull."

19. UCL, JR Papers, box 26, folder 6, Henry Morgenthau to Herman Bernstein, April 24, 1928.

20. UCL, JR Papers, scrapbook 5, 80, article in a Springfield newspaper.

21. UCL, JR Papers, box 48, folder 8 (Werner Notes), Samuel Rosenwald to Mrs. Bernhard Rosenwald and Family, March 11, 1884 (original in German).

22. UCL, JR Papers, box 48, folder 8, M. Werner interview with Mo Newborg, 1934.

23. UCL, JR Papers, addendum II, box 1, folder 5, JR to L. B. Philip, December 19, 1916.

24. UCL, JR Papers, box 48, folder 8 (Werner Notes).

25. Werner, *Rosenwald,* 22.

26. UCL, JR Papers, box 48, folder 8 (Werner Notes), Samuel Rosenwald to Bernhard Rosenwald, December 11, 1880 (original in German).

27. Dun Papers, Harvard Business School Library, Department of Special Collections, Sangamon County, Illinois, vol. 200, 646.

28. For an excellent picture of Chicago in the period 1871–1900, see Donald L. Miller, *City of the Century: The Epic of Chicago and the Making of America* (New York: Simon & Schuster, 1997).

29. On Ward, see ibid., 244–47, and David Blanke, *Sowing the American Dream: How Consumer Culture Took Root in the Rural Midwest* (Athens: Ohio University Press, 2000), 181–214.

30. UCL, JR Papers, box 48, folder 8 (Werner Notes).

31. On Emanuel Nusbaum, see Christopher Ogden, *Aaron's Gift* (New York: privately published, 2002), 3–45.

32. Dun Papers, Harvard Business School, Department of Special Collections, New York City, Clinton County volume, 57.

33. UCL, JR Papers, box 48, folder 8 (Werner Notes), JR to Gussie, August 17, 1890.

34. UCL, JR Papers, box 48, folder 8 (Werner Notes), JR to Gussie, September 22, 1890.

35. UCL, JR Papers, box 48, folder 8 (Werner Notes), JR to Gussie, September 25, 1890.

36. UCL, JR Papers, box 48, folder 8 (Werner Notes), JR to Gussie, December 15, 1890.

37. UCL, JR Papers, box 48, folder 8 (Werner Notes), JR to Gussie, December 29, 1890.

38. UCL, JR Papers, box 48, folder 8 (Werner Notes), JR to Gussie, December 30, 1890.

39. LV, JR to Gussie, September 11, 1891.

40. UCL, JR Papers, box 48, folder 8 (Werner Notes), telegram from Julius Weil to JR, February 9, 1891.

41. UCL, JR Papers, box 48, folder 8 (Werner Notes), Samuel Rosenwald to JR, January 7, 1892.

42. UCL, JR Papers, box 48, folder 8 (Werner Notes), Samuel Rosenwald to JR and Julius Weil, July 9, 1892.

43. UCL, JR Papers, box 48, folder 8 (Werner Notes), Samuel Rosenwald to JR and Julius Weil, July 10, 1892.

44. LV, Gussie to JR, July 7, 1892.

45. LV, Gussie to JR, July 15, 1890.

46. LV, Gussie to JR, July 23, 1890.

47. LV, Gussie to JR, September 19, 1890.

48. LV, Gussie to JR, January 11, 1892.

49. LV, Gussie to JR, January 13, 1892.
50. LV, Gussie to JR, September 8, 1891.
51. UCL, JR Papers, box 48, folder 8 (Werner Notes), JR to Gussie, September 14, 1891.
52. LV, Gussie to JR, September 19, 1891.
53. LV, JR to Gussie, February 2, 1891 (2).
54. LV, JR to Gussie, February 2, 1891 (1).
55. LV, JR to Gussie, September 13, 1891, September 21, 1891.
56. LV, JR to Gussie, September 12, 1891.
57. LV, JR to Gussie September 21, 1891.
58. LV, Gussie to JR, January 7, 1892.
59. LV, Gussie to JR, September 18, 1890.
60. LV, Gussie to JR, January 9, 1892.
61. LV, Gussie to JR, September 21, 1890.
62. LV, Gussie to JR, January 12, 1892.
63. LV, Gussie to JR, July 15, 1890.
64. LV, Gussie to JR, July 6, 1892.
65. Sterling Library, Yale University, Jerome Frank Papers, box 6, folder 158, interview of Oscar J. Friedman by Florence Kiper Frank.
66. LV, Gussie to JR, September 22, 1891.
67. LV, Gussie to JR, September 14, 1891.
68. LV, Gussie to JR, May 24, 1892.
69. UCL, JR Papers, box 48, folder 8 (Werner Notes), following transcription of Gussie's letter to JR of January 18, 1893.
70. UCL, JR Papers, box 48, folder 8 (Werner Notes), Gussie to JR, July 9, 1893.
71. UCL, JR Papers, box 48, folder 8 (Werner Notes), Werner interview with Mo Newborg, 1934.
72. UCL, JR Papers, box 48, folder 8 (Werner Notes), JR autobiographical fragment.
73. An excellent description of the early history of Sears, Roebuck & Co. can be found in Boris Emmet and John E. Jeuck, *Catalogues and Counters: A History of Sears Roebuck & Co.* (Chicago: University of Chicago Press, 1950), esp. chap. 3.
74. Ibid., 26.
75. Ibid., 36.
76. Ibid., 46.
77. Leon Harris, *Merchant Princes* (New York: Berkley Books, 1979), 268. See also Ogden's *Aaron's Gift,* 55–57.
78. Werner, *Rosenwald,* 40.
79. Ibid., 39–40, and UCL, JR Papers, box 48, folder 8 (Werner Notes), interview with Mo Newborg.
80. Emmet and Jeuck, *Catalogues and Counters,* 49.

2. Early Sears Years, 1895–1908

1. Alfred D. Chandler Jr., *The Visible Hand: The Managerial Revolution in American Business* (Cambridge: Belknap Press of Harvard University, 1977).
2. William Cronon, *Nature's Metropolis: Chicago and the Great West* (New York: W. W. Norton, 1991), 337, 339–40.
3. UCL, JR Papers, box 55, folder 3 (Werner Notes), memo written by R. Buchner, July 11, 1918.
4. This excerpt is from the first, unpublished biography of JR by Florence Kiper Frank. It is quoted in Boris Emmet and John E. Jeuck, *Catalogues and Counters: A History of Sears Roebuck & Co.* (Chicago: University of Chicago Press, 1950), 129–30.
5. Cecil C. Hoge Sr., *The First Hundred Years Are the Toughest: What We Can Learn from the Century of Competition between Sears and Wards* (Berkeley: Ten Speed Press, 1988), 54.
6. Emmett and Jeuck, *Catalogues and Counters,* 113.

7. William Leach, *Land of Desire: Merchants, Power, and the Rise of a New American Culture* (New York: Vintage Press, 1993), 36.

8. Quoted in Louis E. Asher and Edith Head, *Send No Money* (Chicago: Argus Books, 1942), 10.

9. David Blanke, *Sowing the American Dream: How Consumer Culture Took Root in the Rural Midwest* (Athens: Ohio University Press, 2000), 200–15.

10. Frederick Asher, *Richard Warren Sears: Icon of Inspiration* (New York: Vantage Press, 1997), 60–61.

11. Asher and Head, *Send No Money,* 20.

12. Werner, *Rosenwald,* 49.

13. Emmett and Jeuck, *Catalogues and Counters,* quoting Asher in a letter to Florence K. Frank, 51.

14. Louis Rosenfield to Aaron Nusbaum, February 24, 1901. I owe this and other letters to Nusbaum to the kindness of Frank Weil, Nusbaum's grandson.

15. Louis Rosenfield to Nusbaum, February 26, 1901.

16. Louis Rosenfield to Nusbaum, April 29, 1901.

17. Sears to Nusbaum, March 25, 1901.

18. LV, Gussie to JR, May 4, 1904.

19. LV, Gussie to JR, May 11, 1904.

20. See Christopher Ogden, *Aaron's Gift* (New York: privately published, 2002), 92–121, for a description of Aaron Nusbaum's life after his ouster.

21. JoAnne Yates, *Control through Communication: The Rise of System in American Management* (Baltimore: Johns Hopkins University Press, 1993).

22. UCL, JR Papers, box 48, folder 12 (Werner Notes), JR to Mo Newborg, July 23, 1900.

23. Theodore Starett, "The Building of a Great Mercantile Plant," *Architectural Record* 19 (April 1906): 269.

24. Ibid., 273.

25. Ibid., 269.

26. George F. Nimmons and William K. Fellows, "Designing a Great Mercantile Plant," *Architectural Record* 19 (June 1906): 408.

27. In *Creating the Corporate Soul: The Rise of Public Relations and Corporate Imagery in American Business* (Berkeley: University of California Press, 1998), Richard Marchand notes that one important way that a business could create an image in the public mind was through its factory. Richard Sears was very successful in publicizing the pictures and descriptions of the new Sears, Roebuck plant and in personalizing the enterprise, so that visitors in those early days would come to the Homan Avenue facility expecting to see Mr. Sears himself.

28. Sears, Roebuck catalog, spring 1908, 5.

29. Stuart D. Brandes, *American Welfare Capitalism, 1880–1940* (Chicago: University of Chicago Press, 1976).

30. UCL, JR Papers, box 55, folder 5 (Werner Notes), Louis Asher to Mrs. Jerome Frank, September 8, 1932.

31. Asher and Head, *Send No Money,* 88.

32. Emmet and Jeuck, *Catalogues and Counters,* 78.

33. LV.

34. UCL, Louis E. Asher Papers, box 1, Asher to Sears, August 16, 1908. Underlining and punctuation in the original.

35. LV, Sears to JR, July 26, 1907.

36. F. Asher, *Richard Warren Sears,* 62.

37. Hoge, *First Hundred Years,* 62.

38. UCL, JR Papers, box 33, folder 6, JR to Messrs. Rosenwald and Benjamin, November 1, 1900.

39. Werner, *Rosenwald,* 70–71.

40. No comprehensive biography of Hirsch exists. The only one available is sketchy and lacks footnotes. It is by Hirsch's son, David Einhorn Hirsch: *Rabbi Emil G. Hirsch: The Reform Advocate* (Northbrook, Ill.: Whitehall, 1968). There are two articles on Hirsch's teachings by Bernard Martin originally printed in the *American Jewish Archives* and reprinted in *Critical Studies in American Jewish History,* vol. 1 (Cincinnati: American Jewish Archives, 1971). These articles are "The Religious Philosophy of Emil G. Hirsch" (186–201) and "The Social Philosophy of Emil G. Hirsch" (202–16). Hirsch's writings have been collected in *My Religion* (New York: Macmillan, 1925) and *The Theology of Emil G. Hirsch,* ed. David Einhorn Hirsch (Wheeling, Ill.: Whitehall, 1977).

41. Hirsch, ed., *Theology,* 318.

42. Marc Lee Raphael, *Profiles in American Judaism: The Reform, Conservative, Orthodox, and Reconstructionist Traditions in Historical Perspective* (San Francisco: Harper & Row, 1984), chaps. 1 and 2.

43. Hirsch, *Rabbi Emil G. Hirsch,* 4.

44. Gerson B. Levi, introduction to Hirsch, *My Religion,* 13.

45. American Jewish Archives, "Address of Mr. Julius Rosenwald, at the Euclid Avenue Temple [Cleveland], Friday evening, November 26, 1920, speaking in behalf of the Hebrew Union College at Cincinnati, Ohio," 4.

46. Bernard Martin, "The Social Philosophy of Emil G. Hirsch," *American Jewish Archives* 6 (1954): 161.

47. Hirsch, ed., *Theology,* "Ethics," 156.

48. Werner, *Rosenwald,* 30.

49. Typewritten list entitled "Julius Rosenwald Gifts," in the possession of the author.

50. UCL, JR Papers, scrapbook 1, 43, Jane Addams to JR, December 20, 1902; UCL, JR Papers, box 20, folder 2, Jane Addams to JR, December 15, 1906.

51. LV, Jane Addams to Gussie, January 4, 1907.

52. UCL, JR Papers, box 18, folder 8, JR to Edward Heinsheimer, January 24, 1905.

53. Hebrew Union College Archives, President of the Board of Governors of Hebrew Union College (Kohler) to JR, October 2, 1905.

54. Chicago Jewish Archives, Michael Reese Papers, box 3, folder 2. See also Hyman L. Meites, *History of the Jews of Chicago* (1924; reprint, Chicago: Chicago Jewish Historical Society, 1990), 207.

55. UCL, JR Papers, box 22, folder 11, JR to George Lytton, February 8, 1905.

56. UCL, JR Papers, box 13, folder 10, JR to Marvin B. Pool, April 26, 1906.

57. UCL, JR Papers, box 7, folder 4, Sadie T. Wald to JR, February 6, 1905.

58. UCL, JR Papers, box 7, folder 4, JR to Sadie Wald, December 2, 1905.

59. UCL, JR Papers, box 49, folder 1 (Werner Notes), JR to Henry Tibbets and appended note from Tibbets, July 12, 1906.

60. UCL, JR Papers, box 48, folder 14 (Werner Notes), JR to Gussie, June 6, 1904.

61. Meites, *Jews of Chicago,* 222.

62. UCL, JR Papers, box 18, folder 2, Dr. E. A. Fishkin to JR, March 11, 1908.

63. Meites, *Jews of Chicago,* 224.

64. Ibid.

65. UCL, JR Papers, box 18, folder 2, JR to Isador Strauss, September 20, 1908.

66. UCL, JR Papers, box 49, folder 2 (Werner Notes), Samuel B. Goldberg to JR, May 4, 1908.

67. Chicago Jewish Archives, Jewish Home Finding Society box, folder 1, letter from the Secretary to H. L. Meites, November 28, 1925, and Meites, *Jews of Chicago,* 598.

68. Meites, *Jews of Chicago,* 211.

69. UCL, JR Papers, box 48, folder 11 (Werner Notes), JR to Gussie, September 29, 1907.

70. LV, Gussie to Teddy and Lena, n.d.

71. Commission on Chicago Historical and Architectural Landmarks, *The Julius Rosenwald House: Preliminary Survey of Information,* May 2, 1977, in the Chicago Historical Society.

72. UCL, JR Papers, box 48, folder 12 (Werner Notes), Gussie to JR, November 11, 1900.

73. LV, Gussie to Adele, August 7, 1906.

74. UCL, JR Papers, box 49, folder 1, *Reform Advocate* (1906).

75. LV, Gussie to JR, May 20, 1904.

76. UCL, JR Papers, box 48, folder 11 (Werner Notes), JR to Gussie, April 26, 1897.

77. UCL, JR Papers, box 49, folder 1 (Werner Notes), JR to Gussie, April 4, 1903.

78. UCL, JR Papers, addendum II, box 1, folder 1, JR to Lessing, July 21, 1908.

79. Ron Chernow, *Titan: The Life of John D. Rockefeller Sr.* (New York: Random House, 1998), chap. 19.

80. LV, JR to Adele, July 7, 1906.

81. UCL, JR Papers, box 33, folder 4, JR to Harry Lipsis, May 4, 1906.

82. UCL, JR Papers, box 33, folder 6, JR to Nettie Lipsis, June 8, 1908.

83. LV, Tessie to Gussie, June 24, 1908.

84. LV, Gussie to her children, January 1900.

85. LV, Gussie to her children, February 1900.

86. LV, Gussie to her children, March 1, 1900.

87. UCL, JR Papers, box 48, folder 14 (Werner Notes), JR to "My dear ones," May 6–7, 1904.

88. UCL, JR Papers, box 48, folder 14 (Werner Notes), JR to Gussie, June 19, 1904.

89. UCL, JR Papers, box 48, folder 7 (Werner Notes).

90. UCL, JR Papers, box 48, folder 14 (Werner Notes), JR to Gussie, May 14, 1904.

91. UCL, JR papers, box 48, folder 14 (Werner Notes), JR to Gussie, May 19, 1904.

92. LV, Gussie to JR, May 23, 1904.

93. LV, Gussie to "My dear Girls," July 3, 1907.

94. LV, Gussie to "My dear ones all," August 3, 1907.

95. LV, JR to "Dear Folks," n.d., but clearly from aboard ship.

96. UCL, JR Papers, box 49, folder 1 (Werner Notes), JR to Sears and Loeb, August 16, 1907.

97. LV, Gussie to Adele, July 31, 1906.

3. Blacks, Politics, and Philanthropy, 1908–1912

1. Emmet and Jeuck, *Catalogues and Counters,* 233.

2. Ibid., 231.

3. UCL, JR Papers, scrapbook 1, 58, article from *National Food Magazine,* "Back to the Fountain Source," by Victor Ayer.

4. Peter Drucker, "Good Works and Good Business," in *Across the Board* 21 (October 1984): 12.

5. UCL, JR Papers, scrapbook 3, 85, article in the *Chicago Examiner,* January 12, 1913.

6. "Julius Rosenwald Gifts," folder in the possession of the author.

7. UCL, JR Papers, box 49, folder 2 (Werner Notes).

8. Emmett Dedmon, *Great Enterprises: 100 Years of the YMCA of Metropolitan Chicago* (New York: Rand McNally, 1977), 164–65.

9. UCL, JR Papers, scrapbook 1, 7 (*Chicago Tribune,* April 7, 1910).

10. UCL, JR Papers, box 49, folder 3 (Werner Notes), JR to Lessing, January 10, 1910.

11. YMCA Papers, CHS, box 18, folder 17.

12. James R. Grossman, *Land of Hope: Chicago's Black Southerners and the Great Migration* (Chicago: University of Chicago Press, 1989), 164.

13. UCL, JR Papers, addendum II, box 1, folder 1, JR to "Dear Ones All," July 25, 1908.

14. LV, Gussie to Adele, February 4, 1910.

15. Werner, *Rosenwald,* 107–108.

16. LV, JR to "My Own Girlies," September 25, 1910.

17. Nina Mjagkij, *Light in the Darkness: African Americans and the YMCA, 1852–1946* (Lexington: University Press of Kentucky, 1994), 67.

18. CHS, YMCA Papers, box 92, folder 4, "Memorandum of Conversation with Julius Rosenwald, A. H. Loeb, L. Wilbur Messer, Wm. J. Parker, and J. E. Moorland."

19. UCL, JR Papers, box 10, folder 21, JR to the YMCA, December 30, 1910.

20. Dedmon, *Great Enterprises,* 186. See also George R. Arthur, *Life on the Negro Frontier* (New York: Association Press, 1934), 40.

21. UCL, JR Papers, box 10, folder 21, Leo Sykes to JR, January 1, 1911.

22. UCL, JR Papers, scrapbook 14, 188, unknown newspaper, no date.

23. CHS, YMCA Papers, Messer to F. W. Ober, editor of *Association Men,* January 5, 1911.

24. CHS, YMCA Papers, box 94, folder 11, Messer to J. Hicks of the New York branch, January 7, 1911.

25. CHS, YMCA Papers, box 92, folder 7, William H. Taft to Messer, January 9, 1911.

26. UCL, JR Papers, scrapbook 14, 241.

27. UCL, JR Papers, box 49, folder 5 (Werner Notes), JR to Gussie, April 24, 1911.

28. UCL, JR Papers, box 49, folder 5 (Werner Notes), JR to Gussie, "Tuesday Morning," a continuation of the letter begun April 24, 1911.

29. UCL, JR Papers, scrapbook 14, 245, Julian W. Mack to JR, May 21, 1911.

30. UCL, JR Papers, scrapbook 14, 243.

31. UCL, JR Papers, scrapbook 14, 245, Judge Mack to JR, May 21, 1911.

32. CHS, YMCA Papers, box 94, folder 11, Henry M. Orme of New York to L. Wilbur Messer, January 24, 1911.

33. CHS, YMCA Papers, box 94, folder 11, JR to William Fellowes Morgan, February 14, 1912.

34. CHS, YMCA Papers, box 93, folder 7, JR to D. B. Meacham, January 10, 1912, and UCL, JR Papers, scrapbook 14, 217, *Chicago News* interview with JR, October 31, 1911.

35. Nina Mjagkij, "A Peculiar Alliance: Julius Rosenwald, the YMCA, and African Americans, 1910–1933," *American Jewish Archives* 44 (1993): 600.

36. UCL, JR Papers, scrapbook 14, 203.

37. UCL, JR Papers, scrapbook 14, 217, *Chicago News* interview with JR, October 31, 1911.

38. CHS, YMCA Papers, box 93, folder 9, Messer to Moorland, November 20, 1916.

39. UCL, JR Papers, scrapbook 14, 36, "Remarks made by Mr. Rosenwald at Booker T. Washington Luncheon," May 18, 1911.

40. UCL, JR Papers, box 49, folder 6 (Werner Notes), JR to Gussie, May 18, 1911.

41. UCL, JR Papers, box 49, folder 5 (Werner Notes), JR to Gussie, May 21, 1911.

42. Louis R. Harlan and Raymond W. Smock, eds., *The Booker T. Washington Papers* (Urbana: University of Illinois Press, 1981), 11:165–66.

43. LC, Booker T. Washington Papers, reel 68, JR to Washington, May 29, 1911.

44. LC, Washington Papers, reel 68, "Program for the Two-Day Visit of Mr. Rosenwald and Party."

45. UCL, JR Papers, scrapbook 14, 37, *Chicago Tribune,* October 29, 1911.

46. LC, Washington Papers, reel 68, container 74, Washington to Theodore Roosevelt, December 12, 1911. See Louis R. Harlan, "Booker T. Washington's Discovery of Jews," in *Region, Race, and Reconstruction: Essays in Honor of C. Vann Woodward,* ed. J. Morgan Kousser and James McPherson (New York: Oxford University Press, 1982), 267–79.
47. LC, Washington Papers, reel 68, Washington to JR, March 29, 1912.
48. UCL, JR Papers, scrapbook 14, 41, *Tuskegee Student,* February 1912.
49. LV, Gussie to "My darling children," February 20, 1912.
50. UCL, JR Papers, scrapbook 14, 47, A. Mitchell Innes to JR, February 27, 1912.
51. LV, Gussie to Adele and Armand, March 10, 1912.
52. LC, Washington Papers, reel 68, JR to Emmett Scott, March 12, 1912.
53. UCL, JR Papers, addendum I, box 1, folder 1, JR to Adele and Armand, March 12, 1912.
54. UCL, JR Papers, scrapbook 14, 48, *Chicago Record-Herald,* March 14, 1912.
55. Werner, *Rosenwald,* 125.
56. LC, Washington Papers, reel 68.
57. Harlan and Smock, eds., *Washington Papers,* 11:562.
58. UCL, JR Papers, box 3, folder 17, JR to Miss C. Neal, secretary of the Berry School, June 3, 1912.
59. UCL, JR Papers, box 37, folder 9, William Edwards to JR, June 7, 1912.
60. LC, Washington Papers, reel 68, Washington to JR, May 2, 1912.
61. UCL, JR Papers, box 14, folder 31, JR to George Gates, November 27, 1911.
62. UCL, JR Papers, scrapbook 14, 16, *Congregationalist* newspaper of Massachusetts, January 10, 1913.
63. UCL, JR Papers, box 19, folder 9, G. W. Hubbard to JR, January 8, 1912, and JR to Hubbard, January 18, 1912.
64. UCL, JR Papers, scrapbook 14, 32, *Northwestern Christian Advocate,* March 13, 1912.
65. UCL, JR Papers, scrapbook 14, 21.
66. UCL, JR Papers, box 15, folder 17, and LC, NAACP Papers, reel 8.
67. UCL, JR Papers, box 26, folder 13.
68. UCL, JR Papers, scrapbook 14, 5, article in *Survey,* May 18, 1912.
69. Louis R. Harlan, *Booker T. Washington: The Wizard of Tuskegee, 1901–1915* (New York: Oxford University Press, 1983); David Levering Lewis, *W. E. B. DuBois: Biography of a Race, 1868–1919* (New York: Henry Holt, 1993).
70. UCL, JR Papers, box 49, folder 7 (Werner Notes), JR to Caesar Cone, December 16, 1911.
71. UCL, JR Papers, box 33, folder 11, JR to M. J. Foreman, November 1, 1911.
72. UCL, JR Papers, scrapbook 6, 150, *Examiner,* June 9, 1910.
73. UCL, JR Papers, addendum II, box 1, folder 1, JR to Lessing October 28, 1909.
74. Chicago Jewish Archives, Minute Book of the Associated Jewish Charities, meeting of April 20, 1911.
75. UCL, JR Papers, box 22, folder 24, JR to Adolph King, March 15, 1910.
76. UCL, JR Papers, scrapbook 6, 152.
77. UCL, JR Papers, box 6, folder 15, Loeb to JR, October 28, 1913.
78. *Reform Advocate,* May 28, 1910.
79. UCL, JR Papers, box 6, folder 14, Loeb to JR, October 28, 1913.
80. UCL, JR Papers, addendum II, box 1, folder 1, JR to Lessing, March 8, October 4, and October 9, 1909.
81. Chicago Jewish Archives, Minute Books of the Associated Jewish Charities, meetings of March 16, 1909, and April 21, 1909.
82. Meites, *Jews of Chicago,* 232.
83. LV, Charles Eisenman to JR, January 19, 1910.

84. UCL, JR Papers, box 49, folder 17 (Werner Notes), JR to Lessing, February 23 and 25, April 29, and November 10, 1910.

85. UCL, JR Papers, box 49, folder 17 (Werner Notes), JR to Lessing, November 10, 1910.

86. LV, Jacob Billikopf to JR, November 8, 1910.

87. J. J. Goldberg, *Jewish Power: Inside the American Jewish Establishment* (New York: Addison Wesley, 1996), 102.

88. Naomi W. Cohen, *Not Free to Desist: The American Jewish Committee, 1906–1966* (Philadelphia: Jewish Publication Society of America, 1972), 563.

89. UCL, JR Papers, scrapbook 3, 90–91, *New York Times,* December 19, 1911. See also Cohen, *Not Free to Desist,* chap. 4, "The Abrogation Campaign."

90. Charles Reznikoff, ed., *Louis Marshall: Champion of Liberty* (Philadelphia: Jewish Publication Society of America, 1957), 704.

91. UCL, JR Papers, addendum I, box 1, folder 1, JR to Lessing, February 8, 1909.

92. UCL, JR Papers, box 23, folder 1.

93. Carl Alpert, *Technion* (New York: Sepher Hermon, 1982), 54.

94. Werner, *Rosenwald,* 96–97. See Harry Barnard, *The Making of an American Jew* (New York: Herzl Press, 1974), 106.

95. UCL, JR Papers, addendum II, box 1, folder 1, JR to Lessing, November 2, 1909.

96. *Reform Advocate,* May 7, 1910.

97. UCL, JR Papers, scrapbook 1, 44, Jane Addams to JR, May 10, 1910.

98. UCL, JR Papers, scrapbook 11, 14.

99. UCL, JR Papers, scrapbook 1, 44, Jane Addams to JR, May 10, 1910, and scrapbook 5, 7, Jane Addams to Julian Mack, August 5, 1912.

100. Newberry Library, Chicago, Graham Taylor Papers, folder: "Julius Rosenwald and Family," JR to Graham Taylor, January 6, 1911.

101. Louise C. Wade, *Graham Taylor: Pioneer for Social Justice* (Chicago: University of Chicago Press, 1964), 166–69.

102. UCL, JR Papers, box 20, folder 2, JR to Julia Lathrop, September 27, 1910.

103. UCL, JR Papers, box 7, folder 16, JR to Julia Lathrop, May 25, 1911.

104. UCL, JR Papers, box 7, folder 16, JR to Emil Hirsch, March 22, 1912.

105. Jane Addams Papers, reel 6, letters signed by JR and Jane Addams to Julian Mack and Lillian Wald, April 12, 1912. The Mack letter is in the William H. Taft Papers in the Library of Congress, and the Wald letter is in the Grace and Edith Abbott Papers at the University of Chicago.

106. UCL, JR Papers, box 7, folder 8, JR to S. T. DeLee, October 19, 1909.

107. UCL, JR Papers, box 8, folder 23, JR to Mayor Carter Harrison, July 22, 1912.

108. UCL, JR Papers, box 13, folder 17, Henry H. Schuhmann to JR, March 11, 1911.

109. UCL, JR Papers, box 13, folder 17, JR to Henry Schuhmann, October 11, 1911, but quoting an earlier letter of his dated March 31, 1911.

110. UCL, JR Papers, box 13, folder 12, JR to Rufus G. Dawes, March 9, 1912.

111. UCL, JR Papers, box 13, folder 17, JR to C. N. Johnson, April 13, 1912.

112. UCL, JR Papers, box 13, folder 17, C. N. Johnson to JR, October 8, 1912.

113. UCL, JR Papers, box 15, folder 16, JR to Fabian Franklin of the *New York Evening Post,* November 22, 1910.

114. During this period it was unusual for a major research university to have any Jewish trustees. But Jews had been involved with the University of Chicago from the very beginning, giving William Rainey Harper money at a critical time.

115. UCL, JR Papers, box 24, folder 1, Julian Mack to JR, May 11, 1911.

116. UCL, JR Papers, box 55, folder 12 (Werner Notes), JR to Gussie, May 11, 1911.

117. UCL, JR Papers, box 49, folder 9 (Werner Notes), Charles Beale to JR, June 11, 1912.

118. UCL, JR Papers, box 49, folder 3 (Werner Notes), JR to Lessing, March 7, 1910.

119. Werner, *Rosenwald,* 149; Illinois State Senate, *Report of the Senate Vice Committee* (Springfield, 1916), 179. See also JR Papers, scrapbook 2, 3, article in the *Chicago Tribune* of March 16, 1910.

120. UCL, JR Papers, scrapbook 2, 53, JR quoted in the *Chicago Tribune,* May 30, 1913.

121. UCL, JR Papers, scrapbook 2, 87, Sherman P. Cody to JR, June 4, 1910.

122. Werner, *Rosenwald,* 142.

123. UCL, JR Papers, box 49, folder 5 (Werner Notes), JR to Gussie, March 19, 1911.

124. UCL, JR Papers, box 49, folder 5 (Werner Notes), JR to Gussie, March 26, 1911.

125. UCL, JR Papers, box 49, folder 5 (Werner Notes), JR to Gussie, April 2, 1911.

126. UCL, JR Papers, box 48, folder 5 (Werner Notes), JR to Gussie, March 23, 1911.

127. UCL, JR Papers, scrapbook 3, 2.

128. UCL, JR Papers, box 49, folder 5 (Werner Notes), JR to Gussie, April 5, 1911.

129. Ibid.

130. Newberry Library, Chicago, Carter Harrison Papers, JR to Carter Harrison, December 22, 1911.

131. Werner, *Rosenwald,* 146.

132. UCL, JR Papers, scrapbook 2, 101, Taft to JR, February 13, 1912.

133. Werner, *Rosenwald,* 146–47.

134. UCL, JR Papers, scrapbook 3, 35–36.

135. UCL, JR Papers, box 20, folder 2, JR to Jane Addams, August 12, 1912.

136. Quoted in Werner, *Rosenwald,* 147.

137. UCL, JR Papers, box 49, folder 3 (Werner Notes), JR to Lessing, October 26, 1910.

138. UCL, JR Papers, addendum II, box 1, folder 1, JR to Lessing, October 23, 1909.

139. UCL, JR Papers, addendum II, box 1, folder 1, JR to Adele, November 27, 1909.

140. UCL, JR Papers, box 49, folder 5 (Werner Notes), JR to Gussie, April 4, 1911.

141. UCL, JR Papers, box 49, folder 6 (Werner Notes), JR to Gussie, May 2, 1911.

142. UCL, JR Papers, addendum III, box 1, folder 4.

143. According to the memoirs of William Rosenwald, the name "Tel Aviv" only appeared on stationery. The children always called the estate simply "Ravinia."

144. UCL, JR Papers, addendum II, box 1, folder 1, JR to Adele and Armand, March 29, 1912.

145. LV, JR to "My own girlies," November 1, 1910.

146. UCL, JR Papers, box 49, folder 9 (Werner Notes).

147. Ernest Grunsfeld's diaries are in the Leo Baeck Institute in New York.

148. UCL, JR Papers, box 34, folder 6.

149. Chicago Jewish Archives, Minute Book of the Board of the Associated Jewish Charities, meetings of June 22, 1910, and September 15, 1910.

150. Chicago Jewish Archives, Minute Book of the Board of the Associated Jewish Charities. JR's letter, dated August 12, 1912, is inserted in the book under the October meeting when the Board of the Associated accepted its terms.

151. Hyman L. Meites, ed., *History of the Jews of Chicago* (1924; reprint, Chicago: Chicago Jewish Historical Society, 1990), 595.

152. UCL, JR Papers, box 8, folder 14, JR to the Trustees of the University of Chicago, August 12, 1912.

153. UCL, JR Papers, box 8, folder 23, JR to Mrs. Kellogg Fairbank, July 22, 1929.

154. UCL, JR Papers, box 20, folder 2, JR to Jane Addams, Minnie Low, Judge

Mack, S. C. Kingsley, Father P. J. O'Callaghan, Louis H. Cahn, and William C. Graves, August 12, 1912.

155. UCL, JR Papers, box 6, folder 15, JR to the Officers and Directors of the Chicago Hebrew Institute, August 12, 1912.

156. Meites, *Jews of Chicago,* 236–38.

157. Ibid., 94–95, and the Chicago Jewish Archives, Minutes of the Associated for the meetings of September 30, November 18, and December 16, 1909.

158. UCL, JR Papers, scrapbook 11, 91, *Chicago Examiner,* August 12, 1912.

159. LC, Washington Papers, reel 69, container 76, JR to Washington, July 15, 1912.

160. Washington to JR, July 20, 1912, in *Washington Papers,* 11:562.

161. JR to Washington, August 5, 1912, in *Washington Papers,* 11:576–77.

162. UCL, JR Papers, box 52, folder 6 (Werner Notes).

163. UCL, JR Papers, scrapbook 5, 7, Judge Mack to Jane Addams, August 8, 1912.

164. UCL, JR Papers, scrapbook 11, 91, *Chicago Examiner.*

165. UCL, JR Papers, scrapbook 11, 94, *Chicago Tribune,* August 13, 1912.

166. UCL, JR Papers, scrapbook 11, 103, a New York newspaper, August 20, 1912.

167. UCL, JR Papers, scrapbook 11, 166–67, Graham Taylor to Mr. and Mrs. Julius Rosenwald, August 3, 1912.

4. Black Schools, Political Attacks, and the Profit Sharing Plan, 1912–1916

1. Adam Fairclough, "Liberation or Collaboration? Black Teachers in the Era of White Supremacy," in *Teaching Equality: Black Schools in the Age of Jim Crow* (Athens: University of Georgia Press, 2001).

2. Raymond B. Fosdick, *Adventures in Giving: The Story of the General Education Board* (New York: Harper & Row, 1962), 93.

3. UCL, JR Papers, box 33, folder 1, Carter Woodson, "The Story of the Fund," chapter 2, 10–11. See also the forthcoming book on Rosenwald schools by Mary Hoffschwelle, *Rosenwald Schools of the American South,* to be published by the University Press of Florida.

4. LC, Booker T. Washington Papers, reel 68, Washington to JR, August 31, 1912.

5. LC, Washington to JR, September 12, 1912.

6. LC, JR to Washington, September 16, 1912.

7. LC, Washington Papers, reel 70, Washington to JR, December 20, 1912.

8. LC, JR to Washington, December 26, 1912.

9. LC, Washington to JR, May 21, 1913. Other letters noted above are from January 17 and April 10, 1913.

10. LC, Washington to JR, May 31, 1913.

11. LC, JR to Washington, June 10, 1913.

12. UCL, JR Papers, scrapbook 14, 49, article by Clement Richardson, "Schools for Negro Great Boon for Race," *Inter-Ocean,* September 15, 1913.

13. UCL, JR Papers, box 53, folder 12 (Werner Notes), William C. Graves to JR, April 23, 1914.

14. UCL, JR Papers, box 53, folder 7 (Werner Notes), Washington to JR, June 1, 1914.

15. LC, Washington Papers, Washington to JR, October 2, 1914.

16. UCL, JR Papers, box 53, folder 7 (Werner Notes), Washington to JR, September 17, 1914.

17. LC, Graves to Washington, November 30, 1914.

18. LC, Washington to Graves, January 20, 1915

19. Washington to Graves, December 7, 1914, in *Booker T. Washington Papers,* 13: 196–97.

20. LC, Washington to JR, December 5, 1914.

21. LC, James L. Sibley to JR, January 8, 1915.

22. UCL, JR Papers, scrapbook 14, 62, an account of the Tuskegee trip by Jenkin Lloyd Jones in *Unity,* February 28, 1915.
23. UCL, JR Papers, scrapbook 14, 60, article from the *Montgomery Advertiser,* February 22, 1915.
24. UCL, JR Papers, box 54, folder 1 (Werner Notes), JR to Julian W. Mack, March 1, 1915.
25. UCL, JR Papers, scrapbook 14, 65, Jenkin Lloyd Jones to JR, April 16, 1915.
26. UCL, JR Papers, scrapbook 14, 64, 69, the account of Mary Jackson is in an article from the *Boston Transcript,* March 24, 1915. Quotes from Ms. Johnson are in dialect, which I chose to render into standard English.
27. UCL, JR Papers, box 54, folder 1 (Werner Notes), Washington to JR, March 17, 1915.
28. LC, Washington Papers, JR to Washington, March 20, 1915.
29. LC, report of Booker T. Washington Jr. for June 1915.
30. LC, Washington Papers, excerpts from the report for July 1915 by Washington Jr.
31. LC, Washington Papers, excerpts from report for August 1915 by Washington Jr.
32. These were blacks whose salaries and traveling expenses were paid for by JR and whose job was to spend their "entire time in bringing to the attention of backward communities, Mr. Rosenwald's offer and also lead in the organization necessary to get the people to raise their part of the funds for schoolhouse building." LC, Washington Papers, Clinton Calloway to Washington, October 14, 1915.
33. *Booker T. Washington Papers,* 14:294.
34. LC, Washington Papers, Washington to Graves, July 30, 1915.
35. LC, Washington Papers, Washington to Graves, October 7, 1915.
36. James D. Anderson, *The Education of Blacks in the South, 1860–1935* (Chapel Hill: University of North Carolina Press, 1988), esp. chap. 5.
37. LC, Washington Papers, Washington to JR, October 1, 1915.
38. *Washington Papers,* 14:386.
39. UCL, JR Papers, box 54, folder 1 (Werner Notes), JR to Gussie, November 12, 1915.
40. LC, Washington Papers, Washington to JR, November 7, 1912, and JR's reply on November 13, 1912.
41. LC, Washington Papers, JR to Washington, March 10, 1915.
42. UCL, JR Papers, scrapbook 14, 63, speech quoted in the *Tuskegee Messenger,* March 6, 1915.
43. *Washington Papers,* 14:277.
44. LC, Washington Papers, Seth Low to JR, May 20, 1915.
45. LC, Washington Papers, Washington to JR, May 10, 1915.
46. UCL, JR Papers, addendum III, box 1, folder 15, George Washington Carver to JR, May 10, 1915.
47. *Washington Papers,* 14:342–44.
48. Ibid., 409–10.
49. Ibid., 435.
50. UCL, JR Papers, box 34, folder 7, "Address of Mr. Julius Rosenwald at the Memorial Services in Memory of Principal Booker T. Washington, Tuskegee Institute Chapel, December 12, 1915."
51. *Washington Papers,* 14:459.
52. Louis R. Harlan, *Booker T. Washington: The Wizard of Tuskegee, 1901–1915* (New York: Oxford University Press, 1983), 221.
53. UCL, JR Papers, box 26, folder 1, JR to Isaiah Montgomery, June 3, 1912.
54. Harlan, *Washington,* 223.
55. On Mound Bayou, see ibid., 221–24. See also August Meier, "Booker T. Wash-

ington and the Town of Mound Bayou," in *Along the Color Line: Explorations in the Black Experience,* ed. August Meier and Ellen Rudwick (Urbana: University of Illinois Press, 1976), 217–23.

56. UCL, JR Papers, box 4, folder 1, Graves to JR, April 9, 1915.

57. UCL, JR Papers, box 4, folder 1, JR to William Hale Thompson, May 15, 1915.

58. UCL, JR Papers, box 4, folder 1, JR to Edwin Barker, September 14, 1916.

59. UCL, JR Papers, scrapbook 14, 1.

60. UCL, JR Papers, box 27, folder 18. See especially JR to Paul Sachs, June 30, 1914.

61. UCL, JR Papers, scrapbook 14, 239, article in the *St. Louis Star,* December 21, 1915.

62. CHS, YMCA Papers, box 94, folder 11, L. Wilbur Messer to Henry Orme of New York, March 27, 1915.

63. UCL, JR Papers, scrapbook 14, 209, *Calendar,* August 1913.

64. UCL, JR Papers, scrapbook 14, 184, "A Fair Chance for the Colored Man," by Julius Rosenwald, *Association Men,* January 1914.

65. CHS, YMCA Papers, box 94, folder 16, JR to Walter W. Wood, October 29, 1913.

66. James R. Grossman, *Land of Hope: Chicago's Black Southerners and the Great Migration* (Chicago: University of Chicago Press, 1989), 170.

67. Emmett Dedmon, *Great Enterprises: 100 Years of the YMCA of Metropolitan Chicago* (New York: Rand McNally, 1977), 188.

68. UCL, JR Papers, scrapbook 14, 2, article from the *Cleveland Gazette,* June 23, 1913.

69. UCL, JR Papers, scrapbook 14, 209, "A Remarkable Triple Alliance: How a Jew Is Helping the Negro through the YMCA," by Booker T. Washington, *Outlook,* 1914, 485.

70. UCL, JR Papers, "Statement for Mr. Graves."

71. *Report of the Senate Vice Committee,* 37.

72. Ibid., 182.

73. A 1908 survey of retail workers indicated that the lowest paid females received wages of $4.69 a week. Allowing for inflation, that would indicate that Sears was paying the going rate. See Joanne J. Meyerowitz, *Women Adrift: Independent Wage Earners in Chicago, 1880–1930* (Chicago: University of Chicago Press, 1988), 37.

74. *Report of the Senate Vice Committee,* 180.

75. Ibid., 182.

76. UCL, JR Papers, scrapbook 2, 3, article in the *Inter-Ocean,* 1914.

77. UCL, JR Papers, box 52, folder 9 (Werner Notes), JR to Woodrow Wilson, March 20, 1913.

78. UCL, JR Papers, scrapbook 12, 44, *Inter-Ocean,* June 7, 1913.

79. *Report of the Senate Vice Committee,* 183.

80. Ibid., 146.

81. Stuart D. Brandes, *American Welfare Capitalism, 1880–1940* (Chicago: University of Chicago Press, 1976), 83–91.

82. Werner, *Rosenwald,* 159.

83. Emmet and Jeuck, *Catalogues and Counters,* 681.

84. Brandes, *American Welfare Capitalism,* 23.

85. Emmet and Jeuck, *Catalogues and Counters,* 682.

86. James B. Morrow, "The Making of a 'Mail Order Menace,'" *Nation's Business,* December 1917, 19–20.

87. UCL, JR Papers, scrapbook 5, "Personal Interview Letter Series," by Joe Mitchell Chapple (1917), 40.

88. Ibid., 2.

89. Ibid., 4

90. UCL, JR Papers, scrapbook 5, 32–33, B. C. Forbes, "Men Who Are Making America," *Leslie's Weekly,* December 7, 1916. Italics in original.

91. UCL, JR Papers, scrapbook 12, 113, Judge Harry Fisher to JR, January 1, 1915.

92. Werner, *Rosenwald,* 140–42.

93. UCL, JR Papers, scrapbook 6, 107.

94. UCL, JR Papers, box 15, folder 15, Louis Marshall to JR, May 10, 1915.

95. LC, Walter Fisher Papers, container 2, JR to Walter Fisher, May 17, 1915.

96. UCL, JR Papers, box 15, folder 15, Lasker to JR, July 15, 1914.

97. UCL, JR Papers, box 15, folder 15, Leo Frank to JR, July 11, 1915.

98. UCL, JR Papers, scrapbook 12, 6, *New York Evening Post,* August 18, 1915.

99. Abraham Flexner, *Abraham Flexner: An Autobiography* (New York: Simon & Schuster, 1960), 168–70.

100. UCL, JR Papers, box 8, folder 24, JR to Judson, November 6, 1916.

101. UCL, JR Papers, box 8, folder 23, telegram from Flexner to Judson, November 13, 1916.

102. UCL, JR Papers, box 8, folder 23, telegram from Judson to Flexner, November 13, 1916.

103. UCL, JR Papers, box 8, folder 23, JR to Judson, November 21, 1916.

104. UCL, JR Papers, box 49, folders 12 and 13, entry dated January 9, 1914.

105. LV, Edith Rosenwald Sulzberger to Adele, Hotel Semiramis, Egypt, January 20, 1914.

106. LV, Edith Rosenwald to Adele, January 7, 1914.

107. UCL, JR Papers, box 49, folder 12 (Werner Notes), JR diary of Egyptian trip, entries for February 5 and February 13.

108. Ibid., entry for March 3, 1913.

109. Ibid., entries for March 5 and March 6.

110. Ibid., entry for March 2, 1914.

111. UCL, JR Papers, box 49, folder 15 (Werner Notes), April 1, 1919.

112. Ibid., Graves to Lessing Rosenthal.

113. UCL, JR Papers, scrapbook 3, 101.

114. I owe my acquisition of a photocopy of this valuable manuscript to the kindness of Lee Ellen Cromer, a niece of the late Harry Kersey.

5. World War I, 1916–1918

1. In addition to the chapter in Werner's biography on World War I, see the article by Miriam Joyce, "Julius Rosenwald and World War I," *American Jewish Archives* 45 (1993): 208–27.

2. UCL, JR Papers, box 50, folder 1 (Werner Notes), JR to Leo Wormser, February 8, 1916.

3. UCL, JR Papers, scrapbook 2, 67, *Chicago Herald,* October 14, 1916.

4. Robert D. Cuff, *The War Industries Board* (Baltimore: Johns Hopkins University Press, 1973), 39.

5. UCL, JR Papers, box 12, folder 20, Felix Frankfurter to JR, October 12, 1916.

6. Dr. Franklin H. Martin, *The Joy of Living: An Autobiography,* vol. 2 (Garden City, N.Y.: Doubleday, Doran, 1933), 61.

7. Ibid., 2:66.

8. UCL, JR Papers, box 24, folder 16, Kohlsaat to JR, June 18, 1917.

9. UCL, JR Papers, scrapbook 8, interview with the *Chicago Examiner,* March 22, 1917.

10. Martin, *The Joy of Living,* 2:88.

11. UCL, JR Papers, scrapbook 10, 36–37, JR to Charles Eisenman, February 19, 1917.

12. National Archives (Suitland, Md.), Council of National Defense, RG62, box 313, "Statement on Committee on Supplies in *Preliminary Inventory of the Council of National Defense Records* (Washington, 1942)."

13. Cuff, *The War Industries Board,* 236–39.

14. UCL, JR Papers, scrapbook 10, 54, *Chicago Tribune,* July 3, 1917.

15. Ibid., 70, *Chicago Tribune,* July 7, 1917.

16. Ibid., 68, JR to Woodrow Wilson, July 2, 1917.

17. Quoted in Martin, *The Joy of Living,* 2:281–82.

18. UCL, JR Papers, scrapbook 10, 21, *Chicago Tribune,* May 6, 1917.

19. Martin, *The Joy of Living,* 2:121.

20. UCL, JR Papers, box 12, folder 16, JR to Eisenman, November 14, 1917.

21. UCL, JR Papers, box 34, folder 10, JR to A. Loeb & Sears board of directors, July 7, 1917.

22. UCL, JR Papers, scrapbook 10, 115, *Boston Traveler & Evening Herald*, December 31, 1917.

23. Quoted in Martin, *The Joy of Living,* 2:281.

24. National Archives (Suitland, Md.), RG 62, box 314, Goethals to Eisenman, January 24, 1918.

25. UCL, JR Papers, box 12, folder 16, W. A. Rogers to JR, September 20, 1917.

26. National Archives (Suitland, Md.), RG 62, box 314, correspondence between Eisenman and Goethals and attached memos.

27. UCL, JR Papers, box 50, folder 2 (Werner Notes), JR to Gussie, May 4, 1917.

28. AJA, Jacob Schiff Papers, box 454, folder 18, JR to Schiff, October 19, 1917.

29. UCL, JR Papers, box 12, folder 19, George W. Goethals to JR, January 14, 1918.

30. UCL, JR Papers, box 10, folder 19, JR to Benedict Crowell, January 23, 1918.

31. UCL, JR Papers, box 12, folder 21, minutes of the joint meeting of the Advisory Commission and the Council of National Defense, February 4, 1918.

32. UCL, JR Papers, box 12, folder 21, JR to Bernard Baruch, February 20, 1918.

33. Martin, *The Joy of Living,* 2:227.

34. UCL, JR Papers, addendum II, box 1, folder 3, JR to "Dear Children," March 1, 1918.

35. Aside from newspaper clippings in the scrapbooks, there is little one can learn about Gussie's suffrage activity.

36. UCL, JR Paper, box 43, folder 7, JR to Elonzo Tyson, March 5, 1918.

37. UCL, JR Papers, box 12, folder 19, JR to President Wilson, March 6, 1918. Emphasis added by JR.

38. MSI, "Letters in Times of War and Peace," 6, Woodrow Wilson to JR, March 7, 1918.

39. UCL, JR Papers, scrapbook 10, 149.

40. UCL, JR Papers, scrapbook 2, 37 ff.

41. UCL, JR Papers, addendum II, box 1, folder 3, JR to Lessing, March 6, 1916.

42. UCL, JR Papers, box 36, folder 15, JR to Schiff, June 17, 1918.

43. MSI, "Letters in Time of War and Peace," 8, Thomas S. McClane to JR, June 26, 1918.

44. Ibid., 9, Herbert L. Pratt to JR, June 28, 1918.

45. UCL, JR Papers, box 34, folder 9, "Account of Experiences in France told to the Commercial Club."

46. UCL, JR Papers, box 34, folder 10, Newton Baker to JR, July 29, 1918.

47. Ibid., Emmett Scott to JR, July 31, 1918.

48. UCL, JR Papers, addendum II, box 1, folder 3, Lieutenant Harris to his family, August 21, 1918.

49. UCL, JR Papers, scrapbook 16, 27–29, JR to "Dear Ones All," August 24, 1918.

50. UCL, JR Papers, box 34, folder 10, JR to "Dear Ones All," September 24, 1918.

51. Ibid., JR to "Dear Ones All," August 29, 1918. The asterisks represent censored information.
52. UCL, JR Papers, scrapbook 16, 31, "The Man the Boys Call Rosy," *Survey,* November 2, 1918.
53. UCL, JR Papers, box 34, folder 10, JR to "Dear Ones All," September 1–5, 1918.
54. Ibid., F. Gates to Gussie, September 28, 1918.
55. Ibid., Corporal H. R. Kern to L. H. Beall, Dept. 157 of Sears.
56. UCL, JR Papers, scrapbook 5, 36, *Kansas City Sun,* February 3, 1919.
57. UCL, JR Papers, box 34, folder 10, JR to "Dear Ones All," September 15, 1918.
58. UCL, JR Papers, box 50, folder 5 (Werner Notes), part of a diary kept by JR.
59. UCL, JR Papers, box 34, folder 9, "Account of Experiences in France told to the Commercial Club."
60. AJA, Jacob Schiff Papers, box 460, folder 4, Schiff to JR, November 21, 1918.
61. UCL, JR Papers, box 36, folder 15, JR to Schiff, November 25, 1918.
62. Ibid., JR to Schiff, November 27, 1918.
63. Ibid., Schiff to JR, December 6, 1918.
64. AJA, Jacob Schiff Papers, box 460, folder 4, JR to Schiff, December 8, 1918.
65. Hyman L. Meites, *History of the Jews of Chicago* (1924; reprint, Chicago: Chicago Jewish Historical Society, 1990), 292.
66. Quoted in Werner, *Rosenwald,* 175.
67. Quoted in Meites, *Jews of Chicago,* 300–301.
68. MSI, "Letters in Time of War and Peace," 7, telegram from President Wilson to JR, March 28, 1917.
69. UCL, JR Papers, scrapbook 8, 36, Herbert Lehman to JR, March 17, 1917.
70. UCL, JR Papers, box 50, folder 2 (Werner Notes), JR to Gussie, April 15, 1917.
71. AJA, Jacob Schiff Papers, box 454, folder 18, JR to Schiff, April 16, 1917.
72. UCL, JR Papers, scrapbook 8, 50, *Chicago Tribune,* May 21, 1917.
73. UCL, JR Papers, box 50, folder 2 (Werner Notes), JR to Gussie May 24, 1917.
74. AJA, Jacob Schiff Papers, box 454, folder 18, JR to Schiff, December 22, 1917.
75. UCL, JR Papers, scrapbook 8, 92, *Chicago Tribune,* December 24, 1918.
76. UCL, JR Papers, box 50, folder 2 (Werner Notes), JR to Gussie, May 24, 1917.
77. Ibid., JR to Gussie, June 20, 1917.
78. Ibid., JR to Gussie, June 22, 1917.
79. UCL, JR Papers, box 34, folder 4.
80. Edwin Embree and Julia Waxman, *Investment in People: The Story of the Julius Rosenwald Fund* (New York: Harper, 1949), 28.
81. Kathleen S. Kelly, *Effective Fund-Raising Management* (Mahwah, N.J.: Lawrence Erlbaum, 1998), 579.

6. The Rescue of Sears and the Consolidation of Philanthropic Endeavors, 1919–1924

1. UCL, JR Papers, addendum II, box 1, folder 3, Lessing to JR, October 9, 1919.
2. Emmet and Jeuck, *Catalogues and Counters,* 198.
3. Werner, *Rosenwald,* 226.
4. UCL, JR Papers, addendum II, box 1, folder 3, Lessing to JR, October 9, 1919.
5. Cecil C. Hoge Sr., *The First Hundred Years Are the Toughest: What We Can Learn from the Century of Competition between Sears and Wards* (Berkeley: Ten Speed Press, 1988), 81.
6. Emmet and Jeuck, *Catalogues and Counters,* 202.
7. Werner, *Rosenwald,* 227.
8. Ibid., 228.
9. Ibid., 225; Emmet and Jeuck, *Catalogues and Counters,* 198.
10. Emmet and Jeuck, *Catalogues and Counters,* 201.
11. Hoge, *First Hundred Years,* 84.

12. Werner (228) says the workforce was cut by 10 percent; Hoge (86) says that Doering and Adler cut the workforce by 30 percent. Among the jobs eliminated were those of 1,200 black female office workers hired as a result of an Urban League initiative. See Joanne J. Meyerowitz, *Women Adrift: Independent Wage Earners in Chicago, 1880–1930* (Chicago: University of Chicago Press, 1988), 36n.

13. Werner, *Rosenwald,* 229.

14. UCL, JR Papers, box 11, folder 2, JR to Henry Goldman, January 3, 1922. Emmet and Jeuck, *Catalogues and Counters,* present a different perspective, 209–10.

15. According to an article eighteen months later, "[JR] bought the Chicago real estate for an amount that was $8,275,539 in excess of its book value." E. Marshall Young, "The Story of Sears Roebuck's Comeback," *Financial World,* February 11, 1923, in UCL, JR Papers, scrapbook 11, 51.

16. JR Papers, scrapbook 11, 68, article in the *Chicago Tribune,* December 30, 1921.

17. Werner, *Rosenwald,* 229–30.

18. UCL, JR Papers, scrapbook 11, 72, *Boston News Bureau,* December 31, 1921.

19. UCL, JR Papers, box 11, folder 2, Bernard Baruch to JR, January 6, 1922.

20. UCL, JR Papers, box 11, folder 2, Henry Goldman to JR, December 31, 1921.

21. UCL, JR Papers, box 11, folder 2, Victor H. Munnecke to JR, December 30, 1921.

22. UCL, JR Papers, box 11, folder 2, Frederick Rawson to JR, December 31, 1921.

23. Emmet and Jeuck, *Catalogues and Counters,* 215.

24. UCL, JR Papers, box 55, folder 7 (Werner Notes), Stanley Rayfield interview with John Higgins.

25. Hoge, *First Hundred Years,* 89, 90.

26. UCL, JR Papers, scrapbook 11, 61, Julius Rosenwald, "What We Have Learned from 6,000,000 Customers," *American Magazine,* July 1920, 191.

27. Ibid., 294.

28. UCL, JR Papers, scrapbook 11, 67, Julius Rosenwald, "Mail Order House, Chicago Product, Fills Public Need," *Christian Science Monitor,* October 10, 1923.

29. UCL, JR Papers, scrapbook 16, 35, B.C. Forbes, "A Man with 7,000 Partners," *Hearst's Magazine,* December 19, 1919.

30. This article by C. T. Lewis appeared in the Petersburg, Illinois, newspaper in late February 1921. I owe this reference to the kindness of Art Finney, a relative of Lewis.

31. Edward E. Purinton, "Satisfaction or Your Money Back," *Independent,* February 5, 1920, 298–99.

32. Rosenwald, "Mail Order House."

33. Julius Rosenwald, "Why You Can't Do Too Much for Customers," *System* 46 (December 1924): 778–79.

34. S. L. Smith, *Builders of Goodwill: The Story of the State Agents of Negro Education in the South, 1910 to 1950* (Nashville: Tennessee Book, 1950), 65.

35. RAC, GEB Papers, box 212, folder 2038, JR to Flexner, December 4, 1917, and attachments.

36. Ibid., George E. Goddard, Special Rural School Supervisor of Georgia to County Superintendents of Schools, January 1, 1919.

37. In her forthcoming book on Rosenwald schools, Mary Hoffschwelle suggests that JR had begun hearing criticism of Tuskegee's handling of the school building program as early as December 1917.

38. LC, Booker T. Washington Papers, James L. Sibley to William C. Graves, May 8, 1915.

39. LC, Booker T. Washington Papers, Washington to Graves, May 26, 1915.

40. The pamphlet *The Rural Negro School and Its Relation to the Community* was printed in 1915. It was probably written by Clinton Calloway.

41. RAC, GEB Papers, box 212, folder 2038, Frank P. Bachman to Abraham Flexner, May 14, 1919.

42. Ibid., N. C. Newbold to Flexner, May 17, 1919, and Flexner to Newbold, May 19, 1919.

43. Ibid., Wallace Buttrick to Dr. Fletcher B. Dresslar, June 18, 1919.

44. Ibid., Dr. Robert Moton to Flexner, July 19, 1919.

45. Ibid., Flexner to Moton, July 26, 1919.

46. Ibid., Flexner to JR, July 31, 1919.

47. Ibid., Flexner to JR, September 17, 1919.

48. Ibid., Dresslar to Flexner, August 30, 1919.

49. Ibid., Leo Favrot to Flexner, December 10, 1919.

50. RAC, GEB Papers, box 212, folder 2039, T. H. Harris to Flexner, March 30, 1920.

51. Ibid., Flexner to JR, April 24, 1920.

52. Ibid., Moton to Buttrick, May 20, 1920.

53. Ibid., Margaret Washington to Buttrick, May 24, 1920.

54. JRFA, box 127, folder 16, S. L. Smith to JR, June 15, 1921.

55. RAC, GEB Papers, box 212, folder 2039, S. L. Smith to Buttrick, June 21, 1924.

56. Edwin Embree and Julia Waxman, *Investment in People: The Story of the Julius Rosenwald Fund* (New York: Harper, 1949), 40–41.

57. William A. Link, *The Paradox of Southern Progressivism, 1880–1930* (Chapel Hill: University of North Carolina Press, 1992), 246.

58. The cities that built YMCAs under the initial offer were Washington, D.C., Chicago, Indianapolis, Philadelphia, Kansas City, Cincinnati, Baltimore, St. Louis, Columbus, Atlanta, and Pittsburgh. New York City had one in Manhattan and one in Brooklyn.

59. UCL, JR Papers, box 44, folder 35, "Report on Colored YMCA Buildings" submitted by J. E. Moorland, January 15, 1920.

60. UCL, JR Papers, box 44, folder 35, William J. Parker to JR, March 15, 1920.

61. Ibid., Parker to Graves, March 19, 1920.

62. Ibid., "Re Proposed Extension Colored 'Y' Offer," memo by W. C. Graves, March 22, 1920.

63. Nina Mjagkij, *Light in the Darkness: African Americans and the YMCA, 1852–1946* (Lexington: University Press of Kentucky, 1994), 81. Mjagkij also has an article on JR and the YMCAs in the *American Jewish Archives* (1993).

64. CHS, YMCA Papers, box 92, folder 5, JR to the YMCA, July 8, 1920.

65. Mjagkij, *Light in the Darkness,* 81.

66. The second round of YMCAs were built in Montclair and Orange, New Jersey, Denver, Detroit, Los Angeles, Buffalo, Dayton, Toledo, Dallas, Youngstown, and Harrisburg.

67. George R. Arthur, *Life on the Negro Frontier* (New York: Association Press, 1934), 41.

68. UCL, JR Papers, box 9, folder 13, Graves to JR, November 23, 1917.

69. UCL, JR Papers, box 9, folder 14, Amanda Sears, Horace Bridges, and T. Arnold Hill to JR, December 11, 1918.

70. UCL, JR Papers, box 9, folder 15, note of April 6, 1920, on a Graves memo to JR of November 28, 1919.

71. UCL, JR Papers, box 9, folder 14, JR to C. E. Jenks, November 6, 1920.

72. William M. Tuttle Jr., *Race Riot: Chicago in the Red Summer of 1919* (Urbana: University of Illinois Press, 1996).

73. Albert I. Waskow, *From Race Riot to Sit-In: 1919 and the 1960s* (Garden City, N.Y.: Doubleday, 1966), 62.

74. UCL, JR Papers, box 6, folder 4, Graves to JR, December 12, 1919.

75. At an executive committee meeting that discussed this issue, JR raised an interesting point: "whether newspapers could be induced, in their reports of the crisis, to omit designating Negro criminals as Negroes, except in cases where such designation would

be helpful for identification." UCL, JR Papers, box 6, folder 4, "Minutes of the Commission Meeting of March 12, 1920."

76. Waskow, *From Race Riot to Sit-In,* 86.

77. Tuttle, *Race Riot,* 257n.

78. Waskow, *From Race Riot to Sit-In,* 70.

79. Werner, *Rosenwald,* 273.

80. UCL, JR Papers, scrapbook 14, 168, Carl Sandburg article in *Chicago News,* July 29, 1919.

81. UCL, JR Papers, scrapbook 14, 166, Julius Rosenwald, "Reconstruction and the Negro," *Chicago Broad Axe,* May 10, 1919.

82. UCL, JR Papers, scrapbook 14, 154, Julius Rosenwald, "The North and the Negro," *New York Times,* March 9, 1925.

83. Thomas Lee Philpott, *The Slum and the Ghetto: Immigrants, Blacks, and Reformers in Chicago, 1880–1930* (Belmont, Calif.: Wadsworth, 1991), 302–303.

84. Hyman L. Meites, *History of the Jews of Chicago* (1924; reprint, Chicago: Chicago Jewish Historical Society, 1990), 336.

85. UCL, JR Papers, scrapbook 6, 175, "It's Up to You, J. R.," *Chicago Chronicle,* December 1, 1922.

86. Meites, *Jews of Chicago,* 229.

87. Ibid., 336.

88. UCL, JR Papers, scrapbook 6, 176, Julius Rosenwald, "The United Drive for $2,500,000," *Sentinel,* April 27, 1923.

89. It is unclear when the Research Bureau came into existence. Meites quotes a speech by James Davis in January 1922, before the merger, which indicates it was already operating. However, in a speech delivered on January 27, 1924, JR said: "The Jewish Charities of Chicago has taken a great step forward in the creation of a Research Bureau." An extract from this speech is contained in the Jewish Federation Archives, R.61, box 2, folder 8.

90. Hoover Presidential Library, West Branch, Iowa, Louis Strauss Papers, box 66, Ms. Filer to Strauss, November 9, 1919.

91. UCL, JR Papers, scrapbook 8, 118, *Chicago Herald,* October 27, 1919.

92. UCL, JR Papers, scrapbook 8, 168–69.

93. According to the memoirs of JR's son, William, JR gleefully banned liquor from his home. However, if he was invited out and was offered an alcoholic beverage, he did not refuse it, for he believed that to do so would have been considered rude.

94. UCL, JR Papers, scrapbook 6, 36, *New York World,* January 25, 1923.

95. UCL, Minutes of the University of Chicago Board of Trustees, vol. 11, 521–22, August 5, 1920.

96. UCL, JR Papers, box 9, folder 7, Ernest Freund to JR, November 23, 1923.

97. UCL, JR Papers, addendum II, box 1, folder 3, JR to "Dear Cousins" in Germany, November 8, 1920.

98. UCL, JR Papers, scrapbook 5, 62.

99. UCL, JR Papers, scrapbook 7, 80.

100. UCL, JR Papers, box 50, folder 10 (Werner Notes), JR to Simon Rosenwald, December 12, 1923.

101. UCL, JR Papers, addendum II, box 1, folder 3, JR to "Dear Cousins" in Germany, November 8, 1920.

102. UCL, JR Papers, addendum II, box 1, folder 3, JR to Mr. and Mrs. Gustav Rosenwald, May 13, 1921.

103. Yale University, Sterling Library, Jerome Frank Papers, box 6, folder 158, "Recollections of Oscar J. Friedman."

104. This document is in the possession of the author.

105. UCL, JR Papers, scrapbook 7, 4, "Obituaries of Morris Rosenwald."

106. UCL, JR Papers, box 50, folder 11 (Werner Notes), "Diary of JR's Trip to Europe, April 3, 1924–May 22, 1924."

107. Manuscript in the possession of the author.

108. Library of Congress, Lessing Rosenwald Papers, container 62, JR to Lessing July 28, 1924.

109. Werner, *Rosenwald,* 234.

110. Quoted in James C. Worthy, *Shaping an American Institution: Robert E. Wood and Sears, Roebuck* (Champaign: University of Illinois Press, 1984), 39.

111. Hoover Presidential Library, West Branch, Iowa, Robert E. Wood Papers, memo signed by Wood and witnessed by Jennie M. Richardson, November 14, 1924.

112. Emmet and Jeuck, *Catalogues and Counters,* 328.

113. Peter Drucker, *Management: Tasks, Responsibilities, Practices* (New York: Harper & Row, 1974), 780. Italics in the original.

7. New Philanthropic Ventures, 1924–1928

1. Most of the material in this section appeared in my article "Julius Rosenwald and the Founding of the Museum of Science and Industry," *Journal of Illinois History* 2 (1999): 163–82.

2. Edward P. Alexander, *Museum Masters: Their Museums and Their Influence* (Nashville: American Association for State and Local History, 1983), chap. 12, esp. 367–68.

3. According to William Rosenwald's unpublished autobiography. I owe this reference to William Rosenwald's daughter, Elizabeth Varet.

4. Werner, *Rosenwald,* 281; Herman Kogan, *A Continuing Marvel: The Story of the Museum of Science and Industry* (New York: Doubleday, 1973), 10–11.

5. Werner, *Rosenwald,* 281.

6. The South Park Commission oversaw one of three autonomous park districts in Chicago. See Helen Lefkowitz Horowitz, *Culture and the City: Cultural Philanthropy in Chicago from the 1880s to 1917* (Lexington: University Press of Kentucky, 1976), 214.

7. Kogan, *A Continuing Marvel,* 15–16.

8. Jay Pridmore, *Inventive Genius* (Chicago: Museum of Science and Industry, 1996).

9. UCL, JR Papers, scrapbook 15, 3, *Chicago Tribune,* April 17, 1926.

10. MSI Papers, William Rosenwald letter (excerpt), May 13, 1926.

11. MSI Papers, Wormser to the South Park commissioners, August 18, 1926.

12. MSI Papers, "To the Executive Committee of the Commercial Club of Chicago," July 8, 1926.

13. The museum was free until 1991.

14. UCL, JR Papers, scrapbook 15, 6, *Chicago Journal,* August 17, 1926.

15. UCL, JR Papers, scrapbook 15, 6, *New York Times,* August 19, 1926.

16. MSI Papers, Frank Wetmore to Wormser, July 21, 1926.

17. MSI Papers, Wormser to JR, September 11, 1926.

18. MSI Papers, JR to Wormser, September 13, 1926.

19. MSI Papers, Wormser to JR, September 14, 1926.

20. MSI Papers, JR to Wormser, September 16, 1926.

21. Ibid.

22. MSI Papers, Piez to Wormser, July 19, 1926.

23. MSI Papers, Letters of Wormser to JR, September 15, 1926, and Wormser to Sewell Avery, February 23, 1927.

24. MSI Papers, Wormser to JR, February 1, 1927.

25. MSI Papers, JR to Wormser, February 6, 1927.

26. Kogan, *A Continuing Marvel,* 25–26.

27. MSI Papers, Wormser's "Conversation with Mr. E. J. Kelly, May 27, 1927."

28. MSI Papers, Louis Behan to Wormser, April 26, 1927.

29. MSI Papers, Wormser to JR, July 14, 1927.

30. MSI Papers, Wormser's "Notes on Luncheon with Mr. Kelly, April 24, 1927."

31. MSI Papers, Calvin W. Rice to JR, July 19, 1927, and JR's reply, July 26, 1927.

32. Werner, *Rosenwald,* 247.

33. UCL, JR Papers, box 35, folder 15, Rosen report, 49.

34. AJA, Felix Warburg Papers, box 223, folder 24, JR to Felix Warburg, September 8, 1925.

35. UCL, JR Papers, box 35, folder 8, Billikopf to JR, September 8, 1925.

36. UCL, JR Papers, box 35, folder 13. JR's speech is in the *Jewish Daily Bulletin,* September 15, 1925.

37. UCL, JR Papers, box 35, folder 8, JR to Morris Wolf, September 25, 1925.

38. UCL, JR Papers, box 35, folder 14, Billikopf to JR, June 4, 1926. JR's reply is in box 35, folder 8, dated June 16, 1926.

39. Werner, *Rosenwald,* 253.

40. UCL, JR Papers, box 35, folder 8, William to JR, August 20, 1926.

41. UCL, JR Papers, box 35, folder 13, Samuel Cahan to JR, October 25, 1926.

42. UCL, JR Papers, box 35, folder 14, Billikopf to JR, June 4, 1926.

43. UCL, JR Papers, box 16, folder 11, Graves memo, October 11, 1926.

44. JDCA, David Bressler to Paul Baerwald, November 16, 1926.

45. JDCA, David A. Brown to JR, December 7, 1926.

46. JDCA, Brown to Felix Warburg, December 13, 1926.

47. JDCA, Graves to Marcy A. Berger, April 6, 1927.

48. JDCA, speech of JR at Warburg dinner, November 5, 1927.

49. JDCA, speech of Herbert Hoover at Warburg dinner, November 5, 1927.

50. JDCA, Rosenberg to Rosen, December 19, 1927.

51. See Kathleen S. Kelly, *Effective Fund-Raising Management* (Mahwah, N.J.: Lawrence Erlbaum, 1998), 143–47.

52. UCL, JR Papers, box 8, folder 15, JR to Harold Swift, January 5, 1925.

53. UCL, Harold Swift Papers, box 76, folder 23, Harold Swift to JR, October 6, 1926.

54. UC Oriental Institute Library, Breasted Papers, Breasted to President Judson, March 29, 1919. I owe this material to the kindness of John Larson of the Oriental Institute.

55. Ibid., Breasted to JR, June 22, 1919.

56. Ibid., JR to Breasted, July 14, 1919.

57. UCL, Harold Swift Papers, box 169, folder 3, JR to Max Mason, March 4, 1926.

58. UCL, U. of C. Presidents' Papers, 1889–1925, box 57, folder 5, Harold Swift to President Burton, February 7, 1925.

59. UCL, JR Papers, box 8, folder 14, memo of R. F. Duncan to JR, February 28, 1925.

60. UCL, JR Papers, box 17, folder 19, Frankfurter to JR, May 13, 1927.

61. Werner, *Rosenwald,* 303.

62. UCL, JR Papers, box 51, folder 6 (Werner Notes), *Chicago Tribune,* August 17, 1931.

63. UCL, JR Papers, box 51, folder 6 (Werner Notes), *Chicago Tribune,* August 18, 1931.

64. Carroll Wooddy, *The Case of Frank Smith: A Study in Representative Government* (Chicago: University of Chicago Press, 1931), 221.

65. For a modern historical look at Moton, see Adam Fairclough's essay "Robert R. Moton and the Travail of the Black College President," in his book *Teaching Equality: Black Schools in the Age of Jim Crow* (Athens: University of Georgia Press, 2001).

66. UCL, JR Papers, box 53, folder 2 (Werner Notes).

67. UCL, JR Papers, box 54, folder 5 (Werner Notes), JR to Challis Austin, January 4, 1926.

68. UCL, JR Papers, box 17, folder 6, JR to George Foster Peabody, January 4, 1926.

69. UCL, JR Papers, box 53, folder 2. The words are Werner's. He does not elaborate.

70. UCL, JR Papers, box 54, folder 6 (Werner Notes), JR to William Jay Scheiffelin, January 6, 1926.

71. UCL, JR Papers, box 51, folder 1 (Werner Notes), JR to "My Dear Ones, Wherever You May Be," February 18, 1927.

72. UCL, JR Papers, scrapbook 14, 15, *Nashville Tennessean,* December 1, 1926.

73. Werner, *Rosenwald,* 361.

74. UCL, JR Papers, box 54, folder 5 (Werner Notes), JR to Challis Austin, January 4, 1926.

75. Memoirs of Harry Kersey (photocopy), 6.

76. UCL, JR Papers, box 22, folder 5, JR to Otto Herstett, November 4, 1925.

77. Tulane University, Edgar Stern Papers, box 7, folder 6, JR to Edith and Edgar Stern, March 3, 1927.

78. UCL, JR Papers, box 33, folder 12, JR to Selma and Sig Eisendrath (n.d., probably June 1928).

79. UCL, box 51, folder 1 (Werner Notes), JR to "Dear Ones All," February 17, 1927.

80. UCL, JR Papers, box 34, folder 4.

81. UCL, JR Papers, box 51, folder 1 (Werner Notes).

82. UCL, JR Papers, box 15, folder 2, Flexner to JR, November 28, 1925.

83. Ibid., JR to Flexner, October 12, 1927.

84. This amusing incident is in a draft of an article on Embree found in the Edwin Embree Papers, Sterling Memorial Library, Yale University, reel 3, folder 30.

85. Yale University, Sterling Memorial Library, Embree Papers, reel 2, folder 14, Embree to Clarence Day, December 1, 1927.

86. JRFA, box 106, folder 31.

87. Embree to Clarence Day, December 1, 1927.

88. JRFA, box 104, folder 31, Embree to JR, December 1, 1927.

89. Yale University, Sterling Memorial Library, Embree Papers, reel 3, folder 34, JR to Embree, December 5, 1927.

90. JRFA, box 104, folder 34, E. F. Keppel to JR, December 22, 1927.

91. Yale University, Sterling Memorial Library, Embree Papers, reel 3, folder 34, Henry Jaggelon to Embree, December 22, 1927.

8. The Julius Rosenwald Fund, Hoover, and the Depression, 1928–1930

1. JRFA, box 104, folder 32, Embree to JR, March 6, 1928.

2. Ibid., Embree to JR, March 1, 1928.

3. William A. Link, *The Paradox of Southern Progressivism, 1880–1930* (Chapel Hill: University of North Carolina Press, 1992), 229–30.

4. Yale University, Embree Papers, Embree to Clarence Day, May 22, 1928.

5. JRFA, box 133, folder 2, JR to Embree, March 12, 1928.

6. UCL, JR Papers, addendum I, box 2, folder 1, docket for meeting of April 29, 1928, 13.

7. Edwin Embree and Julia Waxman, *Investment in People: The Story of the Julius Rosenwald Fund* (New York: Harper, 1949), 30–31.

8. UCL, JR Papers, addendum I, box 4, folder 2, *Chicago Tribune,* May 17, 1928, editorial entitled "Mr. Rosenwald's Wise Giving."

9. UCL, JR Papers, box 33, folder 7, B. F. Sunny to JR, May 14, 1928.

10. UCL, JR Papers, addendum I, box 2, folder 2, docket for meeting of April 30, 1928.

11. Ibid., folder 5, docket for meeting of May 11, 1929.
12. Ibid., folder 11, meeting of November 30, 1928.
13. On the Commission on Interracial Cooperation, see Link, *Paradox,* 248–61.
14. UCL, JR Papers, addendum I, box 2, folder 11, minutes of meeting of November 30, 1928.
15. Ibid., folder 3, docket for meeting of November 4, 1928.
16. Ibid., folder 11.
17. JRFA, box 90, folder 9, Embree to JR, March 29, 1929.
18. UCL, JR Papers, addendum I, box 2, folder 5, docket for meeting of May 22, 1929.
19. James H. Jones, *Bad Blood: The Tuskegee Syphilis Experiment* (New York: Free Press, 1981).
20. JRFA, box 90, folder 10, Embree to JR, December 12, 1929.
21. John D. Rockefeller's *Random Reminiscences* were ghostwritten articles that appeared in book form, but they were an example of public relations rather than a serious attempt by Rockefeller to explain his philanthropy. Chernow calls these articles "quaint superficial pieces." Ron Chernow, *Titan: The Life of John D. Rockefeller Sr.* (New York: Random House, 1998), 531.
22. UCL, JR Papers, box 32, folder 15, "The Burden of Wealth" by Julius Rosenwald as told to Elias Tobenkin, *Saturday Evening Post,* January 5, 1929.
23. UCL, JR Papers, box 3, folder 6, Ellery Sedgwick to JR, May 15, 1928.
24. Ibid., folder 7, Embree to John Gray, June 18, 1929.
25. Julius Rosenwald, "The Principles of Public Giving," *Atlantic Monthly,* May 1929, 599–607.
26. UCL, JR Papers, box 3, folder 4, A. Lawrence Lowell to JR, June 24, 1929.
27. Ibid., folder 8, Bernhard Osterlonk to JR, May 7, 1929.
28. Ibid., folder 10, JR to Ellery Sedgwick, June 28, 1929.
29. Martin Morse Wooster, "Debates on Perpetuity," *Philanthropy* (1998), 29–32.
30. Waldemar A. Nielsen, *Inside American Philanthropy* (Norman: University of Oklahoma Press, 1996), 246–47.
31. UCL, JR Papers, box 3, folder 6, Thomas Cochran to JR, May 14, 1929.
32. UCL, JR Papers, box 19, folder 14, Thomas Cochran to JR, June 21, 1929.
33. Werner, *Rosenwald,* 333.
34. UCL, JR Papers, box 19, folder 14, JR to Calvin Coolidge, September 19, 1929.
35. Ibid., folder 11, Embree to JR, September 29, 1929.
36. Ibid., folder 13, list of the grants from the Hubert estate.
37. UCL, JR Papers, box 39, folder 15, "Jedidiah Tingle" to JR, October 10, 1927.
38. Ibid., JR to "Tingle," October 20, 1927.
39. Ibid., Embree to JR, December 2, 1927.
40. LC, Harmon Foundation, box 22, "Celebration—Washington."
41. LC, Harmon Foundation, box 58, "Julius Rosenwald."
42. UCL, JR Papers, box 17, folder 11, George E. Hayes to JR, January 14, 1928.
43. MSI Papers, William E. Harmon to JR, March 15, 1928.
44. LC, Harmon Foundation, box 22, "Celebration—Washington," JR to William E. Harmon, March 24, 1928.
45. MSI Papers, Wormser to JR, January 4, 1928.
46. MSI Papers, JR to Wormser, March 3, 1928.
47. MSI Papers, Kaempffert to JR, Sewell Avery, and Wormser, October 3, 1928.
48. MSI Papers, JR to Kaempffert, October 4, 1928.
49. MSI Papers, press release, July 6, 1929.
50. Quoted in Herman Kogan, *A Continuing Marvel: The Story of the Museum of Science and Industry* (New York: Doubleday, 1973), 32.
51. MSI Papers, *Chicago Daily News* article, April 14, 1928.

52. MSI Papers, JR to Wormser, December 19, 1928. See also Kogan, *A Continuing Marvel,* 29–30.

53. Kogan, *A Continuing Marvel,* 30; Jay Pridmore, *Inventive Genius* (Chicago: Museum of Science and Industry, 1996), 40.

54. MSI Papers, Wormser to JR, August 19, 1930; Pridmore, *Inventive Genius,* 46.

55. MSI Papers, Wormser to Arthur Anderson & Co., April 8, 1930.

56. MSI Papers, Wormser to Miss Stinson, JR's secretary, December 6, 1930.

57. MSI Papers, Waldemar Kaempffert, "Revealing the Technical Ascent of Man in the Rosenwald Industrial Museum," *Scientific Monthly* 28 (June 1929): 482–98.

58. MSI Papers, *Chicago Tribune,* February 29, 1928. See also Charles G. Abbott, *The Relations between the Smithsonian Institution and the Wright Brothers,* Smithsonian Miscellaneous Collections, vol. 81, no. 5 (Washington, D.C., 1930).

59. MSI Papers, JR to Wormser, March 3, 1928.

60. JDCA, James N. Rosenberg in an article published in the *American Hebrew* shortly after JR's death.

61. JDCA, folder 561, Hoover to JR, February 13, 1928, and UCL, JR Papers, box 18, folder 25. See also Werner, *Rosenwald,* 254.

62. UCL, JR Papers, box 18, folder 25, JR to Hoover, February 16, 1928.

63. JDCA, "Rosenwald's Five Million Dollars," *Chicago Chronicle,* April 20, 1928.

64. UCL, JR Papers, box 16, folder 11, Felix Warburg to JR, April 30, 1928.

65. UCL, JR Papers, box 54, folder 11 (Werner Notes), interview in *The Day,* July 3, 1928.

66. UCL, JR Papers, box 51, folder 5 (Werner Notes), JR to Julian W. Mack, November 17, 1930. Also quoted in Werner, *Rosenwald,* 262.

67. Hoover Presidential Library, Campaign and Transition, box 59, Rosenberg to Hoover, September 5, 1928, Hoover to Rosenberg, September 19, 1928, and a clipping from a newspaper, unknown and undated.

68. JDCA, folder 561, Rosenberg to Embree, January 14, 1930. The idea that JR was giving five-eighths rather than half of the $10 million seems to have come from Embree, who, in the first report of the Rosenwald Fund, announced that JR was giving $6 million to the Russian colonies. Perhaps he added JR's initial $1 million pledge to the subsequent $5 million pledge. This public announcement caught the JDC staff by surprise (see memo from Joseph Hyman to Rosenberg, Warburg, and Baerwald, January 21, 1929), but the five-eighths idea stuck.

69. JDCA, folder 561, memo from Paul Low to Paul Baerwald, December 21, 1930.

70. UCL, JR Papers, box 9, folder 12, John P. Wilson Jr. to JR, October 16, 1929.

71. UCL, JR Papers, box 8, folder 17, Swift to Embree, January 20, 1928.

72. Ibid., folder 16, Swift to JR, May 31, 1928.

73. Ibid., folder 17, Frederic Woodward to Embree, July 28, 1928.

74. Ibid., folder 16, JR to the university board of trustees, November 7, 1928.

75. Ibid., folder 17, John T. Moulds, secretary of the board, to JR, November 30, 1928.

76. UCL, JR Papers, box 9, folder 3, W. R. Harrell to JR, July 13, 1929.

77. UCL, JR Papers, box 7, folder 9, Nathan Levin to JR, November 20, 1929.

78. UCL, JR Papers, box 9, folder 3, Embree to Woodward, March 25, 1929.

79. Ibid., JR to Hutchins, September 2, 1929.

80. UCL, JR Papers, box 8, folder 20, Hutchins to JR, October 2, 1929. The Rockefeller group refers to the various foundations under the Rockefeller umbrella, including the General Education Board.

81. Ibid., JR to Hutchins, October 2, 1929.

82. Ibid., Hutchins to JR, October 4, 1929.

83. UCL, Harold Swift Papers, box 185, folder 8, a memo marked "excessively confidential" of a conversation between Robert M. Hutchins and Julius Rosenwald on October 10, 1929.

84. UCL, JR Papers, box 8, folder 20, Hutchins to JR, October 30, 1929.

85. UCL, JR Papers, box 15, folder 3, JR to Flexner, July 15, 1930.

86. UCL, Harold Swift Papers, box 185, folder 8, Hutchins memo on a meeting with Embree, September 18, 1930.

87. UCL, JR Papers, box 52, folder 5, Arthur Morris to M. Werner, March 10, 1937.

88. UCL, JR Papers, scrapbook 6, 10. There are numerous articles about Morris Plan Banks here and also in scrapbook 16.

89. UCL, JR Papers, addendum I, box 2, folder 3, docket for the November 4, 1928, meeting of the Julius Rosenwald Fund, 41.

90. Ibid., 41–42.

91. UCL, JR Papers, box 7, folder 2, JR to Benjamin Rosenthal, June 21, 1919; Thomas Lee Philpott, *The Slum and the Ghetto* (Belmont, Calif.: Wadsworth, 1991), 242. Philpott contends (236) that JR was fearful that Rosenthal wanted to mix whites and blacks in his planned community, but his "proof" of this is a letter from Rosenthal to JR answering a question that has been lost. It is based on a supposition.

92. UCL, JR Papers, box 7, folder 2, JR to E. J. Buffington, president of the Illinois Steel Company, August 13, 1920.

93. Devereux Bowley Jr., *The Poorhouse: Subsidized Housing in Chicago, 1895–1976* (Carbondale: Southern Illinois University Press, 1978), 6.

94. Philpott, *The Slum and the Ghetto,* 244.

95. UCL, JR Papers, scrapbook 14, 172, *Chicago News,* December 18, 1916.

96. Philpott, *The Slum and the Ghetto,* 208–209.

97. Ibid., 255–56.

98. "Better Housing Seen as Way to Win Prosperity," *Chicago Tribune,* June 15, 1931.

99. Bowley, *The Poorhouse,* 11.

100. Philpott, *The Slum and the Ghetto,* 262.

101. JRFA, box 92, folder 1, Alfred K. Stern to JR, November 17, 1928.

102. UCL, JR Papers, addendum I, box 2, folder 3, docket for the November 4, 1928, meeting of the Rosenwald Fund, 42.

103. UCL, JR Papers, box 6, folder 1, JR to Dr. Arnold H. Kegel, January 12, 1929.

104. UCL, Harold Swift Papers, box 185, folder 8, *Chicago Tribune,* June 10, 1937.

105. Philpott, *The Slum and the Ghetto,* 270–71.

106. These remarks by former residents were made in a meeting with the author on June 16, 2001, at Chicago State University. My thanks to Kay Johnson for arranging this meeting.

107. UCL, JR Papers, box 15, folder 19, Alfred K. Stern to Irene J. Graham, October 24, 1930.

108. Philpott, *The Slum and the Ghetto,* 303–16.

109. Joan Huff Wilson, *Herbert Hoover: Forgotten Progressive* (Boston: Little, Brown, 1975).

110. UCL, JR Papers, box 18, folder 25, notes of William C. Graves.

111. Hoover Presidential Library, Campaign and Transition, box 59, JR to Hoover, August 12, 1928.

112. UCL, JR Papers, box 55, notebook 2 (Werner Notes), Hoover to JR, November 7, 1928.

113. UCL, JR Papers, box 18, folder 26, "Statement Prepared for the *Chicago Daily News* by Julius Rosenwald."

114. Ibid., "Why I Am for Hoover," by Mrs. Julius Rosenwald.

115. Ibid., JR's radio address, given October 27, 1928.

116. UCL, JR Papers, box 51, folder 2 (Werner Notes), JR to "Bunder Old and Young," October 29, 1928.

117. JRFA, box 92, folder 1, Alfred K. Stern to JR November 17, 1928, for the story in *Time;* Hoover Presidential Library, Campaign and Transition, box 89, clipping from the *Washington Times,* February 4, 1929.

118. Hoover Presidential Library, Campaign and Transition, box 89, Heineman to Hoover, January 2, 1929.

119. Ibid., Jason Rogers to Hoover, January 2, 1929.

120. Ibid., unsigned and undated cable to Hoover.

121. UCL, JR Papers, box 51, folder 3 (Werner Notes), JR to Frau Emma Rosenwald, January 29, 1929.

122. Hoover Presidential Library, Campaign and Transition, box 59, JR to Julius Klein, January 12, 1929.

123. UCL, JR Papers, box 51, folder 3 (Werner Notes), JR to "Dear Ones," March 6, 1929.

124. MSI Papers, Hoover to JR, July 3, 1930.

125. Hoover Presidential Library, Presidential Papers, French Strother to JR, July 9, 1929.

126. Ibid., memo from the secretary of the interior to the president, November 7, 1929.

127. Hoover Presidential Library, Presidential Papers, box 158, JR to Hoover, December 12, 1929, and Hoover's reply, December 16, 1929.

128. Wood's letter to Endicott is quoted in Worthy, *Shaping an American Institution,* 41–42.

129. Emmet and Jeuck, *Catalogues and Counters,* 330.

130. UCL, JR Papers, addendum II, box 1, folder 9, JR to an unknown correspondent asking for his "view on . . . the outlook for a continuation of prosperity," July 6, 1928.

131. UCL, JR Papers, box 51, folder 2 (Werner Notes), JR to "All German cousins," August 23, 1928.

132. Emmet and Jeuck, *Catalogues and Counters,* 343.

133. Werner, *Rosenwald,* 242.

134. UCL, JR Papers, addendum II, box 2, folder 3, newspaper story headlined "Rosenwald Aid Brings Song to Workers' Lips," from an unknown newspaper of uncertain date.

135. Quoted in Werner, *Rosenwald,* 239–40.

136. UCL, JR Papers, addendum II, box 2, folder 3, *Chicago Herald and Examiner,* October 31, 1929.

137. Werner, *Rosenwald,* 241.

138. UCL, JR Papers, box 39, folder 3, Henrietta Szold to JR, November 28, 1929.

139. UCL, JR Papers, box 38, folder 13, JR to Homer Guck, November 7, 1929.

140. Nathan W. Levin and Robert M. Vega, *Report on the Estate of Julius Rosenwald* (privately printed, 1949), 9.

141. Sears Roebuck Archives, memo from JR to Mr. Powell and Mr. Pollock, October 17, 1930.

142. UCL, JR Papers, box 26, folder 8, press release headed "Rosenwald Talks on Success in Movietone."

143. Ibid., Fox Movietone speech, October 31, 1929.

144. UCL, JR Papers, box 51, folder 2 (Werner Notes), JR to "All German Cousins," August 23, 1928.

145. Tulane University Department of Special Collections, Edgar B. Stern Papers, box 7, folder 6, Edgar B. Stern to Gussie, April 27, 1929.

146. Memoirs of Harry Kersey, 6.

147. UCL, JR Papers, box 51, folder 2 (Werner Notes), "Funeral of Mrs. Rosenwald, May 23, 1929."

148. UCL, JR Papers, addendum II, box 1, folder 8, Hoover to JR, May 30, 1929.

149. UCL, JR Papers, box 51, folder 4 (Werner Notes), JR to Bunde relatives, June 18, 1929.

150. MSI Papers, clipping from the *New York City American,* March 19, 1930.

9. Final Year and Postmortem, 1931–1948

1. UCL, JR Papers, box 51, folder 5 (Werner Notes), JR to "Dear Ones All," December 24, 1930.

2. Tulane University, Edgar Stern Papers, box 7, folder 6, JR and Addie to Edgar Stern, January 5, 1931.
3. UCL, JR Papers, box 51, folder 5 (Werner Notes), December 29, 1930.
4. Ibid., folder 6 (Werner Notes), JR to his children, January 16, 1931.
5. JRFA, box 90, folder 12, JR to Embree, February 6, 1931.
6. UCL, JR Papers, box 51, folder 6 (Werner Notes), Addie to the family, February 10 and February 20, 1931.
7. JDCA, Levin to Baerwald, March 21, 1931.
8. MSI Papers, W. Rufus Abbott to Leo Wormser, April 20, 1931.
9. JRFA, box 90, folder 12, Embree to JR, January 27, 1931.
10. Ibid., JR to Embree, February 6, 1931.
11. James D. Anderson, *The Education of Blacks in the South, 1860–1935* (Chapel Hill: University of North Carolina, 1988), chap. 6.
12. JRFA, box 90, folder 12, Embree to JR, January 31, 1931.
13. Ibid., JR to Embree, February 13, 1931.
14. Embree and Waxman, *Investment in People,* 54.
15. UCL, JR Papers, box 33, folder 9, Embree to JR, May 4, 1931.
16. This was the father of Julian Bond, the noted civil rights leader.
17. Embree and Waxman, *Investment in People,* 57.
18. UCL, JR Papers, box 33, folder 9, Embree to JR, May 6, 1931.
19. JRFA, box 90, folder 13, Embree to JR, November 30, 1931.
20. JRFA, box 90, folder 14, undated note in JR's handwriting.
21. Nathan W. Levin and Robert M. Vega, *Report on the Estate of Julius Rosenwald* (privately printed in 1948), iii.
22. UCL, JR Papers, box 33, folder 9, Embree to JR, April 10, 1931. JR's emphasis.
23. UCL, JR Papers, box 33, folder 9, Embree to JR, May 4, 1931.
24. Ibid., Embree to JR, August 21, 1931.
25. JRFA, box 90, folder 13, Embree to JR, October 19, 1931.
26. Ibid., Embree to JR, November 27, 1931.
27. UCL, JR Papers, box 33, folder 9, Embree to JR, August 21, 1931.
28. JRFA, box 90, folder 13, Embree to JR, November 27, 1931.
29. MSI Papers, minutes of the meeting of the executive committee, January 5, 1931.
30. MSI Papers, Wormser to JR, January 3, 1931.
31. MSI Papers, JR to Wormser, January 7, 1931.
32. MSI Papers, Abbott to JR, June 24, 1931.
33. MSI Papers, JR to Rufus Abbott, June 25, 1931.
34. MSI Papers, minutes of the executive committee meeting, May 26, 1930.
35. MSI Papers, Rufus Abbott to JR, June 23, 1931.
36. MSI Papers, JR to Wormser, in letter from Wormser to Abbott, July 21, 1931.
37. Pridmore, *Inventive Genius,* 49–51.
38. Levin and Vega, *Report on the Estate of Julius Rosenwald,* 73:

Donations to the Museum of Science and Industry

	Cash	55,000 shares of *Sears stock*	*Total*
JR during his lifetime	$3,836,893		$3,836,893
Estate of JR	2,757,500	$2,242,500	5,000,000
Rosenwald Family Assn.	563,332	1,600,625	2,163,957
Totals	$7,157,724	$3,843,125	$11,000,850

39. Herman Kogan, *A Continuing Marvel: The Story of the Museum of Science and Industry* (New York: Doubleday, 1973), 43.

40. JDCA, Morris C. Troper to Nathan Levin, May 9, 1931.

41. JDCA, Paul Baerwald to Levin, December 28, 1931.

42. UCL, Harold Swift Papers, box 185, folder 7, Embree to Robert M. Hutchins, January 4, 1932.

43. James C. Worthy, *Shaping an American Institution: Robert E. Wood and Sears Roebuck* (Urbana: University of Illinois Press, 1984), 44.

44. Hoover Library, West Branch, Iowa, General Robert E. Wood Papers, Wood to JR, May 28, 1931.

45. Ibid., JR to Wood, October 24, 1931.

46. UCL, Harold Swift Papers, box 185, folder 6, "Memorandum Concerning the Relationship of the University of Chicago and Franklin C. McLean to the Case of Mr. Julius Rosenwald," July 1, 1931.

47. UCL, JR Papers, box 51, folder 6 (Werner Notes), JR to Arthur Lehman, July 22, 1931.

48. UCL, JR Papers, box 51, folder 6 (Werner Notes), Addie to Abraham Flexner, July 20, 1931.

49. UCL, Harold Swift Papers, box 185, folder 6, Franklin McClean to Adele Levy, September 3, 1931.

50. Tulane University, Edgar Stern Papers, box 6, folder 10, Edith Stern to Edgar Stern's mother.

51. UCL, JR Papers, box 61, folder 13, *New York Times,* January 7, 1932, 18.

52. MSI Papers, Graham Taylor, "Julius Rosenwald—Fellow Citizen," *Survey Graphic* (February 1932).

53. UCL, JR Papers, box 61, folder 6, Dr. Louis L. Mann, *Julius Rosenwald* (A Memorial Address at Chicago Sinai Congregation, January 17, 1932).

54. UCL, JR Papers, box 51, folder 7 (Werner Notes), 2.

55. Ibid., 3.

56. *Crisis* (February 1932), 58.

57. Emmet and Jeuck, *Catalogues and Counters,* 689.

58. Nathan W. Levin and Robert M. Vega, *The Estate of Julius Rosenwald,* iii.

59. Ibid., 4.

60. UCL, JR Papers, box 61, folder 13, *New York Times,* January 7, 1932, 18.

61. Levin and Vega, *Report on Estate,* 8.

62. RAC, GEB Papers, box 212, folder 2041, Embree and Lessing Rosenwald to Raymond Fosdick, May 25, 1932.

63. Ibid., excerpt from the diary of Thomas B. Appleget: "Thomas M. Debevoise."

64. Ibid., "Max Mason."

65. Ibid., Max Mason to Trevor Arnett, June 10, 1932.

66. RAC, GEB Papers, box 213, folder 2049, S. L. Smith to Jackson Davis, June 27, 1932, and Davis's reply, June 29, 1932.

67. Ibid., S. L. Smith to Jackson Davis, July 8, 1932, and "I-2580 Emergency Assistance to Institutions or Agencies," the formal resolution voted by the GEB Board July 14, 1932.

68. RAC, GEB Papers, box 212, folder 2041, Janet M. Warfield to Thomas M. Appleget, July 26, 1932.

69. Ibid., Thomas Appleget to Janet Warfield, July 29, 1932.

70. Ibid., "Repayment of Advances by the General Education Board," an undated memo by Embree, date-stamped April 10, 1934, in the GEB offices.

71. Embree and Waxman, *Investment in People,* 206–207.

72. Ibid., 21.

73. Ibid., 57.

74. Ibid., 153–54.

75. Ibid., 55.

Conclusion

1. Boris Emmet and John E. Jeuck, *Catalogues and Counters: A History of Sears Roebuck & Co.* (Chicago: University of Chicago Press, 1950), 671.

2. Peter Drucker, *Management: Tasks, Responsibilities, Practices* (New York: Harper & Row, 1974), 52.

3. Raymond D. Smith and William P. Darrow, "Strategic Management and Entrepreneurial Opportunity: The Rise of Sears, Inc.," *Journal of Business and Entrepreneurship* 11, no. 1 (March 1999): 7–8.

4. Gordon L. Weil, *Sears, Roebuck, U.S.A.: The Great American Catalog Store and How It Grew* (New York: Stein and Day, 1977), 60.

5. Richard S. Tedlow, *New and Improved: The Story of Mass Marketing in America* (Cambridge: Harvard Business School Press, 1996), 276–77.

6. Ibid., 341, 350.

7. Kathleen D. McCarthy, *Noblesse Oblige: Charity and Cultural Philanthropy in Chicago, 1849–1929* (Chicago: University of Chicago Press, 1982), 106.

8. Ibid., 110.

9. Waldemar A. Nielsen, *Inside American Philanthropy* (Norman: University of Oklahoma Press, 1996), 31–32.

10. Ibid., 32, 34.

11. Ibid., 39, 42, 48.

12. Judith Sealander, "Curing Evils at Their Source: The Arrival of Scientific Giving," in *Charity, Philanthropy, and Civility in American History,* ed. Lawrence Friedman and Mark D. McGarvie (Cambridge: Cambridge University Press, 2003), 221, 226.

13. Ibid., 233–34.

Bibliography

Alexander, Edward P. *Museum Masters: Their Museums and Their Influence.* Nashville: American Association for State and Local History, 1983.

Alpert, Carl. *Technion.* New York: Sepher Hermon, 1982.

Anderson, James D. *The Education of Blacks in the South, 1880–1935.* Chapel Hill: University of North Carolina Press, 1988.

Arthur, George R. *Life on the Negro Frontier.* New York: Association Press, 1934.

Asher, Frederick. *Richard Warren Sears: Icon of Inspiration.* New York: Vantage Press, 1997.

Asher, Louis E., and Edith Head. *Send No Money.* Chicago: Argus Books, 1942.

Barnard, Harry. *The Making of an American Jew.* New York: Herzl Press, 1974.

Blanke, David. *Sowing the American Dream: How Consumer Culture Took Root in the Rural Midwest.* Athens: Ohio University Press, 2000.

Bowley, Devereux, Jr. *The Poorhouse: Subsidized Housing in Chicago, 1895–1976.* Carbondale: Southern Illinois University Press, 1978.

Brandes, Stuart D. *American Welfare Capitalism, 1880–1940.* Chicago: University of Chicago Press, 1976.

Burrows, Edwin G., and Mike Wallace. *Gotham: A History of New York City to 1898.* New York: Oxford University Press, 1998.

Chandler, Alfred D., Jr. *The Visible Hand: The Managerial Revolution in American Business.* Cambridge: Belknap Press of Harvard University, 1977.

Chernow, Ron. *Titan: The Life of John D. Rockefeller Sr.* New York: Random House, 1998.

Cohen, Naomi W. *Not Free to Desist: The American Jewish Committee, 1906–1966.* Philadelphia: Jewish Publication Society of America, 1972.

Cronon, William. *Nature's Metropolis: Chicago and the Great West.* New York: W. W. Norton, 1991.

Cuff, Robert D. *The War Industries Board.* Baltimore: Johns Hopkins University Press, 1973.

Dedmon, Emmett. *Great Enterprises: 100 Years of the YMCA of Metropolitan Chicago.* New York: Rand McNally, 1977.

Diner, Hasia R. *A Time for Gathering: The Second Migration.* Baltimore: Johns Hopkins University Press, 1992.

Drucker, Peter. *Management: Tasks, Responsibilities, Practices.* New York: Harper & Row, 1974.

Embree, Edwin, and Julia Waxman. *Investment in People: The Story of the Julius Rosenwald Fund.* New York: Harper & Brothers, 1949.

Emmet, Boris, and John E. Jeuck. *Catalogues and Counters: A History of Sears Roebuck & Co.* Chicago: University of Chicago Press, 1950.

Fairclough, Adam. *Teaching Equality: Black Schools in the Age of Jim Crow.* Athens: University of Georgia Press, 2001.

Flexner, Abraham. *Abraham Flexner: An Autobiography.* New York: Simon & Schuster, 1960.

Fosdick, Raymond B. *Adventures in Giving: The Story of the General Education Board.* New York: Harper & Row, 1962.

Goldberg, J. J. *Jewish Power: Inside the American Jewish Establishment.* New York: Addison Wesley, 1996.

Grossman, James R. *Land of Hope: Chicago's Black Southerners and the Great Migration.* Chicago: University of Chicago Press, 1989.

Harlan, Louis R. *Booker T. Washington: The Wizard of Tuskegee, 1901–1915.* New York: Oxford University Press, 1983.

Harlan, Louis R., and Raymond W. Smock, eds. *The Booker T. Washington Papers.* Vols. 11, 13, 14. Urbana: University of Illinois Press, 1981.

Harris, Leon. *Merchant Princes.* New York: Berkley Books, 1979.

Hirsch, David Einhorn. *Rabbi Emil G. Hirsch: The Reform Advocate.* Northbrook, Ill.: Whitehall, 1968.

Hirsch, David Einhorn, ed. *The Theology of Emil G. Hirsch.* Wheeling, Ill.: Whitehall, 1977.

Hirsch, Emil G. *My Religion.* New York: Macmillan, 1925.

Hoge, Cecil C., Sr. *The First Hundred Years Are the Toughest: What We Can Learn from the Century of Competition between Sears and Wards.* Berkeley: Ten Speed Press, 1988.

Horowitz, Helen Lefkowitz. *Culture and the City: Cultural Philanthropy in Chicago from the 1880s to 1917.* Lexington: University Press of Kentucky, 1976.

Illinois State Senate. *Report of the Senate Vice Committee.* Springfield, Illinois, 1916.

Jones, James H. *Bad Blood: The Tuskegee Syphilis Experiment.* New York: Free Press, 1981.

Kelly, Kathleen S. *Effective Fund-Raising Management.* Mahwah, N.J.: Lawrence Erlbaum, 1998.

Kogan, Herman. *A Continuing Marvel: The Story of the Museum of Science and Industry.* New York: Doubleday, 1973.

Leach, William. *Land of Desire: Merchants, Power, and the Rise of a New American Culture.* New York: Vintage Press, 1993.

Lewis, David Levering. *W. E. B. DuBois: Biography of a Race, 1868–1919.* New York: Henry Holt, 1993.

Link, William A. *The Paradox of Southern Progressivism, 1880–1930.* Chapel Hill: University of North Carolina Press, 1992.

Marchand, Richard. *Creating the Corporate Soul: The Rise of Public Relations and Corporate Imagery in America.* Berkeley: University of California Press, 1998.

Martin, Bernard. *Critical Studies in American Jewish History,* Vol. I. Cincinnati: American Jewish Archives, 1971.

Martin, Dr. Franklin H. *The Joy of Living: An Autobiography.* 2 vols. Garden City, N.Y.: Doubleday, Doran, 1933.

McCarthy, Kathleen D. *Noblesse Oblige: Charity and Cultural Philanthropy in Chicago, 1849–1929.* Chicago: University of Chicago Press, 1982.

Meites, Hyman L. *History of the Jews of Chicago.* 1924; reprint, Chicago: Chicago Jewish Historical Society, 1990.

Meyerowitz, Joanne J. *Women Adrift: Independent Wage Earners in Chicago, 1880–1930.* Chicago: University of Chicago Press, 1988.

Miller, Donald L. *City of the Century: The Epic of Chicago and the Making of America.* New York: Simon & Schuster, 1997.

Mjagkij, Nina. *Light in the Darkness: African Americans and the YMCA, 1852–1946.* Lexington: University Press of Kentucky, 1994.

Nielsen, Waldemar. *Inside American Philanthropy.* Norman: University of Oklahoma Press, 1996.

Ogden, Christopher. *Aaron's Gift.* New York: privately published, 2002.

Philpott, Thomas Lee. *The Slum and the Ghetto: Immigrants, Blacks, and Reformers in Chicago, 1880–1930.* Belmont, Calif.: Wadsworth, 1991.

Pridmore, Jay. *Inventive Genius: The History of the Museum of Science and Industry.* Chicago: Museum of Science and Industry, 1996.

Raphael, Marc Lee. *Profiles in American Judaism: The Reform, Conservative, Orthodox and Reconstructionist Traditions in Historical Perspective.* San Francisco: Harper & Row, 1984.

Reznikoff, Charles, ed. *Louis Marshall: Champion of Liberty.* Philadelphia: Jewish Publication Society of America, 1957.

Sealander, Judith. *Private Wealth and Public Life: Foundation Philanthropy and the Reshaping of American Social Policy from the Progressive Era to the New Deal.* Baltimore: Johns Hopkins University Press, 1997.

Smith, S. L. *Builders of Goodwill: The Story of the State Agents of Negro Education in the South, 1910 to 1950.* Nashville: Tennessee Book Co., 1950.

Spear, Allan H. *Black Chicago: The Making of a Negro Ghetto, 1890–1920.* Chicago: University of Chicago Press, 1967.

Tedlow, Richard S. *New and Improved: The Story of Mass Marketing in America.* Cambridge: Harvard Business School Press, 1996.

Tuttle, William M., Jr. *Race Riot: Chicago in the Red Summer of 1919.* Urbana: University of Illinois Press, 1996.

Wade, Louise C. *Graham Taylor: Pioneer for Social Justice.* Chicago: University of Chicago Press, 1964.

Waskow, Albert I. *From Race Riot to Sit-In: 1919 and the 1960s.* Garden City, N.Y.: Doubleday, 1966.

Wiebe, Robert H. *The Search for Order, 1877–1920.* New York: Hill and Wang, 1967.

Weil, Gordon L. *Sears, Roebuck, U.S.A.: The Great American Catalog Store and How It Grew.* New York: Stein and Day, 1977.

Werner, M. R. *Julius Rosenwald: The Life of a Practical Humanitarian.* New York: Harper & Brothers, 1939.

Wilson, Joan Huff. *Herbert Hoover: Forgotten Progressive.* Boston: Little, Brown, 1975.

Woody, Carroll. *The Case of Frank Smith.* Chicago: University of Chicago Press, 1931.

Worthy, James C. *Shaping an American Institution: Robert E. Wood and Sears Roebuck.* Urbana: University of Illinois Press, 1984.

Yates, JoAnne. *Control through Communication: The Rise of System in American Management.* Baltimore: Johns Hopkins University Press, 1993.

Articles

Ascoli, Peter M. "Julius Rosenwald and the Founding of the Museum of Science and Industry." *Journal of Illinois History* 2 (1999): 163–82.

Drucker, Peter. "Good Works and Good Business." *Across the Board* 21 (October 1984): 12–15, 64.

Harlan, Louis R. "Booker T. Washington's Discovery of Jews." In *Region, Race, and Reconstruction: Essays in Honor of C. Vann Woodward,* ed. J. Morgan Kousser and James McPherson, 267–79. New York: Oxford University Press, 1982.

Joyce, Miriam. "Julius Rosenwald and World War I." *American Jewish Archives* 45 (1993): 208–27.

Martin, Bernard. "The Religious Philosophy of Emil G. Hirsch." In *Critical Studies in American Jewish History,* 3 vols., comp. Jacob R. Marcus (Cincinnati: American Jewish Archives, 1971), 1: 186–201.

———. "The Social Philosophy of Emil G. Hirsch." In *Critical Studies in American Jewish History,* 3 vols., comp. Jacob R. Marcus (Cincinnati: American Jewish Archives, 1971), 1:202–16.

Meier, August. "Booker T. Washington and the Town of Mound Bayou." In *Along the Color Line: Explorations in the Black Experience,* ed. August Meier and Ellen Rudwick, 217–23. Urbana: University of Illinois Press, 1976.

Mjagkij, Nina. "A Peculiar Alliance: Julius Rosenwald, the YMCA, and African Americans, 1910–1933." *American Jewish Archives* 44 (1993): 585–600.

Nimmons, George F., and William K. Fellows. "Designing a Great Mercantile Plant." *Architectural Record* 19 (June 1906): 403–12.

Purinton, Edward E. "Satisfaction or Your Money Back." *Independent,* February 5, 1920, 298–99.

Rosenwald, Julius. "The Principles of Public Giving." *Atlantic Monthly,* May 1929, 599–607.

Sealander, Judith. "Curing Evils at Their Source: The Arrival of Scientific Giving." In *Charity, Philanthropy and Civility in American History,* ed. Lawrence Friedman and Mark D. McGarvie, 217–39. Cambridge: Cambridge University Press, 2003.

Smith, Raymond D., and William P. Darrow. "Strategic Management and Entrepreneurial Opportunity: The Rise of Sears, Inc." *Journal of Business and Entrepreneurship* 11, no. 1 (March 1999): 1–16.

Starett, Theodore. "The Building of a Great Mercantile Plant." *Architectural Record* 19 (April 1906): 265–74.

Wooster, Martin Morse. "Debates on Perpetuity." *Philanthropy,* 1998, 29–32.

Index

Italicized page numbers indicate illustrations.

Peter M. Ascoli is on the faculty of Spertus College in Chicago. He taught at Utah State University and later served as director of development for Chicago Opera Theater and Steppenwolf Theater Company. He worked in the development offices of both the University of Chicago and the University of Illinois at Chicago. He is a graduate of both the University of Chicago and St. Catherine's College, Oxford and has a Ph.D. in history from the University of California, Berkeley, and a Master of Management from the Kellogg Graduate School of Management, Northwestern University. He is a grandson of Julius Rosenwald.